T. Bonar 174 Nassau St.

Old Stone Mill At Newport.

BY REV. EDWARD PETERSON.

NEW YORK.
JOHN. S. TAYLOR
17 Ann St.

HISTORY

OF

RHODE ISLAND.

BY REV. EDWARD PETERSON,

AUTHOR OF "THE WORLD IN THE ASCENDANT," "PRIMITIVE CHRISTIANITY CONTRASTED WITH MODERN," "BIBLE TEMPERANCE REVIEW," &c., &c.

New-York:
JOHN S. TAYLOR, 17 ANN-STREET.
1853.

JOHN J. REED, PRINTER,
16 Spruce-street.

TO

THE PEOPLE,

THIS

WORK IS MOST RESPECTFULLY DEDICATED,

BY

THE AUTHOR.

PREFACE.

IN SEEKING out Materials for a work of this kind, embracing a period of nearly two centuries, it must be obvious to the reader, that it has been attended with much difficulty, as valuable Records have been lost, which would have greatly aided and facilitated the publication.

Tradition has been the source, from whence much information has been derived, of a highly interesting and amusing character, and which could not, possibly, have been obtained from authentic records.

We have, however, under every discouragement, labored to present a variety of subjects of the deepest interest, from the Settlement of the Island, to the breaking out of the American Revolution; at which period we have shewn, that Newport had attained to a high degree of celebrity, and stood unrivalled by any City or Town in the Colonies.

We have, also, brought down events until within a few years, in order to give the reader the opportunity of enjoying all the advantage which was to be gathered from the reminiscenses of the past.

To the Antiquarian, this work will be highly interesting, as it will be found to contain much valuable information; and prove extremely amusing to every class of readers, from the variety of subjects which it contains.

This work being published by subscription, we have added a list of those subscribing, whose names were transmitted to us prior to its going to press, since which numerous others have been handed to the Agents, but not as yet transmitted to us, which precludes their appearing with the rest.

As we have among our Subscribers many celebrated names, either in connection with Rhode Island, or from other causes, we have, in order to add to the interest of the work, given a fac-simile of their respective signatures.

The Author's acknowledgments are due to the many friends who have aided him in the progress of the work, and more particularly to DAVID MELVILLE, Esq., and B. B. HOWLAND, Esq.; also for information gleaned from the Notes of the late HENRY BULL, Esq., and Ross's "Historical Discourse"; also to many other gentlemen, who have taken a lively interest in this enterprize.

Newport, R. I., 1853.

CONTENTS.

HISTORY OF RHODE ISLAND.

THE ISLAND OF AQUEDNECK, NOW RHODE ISLAND.

"My lovely island home,
 I love thy sea-girt shore,
Thy rocks and sunny hills,
 And foaming billows' roar.

The harvest proudly waves,
 And gently fan each breeze,
The sweet birds hover round the spot,
 And warble in the trees.

To thee my memory turns,
 In sorrow and in care:
My native island home,
 I love to linger there.

My home o'er the dark-blue sea,
 Thy charms shall near depart;
But linger round my memory,
 And twine about my heart."

The Island of Aquedneck, now Rhode Island, from whence the State derives its name, was so called from the celebrated Isle of Rhodes, in the Mediterranean Sea. It is fifteen miles in length, and about three miles and a half in width. Its bay, or harbor, is universally acknowledged to be one of the finest in the world, being easy of access at all seasons of the year. A number of small islands lie near, covered with the richest verdure; viz.:—Goat Island, directly opposite the town, which was formerly garrisoned, but is at present in a dismantled and dilapidated state. The first fort erected on this island, was built by the proceeds of the tenth, or King's part of the privateers captured by him. Rose Island, once fortified, but now in ruins. Cannonicut, lying west, on which is Fort Dumpling, erected under the administration of the elder Adams, but never occupied as a fortress; with Prudence and Gould Island, at the north, present a pleasing and highly picturesque scenery.

On the southern extremity, it is bounded by the broad Atlantic, whose heaving billows, so grand and imposing, are every way suited to convey a just impression of the power and majesty of that Divine Being, who "directs the whirlwind and the storm."

At its northern extremity stands out, in bold relief, Hog Island, with Mount Haup in the distance, once the residence of Philip, the King of the Wanpanouages.

On the north-east, a stone bridge, one-quarter of a mile long, connects the island with the main. At this point also, the scenery is pleasing and attractive. The climate is salubrious, and its soil rich and fertile; producing every variety to be found in northern latitudes. The island was once covered with a heavy growth of timber, at the period when the Indian was its lawful proprietor, and the sound of the war-whoop rung from out the forest, and reverberated through the vallies, and his bow and arrows supplied him with deer and fowl, which were then abundant. Such is a faint sketch of this island, of which Mr. Neal justly observes, p. 595, that it is deservedly esteemed the Paradise of New England.

Dear Isle of my birth, sweetest gem of the sea,
Now summer revisits thy shore;
My heart's best affection, turns fondly to thee,
Oh, when shall I greet thee once more !"

THE SETTLEMENT OF THE ISLAND.

We are now approaching a subject of deep and vital interest to the inhabitants of the island. When our forefathers fled the father-land, for the sake of enjoying liberty of conscience, and to worship God in more scriptural simplicity,—this was the motive which prompted them to forego the pleasures of kindred and home, and cross the Atlantic, and here, in this western world, erect temples to the worship of Almighty God. And, to the honor of the first settlers of this island, be it said, that they possessed, in a much higher degree, the principles of civil and religious liberty, than were to be found in any other portion of New England. They had felt the strong arm of oppression in their native land, and had no wish or desire to see it perpetuated in their new home, which, alas, was too painfully witnessed in many portions of the colonies. There was a consistency in their belief and practice, and to this day there is to be found on the island more of a truly Republican spirit than exists in other sections of New England. It is to be attributed to the impress left by the original settlers of the island, that this mark of distinction still exists. We shall have occasion, as we advance in our work, to draw a contrast between Clarke and Coddington with the settlers of other sections; shewing their great superiority, and the extent of their knowledge in framing laws for the regulation of the settlement. We shall labor to avoid falling into a deep-rooted prejudice, and present the truth in all its bearings, so far as the materials furnished for a history will permit. It cannot, however, be disguised, that full justice has never been awarded to these noble patriots, whose devotion in the sacred cause of civil and religious freedom, has never been surpassed.

The decline of commerce on the island, owing in a great measure to the calamities growing out of the American revolution, has thrown the ancient metropolis quite into the shade. None has had the moral courage, and the patient industry, to present her claims to the world as they justly deserve; and her history has consequently been almost lost. We could have wished that the task had devolved on some one better qualified, and whose *pecuniary means* would have placed them in a situation, to have done ample justice to the subject. But, as no one has stepped forth, to rescue the events of the past from oblivion, we have been constrained, from the strong attachment which we hold to the *place* of our birth, to furnish the world with such evidence of the past history of Newport, as is to be obtained from records, and from tradition, which, we flatter ourselves, will be both pleasing and acceptable to our readers.

We find on the 7th day of March, 1637, the names of eighteen men, who had taken up their residence on Aquedneck, now Rhode Island, viz. :

William Coddington,	Thomas Savage,
John Clarke,	William Dyre,
William Hutchinson,	William Freeborne,
John Coggeshall,	Philip Shearman,
William Aspinwall,	John Walker,
Samuel Wilbour,	Richard Carder,
John Porter,	William Baulston,
John Sanford,	Edward Hutchinson,
Edward Hutchinson, jun.	Henry Bull,

Randall Houldon.

This last person, Randall Houldon, we presume, soon left, as we find his name not mentioned in the records, as being one of the first proprietors of the island. These names were, however, taken from a fac-simile in the author's possession.

The first settlement on the island, was commenced at its northern extremity, where a town was regularly laid out, and first named Pocasset, subsequently Portsmouth. It is that part of the island known as New-Town. But so rapid was the increase of the Colony, during the following summer, that it was deemed advisable for their mutual prosperity, to commence a settlement on some other part of the island. Accordingly, in the following spring, Mr. Clarke, with several others, removed to the south part of the island, and commenced a settlement in or about what is now called Tanner-street, formerly New-Town, to which they gave the name of Newport. The island itself, subsequently, by order of the General Court, was called the Isle of Rhodes, or Rhode Island, in memory, as before remarked, of that celebrated isle of the Mediterranean Sea. Both towns were united under the same simple patriarchal form of government, of which Mr. William Coddington was chosen magistrate, or judge. A few months subsequently they chose Mr. John Coggeshall, Nicholas Easton, and William Brenton, to act as his assistants. Mr. Coggeshall was descended from an ancient and respectable family in England. He came to this country with Mr. Coddington, in 1630, and was admitted a freeman of the town of Boston in 1632. He was a member of the first Board of Selectmen, of Boston, and represented the town in

General Court in 1634–5–6, and the spring session of 1637, but was disfranchised for conscience toward God, that same year. His disfranchisement, with others, created great discontent among his friends, which led to their removal, and finally to the settlement of the island. Mr. Coggeshall enjoyed the confidence of the colony of Rhode Island, and at the time of his death, which occurred in 1647, he was President of the Colony. He lies in the Coggeshall burial place, a little south of Newport. The following is the inscription on his tombstone:

Here lieth the Body of
JOHN COGGESHALL, SEN., ESQ.,
Who died, the FIRST PRESIDENT of the Colony, the 27th of November, 1647,
Aged about 56 years.

His descendants are still numerous on the island; and many of them are among our most respectable citizens. He was a man of a large estate, known as Coggeshall Neck.

Mr. Coddington came to this country with Governor Hutchinson, having been appointed in 1629, by the British government, one of the Assistants of the Massachusetts colony. He engaged in mercantile business in Boston, and built the first *brick* house in that town. But, notwithstanding all the facilities he there enjoyed of promoting his own temporal prosperity, yet he chose to relinquish all of them, for the sake of religious freedom. Accordingly, in 1638, with the *beloved Clarke*, and sixteen others, he left the colony of Massachusetts, and commenced the settlement of Rhode Island; and was, by his companions in tribulation, unanimously elected chief magistrate, or Judge of the colony, which office he held until the island was incorporated with Prudence and Warwick. In 1651, he was appointed by the supreme authority of England, Governor of the island, pursuant to a power reserved in the patent, by which the island became again separated from the Providence Plantation, which we shall have occasion to speak of more fully. But the people, jealous of their rights, and fearful that their freedom might be endangered, dispatched Mr. Williams and Mr. Clarke to England, to have it revoked. On receiving due notice from England, Mr. Coddington surrendered up his commission, and retired into private life, when the island again became united with the Plantation. Mr. Coddington was again elected

Governor of the colony in 1674–75, and 1678, in which year he died, aged 78 years. He is said to have been a man of profound learning, and assisted in framing the body of laws, which has been the basis of our Constitution and government ever since.

Governor Coddington was interred in the family burial place, which, at his death, he gave the Society of Friends in Farewell-street, just south of the North Baptist meeting-house. The freemen of Newport, in town meeting, August 30th, 1836, appointed a committee to repair the monument at the head of the grave of this distinguished friend and advocate of civil and religious freedom. His likeness, which is still in good preservation, shews him to have been a most elegant and accomplished gentleman.

It may be instructive to read the laws passed by our ancestors, on the subject of religion. But every good man and lover of his country, blushes at the superstition, bigotry, and intolerance, with which they were too often tainted. Need we refer to history? Let us look for a moment to the pilgrim fathers, to the colony at Plymouth. Speaking of them, a judicious writer observes:

"Much as we respect that noble spirit which enabled them to part with their native soil—by some held dearer than friends, relatives, or children, and by every generous bosom preferred even to life itself,—we must condemn the proceedings which ensued. In the first moment when they began to taste of Christian liberty themselves, they forgot that others had a right to the same enjoyment. Some of the colonists, who had not emigrated through motives of religion, retaining a high veneration for the ritual of the English church, refused to join the colonial state establishment, and assembled separately to worship. But their objections were not suffered to pass unnoticed, nor unpunished. Endicott called before him the two principal offenders, and though they were men of respectability, and amongst the number of original patentees, he expelled them from the colony, and sent them home in the first ship returning to England. Had this inquisitorial usurpation been no further exercised, some apology, or at least palliation, might be framed. More interesting and painful consequences, however, not long afterwards, resulted. The very men who had countenanced this violation of Christian duties, lived to see their descendants excluded from church communion; to behold their grand-children, the smiling infants at the breast, denied the sacred right of baptism!" * * *

Coddington, an eminent merchant of Boston, was banished, for holding what they conceived to be erroneous sentiments, and for favoring the views of Mrs. Hutchinson.

"The first general court was held at Charlestown, on board the ship *Arabella*. A law was passed, declaring that none should be admitted as freemen, or be entitled to any share in the government, or even to serve as jurymen, except those who had been received as members of the church; *by which measure, every person whose mind was not of a particular structure, or accidentally impressed with peculiar ideas, was at once cast out of society, and stripped of his civic rights.*

"In 1656, a number of Quakers, having arrived from England and Barbadoes, and given offence to the clergy of the established church, by the novelty of their religion, at that time, certainly, a little extravagant, were imprisoned, and by the first opportunity sent away. A law was then made, which prohibited masters of vessels from bringing any Quakers into Massachusetts, and themselves from coming there, under a penalty, in case of a return from banishment, as high as death. In consequence of this several were hanged. Toleration was preached against, as a sin in rulers, that would bring down the judgment of heaven upon the land. Mr. Dudley died with a copy of verses in his pocket, of which the two following lines make a part:

'Let men of God, in court and churches watch,
O'er such as do a toleration hatch.'

The Anabaptists were the next object of persecution. Many were disfranchised, and some banished."

American Quarterly Review, June, 1835.

The principles which governed the early settlers of the island of Rhode Island, embraced all of every sect, whether Jew or Gentile.

The last of the original purchasers and proprietors of this island, was Henry Bull, Esq., who died in 1693, aged 84 years. He held various public offices in the colony, from its first settlement, until a few years before his death. He was Governor of the colony in 1685, after which, being at a very advanced age, he relinquished public employment, to end his days in domestic peace ; but after the revolution in England, the colony charter having been vacated, and Rhode Island put under the grant of Sir Edmund Andros, who held it until the spring of 1689 ; he was induced again to come forward into public life, thereby shewing a moral courage which was wanting in others.

The house erected by Governor Bull, in Newport, is of stone, and still standing on the east side of Spring-street, near the junction of Broad-street. It was, in 1642, used as a place of defense against the attacks of the Indians.

Governor Bull lies buried in the Coddington burial place, where a plain and unostentatious slab, points the passing stranger to the spot where sleep the mouldering ashes of this bold and fearless patriot. His descendants are now in possession of the patrimonial estate of their ancestor.

The character of the men who have already been brought into view, proves them to have been actuated by the best motives, in their attempts to found this colony. They recognized a superintending Providence, as will appear in the original charter of the American Isle of Rhodes :

" We, whose names are underwritten, do swear, solemnly, in the presence of the Great Jehovah, to incorporate ourselves into a body politic ; and He shall help us,—will submit our persons, lives, and estates, unto the Lord Jesus Christ, the King of kings, and Lord of lords ; and to all those perfect laws of his, given us in his most holy word of truth, to be guided and judged thereby.

(" Signed,)

William Coddington,	Richard Carder,
John Clarke,	William Baulston,
William Dyre,	Edward Hutchinson,
William Freeborn,	William Hutchinson,
Philip Shearman,	Henry Bull,
John Walker,	John Coggeshall."
Samuel Wilbour,	

And six others, whose names have already been mentioned.

Such were the principles, and such the sentiments, which distinguished the men, *who first planted* civil and religious liberty in this western world. We shall have occasion to dwell more at length on the dignity of their character, as we progress in the history of the island. The subject opens a wide field for reflection. It proves what men are capable of doing, under the influence of moral and christian principles.

Their object in coming to this continent was not merely to acquire gain, as is too apt to be the case with all adventurers, but rather to establish a refuge from persecution, where each should have the liberty of enjoying his opinion without fear; and even at this day, after a period of more than two centuries, there is possessed by the inhabitants of the island, more liberty than is enjoyed by any other portion of the State. The cause we shall attempt to show by and by, which will convince the mind of the impartial reader, that the position here assumed is correct.

THE PURCHASE OF THE ISLAND.

Without adverting to this subject, it would look as though the early settlers took possession of it by conquest, without affording the native Indians any remuneration for their lands. But so far from this, they actually purchased the island, as will appear by the receipt given by the two Sacems:

"22nd November, 1639.

"Received by me, Miantunomu, of Mr. William Coddington, and his friends united, twenty and three coats, and thirteen hoes, to be distributed to the Indians that do inhabit the island of Aquedneck, in full of all promises, debts, and demands, for the said island, as also two torkepes.

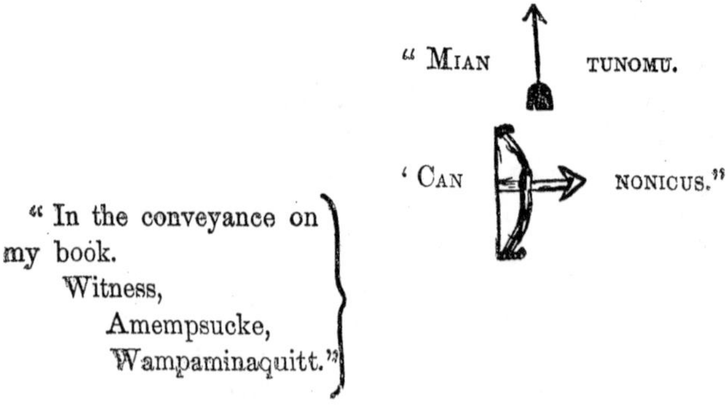

"MIAN TUNOMU.

'CAN NONICUS."

"In the conveyance on my book.
Witness,
Amempsucke,
Wampaminaquitt."

"A true copy of the original, entered, and recorded by me,
"JOHN SANFORD, *Recorder*."
[Colony Records.]

"The 11th of May, 1639, Received by me, Miantunomu, (as a gratuity,) of Mr. Coddington, and his friends united, for my pains and travel, in removing the natives off the island of Aquedneck, ten fathoms of wampum peage, and one broad-cloth coat.

"MIAN ↑ TUNOMU."

"A true copy of the original, entered, and recorded by
"JOHN SANFORD, *Recorder*."

"June 20th, 1639, Received of Mr. William Coddington, and of his friends united, in full satisfaction of ground broken up, or any other title or claim whatsoever, formerly had of the island of Aquedneck, the full sum of five fathoms of wampum peage.

"WONIMENATONY, X his mark."

"Witness,
Wm. Cowling,
Richard Sawell."

"A true copy of the original, entered, and recorded by me,
"JOHN SANFORD, *Recorder*."

The other seventeen joint purchasers of Aquedneck, whose names are mentioned, expressed their dissatisfaction that the Indian title to the island of Rhode Island, stood in the name of William Coddington, and to pacify them, he executed an instrument, giving them an equal share with himself. Mr. Coddington had no selfish wish to gratify:

"I, the said William Coddington, Esq., have no more in the purchase of right, than either of the purchasers or freemen received, or shall be received in by them, but only for my own proportion.

"In witness hereof, I have put to my hand, this 14th of April, 1652.

"WILLIAM CODDINGTON"

"Signed in the presence of,
Robert Knight,
George Muning."

"A true copy of the original, entered, and recorded the 7th of April, 1673.

"JOHN SANFORD, *Recorder.*"
[Colony Records.]

We think that great injustice has been done the aborigines of this country: whether our fathers viewed them as inferiors, and undeserving of their respect and kindness, it is self-evident that their conduct has been unbecoming, and every way calculated to foster revenge in the breast of the red men of the forest. They are a noble race, and their conduct would often put to the blush civilized man, who stoops to acts of meanness which would not be tolerated for a moment in savage life. Their sufferings have been great; driven from the homes of their fathers, and compelled to take up their abode in a strange land, so affected them with the deepest anguish, as to prove that their sympathies are as great, and their susceptibilities of right as keen as those of ours.

To the praise of the settlers of the island, they were never hostile to the Indians, as were some of the colonists, which we shall have occasion to notice. It should be remembered that they were the rightful owners of the soil, while we have usurped it. Never do we look on the countenance of the Indian, without reverence and respect, for they are nature's noblemen; but it has ever been with the "pale faces," agreeably with the sentiments of the poet Wordsworth:

"The good old plan,—
That they should get who have the power,
And they should keep who can."

Of the original settlers of the island, we find that William Hutchinson died on the island. The other Hutchinson, Aspinwall, and Savage, went back and got reconciled to the Massachusetts colony. In March, 1641, Carder, Houlden, and Porter were disfranchised. R. Houlder settled in Warwick; from him have descended the numerous family of Houldens in this State.

Nicholas Easton arrived in New England, with his two sons, May 14th, 1634. He first settled at Ipswich, and was a deputy to the General Court. The next year he removed to Newburg, and afterwards to Hampton, where he built the first house. In 1638, in consequence of the religious intolerance, he removed to Rhode Island, and settled in Portsmouth. The next year he removed to Newport, where he built the first house. It stood where the house now stands belonging to the heirs of the late Jonathan Southwick, in Farewell-street. As late as 1641, the Indians burnt the house of Nicholas Easton, on Lord's day, by kindling a fire on his lands. It alarmed the people, and, among other measures, they fitted out *an armed boat*, to ply round the island, to prevent the Indians from landing. They likewise appointed garrison houses, to which the people were to repair on an alarm. But the rupture lasted not long, before peace was restored.

Nicholas Easton and his two sons, Peter and John, on their way to the south part of the island, in a boat, landed on a small island, which they called Coaster's Harbor.

Mr. Easton and Mr. Clarke were appointed to write to Mr. Vane, and direct him about the obtaining of a patent of the island from his Majesty. The neck of land by Mr. Easton's house, was ordered to be sufficiently fenced, and to remain as a common field belonging to the town. Governor Easton died in 1675.

John Easton was the son of Governor Nicholas Easton, who came to Rhode Island with his father and brother, soon after the settlement, as before remarked. He was, for fifteen years, Attorney-General of the Colony. In 1674 and 1675, he was elected Deputy-Governor. He died on the 12th December, 1705, aged 88 years, and was buried in the Coddington burial-place. The family have been highly respectable, and, until within a few years, quite numerous. Governor Easton was an extensive landholder, and some of the original property is now in the possession of his descendants.

We have already observed, that the settlement of Newport

began in what is now called Tanner-street, and extended through to Marlborough-street. Here stood Governor Coddington's house, one of the oldest, and which remained until within a few years, when it was unfortunately *pulled* down, much to the regret of many of the present inhabitants. It should have been preserved, as a *memento* of the past.

There was a degree of generosity displayed, in laying out the town, as we learn from the records:

"At a General meeting it was ordered, that the home allotments shall be four acres apiece, laid out conveniently where the ground affords, and that Mr. Coddington shall have six acres for an orchard."

The original estate of Governor Coddington, in Newport, embraced all the land between Malborough, Farewell, North Baptist, and Thames streets. His mansion stood in Malborough, fronting Duke-street.

"It was ordered that the town shall be laid out, and built on both sides of the Spring, and by the sea-side southward," (now Thames street.) This spring runs through Tanner-street, a little below the jail, and empties into the harbor. The source of this river is Vaughn's Pond, a little north-west of Broad-street. At one period it flowed so rapid as to propel a water mill, which was erected within eight years of the formation of the settlement, in what is now known as Malborough-street. One of the mill-stones lays in front of the steps to the house of the late Benjamin Pierce, Esq. This portion of the town was originally a swamp, and the flow of water, within the memory of some of the older inhabitants, was much more abundant than at the present time.

As the town increased in population, improvements continued to be made, in the way of filling up and making land. The flow of the ocean at the first settlement, extended north of Elm-street on the Point. Bridge-street is made land, as is also Washington to Bridge. Before the extension of the long wharf, and the south part of Washington-street was made, it was an *open* passage to the Cove. Gravelly Point was then surrounded by water.

Vessels of ninety, and even one hundred tons were formerly built in the Cove. Subsequently, the ingress and egress to and from the Cove, was through a drawbridge, twenty-six feet wide. It is now only navigable for small boats.

It was the intention, originally, to have made Thames-street, equal in width to the houses which stand back from the street, viz.: the Atkinson, Cotton, &c.; why they encroached on the street to its present narrow limits, no good and sufficient reason can be offered.

"1640,—Rev. Robert Lenthel, was, by a vote, called to keep a public school for the learning of youth, and for his encouragement, there was granted him and his heirs, one hundred acres of land, and four more for a house lot, in Newport. It was also voted, that one hundred acres should be laid forth, and appropriated for a school, for encouragement of the poorer sort to train up their youth in learning; and Mr. Lenthel, while he continues to teach school, is to have the benefit thereof."

Thus, at an early period, the reader will perceive, that the attention of the first settlers was directed to the subject of education. Children were not permitted to grow up "like the wild ass's colt," without *moral* culture, and to pay no deference and respect to their superiors in age, and in knowledge. With all the means and facilities of education, now enjoyed, there is evidently a want of attention to the moral qualities of the mind, which *alone* make the good man and the good citizen.

In May, 1650, the Legislature, by the following act, first created the offices of Attorney and Solicitor-General of the Colony, viz:—

"It is ordered that this Court appoint one Attorney-General for the Colony, as also a Solicitor. That the Attorney-General shall have full power to implead any transgression of the State, in any court in the State, but especially to bring all such matters of penal laws, to the trial of the General Court of trials, as also for the trial of the officers of the State, at the General Assemblies; and to implead, in full power and authority of the free people of this State, their prerogatives and liberties; and because envy, the cut-throat of all prosperity, will not fail to *gallop* with its full career, let the said Attorney be faithfully engaged, and authorized, and encouraged, engaged for the people, by, or in the people's name, and with their full authority assisted, authorized that upon information of transgressions and transgressors of the laws, prerogatives, and liberties of the people, and these penal laws, he shall underhand and seal, take forth summons from the President or General Assistant, to command any delinquent, or vehemently suspected of delinquency, in what kind soever, according to the premises, to appear at the General Court, if it be thereunto belonging, or to the General Assembly in those matters proper thereunto; and if any refuse to appear at that mandamus, in the State of England's name, and the people of this State, he shall be judged guilty, and so proceeded against by fine and penalty.

"It is ordered, that in case of prohibitions, (any concerning guns, powder, lead, &c., it being proved that such and such, or any one, had a gun, &c.,) or the Solicitor, *bona fide*, in his own knowledge, do know or can swear, &c., that such a one was possessed of a gun, &c., as his own proper goods, and upon demand of the Solicitor, cannot produce or cannot give a good account of what has become of it, before one or two persons, or the Attorney, he shall be judged guilty of the breach of the law, and to be accordingly dealt withal; and that the law shall extend to inquiry, especially to guns and other prohibitions, as powder, shot, lead, wine, or liquors, that hath been merchandized or conveyed away to the Indians, since the law made on that subject."

And the people, by general ticket, elected in May, 1650, William Dyre, Attorney-General, and Hugh Burt, Solicitor-General.

Mr. Dyre was one of the original settlers, and owned the farm north of Easton's Point, at present owned by Charles Hunter, Esq., of the U. S. N. Mr. Dyre was highly respected for his talents, which is clearly shown by his appointment to so important an office as that of Attorney-General of the Colony. He also held a commission from the English Government, as Surveyor and Searcher-General. His commission extended to New-York.

Mr. Dyre, in the active part which he took with Wm. Coddington, in advocating and justifying the separation of the Islands from the Plantation, incurred the hatred and the displeasure of the people in that section. But there was no just and valid cause, why he should be charged with a "want of *public* spirit, and being ruined by party purposes," in his adherance to Mr. Coddington. He no doubt acted conscientiously, as did Mr. Coddington, believing in the then present condition of affairs, that it would prove for the interest of the Islands to maintain a separate and distinct form of government.

The jealousy of the Plantations, was, however, awakened, and it called forth the indignation of some of the *leaders*, as appears by Staple's "History of Providence," who looked on the measure as a gross insult offered to the people of the North. Mr. Dyre felt called upon to uphold a government with such an *able* leader as Coddington, a man of unblemished reputation, and whose reasons for his course of conduct, were founded on the immutable principle of right.

And whatever invidious reflections may be cast on the measures of these men, it will only recoil on the heads of those who made them. The charge preferred against Mr. Dyre being actuated by sinister motives, had no doubt its rise in that feeling of jealousy before mentioned, which existed between the Plantations and the Islands, which were independent, and which owed no allegiance, only to the Prince.

There is but *one* male descendant of Mr. Dyre, now living in Newport. It will be seen that the manner of spelling the name is different from those in other parts of the State, which shows that there was no connection between them.

Mr. Dyre's grave is to be found on the Dyre farm, for by that name it has always been known, as the inhabitants of Newport respect and venerate antiquity.

It was ordered that "Persicus, the Indian Sachem, shall have liberty to get as many chesnut bush, upon the commons of the Island, as may cover him a wigwam." How humiliating the thought, that the once rightful owners of the island, must now *supplicate* for permission from the "new-comers," for materials to cover them from the pelting storm! But these vicissitudes are of every day occurrence, and teach a salutary lesson of the uncertainty of all terrestrial things.

In 1651, the inhabitants, on the main, refused submission to Coddington's government.

THE ISLAND INDEPENDENT.

Before we proceed to notice this event, we will go back a little, and show the reader the position which the Island occupied from the settlement in 1638, to 1644.

"The towns of Portsmouth and Newport, erected their own separate governments, independent of that of the Plantations, and there was no political connection between them from the settlement in 1638 to 1644, and during these six years they were independent governments, free from every other power but the mother country. During this period, they enacted many laws, which were the foundation of the future statues and bill of rights, which distinguished the early laws and character of the State and people of Rhode Island, from the other English Colonies in America. For when the government of the Island was united with the Providence Plantations, by the Charter of 1643, and in General Assembly they enacted laws for the Colony of Rhode Island and Providence Plantations, the town of Providence instructed their commissioners to hold correspondence with the whole Colony, 'in the model that hath been lately shown unto us by our worthy friends of the Island.' And it appears that the plan of the government was formed by the people of the Island, and shown to those of Providence, who agreed to adopt them; and thus from the legislation of the people of the Island, the free institutions emanated."

This being an established fact, "that the plan of government formed by the people of the Island," and subsequently adopted by the Plantations, was a virtual admission of the profound wisdom, which dwelt in the minds of the Islanders; and proves in a word, any or every attempt made to engraft new principles, conflicting with those which they held as most sacred and binding, should be resisted at every hazard by the people of the Island, as they valued their peace, liberty and happiness.

The legislative acts, many of which seem to approximate to the former *blue* laws of Connecticut, and which is in direct conflict with the letter and spirit of the laws which originated from the Island, and which were made the basis of the government of the State, has led us to doubt the propriety of ever having formed an alliance with the Plantations after the Island had once become independent. For however tolerant the Island may be in the execution of laws, associated and confederated as they are with the Plantations, involves them in the disgrace and obloquy of sanctioning such arbitrary measures as are in force in the Plantations.

To obviate the difficulty as far as possible, the Islanders

should instruct their representatives in General Assembly, to oppose every law introduced into that body, which has the least appearance of despotism, and as aiming to subvert and to overthrow the rights and liberties of the people; and in case of their not doing it, and making it imperative on their legislators to act in accordance with the principles of their fathers, they in fact become a party concerned in upholding such tyrannical and unjust measures, which are at war with every principle of moral right.

ENCOURAGEMENT OF SETTLERS.

The proprietors, to encourage the settlement of the Island, sold out at a small price, and on easy terms, to such as were inclined to build and to whom they saw fit to admit to ownership of the soil. Those whom they considered turbulent aud unruly, they would not admit to "ownership, or to exercise the privileges of freemen." A very proper precaution, and calculated to avoid much evil. The spirit which animated the minds of the early settlers of the Island, was enlarged and liberal, and prompted them to render aid and assistance to all worthy persons who desired to take up their abode with them.

In March, 1641, in General Assembly, it was determined unanimously, that this government was a Democracy, saving only the right of the king. And it was ordered that none be accounted a delinquent for doctrines, provided it be not repugnant to government established, which was again confirmed at the next General Court, as follows:

"It is ordered that the law of the last Court, made concerning conscience, in point of doctrine, be perpetuated."

Mr. Bull says: "This appears to be the first act allowing every man *free* to act and advocate what religious opinions he chooses, and which has highly distinguished the State of Rhode Island."

The principles adopted by Clark and Coddington operated like leaven in diffusing itself through the minds of the masses, and was the *neucleus*, out of which ultimately sprang the Declaration of American Independence, and the freedom of the Colonies British misrule and oppression.

It has been already remarked that the Island had a separate

form of government for six years. It then become united with the Plantations, but in 1657, William Coddington went to England and procured a commission constituting him Governor, for life, of Rhode Island, of Cannanicut, and Prudence, and these islands again became separated from the towns on the main land. This continued for three years, when they again became united.

A SEAL FOR THE STATE.

A Seal was ordered to be provided for the State, viz., the government of the islands, with the device of a sheaf of arrows bound up with a motto: "*Amor vincit omnia.*" Love conquers every thing.

"In General Court, held at Newport, Sept. 17th, 1641, it was ordered that if any person or persons on the Island, whether freeman or inhabitant, shall by any means, open or covert, endeavor to bring any other power than what is here established, except it be from our prince, by lawful commission, shall be accounted a delinquent under the head of perjury."

The inhabitants living on islands, and consequently being isolated, and generally *clanish* in their views and feelings, and more opposed to innovations of every form, than those who live on the main, practices which originated with the early settlers have been transmitted down to the present generation. The inhabitants of Newport have felt a reverence for their ancestors which rendered them remarkably sensitive in relation to changes of evey kind, and it is evidence of stability of character which we hope to see perpetuated. We are aware that in this age of *progress*, it is thought sensible to disdain conventional rules, and long established usages of antiquity, and to substitute a licentious course of policy, baptized by the sacred name of Liberty, and thus open wide the floodgates of anarchy and misrule, which will ultimately overwhelm us in an avalanche of desolation. To dissent from the popular opinions of the day, would be to place ourselves in battle array with the march of improvement, and consequently subject us to the anathemas and reproaches of the *new lights* of the age, whose vanity has become so much inflated as to render it almost presumptuous to differ from them.

A certain class of men and mind make the "nineteenth century," a frequent topic of eulogistical declamation, not only common-place, but even disgusting to our feelings. "Surfeiting is one of the effects of profusion."

The spirit which animated our fathers, show that they valued their rights, and the rights of the Colonies, and were disposed to come forward in the hour of exigency, and bare their bosom to the storm, while others with far greater resources, held back through a servile fear. "For when the Colonies of New-Plymouth, and New Haven, shrunk from the war, unless Massachusetts would support them, which she refused to do, the little island of Rhode Island, threw herself into the breach, and took upon herself the responsibility of authorizing in her name, the defence of Long Island against the Dutch and Indians."

Such was the spirit which fired the heart and nerved the arm of our ancestors, and which God grant may be revived in their descendants, and not forever extinguished.

Newport, though settled last of the three, had arrived, in the space of eight years, to a degree of wealth and strength as to be equal with the other two. Many houses had been built at that time, and some wharves, and commercial pursuits on a small scale had been entered into.

"The trade and business of the town, at first, was very little and inconsiderable, consisting of a little corn, pork, and tobacco, sent to Boston, for a few European and other goods, they could not subsist without, and all at the mercy of the traders thereto. At present there are above one hundred sail of vessels belonging to the town. God grant, that as we increase in numbers and riches, we may not increase in sin and wickedness; but that we may rather be led by the divine goodness to reform whatever may have been amiss, or wanting among us."

Callender's Historical Discourse.

1654.—This year there was a schism in the Baptist Church, in Newport,—some of the brethren embracing the opinion that laying on of hands was necessary for all baptized persons.

1656.—This year, some of the people called Quakers came to this colony, being persecuted and abused in the other colonies, and many of the principal inhabitants embraced their doctrines, among whom were William Coddington, Nicholas Easton, and his two sons; Philip Shearman, Adam Matt, and many others.

In 1657, the island of Connanicut, or Quaonoquet, was purchased of the Indians. Koskotep, one of the Narragansett Sachems, sells to Thomas Gould, of Newport, Aguspemokick, or Gould Island.

1696.—This year, Coaster's Harbor and Goat Island was conveyed to the town of Newport, for the sum of ten pounds, by Benedict Arnold; he having purchased them some years before of the Indians.

Conskuet, or Rose Island, (the latter name derived from the abundance of wild roses, which once grew on the island,) was purchased of Mausup, an Indian Sachem, by Peleg Sanford, of Newport. It afterwards became the property of the Giddards, on the Point, and was finally sold by Thomas Giddard, Esq., to the general government, for the sum of $1500.

In 1658, at a General Court of Commissioners, an act was passed, declaring the prison building, in Newport, should be the prison for the whole colony.

On the 18th of May, an act was passed, to receive *peage*, (Indian money,) eight for a penny, in payment of all cost of court.

MASSACHUSETTS' INTOLERANCE AND CRUELTY.

In 1660, Mary Dyre, of Rhode Island, one of the people called Quakers, having returned to Boston, contrary to the *tyrants'* orders, was publicly executed on the 1st of June, agreeably to her former sentence. Mary Dyre was the wife of William Dyre, one of the eighteen associates who first came to Rhode Island. Before their removal from Massachusetts, she was a milliner in Boston, and one of the principal followers of the famous Mrs. Hutchinson.

The year previous, (the 20th of October,) William Robinson, and Marmaduke Stephenson, received sentence of death, which was executed upon them the 27th of June. At that time, Mary Dyre was brought with them to the gallows; but at the intercession of her son, of Newport, and others, she was reprieved, and sent away. Feeling it to be her duty to visit her friends, she returned again the next spring, and, as the reader has been already informed, she was executed under the sanction of men who *dare* call themselves Christians. She died, however, in the triumph of faith, feeling conscious that she had done nothing "worthy to warrant such a course of procedure towards her."

If there is one spot more than another, where the principles of liberty of conscience should be cherished, it is Newport. For, when we reflect on the *baseness* of Massachusetts, in thus putting to death their own citizens, merely for conscience' sake, it is calculated to arouse into action every power of the human mind, to put down intolerance for opinion's sake. Much has been said and written in favor of puritanical measures. The Roundheads of Cromwell's time have been eulogized, and the Cavaliers condemned. But the spirit which could influence such barbarity, must be nearly allied to the inhabitants of the "*pit.*" These men left the mother-country for *conscience'* sake, and came to America, where they could enjoy civil and religious liberty. But what kind of conscience did they possess? The *india-rubber* kind, which can contract, as easily as expand; for, if they had been sincere in their professions of love to the cause of righteousness, free toleration would have been allowed to all who came within their jurisdiction. But, assuming themselves to be right, they stood ready to inflict punishment on all who were unprepared to sanction and approve of their bigoted views. The religion established was Congregational, which, in theory, was Democratic, but, in practice, Aristocratical, and opposed to the principle of civil and religious freedom. And *too much* of the same ungodly spirit exists at the present day, though not permitted to be carried out to its full measure. Mary Dyre, and those associated with her, had been guilty of no crime; they had never opposed wholesome laws, but in matters of conscience touching God, they felt that they had a perfect right to worship Him, agreeably to their views of Christian duty; and in this they were correct. It will ever be a stigma of reproach on Massachusetts, for suffering such high-handed wickedness against the subjects of another colony. Let Newport rejoice in the names of her former legislators, who held to no restrictions in matters of religion, but left to each individual the liberty of forming his own views of religious truth and duty. Tyranny can never vegetate on the soil, which has been consecrated by the prayers of a Clarke and a Coddington.

The period of the transfer of what is now Providence, bears the same date, 1638, with the deed of this island, and the ownership of the land commenced at the same time. But government and laws were established by those of the island, seven months and one day *sooner* than at Providence. Portsmouth had admitted, or added to, the eighteen who first incorporated themselves, thirty other heads of families as settlers, whose names appear on the records, making forty-eight, and before the last of December following, twenty-nine more were admitted.

The first quarterly meeting of Friends in New England, and probably in America, was held at the house of Governor Coddington, before their meeting-house was erected. In 1700, the yearly meeting was then established at Newport, where it has ever since continued; and no situation is better adapted for it than Newport.

There was at the first settlement but two towns on the island, Portsmouth and Newport; but in 1743, Middletown was set off from Newport. This is a fine farming town, and produces a large amount for the Newport market. This town has an asylum, with "one acre of ground for the poor. It is occupied and improved by a family, who contract to board such of the poor as the overseers may think proper. A part of them receive pensions, and live with their friends or relatives. The town council are the overseers of the poor.

"The town receives an annuity of $40, given by the late Andrew Freebody, for the relief of the poor. About $400 was paid for the support of the poor the past year."

In 1640, Samuel Gorton, who came to Rhode Island, in June 1638, was, on some contention, banished from the island.

Samuel Gorton came to this country from London. In one of his printed works, he adds to his name the appellation of "Gentleman." In one conveyance he styles himself "Citizen of London, clothier," and in another, "Professor of the mysteries of Christ." He landed in Boston in 1636, and from that place removed in a short time to Plymouth. Here it seems his heterodoxy in religion was first discovered, and he was complained of and required to find sureties, and fined. From Plymouth, Gorton removed to Rhode Island, and shortly after settled in Warwick. In 1642 he was seized by Massachusetts' forces, and was confined in prison. After his release, he returned to Rhode Island, and then went to England and preferred a memorial respecting his treatment, against Massachusetts. In 1646, he came back to Rhode Island and settled in Warwick.

His religious opinions were peculiar. It is impossible, perhaps, for any one at this day, fully to comprehend them. During his life they were the subject of much speculation. That he was an enthusiast in his religious opinions, there can be no doubt. "A real come-outer, in its true sense." Of the private history of Gorton, very little can be gleaned even from tradition. The following is from the manuscript itinerary of the late Dr. Stiles: "I visited a Mr. Angel, aged eighty, born October 18th, 1691, a plain, blunt spoken man, of right old English frankness. He is not a Quaker, nor Baptist, nor Presbyterian, but a Gortonist, and the only one I have seen. Gorton lives only in him, his only disciple left. He says he knew of no other, and that he is alone. He gave me an account of Gorton's disciples, first and last, and showed me some of Gorton's printed books, and some of his manuscripts.

"He said Gorton had beat down all outward ordinances of baptism and the Lord's Supper, with unanswerable demonstration. That Gorton preached in London, in Oliver's time, and had a church and living of £500 a year offered him, but he believed no sum would have tempted him to take a farthing for preaching. He was at the head of a sect called Gortonians, now extinct—it did not, as the reader will perceive long survive him." —*Extract from Staple's Gorton.*

Though it has been said that he was not "intolerant towards those who differed from him," yet we should rather infer that there must have been something very peculiar, to have led our fathers to have banished him from their jurisdiction. They were eminently tolerant, and favored the largest liberty, where it did not conflict with the rights of others. A man of Gorton's temperament, and strongly biased in favor of his own peculiar notions of religion, would naturally lead him to obtrude his dogmas on the minds of others, however unpleasant it might be; and as our fathers studied peace, and wished no malcontents to remain among them, is the propable cause of his banishment.

It is highly probable that he possessed the spirit which now animates the ultras of the present day, who prefer to rule in h–l, than serve in heaven. On no other ground can we reconcile his banishment from the island.

In 1638, William Baulston was authorized to set up a house of entertainment for strangers, and also to brew beer, and sell wine and *strong* waters. Our fathers would be condemned, in this day of light and knowledge, by a class of fanatics, as being destitute of moral principle, in thus favoring the sale of an article which goes to destroy the bodies and the souls of men.

But it proves them to have been men of common sense, in regulating the sale of an article which they well knew would be used. And to the credit of Newport, there has been far less fanaticism and intolerance on this, as well as on other moral questions, than is to be found in any portion of New-England.

Newport has continued, down to the present day, the sale of spiritous liquors, and without flattery, we challenge the country to produce a more sober and moral community, with a population of nearly ten thousand, than is to be found in the ancient metropolis. Jefferson's motto was, that "that government is best which governs least." But this motto was designed to apply to the attempts of legislators to cure the moral and intellectual evils of society. So far as these attempts are concerned, the less legislation the better.

FIRST INSOLVENCY.

John Luther, a carpenter, having absconded from the island, and being found indebted to several persons, it was ordered that "Mr. Brenton and Mr. Coggeshall, shall take possession of his effects, and shall satisfy his creditors as far as it shall go." They generally, at the present time, take their effects with them, or the proceeds, and thus leave their creditors minus. The age, however, is one of improvement.

"It was ordered that all the sea-banks is free for fishing to the town of Newport." This right was acknowledged to the people under the charter of king Charles II., and preserved in the constitution which is now the fundamental law of the State.

And no proprietor of land has the legal right to prohibit the inhabitants from the enjoyment of the privilege. It is a great public blessing.

June.—It was ordered at a general meeting, that a house for a prison, twelve feet in length and ten in breadth, should be built. Would to God that its limited dimensions could have continued. But as population increased, selfishness became predominant, and as a natural consequence, immorality and crime succeeded, until it was found expedient to enlarge the prisons. In 1772, the present county jail in Newport, was built. It is a substantial brick edifice. The building committee was Oliver Ring Warner. It is pleasantly located in Malborough street. The inmates who are so unfortunate as to be found within its walls, as a general thing, have been treated kindly by the keeper. It is, however, to be lamented that the spirit of the Gospel has not more generally influenced the minds of men, which would have had a salutary tendency in preventing the increase of much evil in the world. As soon as the great law of doing to others as we would others should do to us, begins to be exemplified, the reign of wrong, and injury, and suffering, (leading as it often does to crime,) will rapidly come to an end. Instead of one Howard, one Mrs. Fry, and one Miss Dix, in a century, we should have thousands upon thousands in every department of charity. When we look at what these three individuals have accomplished, what might we not expect from millions laboring with united strength and intellect, in the great work of human welfare! It will be a glorious period when the "fatherhood of God and the brotherhood of man," shall be recognized by all classes. Then will the reign of evil cease, and not before.

Every town was authorized to choose a council of six persons, to manage their town affairs, and to have the trial of small cases.

June 4, 1647.—Cannonicus, the chief Indian Sachem, died this year in a good old age, honored by his tribe, and respected and beloved by the whites who had settled in his territories.

AQUEDNECK INDIANS.

The battle which decided the fate of the Aquedneck Indians, is believed to have been fought in a place about three miles and a quarter from the State House, in Newport, in the town of Middletown, in a swamp, or low ground, near the west road leading to Bristol ferry. The tradition is substantiated by the fact, that very many arrow heads, hatchets, &c., made of a hard stone, have frequently been dug up on the spot, designated in the tradition as the battle field. This was before the purchase of the island. They were subject to the Narragansetts. The seat of Miantunomu was at " Tomony Hill," near Newport. There was formerly a " block-house," built of brick, on this hill. The land fronting on the harbor, where Thames-street now is, was then an impenetrable swamp.

It is well to dwell on the reminiscences of the past, as they carry the mind back to the period when none but the natives were the inhabitants of the island. The sufferings of the aborigines of this country are painful to contemplate, and while many pretend to have their sympathies strongly enlisted on the side of negro slavery, let them reflect, how much greater have been the sufferings of the poor Indian, arising, as it does, from his superior understanding.

Let me inquire of the reader, whether there was ever a nobler character than Philip, the King of the Wampanouages, and one whose sad fate has often been the theme of the poet ? According to the prediction of the Panacos, that he should never fall by the hand of the white man was realized in his death. A renegade Indian shot him in a swamp, at the foot of Mount Haup.

Philip's war lasted more than a year, and was the most distressing period that New England had ever seen, and threatened the total extirpation of her colonies. About six hundred men, the flower of her strength, fell in battle, or were butchered by the savages. In Massachusetts, Plymouth, and Rhode Island, twelve or thirteen towns were utterly destroyed. About six hundred dwelling-houses were burnt, a heavy debt contracted, and a vast amount of property destroyed. There were few families who did not lose some beloved relative in this calamitous war; and a general gloom spread through the country.

The Indians acted on the *defensive;* they felt jealous of their rights, and did not admit the justice and equity of the claim set up by the *pale faces*, to the soil which they had received as a *grant* from the Great Spirit,—and it is no way surprising that Philip and his tribe displayed a hostile attitude towards the enemy of their peace, when they perceived that their domain was passing into other hands, and that they would soon melt away before a superior force. This is a sufficient apology for the course which they pursued towards the colonists; and instead of our exulting and triumphing over their weakness, it should rather be a matter of grief and sorrow, that the possession of this continent was purchased at the expense of the destruction of the Indians.

PHILIP OF MOUNT HAUP.

(BY MISS CASS.)

Philip's head was sent to Plymouth, where it was exposed on a gibbet twenty years, and one of his hands to Boston, where it was exhibited in savage triumph, and his mangled body was denied the right of sepulture, it having been quartered, and hung upon four trees, where it was left, a monument of shocking barbarity.

"To say the least of Philip's humanity, it was as great towards captives, so far as we have any knowledge, as that of the English towards the captive Indians."—*Drake's Biography of Indians.*

"Ye write the white man brave,
When on his native sod,
He lifts his sword to guard and save
His heritage of God.
And earth rings loud, with the deep startling cry—
Of patriots, warring for their liberty.

Ye bid the marble rise,
To shrine his sacred fame;
And loud winds bear along the skies,
His high and holy name.
And ever your children's hearts beat full and strong,
All freedom shout, and glorious triumph sing.

The outrag'd Indian rears
His madden'd battle brand;
And tracks with flame, and blood, and tears,
The oppressors of his land.
And he is savage! and ye give his name
To wear his curse, and be a word for shame.

And even his soulless clay,
Finds not a quiet bed;
The storms may waste it, birds of prey
Feast on the helpless dead—
As if the poor insensate dust could be
A thing for hate, and fiendish mockery.

The gentle Quaker came,
With justice in his hand;
And the whoop lay hush'd, the war-knife's flame
Gleam'd not within the land.
But spread the *Calumet's* soft incense wide,
And rose the olive of the wigwam's side.

Wo! for the red man's wail,
Sweeps o'er New England's hills;
It rides her haughty ocean gale,
And tunes her forest rills.
One jarring echo in the grand old strain,
That ne'er can die along her hallow'd plain."

THE DEATH OF MIANTUNOMU.

As we have noticed the death of Cannonicus, we will also allude to the sad fate of Miantunomu, as they were the two Sachems who conveyed the island of Aquedneck to Mr. Coddington and his friends. Miantunomu was uncle to Cannonicus, and they exercised an important part in the government of the great nation of the Narragansetts.

In 1642, Connecticut became suspicious of Miantunomu, and urged Massachusetts to join them in a war with Uncas, Sachem of the Mohegans. The broil had long existed; but the open rupture was brought on by Uncas making war upon Sequesson, one of the Sachems under Miantunomu. The English accounts say, (and we have no other,) that about 900 warriors were raised by Miantunomu, and about 500 or 600 Mohegans. The Sachem of the former, Miantunomu, intending to chastise Uncas for his adherence to the English, secretly advanced into his country with an army; but Uncas was aware of his approach, and met him on this plain, where both parties halted. Uncas resorted to a stratagem; he stepped forward alone, and challenged Miantunomu to decide the quarrel single-handed. This, as he expected, was refused, and, while his enemies were unprepared, he gave a signal by falling down, when his men instantly set up a yell, discharged their arrows, and rushed forward.

The Narragansetts fled, and many of them were killed. Uncas captured Miantunomu himself, but the haughty Indian would not ask for quarter nor speak a word. He was taken to Hartford, and, after a trial, was delivered to Uncas for execution. He was brought back to this place, and while marching across the fields was tomahawked, on a spot a little east of the road, where a heap of stones for many years marked the place of his burial.

"The place where the battle was fought, was in the eastern part of the town of Norwich, and the place to this day is called the *Sachem's Plain*."—*Note*, from *Winthrop's Journal*.

The sorrowful part of this tale is yet to be told. The Commissioners of the United Colonies having convened at Boston, "who, taking into serious consideration what was safest and best to be done, were all of the opinion, that it would not be safe to set him at liberty; neither had we sufficient ground for us to put him to death."

The awful design of putting to death their friend, they had not yet fixed upon, but calling to their aid in council—whom? —and must it be told?—it has been told before—"five of the most judicious elders;" such as we read of in the apochrypha, who condemned Susannah to death; "they all agreed that he ought to be put to death." This was the final decision, and to complete the deed of darkness, *secrecy* was enjoined upon all, and their determination was to be made known to Uncas privately, with directions that he should execute him within his own jurisdiction, and without torture.

Dr. Trumbull says that "Uncas cut out a large piece of his shoulder and ate it in savage triumph, saying it was the sweetest morsel he ever ate, it made his heart strong." Thus closed a tragedy, which, for infamy, has never been exceeded. And by whom was it effected? *Puritans*—men calling themselves the friends and the advocates of Him who prayed to his Father to "forgive his enemies, for they know not what they do." He was one who had been their friend, according to their own showing, and yet delivered up to the miserable paltroon, Uncas, who by treachery had overcome his enemy. But the conduct of the savage is purity itself, when compared to the vile and disgraceful conduct of those, who having no bowels of compassion, could thus sacrifice a fellow-being on the altar of hatred, malice, and all uncharitableness. But what could we expect better of such men, whose views of God's character, led them to believe that he delighted in misery! For an example, examine Dr. Increase Mather's (Magnolia,) "Prevalence of Prayer," ibid 7. In speaking of the efficacy of prayer in bringing about the destruction of the Indians, he says, "Nor could they cease crying to the Lord against Philip, until they had prayed the bullet into his heart." And in speaking of the slaughter of Philip's people at Narragansett, he says: "We have heard of the two and twenty Indians slain, all of them, and brought down to hell in one day." This is Christianity with a vengeance.

On the death of Miantunomu, Canonchet, his son, became by inheritance, Chief Sachem of the tribe. In "the great swamp fight," as it was familiarly known, he was intercepted and secured by the whites, delivered over to the Mohegan Sachem, Oneco, the son of his father's murderer, and by him put to death by order of the English captors. He was the last who exercised the supremacy over the Narragansett tribe, and now all that is left to call to remembrance these noble warriors is their names, emblazoned on the wheel-house of the steamboats which navigate the Narragansett Bay.

We bless God that we had our birth and education in the State of Rhode Island, where intolerance, bigotry, and cruelty, never flourished; and though our characters have been assailed by "Simon pures," of Massachusetts, as being destitute of true religion, which merely means orthodoxy in the head and not in the heart, we yet have cause to rejoice that charges such as we have enumerated, have never been laid at our door.

Richard Borden, one of the first settlers of Portsmouth, died 25th of third month, 1670, aged seventy years. He was father of Matthew Borden, who was the first white child born on Rhode Island.

THE FIRST CHARTER OF INCORPORATION FROM THE BRITISH CROWN.

"In 1643, Mr. Williams, an agent of the Colonies of Narragansett Bay, obtained a Charter of Incorporation, from the British crown, granting their permission to make laws for themselves, so far as the nature and constitution of the place would admit, subject to the laws of England."

This charter is for civil government only. There is not one word in it about religion or liberty of conscience. Backey, Vol. 1, page 91. This he says he copied from the original manuscript in Mr. Williams' own handwriting, dated Providence 25th, sixth month, 1658.

"That forasmuch as Mr. Roger Williams has taken great pains, and expended much time in obtaining a charter for this province, we do freely give and grant unto the said Roger Williams, £100, to be levied out of the towns, viz., £50 out of Newport, £30 out of Portsmouth, and £20 out of Providence, which rate is to be levied and paid in by the last of November."

Mr. Williams returned with the charter, September 17, 1644. We have no wish or desire to take from Mr. Williams the praise which justly belongs to him—"honor to whom honor is due"—but we do feel conscious that far more has been said of his merits than they well deserve. He has been held up as the oracle of liberty of conscience, and many have been misled into the belief that Rhode Island is indebted to him more than to any other man, for its civil and religious liberties. But we shall have occasion to convince them to the contrary, when we bring forward a man whose character has been neglected, and whose memory nearly forgotten. And this has arisen from the relative position which Providence and Newport occupies. While the former has had a rapid growth, owing to the crowd of adventurers who have resorted there for the purpose of gain, which has, however, sensibly changed its moral character, the latter has declined in commercial prosperity, which has produced a state of supineness, and an entire indifference to her lawful claims, and permitted matters of a highly important nature to be entirely overlooked.

Providence has aimed to exalt Roger Williams, at the expense of his superior, until his name has become as common as household words. We see it emblazoned on banks, insurance companies, and even steamboats which ply in the Narragansett Bay. His name has been canonized as the *ne plus ultra*, and to call in question his character and merits, would be viewed as sacrilegious.

Every author who has attempted to write his biography, has been very careful to keep out of sight his defects, and to publish his virtues to the world, as the originator of civil and religious liberty, until the public have been made to believe that to Roger Williams, and to no one else, Rhode Island is indebted for her privileges.

Now, every writer who has treated on his character, has stood in fear lest an influence should be brought to bear against him, hence they follow in the same track, and continue to eulogize his name. Mr. Williams was not perfect, and a more eccentric man never lived. He had not a well-balanced mind, which his religious career fully proved.

The Rev. Mr. Adlum, in a pamphlet, which he has recently published, showing the origin of the first Baptist church in Newport, and the first in Providence, says of Mr. Williams, that "he was a Baptist only four months. After he left the Baptists, he lived forty-three years, and yet from the records you would not suspect but he was a Baptist to the day of his death. Here was a man, who in the space of four months, had fully made up his mind that there was neither a true ministry, nor true church upon earth; a conviction so strong that he never wavered in it for the forty-three years of his after life. He had been bred in the belief that a regular succession from the apostles downwards, was necessary to a true church and a true ministry."

The manner of his baptism by a layman, we should have thought would have led him to doubt of its validity, and equally so his ordination, which was wholly unauthorized by ecclesiastical usages.

There is evidence that Mr. Williams was not as Catholic as were some of the first settlers; though he had fled from Massachusetts, owing to persecution, yet he is charged with intolerance towards the Quakers, which illustrates and sets forth poor human nature, as it really is. We should not have animadverted on the character of Mr. Williams, had there not been such an effort made by writers, to exalt him above his equals and even superiors.

The united colonies were not content with using compulsion themselves, towards the Quakers, but wished to draw Rhode Island into their measure—and it is on record that Roger Williams favored the measure—but the people of Portsmouth, on Rhode Island, disowned all connection in such arbitrary doings towards their brethren. Portsmouth has ever been an asylum for Quakers from the earliest period of their coming to this country.

A Quaker, Richard Scott, who had been a neighbor of Mr. Williams for thirty-eight years, says of him, that "he was unsettled in his opinions, that which took most with him was, to get honor amongst men. After his society and he, in a church way, were parted, he went to England and got a charter, and coming from Boston to Providence, at Seekonk, the neighbors of Providence met him with fourteen canoes, and carried him to the town. And the man being hemmed in the middle of the canoes, was so elevated and transported out of himself, that I was condemned in myself, that amongst the rest, I had been an instrument to set him up in his pride and folly. Though he professed liberty of conscience, and was so zealous for it at the first coming home of the charter, that nothing in government must be acted till that was granted, yet he could be the forwardest to persecute against those that could not join with him in it."

About the beginning of 1677, came out Mr. Williams' account of his dispute with the Quakers, upon which Mr. Coddington wrote over to his friend Fox, and said: "Here is a lying, scandalous book of Roger Williams', of Providence, printed at Cambridge, New-England. I have known him about fifty years, a mere *weather-cock*, constant only in inconstancy; poor man, that doth not know what should become of his soul, if this night it should be taken from him. He was for the priests, and took up their principles to fight against the truth, and to gratify them and bad magistrates, that licked up his vomit, and wrote the said scurrilous book, and so has transgressed for a piece of bread. One while he is a Separatist, at New-Plymouth, joining with them till they are weary of him; (as appears from Morton's Memorial,) another time you may have him a teacher or a member of the church at Salem. O! then a great deal of devotion is pleaded in women's wearing of veils in their assemblies, as if the power of godliness was in it; and to have the cross out of the color; and then be against the king's patent and authority, and writeth a large book in quarto against it. And another time he is hired for money, and gets a patent from Long Parliament, so that it is not long but he is off and on it again. One time for water baptism—men and women must be plunged into water—and then throws it all down again; one time for men's wearing caps, and not hats, for covering their faces—and again hats and caps; so that Cotton said of him, that 'he was a *haberdasher* of small questions against the power.'"

Mr. Williams, on the 1st of February, 1657–8, issued a warrant against Mr. William Harris, for the alleged crime of opposing the Protector's government. The warrant ordered his arrest and imprisonment, for the purpose of sending him to England, in accordance, probably, with the act of June, 1665. How far this strong measure was deserved by the conduct of Mr. Harris, we cannot now determine. It has been inferred that it was not sustained by public opinion, because at the next election Mr. Williams was superseded as President, by Mr. Benedict Arnold. It is not improbable that he was urged too far, by a zeal to uphold the charter, and the Protector's authority, and perhaps by personal hostility towards Mr. Harris, between whom and himself, there was for many years a very acrimonius feud.

"It appears that Mr. Williams so disliked Mr. Harris, that he would not write his name at length, but abbreviated it thus, 'W. Har.' This mode of writing is seen in the fac-simile prefixed to this volume."—*Knowles' Memoirs of Williams.*

"Mr. Harris soon after went to England to endeavor to settle the dispute between himself and Roger Williams, but the vessel was captured by an Algerine corsair, and he was sold for a slave. His family, in Rhode Island, redeemed him by the sale of a part of his property. He arrived in England, but died there. He was an able man, and we may hope a good man, notwithstanding some infirmities. His quarrels with Roger Williams were discreditable to them both—on which side the most blame lay, we cannot now decide."—*Backus*, volume 1., page 421.

We should rather be inclined to think that Williams was the most in fault, from the fact of his proneness to get into difficulty. The family of Harris are highly respectable in Rhode Island; some of the original land of William Harris, is still in possession of the family.

Roger Williams was the pioneer in the settlement of Providence, and had he possessed the amiable traits of character which distinguished John Clarke, of Newport, he would undoubtedly have been a public blessing to the Colony. But unfortunately, his disposition was irritable, which often led him into trouble. He had the bump of combattiveness largely developed, and was ever ready to enter into disputation; (this seemed to be his *forte.*) In 1672, George Fox, the founder of the sect called Friends, or Quakers, arrived in Rhode Island, and commenced preaching at Newport. Roger Williams visited Newport, and held public disputations with George Fox and others. He had a zeal, not always tempered with knowledge, or otherwise he would have left to each sect, the right to enjoy their own sentiments undisturbed, and never have been guilty of persecution in the least degree. But it shows that he was fallible, like all other men, and had not attained to Christian perfection.

And yet it seems passing strange, that one who had felt the power of oppression, and who had been compelled to flee from Massachusetts' tyranny, did not extend the hand of fellowship to all, of whatever name or sect, who desired to settle within his jurisdiction. But few, however, are properly qualified to exercise power aright—the passions of the human mind, when not restrained, are apt to break forth in a manner which conflicts with the "higher law," of which so much is said at the present day. Some allowance must, however, be made for the period in which he lived. Undoubtedly, there were difficulties to be encountered, and trials to be borne, which required a large share of philosophy to overcome, and if his temperament was ardent and impetuous, he is to be pitied and not severely condemned.

We have been strongly inclined to the belief, that the impress left by Mr. Williams on the Plantations, has had an influence in forming the character of its inhabitants, for liberty of opinion has been far less enjoyed there, than in Newport and the south counties. In secular matters, there has been a disposition to coerce and to bring the people under the ban of the law in matters, too, which were unconstitutional in their nature, which it behoves every patriot and friend to human rights, to condemn.

It must be conceded that the inhabitants of the Island of Rhode Island, were the most active in procuring the inestimable privileges of civil and religious liberty. Here, true Republicanism existed, without aristocratic domination, and it should be the duty of every citizen, to guard against every encroachment attempted to be made against their dearest rights, and heaven-born privileges. Let them glory in the names of Clarke and Coddington, for to them belongs the honor of rearing the standard of Liberty and Independence.

LONGEVITY OF THE FIRST SETTLERS OF THE ISLAND.

Mr. Nicholas Easton, who came, in 1638, from Hampton to Newport, lived to 1675, when he died a very ancient man. His son, Mr. John Easton, who as his father was divers times Governor of the Colony, died in 1705, in the eighty-fifth year of his age. Mr. H. Bull, one of the eighteen that incorporated themselves at the first, was Governor of the Colony, and lived to an advanced age. Mr. Edward Thurston, who was assistant in 1675, and many times deputy for Newport, died 1786–7, aged ninety years.

Many such instances might be given, and many of the second generation, such I mean as were born within the first twenty or twenty-five years, reached to fourscore and some ninety years. If we consider the longevity of many of the first-comers, notwithstanding the hardships and distresses they underwent, and the change of climate, diet, &c., and to this add the great age of many of their children, we cannot call the country unhealthy, or the inhabitants short-lived; and to this day, perhaps, there is no spot that can be compared to the island for the duration of human life.

SHORTNESS OF PROVISIONS.

January 22d, 1639, it was found that there were but one hundred and eight bushels of corn, to supply ninety-six persons, which, at the proportion of one bushel and half-a-peck to each, was not then sufficient to supply them for six weeks ; and yet it was then more than so many months to harvest. But there was plenty of fish, fowl, and *venison*, and soon after, even to this day, the necessaries of life have been plentiful.

Some of the principal persons who came at first to the island, removed again in a little time, some to Long Island for larger accommodations, and some to Massachusetts again, where three of those families have made a considerable figure ever since, to this day, viz. : Hutchinson, Dunmow, and Savage.

Mrs. Ann Hutchinson, of whom mention has been made, after being banished from Massachusetts, came to Rhode Island. From thence she went with her family to East Chester, in New-York, where they were all killed by the Indians, except one daughter, who, after remaining some time among the Indians, was redeemed, and married to Mr. Cole, and lived to old age. A similar account is given in a history of the Indian wars, written by Mr. Niles.

Edward Hutchinson, jun., was mortally wounded in Philip's war. William Hutchinson came over from England in 1634, and died in Newport in 1642. His wife, Anne, was killed by the Indians in 1643. In the records of the old or first church in Boston, we find Edward Hutchinson, senior, admitted a member in 1663, and Edward Hutchinson, junior, and William Hutchinson, merchant, in 1634. Several of the Hutchinson family came to Newport, in consequence of the religious persecutions in Massachusetts. They owned land both in Newport and Narragansett, and their names are frequently found on the records.

William Hutchinson, jun. (second,) Edward Hutchinson, sen., and Edward Hutchinson, jun., were among the first purchasers of Newport, about 1636, to which allusion has been already made. We also find land allotted there to Samuel Hutchinson, in 1638. Some of the family, as before remarked, returned to Boston. See " Bull's Extracts from the State Records."

Capt. Edward Hutchinson, by his will, proved in Boston, 1675, gave all his Narragansett lands to his daughters, Elizabeth Winslow, Ann Dyre, and Susanna Hutchinson. Susanna afterwards married Nathaniel Coddington, of Newport. Ann afterwards married Daniel Verner, the ancestor of the present family of Vernon, of Newport. See "Deeds in Secretary's office, book 1, 442; Records at Wickford, book 2, 121, 123. Updike's History." There is none of the name now to be found in Newport, although numerous in many of the New England States.

Thomas Clifton was one of the earliest settlers. From him the Clifton burial place takes its name. It is situated at the head of Golden-street; it is an ancient ground.

William Brenton was a native of England, and previous to his removal, was a respectable merchant of Boston. He came to Rhode Island soon after the first settlement. He was Deputy-Governor from 1640 to 1646; President of the Colony from 1660 to 1662, and Governor from 1665 to 1669. He was one of the largest proprietors of land on Rhode Island, and owned the whole of the land called Brenton's Neck. He died in 1674, at an advanced age, leaving three sons and four daughters.

Jaheel Brenton, was the eldest son of Governor William Brenton, and inherited most of the estate. He was the first Collector of Boston appointed by the king. In 1699, in consequence of some personal difficulty with Sir William Phipps, the Governor of Massachusetts, he went to England, when he and others preferred charges against the Governor, who, in consequence, was summoned to Whitehall, to answer for his conduct. Governor Phipps died of fever soon after he had arrived in England, and before the trial could take place.

Mr. Brenton was soon after appointed Agent for the Colony of Rhode Island, and as such remained in England several years. He returned from England with a commission from the

King, appointing him Surveyor-General of the Customs of the American Colonies.

He owned all the land in Newport, which is now known as Brenton's Neck, where he had his residence; he also owned a large tract of land in Narragansett, being one of the original Pettaquamsett purchasers.

He died in Newport, on the 8th of November, 1732, aged 77 years, without issue. He was buried on his own land, in that part which is now the site of Fort Adams. By his will, he gave all his lands in the Neck, known as the Hammersmith and Rocky Farms, to his nephew, the second Jaheel Brenton. In 1720, he built the house in Thames-street, now in the possession of Simmons S. Coe. Among his descendants, was the gallant Jaheel Brenton, Admiral of the British navy, and the Hon. Brenton Halliburton, of the Supreme Court of Nova Scotia, both natives of Newport.

In 1681, Peter Easton, and the Executor of John Clarke, were ordered to lay out the common burial ground in Newport, —from which it would appear that John Clarke gave the land for that express purpose. This burial ground had been suffered to lie neglected for years, until it was painful to witness it, when the suggestion was made, that the subject of renovating and improving the ground should be brought up in town meeting, which was accordingly done, when an appropriation of 200 dollars was made, and subsequently $500; and laborers were employed to right and paint the stones, and to lay out new walks, where no graves were visible. The work was commenced in 1848, and the committee, under whose supervision the praiseworthy undertaking was commenced and completed, were the Hon. Edward W. Lauton, and Wm. C. Clarke, Esq. Mr. Clarke took a lively interest in the matter, and it reflects great credit on the town.

Benedict Arnold, was born in England in 1615; he came to this country with his father, William Arnold. They were among the first settlers of Providence, but afterwards formed a settlement at Pawtuxet. In 1653, Benedict Arnold removed to Newport, and was admitted a purchaser there ia May, the same year; in ,1654, he was appointed a Commissioner for Newport; and, in 1657, was chosen President of the Colony, which he held until 1659. He was an Assistant in 1660 and

1661, and again President in 1662 and 1663. In the Charter of 1663, he was named as the first Governor, and was re-elected by the people, with brief intervals, until 1678. He died on the 9th of June, 1678, aged 63 years, leaving four sons and three daughters. He was a large proprietor of land in Newport, Connanicut, and Narragansett. His house stood where the banking house of the Union Bank, now stands. He was buried in the lot which he directed to be set apart for that purpose, which is now an old burying-ground in the rear of the Unitarian church. The ground which was set apart, was three rods square, with the right of way to it. The entrance is from Pelham street, through the grounds of Captain Littlefield.

As the name of Governor Benedict Arnold, and Benedict Arnold, the traitor, are liable to be blended together, we would state the fact, for the benefit of the reader, that there is not the remotest connection existing between them. Governor Arnold was distinguished for his virtue and integrity; his repeated elections to the first place in the Colony, shows his popularity, and the confidence which was reposed in him by his constituents.

We would suggest the propriety of renovating the ground where repose the mouldering ashes of this devoted patriot. We know not whether any collateral branches of the family exist at present on the island; it is certain, however, that there are none in the male line. The extinction of once numerous and highly respectable families, on the island, shows the uncertainty of worldly glory, and the vanity of relying upon any thing earthly.

A BELL-MAN CHOSEN.

1681. A bell-man was chosen to walk up the streets, one whole year, as the town shall agree, and Richard Barnes was chosen. He came out with Mr. John Clarke, the first settler on the island. He was to ring if any thing be brought into the town, as fruit, or fish, &c., "he shall not need to stop at each place, but going along giving notice thereof by a *loud noise.*" This practice is still kept up in the ancient town, and does not disturb the *nerves* of the inhabitants.

1691. Lawrence Clarke had liberty to dig clay and make brick, on the common near Samuel Cranston's land, he doing no damage; and even before this period, permission was granted to make brick, as early as 1681. Why it was discontinued we have no account.

1693. Arnold Collins petitioned for half an acre of land on the common, to set up a fulling mill, which was granted. John Easton, jr., had one quarter of an acre of land to set up a malting-house, to have it as long as he made malt. John Hicks had an acre of land on Goat Island, for a ship-yard, for him and his heirs and assigns, who follow ship-building, paying such rent as they and the committee of the town shall agree.

In 1696, a Seal for the town was procured, with the device of a sheep.

1699. Benjamin Bears, and John Hervey, had liberty to erect a building on the north end of Goat Island, to cure fish. A law was made to prevent oyster shells from being burnt in the streets, except by the liberty of the town or lime kilns. It appears that shell lime was much used at that day, and many of the ancient buildings now standing, confirm the fact.

Oct., 1710. The petition of Mr. Gallaway, for liberty of teaching a Latin school, in the little rooms in the school-house, was granted. Newport has paid a strict regard to education, from the earliest period of the settlement of the island.

"In 1782, John Mumford, surveyor, was authorized to survey the streets of the town; and the Town Council directed to name the streets, as the town had grown to the admiration of all, and was the metropolitan."—*Town Records.*

It is much to be regretted that the codfishery had not been prosecuted in Newport, as the spot is so admirably adapted to the business. It has been made profitable where it has been carried on, giving employment to seamen, as well as enriching the community, and no good and sufficient reason can be offered why it should not be revived in Newport. It is a safe investment, and requiring far less capital than is needed in many other commercial transactions. The bounty paid by the general government, aids very much in the liquidation of the expenses of the voyage. It would seem from the records, that in the early settlement of Newport, the inhabitants turned their attention to every kind of trade, and the rapid and unexampled growth of the place was an evidence of the enterprise which characterized the inhabitants.

To what an extent brick was made, and how long the business was conducted, we have no means of knowing at this late period. We should rather be inclined to the belief that the material was not of the best kind, or otherwise the work would not have been abandoned.

About twenty-five years ago, a discovery was made of yellow ochre, on the Taylor farm, now owned by the Hon. Wm. B. Lawrence. Some gentleman from abroad experimented upon it, hoping to be able to make a yellow paint of it, but after a fair trial it was given up. This gave to Taylor's Point, the modern name of Ochre Point, though we much prefer the former one for its antiquity, the property having been in possession of the Taylor family from a very early period of the settlement of the island.

EASTON'S POINT.

This Point was originally the property of Governor Nicholas Easton, who, on his marriage with Ann Clayton, gave it by deed to her, and confirmed it in his will to her as his wife.

In 1694, a certain William Edwards, a member of the Society of Friends, gave by will to his executors, who were Daniel Gould, Edward Thurston, William James, John Lurkett, the residue of his estate, for the benefit of that society. In the year 1698, they purchased of Ann Bull, widow of Governor Henry Bull, and previously widow of Nicholas Easton, the Point farm, consisting of about sixty-five acres, part of which, in 1714, they laid out in house lots, and made a second division, in 1725, which they rented out at very low rates. The Society has the original plot and regular minutes of the proprietors ever since. The most of the land has since been disposed of, and but a few acres now belong to the Society.

In early times, the Society of Friends was very large. In 1700, about one-half the population of Newport were of that persuasion, and in that year they built the present meeting-house in which they now worship. There have been many ministers, and other conspicuous members of that Society, who lived in Newport and its vicinity. A large proportion of its Governors and other officers, were of that denomination, amongst whom may be enumerated Wm. Coddington, Nicholas Easton, John Easton, Walter Clarke, Henry Bull, John Wanton, Gideon Wanton, and Governor Hopkins, all members of the Society. Mr. Bull says that there was a Friends' meeting-house in Newport, before this was built, probably soon after they came to this country. It stood opposite Coddington burial-ground, which was taken down and some of the materials worked into that which is now the rear of the present meeting-house, which extends thirty feet north of the main building. The denomination from having been very numerous on the island, are at present greatly diminished.

In 1704, the General Assembly passed an act for fixing the soldiers' wages, whether volunteers or impressed, for the service of Goat Island, at £12 per year.

In 1696, a negro named Peter Pylatt, was executed at Newport, for the crime of rape, after which his body was hung in chains on Tommony Hill.

It was voted to offer one penny for a blackbird's head, and two pennies for a crow.

About 1660, and many years afterward, provision pay was one hundred per cent beneath sterling money.

1739. This year the freemen of the town of Newport, granted a new company the right of extending the Long Wharf from Thames street, westward, across the Cove or Flats, to Sandy Point, called Easton's Point, across the said Point, eight hundred feet westward, to Goat Island, from low-water mark, and the fee and privilege to be vested in the company, together with the privileges of all right which the town had in the water, on the north and south sides of the premises, 45 feet in length, &c.

The income arising from the Long Wharf, was for many years devoted to the support of a school kept in Washington street, on the Point. The building which belonged to the company, and occupied for a school, was subsequently sold; it continued however, until the free school system went into operation in Newport. The wharf is in the hands of trustees, and what disposition is made of the income, after keeping the wharf in repair, we have no means of knowing. It would certainly look, after reading the grant made by the town to the company, that they had the exclusive right to manage it as they please. Present length 2183 feet.

At the North side of Long Wharf was situated Barney's Ferry to Connanicut—at that date there were three ferries to Connanicut—two on the Point, Barney's, Ellery's, and Carr's, the present one from Ferry Wharf—all these ferries were constantly employed in bringing large numbers of cattle, horses and mules, from Connecticut, as well as from all parts of this State; and an endless number of hogs were annually brought from Connecticut to this market, and slaughtered for shipping.

Edward Thurston was a native of England, and came to Rhode Island soon after the first settlement. He held many important offices. He died in 1706, aged ninety years, and was buried in the Coddington burial-place. He left six sons and several daughters, from whom are descended all the Thurstons of this State.

In 1710, Anthony Young had liberty to take limestone from the rocks in the harbor, to make lime with. We presume that the business was not long pursued, or otherwise the rock would soon have disappeared. We are not able to decide on the quality of lime made from the rock, never having seen it tested.

A committee was appointed to grant lots for wharfs round the Cove, and so to Gravelly Point. The first town club in Newport was formed this year, 1726.

In 1733, the first market-house, on the Ferry Wharf in New port was built. This year the Assembly granted £50 towards re-building the Point Bridge in Newport.

COLONY-HOUSE BUILT.

1733. The General Assembly this year voted to erect a new Colony-House, in Newport, on the site where the old one stood. The building to be of brick, eighty feet by forty. Peter Bours, Esbon Sanford, George Goulding, and George Wanton, were appointed to superintend the building. Richard Munday was the architect who drew a plan of the building. In 1743, the Court House was not finished.

The old Colony House was sold and removed to a lot in Prison Lane, where it was converted into a dwelling-house, and is still standing. The Colony House, or the present State House, is a beautiful specimen of architecture. Fronting the Parade, with the Mall on the left, gives to it an imposing appearance.

In 1783, the clock in the State House was put up by Benjamin Dudley, an ingenious clock and watch-maker of Newport. The expense was defrayed by private subscription.

In 1774, Christopher Gardner, a native of Newport, opened a Circus, in which he performed surprising feats of horsemanship. He was the son of Henry Gardner, who was the keeper of a tavern, at the head of Tanner street, in Newport.

"NEWPORT, JUNE 15, 1774.

HORSEMANSHIP,

BY CHRISTOPHER GARDNER,

THE ORIGINAL AMERICAN RIDER,

WHO WILL PERFORM ON

ONE, TWO, AND THREE HORSES,

Nearly all the parts which were exhibited here by the celebrated

MR. BATES.

In several of which parts, it is allowed by good judges, he fully equals, or rather excels, any thing of the kind ever performed in this country.

TO-MORROW,

GRATIS, for the Entertainment of all who please to attend,

If the weather be good, if not, the next day, he will Ride at the north-east part of Newport;

and there will be performed

TAYLOR RIDING TO BRENTFORD.

The doors will be opened at Three o'clock in the Afternoon; and he will mount precisely at Four. The seats are suitable for ladies and gentlemen.

Tickets, at a Quarter-of-a-dollar each, to be had of Messrs. Ichabod Potter, Robert Lillibridge, jun., William Davis, and at the Printing-office, by those who chuse to pay.

'Tis hoped no persons will bring any dogs with them.

Mr. Gardner expects to give entire satisfaction, and will gratefully acknowledge all the favours of those ladies and gentlemen who will oblige him with their company."

[From the original printed Handbill.]

T. Bonar 174 Nassau St

State House and Parade

In 1770. On Wednesday, died at Portsmouth, on the island, Mrs. Mary Thomas, and Mrs. Abigail Burrington, widows, both in the 81st year of their age: they were both born in one year, died in one day, and were both buried the same day.

"Some persons from Connecticut, came to town a few days since, with a large sum of money, in order to purchase goods; but *failing* of a supply here, they proceeded immediately to Newport."—From the *Providence Paper*, 1770.

THE CREWLESS VESSEL.

1750. This year a remarkable circumstance occurred at Newport. A vessel was discovered one morning, apparently coming from the eastward, close in to Easton's Beach, with all sails standing; she seemed suddenly to alter her course, avoiding the rocks, and directly came on shore, at the north-west corner of the beach. No one having been seen on board, she was boarded by some fishermen, who were spectators of the scene, and to their great surprise and astonishment, no person was found on board, but they found the table set for breakfast, the kettle boiling, a *dog* and *cat* in the cabin, and every thing undisturbed, except the long-boat, which was missing, as if the crew had that moment left her.

The vessel proved to be a brig, belonging to Mr. Isaac Steele, a merchant of Newport, which had been hourly expected from the Bay of Honduras. She had been spoken a day or two before, by a vessel which had arrived in port. The brig was commanded by Capt. Huxham. No tidings were ever heard of him or his crew, and what became of them will probably remain forever a mystery.

"It is a fearful mystery,
That lies unfathom'd yet;
There never came a word or sign,
From those we still regret.

I dare not muse upon their fate,
Its horror, its despair;
But all among the gazers knew,
No mortal hand was there!"

The vessel was afterwards got off, and William Lee, the grandfather of Robert P. Lee, Esq., cashier of the Rhode Island Union Bank, assisted in getting her off. She was brought round to Godfrey Melbone's wharf, and sold to Henry Collins, then an eminent merchant of Newport, who changed her name to the *Beach Bird*, by which name she made many voyages. This vessel is said to have been in existence, as late as when the British forces took possession of this island; they found her dismantled at one of the wharves, cut her down, and converted her into an armed galley. The most probable conjecture which can be formed of this singular event is, that the crew, becoming terrified on hearing the sound of the breakers, and considering their danger to be imminent, had recourse to the long-boat, and thus perished.

EXECUTION OF PIRATES.

Two pirate sloops, the *Ranger*, and the *Fortune*, which had committed various piracies on the high seas, being in company, on the 8th of May, 1723, captured the ship *Amsterdam Merchant*, John Welland, master; the day after which capture they plundered and sunk the ship. On the 6th day of June, in lat. 39°, they took a Virginia sloop, rifled her, and let her go, who the next day fell in with His Majesty's ship, the *Greyhound*, Capt. Solgard, of 20 guns, to whom they related the circumstances of their late capture and release. Capt. Solgard immediately pursued, and on the 10th, came up with the pirate sloops, about 14 leagues south of the east end of Long Island, who, mistaking him for a merchant ship, immediately gave chase, and soon commenced firing on the Greyhound, under a black flag, but then hauled down the black flag and hoisted a red one. The Greyhound succeeded in capturing one of the sloops, after having seven men wounded, but the other pirate escaped. The Greyhound came with the prize into the harbor of Newport, and the pirates, thirty-six in number, were committed for trial; twenty-six were sentenced to be hanged, which execution took place on Gravelly Point, opposite the town, on the 19th July, 1723. After execution, their bodies were carried to Goat Island, and buried on the shore, between high and low-water mark.

The names of the pirates that were executed on Friday, July the 19th, 1723, at Newport, on Rhode Island, were—

Charles Harris	Thomas Hugget
Thomas Linniear	Peter Cues
Daniel Hyde	William Jones
Stephen Mundon	Edward Eaton
Abraham Lacy	John Brown
Edward Lawson	James Sprinkly
John Tompkins	Joseph Sound
Francis Laughton	Charles Church
John Fitzgerald	John Waters
William Studfield	Thomas Powell
Owen Rice	Joseph Libbey
William Read	Thomas Hazel
William Blades	John Bright.

Most of these men were foreigners; but one belonged to Rhode Island. They were principally natives of England. Perhaps there never was a greater number executed at any one period, in the history of this country.

Block Island, was named after Adrian Block, a Dutch navigator, who, in the summer of 1644, built on the banks of the Hudson, the first decked vessel ever built within the old United States. The vessel was called *Yatch*, and made her first voyage through Hell Gate, into the Sound, as far as Cape Cod, by the Vineyard. It was on this voyage that Block Island was discovered. The island is about nine miles long, and contains a population of 1,262, according to the last census, in 1850. They are a hardy race of men, engaged principally in fishing and agriculture. It is nine miles to the nearest land.

The codfish cured by the islanders, commands a higher price in the market, than those which are taken and cured elsewhere. The soil is rich and fertile, which enables them to export oats, stock, poultry, &c. Their boats, which are perfectly unique in their construction, will live in a gale, while larger craft have to make a harbor. There is on the island, three places of public worship. One close communion, and two free-will Baptist churches. It lays thirty miles south-west from Newport.

A number of pirates were executed in November, as appears

by an Act of the Assembly, for paying the expense of the conviction and execution. They are said to have been executed in the lot, near the Powder-house, at Newport, which afterwards bore the name of the "Gallow's Field."

William Jeffray, was a native of England; at what time he came to America is unknown, but we find him in Massachusetts as early as 1628. He came to Rhode Island soon after the first settlement, and, in 1639, was one of the persons appointed to set off the lands of the first settlers of Newport.

He appears to have been held in great respect by the colonists, and was consulted on all important occasions, and was several times an assistant or deputy from Newport. He was in England about the time of the trial and execution of Charles I., which it is probable, was the origin of a tradition which has always existed, that he was one of the judges on the trial of that unfortunate monarch, and as such his grave is pointed out to this day. He owned a farm of about seventy acres on the Neck, and the point extending out from the farm, is called Jeffray's Point. The extremes of the Neck belonged to Coggeshall and Brenton, while the centre part embraced Price's Neck. We presume Price was an owner, as well as Jeffray's. He died on the 2d of June, 1675, at the advanced age of eighty-five years, and was buried in the common burial place.

Here lieth interred, the body of

WILL. JEFFRAY, GENT.

WHO DEPARTED THIS LIFE ON YE 2D DAY OF JUNE, 1675.

In the 85th year of his age.

Since every tomb an epitaph can have,
The muses owe their tribute to this grave—
And to succeeding ages recommend
His worthy name, who lived and died their friend.

VIVIT POST TEMERE VIRTUS.

DISTRESSING ACCIDENT.

Sept. 17, 1744, was memorable for a most distressing accident, which took place in Newport. A number of gentlemen had collected on the wharf of Col. Malbern, to view the fitting out of two privateers, when a quantity of powder, which had been placed in one of the stores, by some unaccountable means, exploded, killing or wounding a number of persons.

By this accident, the town lost three of its principal citizens, William Coddington, Esq., Mr. Grant, and John Gidley, Esq., who were either killed or died of their wounds. Mr Coddington was a grandson of Governor Coddington, and had held many offices in the colony. Mr. Grant was a native of Scotland, and a respectable merchant of Newport; he was the maternal grandfather of the late Christopher G. Champlin; and Mr. Gidley was an enterprizing merchant, and son of Judge Gidley, of the Vice-Admiralty Court. The house owned and occupied by Mr. Gidley, passed from his grandson to the late Major Breeze, and is now in possession of the heirs of the late Thomas Breeze, of the United States Navy. The street north, is named Gidley, in honor of that gentleman. To those who are fond of reminiscences, such incidents will prove highly interesting and amusing. Newport has been the scene of many wonderful events, and it would be impossible to embody, in a work of this kind, all of them, but as a record of facts, we have aimed to give the reader the benefit of the most striking incidents which have occurred on the island.

Col. William Coddington, was son of Thomas and Mary Coddington, and grandson of the elder Gov. William Coddington, who emigrated from England to Boston with Gov. Winthrop, in 1630. His first wife was Comfort Arnold, eldest daughter of Benedict, son or grandson of Gov. Benedict Arnold. Col. Coddington was born January 1st, 1690, and was a well-educated and accomplished gentleman. The Rev. John Callender, in his century sermon, delivered in Newport, in 1738, which was dedicated to him, says:

" It is not barely to give you a public testimony of my gratitude for many personal favors, nor yet that esteem and respect which *all* men bear you, for your singular equity and benevolence, not only in private life, but in all the various offices in which you have adorned your country, that I prefix your name to these papers—but because an attempt to recover some account of this happy island, and to make a religious improvement of the merciful providence of God towards it, is justly due to the lineal representative of that worthy gentleman, who was the great instrument of its original settlement.

"If the following discourse has done any justice to the memory and character of the pious people who first settled this colony; or, if it has any tendency to promote the true, original ends of this plantation, I am sure of your patronage. And, as to what relates to some articles, different from your judgment and practice in religious matters, the generosity and candor you inherit from your great ancestors, will easily bear with me in endeavoring to vindicate my own opinions on such an occasion."

Such an eulogium, from the pen of the gifted Callender, on the excellencies of character which were possessed by Col. Coddington, and his ancestor Gov. Coddington, place them in the first rank as the advocates of those sound and liberal principles, which operated in a most remarkable manner, in building up this colony.

It would seem from a perusal of Mr. Callender's sermon, that he was *entirely* free from sectarianism. While he took the liberty to think for himself, and to make his own deductions, he left to others the same inherent right, and hence a mutual good feeling existed among the different branches of Christ's Church in Newport, and which has continued to a great degree, and perhaps greater than in any other spot in New-England.

JOHN CLARKE, AND THE CHARTER OF 1663.

Having already alluded to John Clarke, and the important part which he took in the cause of religious liberty, we now propose to enter more fully on the work, as this is a point of vital interest to the inhabitants of the ancient metropolis. Too long have the laurels been plucked from his brow to grace those of another, without one voice being raised in its condemnation.

Like Americus Vespucius, who stole the glory from Columbus, to enrich and ennoble his own character, so has the merit been bestowed on Williams, which pre-eminently belongs to Clarke. We have said that owing to the decline of commerce in Newport, which was her chief support, and which made her the second commercial emporium in the Colonies, has followed in its train, a want of *self-respect*, in not fearlessly asserting her just claims, of being the first in the sacred cause of human rights. Adverse providences in communities, as well as individuals, are apt to lessen the interest which should ever predominate in the human mind, to stand by the principles which were purchased at a great sacrifice by our pious forefathers, and never permit them to be wrested from us with impunity. This has been sadly realized in the matter now under consideration. There has been a spirit at work in this State which has operated most sensibly against that true independence of character, which ought most especially to distinguish this people above others. A few have assumed to have in possession all the wisdom, to guide and direct the affairs both of Church and State, and to crush the least emotion of patriotism, which has occasionally burst forth from the bosom of others. It is to this cause alone that we attribute the want of talent so obviously witnessed in this State. The question is often asked by those of other States,—" Are there no minds in Rhode Island qualified to compete with men of other sections, whose abilities have assisted them to the highest posts of honor and distinction ?" Our reply has ever been in the affirmative ; and that the only cause has arisen from not encouraging and putting men forward, but rather laboring to hold them back, for fear that their own *ignorance* would be the more apparent. What other valid reason can be offered ? Have we not facilities for education ? Is there not an institution called Brown University, which *professes* to rank high in the scale of literature ? Then what prevents the development of mind ? Is the moral soil sterile and unproductive ? Is this our unhappy lot ? The reason is too plain and obvious to admit of a question—it is the want of independence to speak out boldly our thoughts ; every thing has become *stereotyped*, in morals and in politics, so that the moment a sentiment is advanced, not in agreement with previous views, such minds must be sacrificed on the altar of prejudice. While they prate much of the "land of Roger Williams," as the hallowed spot where liberty of conscience is enjoyed, it is, alas, only in *theory!* while the practical working is *restriction* with a vengeance. Now, this spirit did not formerly exist to that degree in the capital of the State, and God grant that it never may. Never let it be said that on the spot which contains the ashes of a Clarke and a Coddington, the people have become so far recreant to the principles espoused by those sainted patriots, as to permit the light which emanated from them to be extinguished forever.

Mr. Clarke procured the Charter, against the combined influence of Massachusetts, whose appointed agents were Edward Winslow, and John Winthrop.

The honor of obtaining the charter of 1663, belongs to John Clarke alone ; for, as Mr. Backus has observed, "There is not one word in the first charter about 'Religion, or Liberty of Conscience.' But John Clarke's charter of Charles the 2d, has it fully expressed."—Backus, vol. 1, p. 91. Now when it is considered that Mr. Clarke *mortgaged* his property to go on his mission, and was absent twelve years from his family ; and at the court of Charles 2d, labored assiduously to procure the instrument, and did procure it,—who, we ask, has the right to share with him the honor ? It was his conciliating manners, which was the means in the accomplishment of the object. It was a most remarkable instrument, considering the source from whence it emanated. It granted every thing which Mr. Clarke wished or desired, and the State would have been far better off, had they remained under it to this day. For, in throwing it off, so far from improving their liberties, the result has been a diminution of their political rights.

In *Allen's Biographical Dictionary*, article, "CLARKE, JOHN,—On the principles afterwards set forth in the 'Declaration of American Independence,' as you have justly observed ; and, perhaps, Mr. Editor, you may not be aware of the fact, that Mr. Jefferson himself stated to a gentleman of this State, now deceased, who visited him about twenty years ago, that he derived those principles from our ancestors, with whose history and writings he seemed to be minutely acquainted, and especially of Mr. Clarke, of whom he spoke, highly contrasting him with Williams, Locke, &c., and preferring him for his mild, yet firm consistency with which he maintained the great principles which he promulgated contemporaneously with Williams, (while Locke was forty years behind them,) and for his persevering, self-sacrificing, and efficient efforts in establishing them in the charter he procured of Charles II. To Mr. Clarke, he gave the credit of being the *author*, as well as procurer of that charter. And here I would observe, that great injustice has been done to Mr. Clarke, in ascribing to Mr. Williams the authorship of that charter; and why deprive Mr. Clarke, whose ability, diligence, and interest in the hearts of our superiors our fathers praised and confided in, of the credit due to his services? Was he inferior to Mr. Williams in talents, education, weight of character, influence, or efficiency of service? I believe it to be susceptible of proof, that he was not, in either.

Neither was Mr. Williams in England at the time,—he went in company with Mr. Clarke, in 1651, but returned in 1654, while Mr. Clarke continued steadily at his post, to look after the interests of the colony, contending with the agents of Massachusetts and Connecticut, until 1663. And the charter which he procured of King Charles, contains no principles which Mr. Clarke had not maintained before he left Rhode Island. Indeed, as early as the 12th of March, 1640, long before the settlements were united, the Assembly of the island, solemnly recognized the great principles of civil and religious liberty, and passed the "first legislative act on record, relating to liberty of conscience." —Monday's *Courrier*, in relation to the late "New-England Festival" in New-York.

Here is an admission which we are very happy to chronicle. Thus, the claim of Mr. Williams, resting as it does, on the supposed influence of Sir Henry Fane, must fall, and the charter must stand as the charter of John Clarke, and he be allowed to share equally with Mr. Williams, the high honor of establishing the first government in the world, which gave to all, equal civil and religious liberty.

To Mr. Clarke, the colony of Rhode Island was, in our opinion, indebted in a greater degree, than to any other of her founders. He was the original projector of the settlement of the island, and one of its first and oldest civilians. In reducing the government to order, Mr. Clarke was much relied on, and held the first rank in legislative intelligence. He was to the rude and boisterous materials among which his lot was east, what the pendulum is to the time-piece. We never find him engaged in angry controversy with those of different persuasions; but, on the contrary, endeavoring to practice and establish what he professed, toleration to all.—*Memoirs of Rhode Island.*

After Mr. Clarke's return, he was "*improved*" in various public offices, was elected Deputy Governor, three years successively, in two of which he accepted the office, but all the concerns of the State did not prevail with him, as it has done with many, to neglect the affairs of religion.

We think that it would be fully as appropriate to call it the land of Clarke as of Williams, after having read the evidence which has been offered, of who was the actual procurer of the charter of Charles II., in 1663.

It behooves the inhabitants of Newport, to speak of his name and to venerate his worth. Let it be emblazoned on some public building, "to be known and read of all men," that our children may learn to esteem a man who has bequeathed to them, such inestimable privileges. Many scarcely know that such a one ever existed, or fulfilled his part so well. Be it our duty to rescue from oblivion, his name and noble deeds, which were appreciated by so gifted a mind as Jefferson's.

The subject is a fruitful one, and might be extended, but we are reminded that in a work like this, brevity is required, in order to glance at the various events which have occurred in our history.

Let the Plantations exult and triumph in its founder, Roger Williams, while the State of Rhode Island, of which Newport is the capital, should continue to glory in the memory of the sainted, patriotic John Clarke, its founder and benefactor, whose moral character has never been surpassed, and his piety never been questioned.

1666. Dr. John Clarke was appointed by the Assembly to digest the laws.

THE RECEPTION OF THE CHARTER BY THE PEOPLE OF NEWPORT.

This Charter was received with great joy. It was brought from Boston by Capt. George Baxter, and was read publicly at Newport, Nov. 24, 1663. The records say:

"The said letters, with His Majesty's royal stamp, and the

broad seal, with much becoming gravity, were held up on high, and presented to the public view of the people."

Thanks were voted to the King, to the Earl of Clarendon, and to Mr. Clarke, together with a resolution to pay all his expenses, and to present him with £100. It was also voted that £25 sterling be paid to Capt. George Baxter from the colony, for his services as bearer of the Charter. This was a proud day for Newport—she appeared in her true dignity, and felt her superiority.

The first Assembly under the Charter, the fundamental law of the State, was held at Newport, March 4th, 1663–4. Mr. Benedict Arnold was created by the Charter, the first Governor, William Brenton, Lieut. Governor, and William Baulston, William Field, John Greene, John Coggeshall, Joseph Clarke, James Barker, Roger Williams, Thomas Olney, John Porter, Randal Houlden, assistants.

The following are the names of the deputies who were returned from Newport: John Card, Richard Tew, John Cranston, William Dyre, John Gould, and Caleb Car, afterwards Governor of the State.

At this session the Seal of the colony was fixed. An anchor, with the word Hope, over it, and the words Rhode Island and Providence Plantations, as follows:

It was voted that the island called Patience, be added and joined to Portsmouth.

This was the commencement of a new era in the history of the State, and the people continued to venerate this charter until within a few years, when it was thought that too great inequality existed in the representation, and in the elective franchise, but the effects which followed the attempt to change the mode and form of government, being of so painful and ludicrous a character, has rather led us to doubt whether, on the whole, we have actually gained or lost, by throwing aside the charter and adopting a Constitution, which is now the fundamental law of the State.

An extension in theory and in practise, is quite a different thing; there may be the semblance of liberty, while liberty does not in fact, exist. It would have been full as politic to have retained the charter, and extended suffrage to every *native-born* citizen, with such other improvements as were necessary, as to have abandoned an instrument which embodied so many privileges, and under which the State so long enjoyed peace, happiness, and prosperity. But steam power is now in operation, and we must get off the track.

THE CHAIR OF STATE.

The old chair of state, in which Governor Benedict Arnold sat at the reception of the charter in 1663, when it was proclaimed in the presence of all the freemen of the Colony, at Newport, is still in being, though somewhat shorn of its pristine honors. It belongs to our respected fellow-citizen, Isaac Gould, Esq., at whose house in Thames-street, it may at any time be seen.

A TALE OF TIMES PAST,—IN THE DAYS OF GOVERNOR BENEDICT ARNOLD.

"Old chair, no longer aches the head,
Of him who sat in stately pride
On thy oak seat, whilst heralds read
What moderns now deride—
The 'CHARTER!'"

"On a bright summer's day, as sweetly shone the sun,
The streets of Newport echoed, to the sound of gun and drum;
And bravely shone each officer, with pointed bead and lace,
And lovely smil'd each maiden, to all of the olden race.

ARNOLD a brave war-horse strode, which proudly tramp'd the way,
Pursued his course, with tabours bright, look'd decórous and gay;
Loud cheers ascended high, from tower, and tent, and shore,
As troop on troop of soldiers grim, pass'd by with trumpet's roar.

Banner and pennon, waving wide, on arquebuss and blade,
Seem'd proudly brave, and shone with joy, on Newport's gay parade;
On a bright canopy, covered o'er, with crimson cloth and gold,
On which was wrought by skilful hands, heraldic emblems bold.

Stood this Old Chair of by-gone days, the Charter's oaken seat,
Whereon emblazon'd, rich and gay, did England's arms complete
The Chair,—with fitting panoply, high backed, strong, and grand,
That old oak Chaïr, look'd gaily there, forever may it stand.

'Long live King Charles!' the heralds cried, and thousands did reply,
While ARNOLD, with a noble grace, sat in the old chair high;
Lady high-born, and lovely maid, knight, squire, and page were seen,
Disporting on that gala day, in garments rich and sheen.

The heavens smil'd, the birds sang gay, and music fill'd the air,
On that bright day of pageantry, thou olden oaken Chair;
But many a year has long gone by, and all those glories fled,
While he who sat upon that seat, now sleeps among the dead.

And save his crumbling grave-stone dim, with tall grass overgrown,
With letters dim, to tell of him, old Chair, thou art alone;
That dream has fled, and gay no more, the world glides careless by,
The Chair of State no more is great, or glitters in the eye."

Newport being the metropolis, as she was the most *flourishing* and populous town in the Colony, the freemen of the *whole* Colony assembled there, to vote for general officers for the year ensuing, agreeably to "An Act regulating the Elections of General Officers."

LAWS,

Made and passed by the General Assembly of His Majesty's Colony of Rhode Island, and Providence Plantations, begun and held at Newport, the first day of March, 1663–1664 :

" And that each and every person that shall vote by *proxy*, shall, on the Town Meeting-day next preceding the General Election, openly, in said meeting, deliver in his votes to the Town-Clerk of the town wherein he dwells, with his name written at length on the backside or the bottom thereof, which votes so taken shall be immediately sealed up by the Town-Clerk, and by him delivered either to an Assistant Justice, Warden, or Deputy of said town, who shall be by the said Town-meeting appointed for the same; by him delivered to the Governor or Deputy-Governor in open Court, before the Election proceed at Newport."

This was the origin of the word " Prox," or " Proxing-day."

It will be seen that the privilege granted by the above Act of voting by proxy at the General Election at Newport, seems first to have become a law at this time. But voting in person, at Newport, (if the freeman preferred it,) was not abolished until August, 1760, nearly one hundred years afterwards.

This was done for the better accommodation of those who, living at a remote distance from Newport, could not make it convenient always to attend in person. But such were the attractions at the capital, that all that could attend, availed themselves of the privilege of being present, and enjoying the amusements, which were of the most interesting and pleasing character.

Tradition informs us, that a sloop filled with freemen, was purposely run on the Bishop Rock, in order to favor one party, at the expense of the other. It was a common practice to get some of the freemen " half-seas" over, and then land them on Prudence Island, or some other of the intermediate places, in order to prevent their voting.

The head-quarters in Newport, where they immediately repaired on their arrival, was Governor Wanton's, and Governor

Whepple's, in Thames-street, and others, where sumptuous tables were spread, including wines and liquors of the choicest kinds, such as is rarely found at this day, and the effects following their indulgence, often led to angry discussion, and even to fisti-cuffing between the belligerent parties.

It must have been a novel sight, to have witnessed the crowds which congregated at Newport, under their respective champions, nobly "battling" for their political preferences. The largest liberty was then enjoyed, each one felt that they possessed the sovereign right to speak out, and act out, their undisguised sentiments, without fear or favor. Political hypocrites, were not then so abundant; and political principle was not then, as now, "five loaves and two small fishes," as the late Hon. John C. Calhoun once remarked.

It should be borne in mind, that there was no "GAG LAW" in operation, and no proscription tolerated. Moral courage was a virtue, which then animated the breast of man, and which would not allow him to pay a blind devotion at the shrine of Mammon, and thereby barter away his political rights for a "mess of pottage."

Independence of character was the characteristic of the period, agreeably to the principles adopted by the early settlers of the island, and which had been sanctioned and approved by the freemen on the main.

Mr. Callender, in speaking of John Clarke, says, "He was a faithful and useful minister, courteous in all the relations of life, and an ornament to his profession, and to the several offices which he sustained. His memory is deserving of lasting honor, for his efforts towards establishing the first government in the world, which gave to all equal civil and religious liberty. To no man is Rhode Island more indebted than to him. He was the original projector of the settlement of the island, and one of its ablest legislators. No character in New England is of purer fame than John Clarke."

It could scarcely be thought possible that so good a man as Mr. Clarke could have been arrested in the *godly State of Massachusetts*, and THRUST INTO PRISON! and this on Lord's day, July 20th, 1651; and on the 31st of that month, by order of the Court of Assistants, held in Boston, Mr. Clarke and brethren, received the following sentence, viz.: Mr. Clarke pay £20, or be severely whipped; Mr. Holmes, £30, or be whipped; and Mr. Crandall, £5, or be whipped;—and this alone for conscience toward God, in differing from their brethren in Massachusetts, on the subject of "Infant Baptism." None suffered whipping but Mr. Holmes, who received thirty stripes, administered with the greatest imaginable severity."—*Ross's Historical Discourse.*

It is no wonder that Mr. Clarke labored to procure a charter, granting to all civil and religious liberty, after having experienced such intolerance on the part of the Massachusett's rulers.

Mr. Clarke died on the 20th April, 1676, in the 66th year of his age. Mr. Backus says, "he was born October the 8th, 1609; married Elizabeth, the daughter of John Harges, Esq., of Bedfordshire, England. In a power of attorney signed by them, May 12, 1656, he styles himself, 'John Clarke, physician, of London.' It was for the recovery of a legacy of £20 per annum, that was given her by her father, out of the Manor of Westingworth, Bedfordshire. Where he had his education, I know not; but the following clause in his will, may give some idea of his learning, viz.: 'Item,—unto my loving friend, Richard Bayley, I give and bequeath my Concordance, and Lexicon thereto belonging, written by myself, being the fruit of several years' study; my Hebrew Bible, Buxtorff's and Parson's Lexicon, Cotton's Concordance, and all the rest of my books.' His first wife died without issue. His second wife was Mrs. Mary Fletcher, who died April 19th, 1672, leaving an only daughter, who died at the age of 11 years. His third wife was the widow, Sarah Davis, who survived him. Mr. Clarke, according to his request, was buried between his two wives, in the burial ground, on the west side of Tanner-street, (which lot he gave the Church.) He left also an estate of considerable value, in the hands of trustees, empowered to choose their successors, for the relief of the poor and the education of children, according to instructions given in his will,—which instructions are, 'That in the disposal of that which the Lord hath bestowed upon me, and with which I have now entrusted you, and your successors, shall have special regard and care; to provide for those that fear the Lord; and in all things, and at all times, so to discharge the trust which I have reposed in you, as may be most to the glory of God, and the good and benefit of those for whom it is by me especially intended."

Mr. Clarke's estate was prized at £1080 12s., by James Barker, Thomas Ward, and Philip Edes, who made oath to the inventory, May 17, 1696. The farm and neck, they apprized at £530, and its late annual income has been $220, as Josias Lyndon, Esq., one of the assigns, stated. The two farms in Middletown, contain about one hundred and fifty acres, and the rents arising from the same, at the present time, amount to $700 per annum.

It is very evident that Mr. Clarke designed the gift to benefit the poor, and to educate the children of the church. For no language could have been employed, more significant than he has employed: "You, and your successors, shall have special regard and care to provide for those who fear the Lord." They were the objects of his regard, and he felt constrained, as a Christian, that the sheep and lambs of the flock should be provided for, and not permitted to want, which would be a gross reflection on the Christian character. This will, we conceive, has been perverted from the original intent of the donor, by appropriating a portion of the income to the support of the ministry, to the neglect of the poor. We are not apprised whether any case at present exists, where the poor and indigent have occasion to seek shelter in the town Asylum; we trust, for the honor of our native town, that such is not the case. Such, however, has been the painful fact, and so long as the poor of the church are not sought out and made comfortable, not *one dollar* of the Clarke bequest should be appropriated to the support of the ministry. The "glory of God," which has been construed to favor the diversion of this gift, can in no higher sense be promoted, than in feeding the hungry, and clothing the naked; for God's glory consists essentially, in his goodness. Gov. Lyndon owned the house which he gave the Society for a parsonage, but which unfortunately has passed into other hands.

Mr. Clarke left three brothers—Thomas, Joseph, and Carew. The numerous family of Clarkes, of Rhode Island, mostly sprung from them. Joseph Clarke settled in Westerly, R. I. We find that the Rev. Joseph Clarke, jr., was in the Seventh-Day Baptist church of Westerly, now Hopkinton, also the Rev. Joseph Clarke, sen., stands enrolled as a member of said church. In

1692, he was clerk of said church, and resigned that office May 21, 1708, and Joseph Clarke, jr., was appointed to fill that place. Rev. Joseph Clarke was ordained Aug. 12th, 1712. Rev. Thos. Clarke was ordained as elder, Oct. 2, 1750. Rev. Joshua Clarke, his son, was ordained as elder, in May, 1768. All the foregoing Clarkes, except John, have been pastors of the church of Hopkinton, then Westerly.—*From the Church Records.*

Judge Samuel Clarke, of Portsmouth, R. I., is in regular descent from this highly distinguished family. He has six brothers and two sisters, now living at Clarkesville, Brookfield, N. Y. The Hon. John H. Clarke, Senator to Congress, from Rhode Island, is also of the same family, and has distinguished himself in the various important stations which he has been called to occupy. Also W. Edward Clarke, Esq., of Providence, who has in his possession the Bible, formerly belonging to John Clarke.

TO THE MEMORY OF

DOCTOR JOHN CLARKE,

One of the original purchasers and proprietors of this Island; and one of the founders of the First Baptist Church in Newport, its first pastor, and munificent benefactor.

He died on the 20th of April, 1676, in the 66th year of his age; And is here Interred.

THIS MONUMENT WAS ERECTED BY HIS TRUSTEES.

May the descendants of the Clarke's follow the example of their illustrious predecessor.

Jeremiah Clarke.—We have not been able to trace any connection between this family and that of John Clarke, one of the first settlers. It is possible that they were remotely connected, though we should rather be inclined to doubt it. Jeremiah Clarke was Governor of the colony in 1745, and died in Newport, 11th month, 1751, and was buried in a tomb which now stands by the water side.—*Friends' Records.*

He was father of Governor Walter Clarke. Weston Clarke, the Recorder, and Rev. James Clarke, of the Second Baptist church of Newport, were grandsons of Jeremiah Clarke. They were among the early settlers of Newport. Many of their descendants have been highly respectable.

There is a tradition that this family originated from the Hon. Lewis Latham, who was Falconer to His Majesty, King Charles I. This was an office of distinction. He is also said to have been an illegitimate child of King Charles, the sot, and lived to the advanced age of 100 years. This Latham subsequently married, and had two daughters, one of whom married Randal Houlden, of Warwich, one of the original settlers, and the other a Clarke, the father of Jeremiah, and the grandfather of Walter Clarke, and these are the descendants of said Lewis Latham. The name of Latham is often found as the Christian name of families in Newport. We had in our possession, until within a few years, a portrait of Lewis Latham, but by some unaccountable negligence on the part of the person who had it in charge, it cannot be found. He was a venerable looking man, with a long flowing beard reaching to his bosom : there was also a coat of arms appended. We think that, considering all the circumstances, Jeremiah Clarke, the father of Walter, could not have been related to John. Walter Clarke was, however, a distinguished man in the colony. He owned the land from the corner of the Parade, as far as to the Jonathan Marsh estate, afterwards belonging to Wm. I. Tilley, to the water, and extending to Clarke-street, named in honor of him. There is one singular fact connected with the Clarkes of Rhode Island, that the name ends with an "*e*," by which they can be distinguished from the other families who bear the name.

We have said much more of this family, especially of John Clarke, than we otherwise should have done, had there not been a disposition on the part of historians, to treat his name and good deeds with indifference, in order to exalt Roger Williams, and Providence, of which he was the founder, at the expense of the honor and glory of Newport.

THE COMMERCIAL RELATIONS OF NEWPORT.

As late as 1769, Newport outrivalled New-York, in her foreign and domestic commerce. The inhabitants of New-York, New-Haven, New-London, &c., depended entirely on Newport for a market to supply themselves with foreign goods, and here they found a ready market for the produce of their own States.

Her merchants were among the most enterprising and wealthy. Mr. Aaron Lopez, is said to have employed more than thirty sail of vessels, of different descriptions, at one time. Mr. Lopez was the first, or among the first, to push the whaling business as far as the Falkland Islands. Col. Godfrey Malborn, was an extensive ship-owner, and did much in building up the town, of which we shall speak more particularly. Jonathan Nichols was an enterprising merchant of Newport, and son of Deputy-Governor Nichols; he was distinguished for his enterprise, public spirit, hospitality, and charity—rare virtues combined. He was extensively engaged in foreign commerce, and owned at the time of his death, sixteen sail of vessels. His residence was the estate on the Point, now owned by the heirs of the late Hon. William Hunter, which at that time had one of the best wharfs and ranges of stores in Newport, all of which he built. The workmanship of the interior of this house, is truly elegant and costly; the stair-ways being of English oak, and twisted, with the rich carved pannel work, shows the taste of its former owner, and the great superiority of the ancient buildings over the modern. There is also the Cheesborough estate, at present belonging to the heir of the late Hon. C. G. Champlin; the Redwood House, on Bridge-street, now in possession of the widow Pierce; the Tillinghast property, now in possession of Gov. W. C. Gibbs; the Redwood House in Thames street, with its heavy iron gate, now the residence of the widow of S. F. Gardner, Esq.; and the Gov. Wanton estate, in Thames street, with others, which clearly proves that a sad deterioration has taken place in the mode and manner of building, and corresponds well with the *minds* of the present age. Mr. Nichols was for many years a deputy from Newport, afterwards an assistant, and at the time of his death was Deputy Governor of the Colony. He died on the 8th of September, 1756. He was great-grandfather to Edward Hazard, Esq., of the Park House, Newport.

Messrs. E. and F. Malborn, Henry Collins, the Wantons, and many other merchants, also did an immense business before the revolution. The remains of the foundations of old wharves, from Robinson's Wharf on the Point, to Overing's at the extreme south, a distance of one mile, which at that interesting period were crowded with commerce, will give the reader some idea of the prosperity of Newport.

The town at this time was in the zenith of her commercial prosperity. The population is said to have been 12,000. She had about two hundred vessels employed in the foreign trade, and between three and four hundred coasting vessels, including a regular line of London packets, and employing no less than twenty-two hundred seamen.

Such was the amount of business done at that period, that goods were not stored, owing to the want of room, while the wharves were literally covered with merchandize, viz.: sugar, rum, molasses, and every kind of foreign and domestic articles.

The coasters would take on board the merchandize, as before remarked, and proceed to New-York and Connecticut, where there was a quick demand, which went to build up and enrich the town of Newport.

We have been told an anecdote of Capt. Hicks, of Warren, who, coming to this port with a load of hoop-poles, found great difficulty in finding a place to land, having passed every wharf without finding room for his cargo, until he reached Overing's wharf at the extreme south of the town.

Her West India trade was immense. This grew partly out of the quantity of rum which was there distilled, there being, in *full blast*, about thirty distilleries. This gave constant employment to coopers,—their shops were to be found on almost every wharf—brass-founders, and to draymen, and others, for all participated in the benefits resulting from this extensive trade. There was around the Cove, some ten or twelve distilleries, as the remains of the old cisterns plainly show.

Simon Newton owned two; the great-grandfather of the firm of E. F. Newton, brothers, Samuel Johnson, the Richardsons, and William Burroughs, each owned a distillery. In this section of the town, the business done was immense. There was seven wharves in the Cove, and before the Long Wharf were extended, vessels entered the Cove and discharged their cargoes; and subsequently, through the drawbridge.

The town, at the same time, contained seventeen manufacturers of sperm oil and candles, also three sugar refineries, one brewery, and five or more ropewalks.

—— Tweedy, apothecary, a large importer and exporter of drugs; such was his business, that he supplied Rhode Island, a part of Massachusetts, all Connecticut and North Carolina, with drugs, and had an establishment in New-York, where merchants might ascertain his prices; this appeared from his books, when in the hands of the late Dr. Edmund T. Waring.

Stephen Dellois, Esq., had a large wholesale hardware store, as also Stephen Ayrault, Samuel Ayrault, Thomas Wilkinson. These were all importers, and did an extensive business. Newport, at this period, was the grand emporium of trade. We have heard aged men remark, 'that they have known of the arrival of eighteen West Indiamen in one day." It was said, at that period, however strange it may sound, "that possibly New-York might, in time, equal Newport." A degree of activity then prevailed, which would astonish us at this day.

CUSTOM HOUSE RECORDS.

It is to be regretted that the books and papers at this period are lost, in the regular *set*, which would have afforded us correct statistics of the amount of merchandize imported into Newport.

We have procured, quite *incidentally*, from Mrs. Dudley, widow of the late Hon. Charles Dudley, Esq., former Mayor of Albany, who was the only son of Charles Dudley, Esq., Collector under the Crown, some portions of the records of the Customs, which will aid the reader in forming an opinion of the extent of commerce at the period of 1768–9. These quarterly returns were forwarded from England by the executor of Charles Dudley, Esq., a few years since. What became of the regular set of books, and papers, belonging to the Customs, is entirely unknown.

It appears by the books and papers in the author's possession, that in the year 1768–9, the entries and clearances amounted to some hundreds of vessels.

" INSTRUCTIONS,

BY THE COMMISSIONERS OF HIS MAJESTY'S CUSTOMS IN AMERICA,

To CHARLES DUDLEY, Esq.,

Who is appointed Collector of the Customs, at the Port of Rhode Island, in America.

" You being deputed to be Collector of the Customs at the Port of Rhode Island, and you having given bond to His Majesty, with sufficient security, in the sum of *one thousand pounds sterling*, for the due execution of said employment, you are to take the following oath, besides the oaths prescribed by the Act of 1st Geo. 1st, 13, before you enter upon your office.

[FORM OF OATH.]

" I, ——— ———, do swear, *to be true and faithful in the execution, to the best of my knowledge and power, of the trust committed to my charge and inspection, in the service of His Majesty's Customs; and that I will not take any Reward or Gratuity, directly or indirectly, other than my Salary, and what is or shall be allowed me from the Crown, or the regular Fees established by Law, for any service done, or to be done, in the execution of my employment in the Customs, on any account whatsoever.*

" So help me God.

Collectors,
Comptrollers,
Land Surveyors and Searchers,
Land Waiters,
Tide Surveyors,
Tides-men,
Coast Surveyors and Riding Officers,
Waiters and Searchers, and Preventive Officers,
Boatmen or Watermen."

[From the original printed Instructions, in a pamphlet form, containing thirty-nine pages.]

" Amount of Molasses imported into Newport, for the Quarter ending the 10th of October, 1769,—3,000 hogsheads. The Names of the Vessels which brought the same, with the Masters and Owners:

Ship's Name.	Master's Name.	Where from.	Merchant's name.
Sally	Simon Smith	Surinam	
Ranger	Jeremiah Cranston	Hispaniola	Jos. & Wm. Wanton
Recovery	James Rathbone	do.	Peleg Thurston & Son
Industry	John Peters	Jamaica	Aaron Lopez
Betsy	John Stanton	St. Lucia	Silas Cook
Hope	Phineas Gilbert	Hispaniola	Myer Pollock
Adventure	William Ladd	do.	Christopher Champlin
Diamond	Joram Place	do.	John Collins
Nancy	Joseph Littlefield	St. Eustatia	Myer Pollock
Pinnock	Sabinus Palmer	Jamaica	Henry Bowers
Abigail	George Rolland	St. Lucia	John Fletcher
Speedwell	John Briggs	Jamaica	William Reed
Dolphin	James Thomas	Hispaniola	William Vernon
Polly	Joshua Bliven	Jamaica	E. & F. Malborn
Polly	Giles Stanton	do.	George Gibbs
Dolphin	Henry Weeden	do.	Charles Wickham

CHARLES DUDLEY, *Collector*,
JOHN NICHOLL, *Comptroller*.

Port of Rhode Island,
Quarter ending 10th of October, 1769."

The amount of duties paid was $4,000. It should be borne in mind, however, that it was considored just and equitable to rob the king of the revenue. Hence, but a portion of the cargoes was entered at the Custom-house, while the remainder was run. The officers of the Customs under the Crown, were not very conscientious; and it has been said that a guinea, being placed over one eye, had considerable effect, while another guinea rendered them blind to what was going on. The bulk of the cargoes was placed on board of coasters and sent off; this was usually done in the night, as being a more favorable time to accomplish their object. An aged man, who was employed on Col. Malborn's wharf, informed the author, that " the scenes enacted there, indicated spirit and activity, rarely witnessed in any commercial town, even at this day."

"DUDLEY, Appellant,—SHAW, Respondent.

(L. S.) "Colony of Rhode Island, &c. }
COURT OF VICE-ADMIRALTY. }

"George the Third, by the Grace of God, of Great Britain, France, and Ireland, King, Defender of the Faith, &c.

"To the Marshal of our Court of Vice-Admiralty, &c., or to his lawful Deputy,—Greeting:

"*Whereas*, an information was filed in our Court of Vice-Admiralty, by Robert Keeler, Esq., Commander of His Majesty's ship, the Mercury, against one hundred and nine casks of molasses, and two casks of coffee, for violation of the acts of Parliament; and on the twenty-eighth of November last past, the Hon. John Andrews, Esq., decree was promulgated, whereby the said one hundred and nine casks of molasses, and two casks of coffee, were condemned and forfeited, and did further order and decree that said molasses and coffee be sold at a public vendue, and the monies arising from the sale thereof, to be distributed agreeably to act of Parliament, &c.

"You are therefore hereby required, pursuant to the aforesaid decree, to sell the said one hundred and nine casks of molasses, and two casks of coffee, this instant, being the fifth day of March, A. D., 1773, at ten o'clock in the forenoon, to the highest bidder, for sterling money, and you are to make true return of said sale, into the Register's office of said Court.

Witness, JOHN ANDREWS, ESQ.,

Commissary and Judge of said Court, at Newport, the 5th day of March, A. D., 1773, and in the thirteenth year of our reign.

THOMAS VERNON *Deputy Register*."

"*Newport, March* 5, 1773.

"At ten o'clock in the forenoon, pursuant to the within warrant, I have sold one hundred and seven casks of molasses, containing 9,813 gallons, to Charles Dudley, Esq.,

at 10*d* sterling, per gallon,	£408 17 6
And two casks of coffee, to ditto, weight, 364 lbs., at 6*d* per lb.,	9 2 0
	£417 19 6

The said Charles Dudley, Esq., being the highest bidder.

WILLIAM MUMFORD, *Deputy Marshal*."

(A true copy from the original manuscript.)

POWER OF ATTORNEY.

"I, Charles Dudley, of Newport, in the County of Newport, Esq., do hereby make, and appoint, and in my place put James Honyman, and Henry Marchant, both of Newport, aforesaid, Esqrs., my attornies, and each of them my attorney in a certain action of trespass, upon the case commenced and prosecuted by Nathaniel Shaw, jun., of New-London, in the County of New-London, and Colony of Connecticut, merchant, against me, the said Charles Dudley, at the Inferior Court of Common Pleas, to be held at Providence, for the County of Providence, upon the third Monday of June, A. D., 1773. And do hereby empower the said James Honyman, and Henry Marchant, jointly, and each of them separately, and by himself, in my name, and to appear in the Inferior Court aforesaid, or in any other Court whatsoever, and there to plead, defend, and pursue to final judgment and execution, with full power of substitution.

"Witness my hand and seal, the 14th day of June, A. D., 1775, and in the thirteenth year of His Majesty's reign, George the Third, King, &c. CHARLES DUDLEY. (L. S.)

"Signed, sealed, and delivered,
in presence of
John Grelea, jun.,
Ben. Peckham."

"NEWPORT, ss.—At Newport, upon the day and year aforesaid, in his proper person, cometh Charles Dudley, above-named, and acknowledged the above power of attorney to be his act and deed. Before J. GRELEA, jun., *Justice of the Peace.*"

A true copy from the original manuscript in the author's possession. This action grew out of the seizure and sale of the molasses and coffee above-named.

George Rome, Esq., (pronounced Room,) was a native of England, and for several years a successful merchant of Newport. He owned a valuable house, with a wharf and stores, on Easton's Point, on the spot known as Gibbs' ship-yard, where he carried on an extensive business. On the commencement of hostilities, he returned to England, and his valuable property in Newport and Narragansett, was confiscated. He lived in splendor, and entertained his friends with sumptuous hospitality. He had a summer residence in Narragansett, which he styled "Bachelor's Hall." He occasionally gave large parties, at which the ladies and gentlemen of Boston, Newport, and Narragansett, would equally mingle. Punch was the fashionable beverage at that period, and the entertainment at "Bachelor's Hall" was extravagant.

In the Stamp Act excitement, he strongly espoused the cause of the Crown. The gross charge of Mr. Rome, of corruption and partiality, against the Legislature, the Courts and Juries of the Colony, with the advice to annul the charter, and create a government more dependent on the Crown, produced an exasperation too powerful to be withstood, and apprehending danger, soon after his release from prison, he fled on board of the Rose, man-of-war, then lying in Narragansett Bay.

Having noticed the extensive business of Mr. Rome, on the Point, we would also notice the manufacturers of furniture, which at that period was quite extensive on the Point, and which was shipped to foreign markets. On Bridge-street was Constant Bayley, Thomas Townsend, Job, Edmond, Christopher, and John; these all had establishments, and employed a great number of hands, manufacturing furniture, for which a ready market was found in New-York and the West Indies. John Goddard, and Benjamin Peabody, had also cabinet-makers' shops on Washington-street, which carried on a large trade with Surinam.

On the east side of Washington-street and corner of the Long Wharf, stood the store of Joseph Hammond, a shipping merchant, who built the large house, since known as the Washington House.

Next, north, stood the spermaceti works of Myer Pollock, who was extensively engaged in manufacturing oil and candles, and stored large quantities of goods for others.

The stores of David Huntington and Benjamin Barker, were also on the Point; both these men were extensively engaged in manufacturing furniture, which they shipped to New-York and the West Indies. Besides the above, there were three tanneries on the same street, and all in successful operation; they were owned by Robert Taylor, William Potter, and —— Bently.

Holmes' Wharf, was a great place for business; on it stood Carter's cooper's shop, Monroe's block-maker's shop, Graftin's sail-loft, and over that a rigging loft.

Bowen's ship-yard.

John Collin's wharf and store; he was engaged in successful trade until the war, when the British destroyed his property, one house excepted.

During the war, 17 buildings were destroyed on Bridge-street.

It will, no doubt, appear quite novel to the reader to be made acquainted with these facts, when contrasted with present appearances. But in no section of the town, at that day, was there want of employment. It was the great commercial mart, and merchants resorted there, to trade and traffic, as well as to enjoy the hospitality of the inhabitants, which was then unbounded.

HENRY COLLINS, ESQ.

Henry Collins, deserves to be recorded with gratitude and respect. He was a native of Newport, and born March, 1699. He was educated in England, and on his return to his native country, adopted the profession of merchant, in which he was for a time eminently successful. He was a man of cultivated taste, and fond of literature—he animated and encouraged kindred spirits, and in 1730, with several associates, formed a literary and philosophical society in Newport, which was the first that was ever formed in the colony, and probably was one of the earliest in America. This society afterwards comprised many of the prominent men in the colony, and some in Massachusetts and Connecticut. He is said to have been the projector of the plan for a Library Association, in Newport, for which purpose he gave the valuable lot of land on which the edifice of the Redwood Library waserected, and was for many years one of the directors of the Institution.

He was a munificent patron of the arts, and by his patronage to Smybert, Alexander, Tocke, &c., we are indebted for many valuable paintings of the ancient Patriarchs, which are still to be found in Newport.

T. Bonar 124 Nassau St.

Market and Granary Erected 1763.

He formed a gallery of paintings, which the venerable Dr. Waterhouse remembers to have seen in his youthful days. In a letter to the Rev. Romeo Elton, he thus speaks: "Henry Collins was a wealthy merchant and man of taste—the Lorenzi de Medici, of Rhode Island; he caused a painting to be made of Parson Callender, as well as some other divines, as Hitchcox, Clap, and Dean Berkley, which I have often admired in the Collins' collection." The painting of Mr. Clap is now in the possession of the Congregational church in Spring-street, and we would suggest to the First Baptist church of Newport, and of America, too, that they should take immediate measures to obtain the portrait of Mr. Callender, which has been taken from Newport and placed in the Historical Building in Providence, where it does not justly belong. Such things should never be permitted to exist, without obtaining redress.

Mr. Collins was at the head of every public improvement in Newport; as the extension of the Long Wharf, and the building of the Brick Market, or Granary, in the year 1763. The architect was Peter Harrison; it was built after the Ionic order. The upper story, for many years, was used for a theatre, before it was altered into a Town Hall.

"*Whereas*, the Proprietors of the Long Wharf, in Newport, aforesaid, have made a grant, on the twenty-fourth day of July, A. D. 1760, to the said town of Newport, of a lot of land, for erecting a Market House, &c., it is therefore voted, that Martin Howard and Josias Lydon, Esqrs., be a committee, and they are hereby confirmed to make and give a good deed of said lot, to the town of Newport, agreeable to said grant.

"And that the upper part be divided into stores for dry-goods, and let out to the best advantage; and all the rents thereof, together with all the profits that shall arise on said building, shall be lodged in the Town Treasury of said town of Newport, towards a stock for purchasing grain, for supplying a *Public Granary forever*. And that said building be erected agreeably to a plan to be agreed on by said Proprietors, to be estimated at twenty-four thousand pounds, old tenor, to be raised by the lottery now on foot.

"The lower part thereof for a Market House, and for no other use whatsoever, forever; (unless it shall be found convenient to appropriate some part of it for a watch-house.) A handsome brick building, to be thirty-three feet in front, or in width, and about sixty-six feet in length."—*From the Records of the Proprietor of the Long Wharf.*

It is understood that there is a fine portrait of Mr. Collins still in being, which is said to be now in possession of some one of the family of the late Dr. Henry Flagg, of South Carolina. It ought to be placed in the Redwood Library. He was a member of the Seventh-Day Baptist church, and was one of the committee for erecting the house of worship.

Such were the merchants of Newport in the past.

1775. On the 15th of November, Charles Dudley, Esq., the king's Collector of the Customs for Rhode Island, *fled* for refuge on board a ship of war. He married the daughter of Robert Cranston, of Newport. He died in England, and his family returned to America. His son was the Hon. Charles Dudley, of Albany. Mr. Dudley owned, and occupied the seat, a short distance from Newport, called "Dudley Place," at present owned by the heirs of the late Governor Charles Collins. Edward Vanzant, Esq. is the present proprietor of this charming retreat; a gentleman of fine manners, who takes delight in rendering every attention to visitors. Mr. Dudley is said to have been a man of polished manners; his portrait, in the costume of a courtier, shews him off to great advantage,—it is in the possession of Mrs. Dudley, of Albany. In the weekly clubs then held in Newport, which embraced men of distinction, Mr. Dudley was usually one of the guests, and both amused and edified the company. At this memorable period, Newport was far in advance of the other towns and cities in the colonies, in the refined taste and the enlarged hospitality, which characterized the inhabitants. This arose from the nature of the education then enjoyed, for where the mind is suffered to vegetate without moral culture, the fruit borne will resemble the grapes of Sodom, or the fabled apples which grew on the margin of the lake Asphaltites. The education of far too many at the present day, having been so crude and indigested, that the lustre, which is shed on the pathway of the intellectual mind, is not visible.

A fine writer has remarked of Newport, that "there are few towns of any magnitude within our broad territory, in which so little change has been effected in half a century, as in Newport.

Until the vast resources of the interior were developed, the beautiful island on which it stands, was a chosen retreat of the affluent planters of the South, from the heats and diseases of their burning climate. Here they resorted in crowds, to breathe the invigorating breezes of the sea. Subjects of the same government, the inhabitants of the Carolinas and of Jamaica met here in amity, to enjoy free interchange of thought and feeling.

At the interesting period of 1769, the island was never more inviting and lovely. Its swelling crests were still crowned with the wood of centuries: its little vales were covered with the living verdure of the north; and its unpretending, but neat and comfortable villas lay sheltered in groves, and embedded in flowers. The beauty and fertility of the place gained for it a name, which, probably, expressed far more than was, at that early day, properly understood. The inhabitants of the county styled their possessions the "Garden of America." Neither were their guests from the scorching plains of the South, reluctant to concede so imposing a title of distinction.

THE LOSS OF THE BRIG DOLPHIN.

As the commerce of Newport whitened every sea, it was to be expected that disasters would occasionally occur. But this event caused painful anguish to many hearts. This year, 1767, was memorable for a melancholy disaster, that took place on the night of the 26th of August, off Point Judith. The brig Dolphin, Capt. John Malborn, (son of Evan,) from Kingston, Jamaica, with a valuable cargo of rum and sugar, and a number of passengers belonging to a theatrical company, took fire, and the vessel and cargo were entirely consumed; five female passengers perished in the cabin. The officers and crew, with the rest of the passengers, escaped to the shore in boats.

The brig was a new vessel, of 210 tons, belonging to Messrs. E. & F. Malborn, merchants, of Newport. Among the passengers was Mr. Henry, the father of the American stage, and William B. Simpson, afterwards a lawyer of Newport.

Mr. Henry's wife and daughter were among those who were lost. It is stated that the cabin-boy was sent below to draw some rum from a choice cask, and carelessly placing the light too near, it immediately ignited, and the cask burst; the report was like that of cannon.

Capt. John Dennis was a native of England; he came to Rhode island when a boy, having been apprenticed to a ship-master in the London trade, belonging to Newport. Being of an active disposition, he soon became master of a vessel. He greatly distinguished himself by his daring courage, and successful enterprise. In 1741, while cruising in the West Indies, he so greatly annoyed the French islands, by the capture of their vessels and privateers, that the authorities of Martinique fitted out a vessel of 14 guns, and 130 men, expressly for the purpose of ridding themselves of so troublesome an enemy; but in this they were disappointed, for, after an engagement of nearly four hours, in which Capt. Dennis was slightly wounded, she was taken possession of by Capt. Dennis, and carried into St. Kitt's. Here he received the attention which he had so justly merited, from the Governor, and other officers of the island, and who, as a testimony of respect for his valuable services, presented him with a golden oar and a purse of five hundred pistoles.

In the war of 1756, Capt. Dennis was selected to command the privateer ship Tay, of 18 guns, and 180 men, which was fitted out by the merchants of Newport, for the purpose of annoying the Spanish commerce. This vessel sailed from Newport on the 22nd of August, 1756, and was never heard from after sailing.

He left a large family; among his sons was the late Capt. Thomas Dennis, for many years an enterprising merchant of Newport, and the late Capt. William Dennis, a revolutionary patriot, who commanded, during the contest for Independence, no less than thirteen privateers. Their descendants are still found in Newport.

1745. This year two large ships were built, and fitted out from Newport, as privateers, and were intended to cruise in company on the Spanish Main. They mounted 22 guns each, and were commanded, one by Capt. Brewer, and the other by Capt. Cranston. They sailed on the 24th of December, at the commencement of a north-east snow storm, which increased with great violence during the next day. These ships were never heard from after sailing, and the only conjecture that could be formed was, that they must have come in collision with each other during the thick snow storm, and both had gone down with all on board. These ships were fitted out, and principally owned, by Col. Godfrey Malborn, and the loss was considered as one of the greatest calamities that ever befel the town; beside the loss of property, upwards of four hundred lives were sacrificed, and nearly two hundred women became widows by this disaster.

EVENTS IN THE WAR WITH FRANCE.

The legislature of Massachusetts decided, after much discussion, to invite the other Colonies to unite with them, in an expedition against Louisburgh, the Gibraltar of the French American Provinces. Into the spirit of this enterprise, the legislature of Rhode Island entered with patriotic ardor; and, at the May session of that body, passed a resolution to raise a regiment of one hundred and fifty men, exclusive of officers; and that the Colony sloop, Tartar, be fitted out, with a compliment of ninety men, exclusive of officers.

The expedition was crowned with success; and after a siege of forty-nine days, the city of Louisburgh, and the island of Cape Breton, was surrendered by the French, on June 17th, 1745, to his Britannic Majesty.

The capture of Louisburgh, by the Colonies, stung the Court of France with mortification and revenge, and they resolved to chastise them for their insolence. Accordingly, an expedition was fitted out for this purpose, consisting of forty ships of war, and fifty-six transports, with three thousand five hundred men, and forty thousand stand of arms, for the French and Indians. The Colonies saw and acknowledged their danger, from their total inability to defend themselves, in case of an invasion by so numerous and formidable a fleet; and the inhabitants of the sea-port towns were thrown into the greatest consternation.

No people had more to fear from foreign invasion, in New England, than the people of Newport; from the extent of her commercial interests, her local situation, and the facility with which the town might be approached with the largest ships of war, the inhabitants were thrown into the greatest agitation and distress. Nor were these apprehensions allayed, until in October, it was ascertained that God had interposed for the Colonies, and gotten the victory with his own arm.

So disastrous was this expedition to the French, that among all this mighty and formidable fleet, destined to lay in ruins the smiling villages of New England, not more than two or three ships, and a few transports, ever reached her coast. A violent storm at sea either destroyed or damaged many of them. Others were compelled to return, on account of a most fearful pestilence which swept off hundreds of their crews, and made the bravest hearts tremble.

The Admiral, or Commander-in-chief of the whole French squadron, on reaching the coast of New England, died of mortification; or as some say, of poison. The Vice-Admiral came to a similar tragical end, by running himself through the body with his own sword. That part of the fleet which arrived on the coast, sailed with the intent of making an attack upon Annapolis, but a storm scattered them again, and they were forced to return without effecting any part of the work of destruction originally intended.

Thus were the Colonies preserved, not by the policy of their councils, nor the prowess of their arms—but by the providence of God. Preliminaries of peace were soon entered into, between France and England, and a definitive treaty was signed in October, 1748. The privateers of Rhode Island distinguished themselves in this war, and during the year 1745, more than twenty prizes, some of them of immense value, were sent into Newport.

In May, 1758, Great Britain, under George II., formally declared war with France; which declaration was reciprocated by France the following month. The causes which led to this war, commonly distinguished by the name of the "French and Indian war," were the alleged encroachments of the French on the English settlements in America.

This war terminated in 1763, by the cession of Nova Scotia, Canada, the Isle of Cape Breton, and all other islands of the gulph and river of St. Lawrence, to the British Crown. In all these splendid achievements of the British arms, during these long, protracted, and sanguinary conflicts, no town, perhaps, of equal size in New England, contributed more to the glory of the British Crown, than Newport.

In 1723, the town of Newport voted to build an Alms House for the poor of the town.

SAMUEL CRANSTON, ESQ.

As the Cranston family figured largely in Newport, previous to the Revolution, some account of them will, no doubt, prove highly interesting and amusing to the reader, more especially the event we now are about to notice.

Samuel Cranston, Esq., a gentleman of noble descent, and who had highly distinguished himself as a merchant in Newport, on the breaking out of the French war of 1755, finding business completely paralyzed, and being of an active temperament of mind, was induced to start on a voyage for Jamaica, not, however, anticipating the scenes and events which he was destined to endure in the prosecution of the voyage.

When off the Keys of Florida, they were attacked by a piratical vessel; they defended themselves to the utmost, satisfied as they were, that should they fall into their hands, no mercy would be shown them; but all their efforts were in vain, and they were compelled to surrender to the enemy. Such was the savage cruelty of these buccaneers, that neither prayers nor expostulations had the least effect on their hard and obdurate hearts: the passengers and crew were all inhumanly butchered on the spot, with the exception of Mr. Cranston, who was spared, in order to labor on board the vessel as a common menial.

To a mind like his, it must have been deeply humiliating to be suddenly thrown from an elevated position in society, and compelled to herd with *brutes* in human form. In this condition he was doomed to labor for seven years. The thoughts of home would rush on the mind, producing pain and disquietude, and anxiously looking forward to the moment of deliverance, when he should once more participate in the enjoyment of the domestic circle. He had watched every moment, from the time of his captivity, for an opportunity to effect his escape; the propitious hour seemed now to have arrived, and he availed himself of it. Having secured a boat and secreted some provisions, he committed himself to the winds and waves, trusting in Divine Providence for protection. After having been tossed about for many days, he was so fortunate as to fall in with an English ship, bound from Jamaica to Halifax, who kindly took him on board and treated him with marked attention. On his arrival at Halifax, a passage was given him to Boston, and on his arrival there, he was startled at the rumor that his wife was on the eve of being married to a Mr. Russell, of Boston. This was an additional stroke, and rendered his mind a prey to the most gloomy thoughts. Poor and penniless, he started from Boston on foot, for Newport, there to await the issue. On his arrival, he entered the back door of his former residence, in the character of a mendicant, and craved food from the servants, which was readily granted. After appeasing the cravings of hunger, he inquired if Mrs. Cranston was the mistress of the house; on being answered in the affirmative, he stated that he had a message which he wished to communicate to her. On being informed that it would be entirely out of her power to comply with his wishes, as she was then making preparations for her nuptial celebration, which was to take place that evening, the heart of Cranston was seized with the most painful emotion, that his lovely and adored wife was about to espouse another. He requested the servant to say to her mistress, that he had seen her husband that day at 12 o'clock, crossing Howland's Ferry.

Such intelligence, so unaccountable, yet highly interesting, brought Mrs. Cranston from her *toilette*, to look on the bearer of such intelligence. He briefly rehearsed over the sufferings which her husband had endured, which she listened to with the deepest interest. He wished to know of Mrs. Cranston whether she had ever seen him before. Dressed in sailor's garb, with a tarpaulin hat partially drawn over his eyes, she replied in the negative; finding himself a stranger and unknown, in his own mansion, he at last raised his hat and gave her a significant look, at the same moment pointing to a scar on his forehead, and exclaiming: "Did you, Mrs. Cranston, ever see that mark before?" She at once flung herself on his bosom, and exclaimed, in transports of joy, "You are my own, own dear, long lost husband!"

It required, as you may well imagine, some little time for the paroxysm to subside, and for Mr. Cranston to dress himself in a manner becoming his rank and station, before entering the drawing room, where the elegant group had assembled to witness the ceremony.

Mr. Russell, and the officiating clergyman, were already present, and nothing was wanting but the appearance of the bride. Soon, however, she entered, gracefully leaning on the arm of Mr. Cranston, whom she introduced as her long absent husband. The scene was worthy of the chisel of the artist, and produced emotions of delight in the minds of the guests.

Mr. Russell with true magnanimity, insisted that the marriage ceremony should be repeated, he giving the bride to her former husband, and endowing her with the amount which he intended to settle on her as his wife. This is a matter of fact, though assuming the appearance of romance.

Mr. Cranston was the son of the Hon. Samuel Cranston, Governor of the Colony. The Hon. Thomas Cranston, the grandson of Governor Samuel Cranston, and Abraham Redwood, married sisters.

"Three full-length portraits, of Mr. Cranston, wife, and daughter, are hanging up in my house at Kingston. They were painted by Copley, before the Revolution, which, with the carved frames, gilded, cost one thousand dollars at that period." —*History of the Narragansett Church.*

Newport was once rich in paintings, but time and change have scattered and dispersed them.

The residence of Governor Cranston was in the rear of the Hunter estate, in Thames-street, and was called his "Castle." Being built of stone, and cemented with shell lime, gave to it an antique appearance. He died, A. D. 1727.

The following inscription appears on his tomb-stone:

"Here lieth the body of
SAMUEL CRANSTON, Esq.
LATE GOVERNOR OF THIS COLONY,
Aged 68 Years; and
Departed this life, April ye 26, A.D. 1727.
He was son of JOHN CRANSTON, Esq., who also was
Governor here, 1680;
He was descended from the noble Scottish
LORD CRANSTON,
And carried in his viens a stream of the
Ancient Earls of
CRAWFORD, BOTHWELL, & TRAQUAIR'S,
Having had for his Grandfather,
JAMES CRANSTON, CLERK,
Chaplain to King Charles the First.
His Great-Grandfather was
JOHN CRANSTON, of POOLE, Esq.,
This last was Son of
JOHN CRANSTON, Esq.,
Which James was Son to
WILLIAM, LORD CRANSTON.

Rest happy now, brave patriot, without end,
Thy country's father, and thy country's friend."

On the head of the tombstone is emblazoned a rich coat-of-arms, with the motto—

"DUM CURO VIGILO."

The late Rev. Walter Cranston, of the Episcopal Church, a native of Newport, was one of his descendants. The name of Cranston, is still found in Newport, and the Hon. Robert B., and H. Y. Cranston, have both been Representatives in the Congress of the United States, from Rhode Island.

THE MARINE SOCIETY.

The Marine Society was instituted in the year 1756, by the name of the Fellowship Club. It was changed to the name of the Marine Society, by an Act of the Legislature, in 1785. The funds of the Institution have accumulated to about $20,000, the interest of which is appropriated to the relief of widows of deceased mariners, and orphan children, and to indigent members of the Society, agreeable to

ARTICLE XII.

"1st. This Society having been instituted for the relief of unfortunate mariners, their widows and orphan children, its funds are never, in any instance, to be diverted from that object."

Under its present arrangement, far more liberality is displayed towards the unfortunate, than formerly. This happy feature has arisen from the admission of new members, with enlarged and liberal views, and disposed to do ample justice towards applicants, without respect to self. It is a noble institution, reflecting honor on the town, and should be fostered and encouraged by every mariner of Newport.

Its first Secretary was Mr. Benjamin Sayer, and its first President, Mr. Oliver Ring Warner.

MASONIC FRATERNITY.

"In the spring of 1658, Mordecai Campannall, Moses Packeckoe, Levi, and others, in all fifteen families, arrived at Newport from Holland. They brought with them the three first degrees of masonry, and worked them in the house of Campannall, and continued to do so, they and their successors, to the year 1742." —*Taken from Documents now in possession of N. H. Gould, Esq.*

We have noticed this institution from the fact of its having been said to be "the oldest body in the United States." It is in a flourishing condition, numbering about one hundred and fifty members.

"In the year 1768, a lottery was granted by the Assembly, to pave Thames-street; it was called 'the Newport Pavement Lottery.'"—*From the Newport Mercury.*

1774. The entries at the Custom House in Newport, for the months of June and July, were: vessels from foreign voyages, 64; coasters, 134; whalemen, 17; making an aggregate of 215 in the space of two months.

The Rhode Island Greening.—It is stated that the first tree

of the kind, came up spontaneously, near the wall, by the brook which runs through the farm of Joseph I. Baily, Esq., in Middletown, the owner at that time being a Mr. Greene; from him the apple took its name. It is highly celebrated and much sought after.

The Gardner Pear was introduced by Mr. Lucas, a French Huguenot, who, on his arrival at Newport, hired an estate of Mr. R. Gardner, for his residence. About the time the tree began to bear, Mr. Gardner occupied his own estate, and the pear remaining, it obtained the name of the "Gardner Pear." They have nearly run out.

The Tallman Sweeting Apple, is a native of the Island, deriving its name from the family of Tallmans.

ORIGIN OF THE DECATUR FAMILY.

Stephen Decatur, who was a Captain in the United States Navy, and father of the late distinguished Commodore Stephen Decatur, was born in Newport, April, 1752. His grandfather was a native of Genoa, who came to Rhode Island about 1746. He married, in Newport, in 1751, the widow Priscilla Hill. Her maiden name was George. The family had their residence in Broad-street, where the house is still standing. As the mother's character so sensibly affects that of her children, it may not be amiss here to say, that Mrs. Hill possessed a force of mind and energy of character which was a characteristic feature of the George family. Stephen Decatur, the elder, was born in the house which then stood where the splendid mansion of Levi H. Gale, Esq., now stands, directly fronting the Mall.

Previous to the Revolution, they removed from Newport. In the war of the Revolution, Capt. Decatur greatly distinguished himself as the commander of a private ship from Philadelphia, called the "Fair American," by the capture of several British armed vessels. After the peace, he commanded a merchant vessel. At the establishment of the navy, in 1797, he was appointed to the command of the Delaware Sloop of War. He continued in her until the frigate Philadelphia was built, when the command was given him, at the request of the merchants who had built her by subscription.

He remained in command of the Philadelphia, until the settlement with France, when he resigned his commission and retired to his farm, a few miles from Philadelphia, where he resided until his death, which took place in March, 1808, in the 57th year of his age.

He had three sons and several daughters. His sons were, the late gallant Commodore Stephen Decatur, Lieut. James Decatur, who was killed in the Tripolitan war, and Col. John P. Decatur.

Commodore Stephen Decatur was unfortunately killed in a duel with the late Commodore Barron. No eulogy from our pen is needed, to establish the high reputation which Stephen Decatur acquired in his naval career; we feel a pride of character, however, in being able to connect him with the illustrious personages whose origin has been in Newport.

1761. This year a company of commedians arrived in Newport from Williamsburgh, Virginia. They erected a temporary theatre at the upper part of the Point near Dyre's Grove, and the performances were well attended. This is said to have been the first company that ever performed in America. John Whipple, on his return from the theatre, was drowned by falling from the Point Bridge.

SLAVER OF G. AND F. MALBORN.

Godfrey and John Malborn, had a slaver bound to Rhode Island, loaded with slaves: a pirate looking vessel hove in sight, and the captain offered to knock off the irons of the slaves, if they would consent to defend the vessel from the pirates. On their consenting, they were taken up and armed, and succeeding in driving off the enemy, they were rewarded, and afterwards taken to Pomfret, in Connecticut, on the large estate of Godfrey Malborn. Many of their descendants are still living in that neighborhood. An old hanger is now in the possession of Thomas Brinley, Esq., one hundred years old, which was used on that occasion.

John Brown, who was an eminent merchant of Newport, died October, 1753. He married a daughter of the Rev. James Honyman. He was extensively engaged in privateering, in company with Godfrey Malborn and George Wanton.

The enterprise which characterized the inhabitants of Newport, at that period, prove them to have been a superior class of men. There was a stimulus to action—for success crowned their efforts—and they were induced to push on, and to make Newport what she once was—the pride and admiration of the Colonies.

We have not alluded to the Slave Trade, from whence she reaped a golden harvest. The large exportation of New England rum to Africa, which in return brought slaves, increased the wealth of the place to an astonishing degree. There were but few of her merchants that were not directly, or indirectly interested in the traffic. Some forty or fifty sail of vessels were in this employment, and it was thought a necessary appendage to have one or more slaves, to act as domestics in their families.

Many an amusing anecdote is related of the slaves, which show them to have been rather more apt than what is usually the case. In imitation of the whites, the negroes held an annual election on the third Saturday in June, when they elected their Governor. This annual festivity was looked for with great anxiety. Party spirit was as violent and acrimonious with them as with the whites. The slaves assumed the power and pride, and took the relative rank of their masters; and it was degrading to the reputation of the owner, if his slaves appeared in inferior apparel, or with less money, than the slave of another master of equal wealth. At dinner, the Governor was seated at the head of the long table, under trees, or an arbor, with the unsuccessful candidate at his right, and his lady on the left. The afternoon was spent in dancing, games of quoits, athletic exercises, &c. They have for many years ceased the observance of this election.

The owners of slaves in Newport, as a general thing, were indulgent masters, so much so that the blacks were not conscious of being in bondage, but were treated with every mark of kindness befitting their station. Dr. Benjamin Waterhouse, late Professor in Harvard University, &c., in speaking on this subject, says:

In Newport there was a worthy, opulent man, and very respectable member of the Society of Friends, named Joseph Jacobs, advanced in life, who had four or five neat and well-behaved negro domestics, bound together by duty, respect, and gratitude; a pleasant picture of patriarchal government, without fear and without reproach. But being all blacks, it left the master and his wife alone in the parlor and garden; when he invited Mary Callender, daughter of Rev. Mr. Callender, to become their parlor companion; and she did so, to mutual satisfaction, waited on by black female slaves, who wore the plain garb of Quakers. The family was singular, and everything very decorous; relatively respectable, and marked by humble wisdom. To see the negro women, with their black hoods and blue aprons, walking at a respectful distance behind their master, to meeting, was not an unpleasant sight on those days. Friend Jacobs himself was somewhat *unique* in his habits and manners. Easy in his circumstances, and intellectual in taste, he filled up his leisure hours in watching the wind, his clock, and his weather-glasses. At that day, he was the only person on Rhode Island who owned a thermometer."

Newport was not alone in the slave trade; other places contributed their full share, and reaped the profits. It was at that period thought to be just and equitable, and none entertained conscientious scruples against it. It is unbecoming in the North, who have been the means of entailing slavery on the South, to turn round and denounce them as a class of unprincipled men, and deny to them the right which properly belongs to them, to manage their own domestic institutions as they please.

The course which has been pursued, so far from hastening the extinction of slavery, has retarded the event to an indefinite period. If we could be satisfied that immediate emancipation would better the condition of the slave, we would heartily acquiesce in the measure. But what has been the result in the British West Indies? Has the physical and moral condition of the slaves been improved, by granting to them their freedom? We believe it to be susceptible of proof, that it has not been the case; for the value of estates has declined, and both planter and negro, have become infinitely worse off by the premature and hasty measure. The results which have since followed, were not at the time anticipated. Great Britain has no great occasion to glory in the measure, but rather to lament it. In corroboration, heed and hearken to the voice that comes up to us from the ponderous columns of the *London Times*; that journal which of all others, perhaps, speaks most accurately the feelings and opinions of the British people on this, as on most other subjects of public concern :—

"Our legislation has been dictated by the presumed necessities of the African slave. After the Emancipation Act, a large charge was assessed upon the Colony, in aid of civil and religious institutions for the benefit of the enfranchised negro, and it was hoped that these colored subjects of the British Crown, would soon be assimilated to their fellow-citizens. From all the information which reaches us, no less than from the visible probabilities of the case, we are constrained to believe that *these hopes have been falsified.* The negro *has not* acquired with his freedom, any habits of industry or morality. *His independence is little better than that of an uncaptured brute.* Having accepted few of the restraints of civilization, he is amenable to few of its necessities; and the wants of his nature are so easily satisfied, that at the current rate of wages he is called upon for nothing but fitful or desultory exertion. *The blacks, therefore, instead of becoming intelligent husbandmen, have become vagrants and squatters, and it is now apprehended that with the failure of cultivation in the island, will come the failure of its resources for instructing or controlling its population.* So imminent does this consummation appear, that memorials have been signed by classes of colonial society hitherto standing aloof from politics, and not only the bench and the bar, but the bishop, clergy, and ministers of all denominations in the island, without exception, have recorded their conviction, that, in the absence of timely relief, the religious and educational institutions of the island *must be abandoned, and the masses of the population retrograde to barbarism!*"

The *New-York Express* adds some very sensible remarks, which we here subjoin :

"Would that those in our own country, who profess to be the only real friends of the African, would study these painful truths, and lay them to heart. Would that they abandon their wild chimeras of immediate, compulsory emancipation, to benefit the African, and betake themselves to the more humane, enlightened, and practical cause of Colonization, now seemingly the only door left open for the regeneration of the race. The bitter experience of Great Britain should teach us wisdom. The mistaken philanthropy which gave to the West India negroes the boon of freedom, which they neither knew nor cared how to value, has been fruitful of evils which, for the true welfare of the slave population in our own country, it were prudence and wisdom to guard against. English emancipation has done for the slave population of the West Indies, just what Abolitionism at home seeks to do for the same class of population in our Southern States, (only in a more aggravated form,) the bestowing upon them of an independence but 'little better than that of an *uncaptured brute*,' and a condition which, so far from enabling them to become intelligent, comfortable, and happy, will as inevitably reduce them to '*mere squatters and vagrants*', among the rest of mankind."

Could the Abolitionists succeed in carrying out their plans, in giving freedom to the slaves, what, we inquire, would be the moral and physical condition of the North? Already, the population has become so dense in our cities and larger towns, and such the competition in labor, with the low prices paid, that the poor man can hardly sustain himself and family. This incendiary measure would flood the North with emancipated negroes, and the collision would be painful to contemplate.

But the Abolitionists say, in reply: "Let the masters employ them and compensate them for their labor, and this would obviate the difficulty." This is mere theory. They having heard so much of the sympathy expressed for them by their Anti-Slavery friends of the North—who, bye-the-bye, would not contribute one dollar to ameliorate their condition—would, however, be induced to come among them and enjoy their *hospitality*, and that liberty of which they have heard so much; but which, alas! would only be imaginary in its nature, for their condition, instead of being improved, would be infinitely worse by the change.

There are certain laws in the physical and moral world, which we can never change, and it is not for us to arraign Omnipotence, and attempt to impeach his divine character. His wisdom is infinite, and out of these discordant materials good will ultimately arise. Our Saviour illustrates the kingdom of heaven, by "a woman's putting a piece of leaven into a measure of meal, until the whole was leavened." This implied the process of fermentation, and it required time. To have attempted to change the order of nature would only have effectually destroyed the article and rendered it useless. So in the moral elements, they are at work, and operating to the final consummation and overthrow of all evil in the world. But we cannot successfully hasten the time, by our own plans and purposes, but must leave it to Infinite Wisdom, at the same time employing the means which his Word and teaching furnish.

While the North held slaves, she took her own time to free them, and this was not done until she had become convinced that they were no longer *profitable.* It was a mere matter of *dollars and cents*, and not a conviction of its moral wrong, which urged them to the measure. No one attempted to coerce the North, which they were then satisfied they had no moral or political right to do. Let the North, then, leave the South to manage her domestic institutions in a manner most agreeable to her wishes, and hence put an end to *agitation*, which has already caused the temple of liberty to tremble to its very base. The union of these States should be dear to every American, and the individual who would put forth a suicidal hand to destroy the work of ages, should be denounced as a traitor of the "*first water*," far beyond Benedict Arnold in infamy and crime. Colonization is the only feasible plan devised, to ultimately free the country from slavery. And we believe it to be God's plan, for in no other possible way, can we conceive of the civilization and Christianizing of the dark Continent of Africa.

It should be borne in mind by the reader, that Slavery was entailed upon us while we were Colonies to Great Britain; and her interference with our institutions—now that we are free and independent—is an assumption of power which should not for a moment be countenanced by these United States. Her emissaries sent forth to stir up strife and sedition between the members of this Confederacy, should be told to go back instanter, and reform the abuses which exist in their own country, and which are most revolting in their nature—infinitely surpassing Southern slavery, which their imagination has *conjured up* as the greatest evil existing in the world.

Nations are very much like individuals; their own wrongs are not seen, while the wrongs and errors of others are magnified to the utmost stretch of a morbid mind. Let Great Britain survey the deep and damning misery which is to be found among the underground subjects of the realm, laboring and toiling in those hells, *the coal-mines*, shut out from the light of heaven, and crouching under their burden, until their limbs becoming contracted, premature old age follows, and death is their only hope of relief from the wretchedness of their condition.

This is the nation which it was once said was "the bulwark of the Christian religion!" When Great Britain will make some effectual effort to free her *white* slaves, we of this nation may feel more inclined to receive council and instruction from her, in relation to real or imaginary wrongs, which are to be found in this country. With her present policy, we have reason to believe that her aim and object is, to divide, if possible, these United States, regardless, *entirely*, of the state and condition of the slaves, which, if they had the control, would *still* be found in the cotton-fields, laboring to keep in successful operation their extensive manufacturing establishments.

The writer to whom we are to refer as evidence of the truth of the above remarks, is the Rev. William Sewell, B. D., Author of "Christian Politics," and late Professor of Moral Philosophy in the University of Oxford :—

"We sigh over the imprisonment of the canary-bird, exclaim against the cruelty of its oppressor, unbar the doors of its cage without a moment's delay, and the poor bird claps its wings with joy, flutters into open air, regains its liberty, its blessed liberty,—and the next day is found dead of cold and hunger. It is not for a Christian to argue in favor of slavery; still less to speak of it, except with abhorrence, when the master abuses his power, and the slave, instead of being raised by him by degrees, to the capability and enjoyment of his freedom, is riveted in his chains forever. But a Christian may indeed ask, whether the total exclusion of all restraint, of all fear, of all positive external obligation from the relation of master and servant, has not ended in reducing the servant in this country to a condition far worse, far more abject and degraded, far more hopeless, far more vitiated, than that of any slave in any period or country of the world? Our mines, our factories, our common workshops,—even our farms and agricultural cottages, full of crippled children and deformed women, of famine and fever, of drunkenness and vice,—of depraved, miserable, hopeless beings, doomed by their own free act, the free act of a being in the agony of starvation,—to the severest toil in darkness, at midnight; deprived of rest, stinted in food, selling their children to the same misery with their own for a few shillings, or sickening over hours of toil to earn their pence,—all the horrible scenes revealed by late inquiries into the state of our lower classes,—what is there in the records of slavery to be found more heart breaking or more appalling, to those who believe that nations, like individuals, are visited by curses from the Almighty,—and that the first curse denounced in His commandments is uttered against those who depart, even in the slightest degree, from His positive, external, revealed truth, and shape out ideas of the divine nature after their own fancy." —pp. 313–328.

In the year 1768, March 21st, it being the anniversary of the repeal of the Stamp Act, the day was celebrated with public exhibitions of joy. A flag was displayed on the top of the noble wide spreading tree of liberty, and a copper-plate affixed to its venerable trunk, in the room of that which was infamously taken from it on the 25th of August preceding. A flag was hoisted at Fort George, at Liberty Mast, on the Point; and the shipping in the harbor displayed their colors. The bells rung a merry peal, and every thing wore a joyous aspect. In the evening, rockets were discharged from the tree of liberty, at Liberty Mast; and at the house of John Madsly, Esq., a number of gentlemen were politely entertained, and the glass circulated in honor to the British and American patriots. Many other gentlemen assembled, in different parts of the town, to commemorate the glorious event, and the whole day was spent in decent festivity.

John Madsly owned and occupied the house, now in the possession of Dr. Watson, at the head of King-street. He is said to have been a polished gentleman, and distinguished for his benevolence, ever ready to confer favors on those who stood in need. The French fleet, in firing on the British batteries, threw several shot unintentionally into the town; Mr. Madsly had apprehended such an event, and had fitted up his oil-house cellar, adjoining his mansion, and invited the neighbors to take shelter there. A bullet entered the building, and lodged, without causing damage to any person in the cellar. It remained where it lodged, until the building was repaired and fitted up as a dancing hall for Carpentiere.

We find, as a matter of record, that " many persons were determined to use their influence in putting a stop to the destructive and pernicious effects attending the immense consumption of foreign teas, which must, otherwise, soon render us a poor, weak, debilitated people. The Hyperion, or Labrador tea, is much esteemed, and by great numbers vastly preferred to the poisonous Bohea."

Newport, in 1767, passed resolutions to discourage, as much as possible, further importations of European manufactures.

" We have heard of many gentlemen in town, of figure and fortune, who are determined to clothe themselves and families for the future, with the manufactures of this country. These resolutions were responded to by other sections of the country."

The *New York Journal*, May 30, 1768, says, " What a glorious example Newport has set us. Rouse, O my countrymen! We are well informed that one married lady and her daughter, of about sixteen, have spun full sixty yards of good fine linen cloth, nearly a yard wide, since the first of March, beside taking care of a large family. The linen manufacture is promoted and carried on, with so much spirit and assiduity, among all ranks, that we are assured there is scarcely flax enough to be had in town, to supply the continued consumption of that article."

King Lemuel says, Prov. 31 : 28, " Her children arise up, and call her blessed." v. 19, " She layeth her hand to the spindle, and her hands hold the distaff," &c.

Spinning and weaving was for ages an art of distinguished life, and was considered in the same light as needle-work now is with us. Accordingly, it was customary to represent those most distinguished, as excelling in the art of spinning, and poets sang of the distaff and loom. Homer alluded to it in the address of Alcondra to Helen ; so also Theocritus, in presenting a distaff to his friend's wife, says,

" O distaff; friend to warp and woof,
Minerva's friend in man's behoof."

It is said that Augustus, at the height of his regal splendor, appeared among his nobles in a robe, made for him by the queen.

Dr. Bushnell has wisely remarked, in his centennial address, that "the age has been called a homespun age;" and we would add, one of simplicity, and of comparative happiness, when those artificial distinctions, the result of mere wealth, was then in a great degree unknown." The homespun age produced economy in every member of the family, and they were contented with small things.

The expense of living, prior to the revolution, was far less than now, and what would then have been considered a sufficient sum to have rendered a man independent, would be looked upon at the present time as quite insignificant. Simon Pease, of Newport, one of the "upper ten thousand" at that day, who lived in a state of elegance befitting his station, was accosted by a William Hookey, a silversmith, who had witnessed the expensive living of Mr. Pease: "It must cost you a great deal to support your family." Mr. Pease replied, "that it cost him the enormous sum of $500 per annum." A person then worth ten thousand dollars, was considered a rich man, and even at this day of extravagance in the price of living, perhaps there is no maritime town, where the income arising from ten thousand dollars, would go as far in supporting a family, as it would in Newport.

EXTRACT FROM A SERMON

Preached in Trinity Church, Newport, Rhode Island, on MONDAY, June 3rd, 1771, at the Funeral of Mrs. ABIGAIL WANTON, late Consort of the Hon. JOSEPH WANTON, Jun., Esq., who departed this life on Friday, May 31st, 1771, in the 36th year of her age.

BY GEORGE BISSET, M.A.

"St. Luke xii. 40.—'BE YE THEREFORE READY ALSO.'

"IT is to be remembered to her honor, that in the day of prosperity, and in an age noted for its thoughtlessness and dissipation, her heart was lifted up in the ways of the Lord, to keep his commandments. It was a practical maxim with her, that as God is our chief benefactor, and can alone be our exceeding joy, so he is justly entitled to our highest veneration and regard; and that, consequently, it is surely good for us on every occasion, to draw near to him, both in his word and in his sacraments. Constant and regular was her attendance here, where her behaviour was remarkably composed and serious, equally distant from the indecent levity of those who come hither solely to comply with custom, not having God in all their thoughts, and from that constraining stiffness of the gloomy and superstitious, who imagine the object of their worship to be altogether such a one as themselves.

"She carefully and steadily observed the precept of the wise man, 'Keep thy foot when thou goest to the house of God;' and the whole of her deportment here always discovered that happy mixture of religious awe and filial confidence, which necessarily arises from just and worthy conceptions of the greatest and best of Beings, who is greatly to be feared in the meeting of his saints, and to be had in reverence of all that are about him.

"But her sense of religion was not confined to the Church, nor to the closet, but as she set God always before her, so that great Being, who honoreth those who honor him, kindly conducted her, with dignity and applause, through the several connections and relations of life. She was a grateful and dutiful daughter, a prudent and affectionate wife, a tender and indulgent parent, a mild and gentle mistress, a sincere and constant friend. She was a safe and easy companion, and possessed, in an eminent degree, the happy art of pleasing and entertaining in conversation, without ever having recourse to the fashionable topics of slander and defamation. Her most intimate friends knew not, indeed, whether to admire more her sweet and engaging compliance towards those who were present, or her tender regard for the character of the absent. Being highly sensible of the value of a good name, she always looked upon it as base and ungenerous meanness to hurt any one in that respect, either through malice, or a vain and unmeaning spirit of censoriousness; and if wit and good nature be incompatible, it must be honestly acknowledged, that she had no pretensions to the former, as she was never able in the least to relish the horrid pleasure of exposing the mangled reputation of a neighbor for the amusement of the company; on the contrary, it was her constant study and endeavor, to promote the interest of good will and friendship, by giving to merit its due praises, by endeavoring to remove all causes of dissentions, by hiding the faults of those with whom she conversed, and by putting the best construction upon their words and actions, which they could possibly admit of; and thus her excellent accomplishments, constantly employed in the cause of virtue, were really a blessing to herself and to society; being agreeably recommended and set off by the still more valuable ornament of a meek, a candid, and a quiet spirit. Those who moved in the higher spheres admired, and were charmed with that elegant simplicity, and unaffected gracefulness of manners, with that solidity of judgment, and benevolence of heart, and with those thousand inexpressible decencies, which uniformly appeared in all her words and actions; and the poor, encouraged by her condescensions, and refreshed and cherished by her extensive charity, rose up and called her blessed, and with heart-felt gratitude, almost adored the liberal hand which was so ready to supply their wants; of which that universal gloom and dejection, which has now so remarkably overspread their faces, give a much more ample and noble testimony, than any encomiums from this place.

"As her life was thus, in all respects, useful and agreeable, so it happily serves to confirm a truth, highly important to the interest of morality, that whoever is pitiful and courteous, and anxious to promote the happiness of others, will be universally beloved, and universally regretted. It was unnecessary, and perhaps impertinent, to have said so much of this amiable and universally admired character; you all knew her worth, and I trust will long respect her memory; and those who were most intimately connected with her, have no need to be put in remembrance, that these things were, and were most dear to them."

In the past, it was not the drapery alone which charmed the beholder, but rather the moral and intellectual acquirements of the mind; these were the gems which rendered the casket, in comparison, valueless. The expenditures for Schools and

Academies were far less than at the present period, and the progress in knowledge as in actual accomplishment, far in advance of this age. There was a solidity of judgment, a fixedness of purpose, a devotion to principle, which distinguished the minds of a former age, and which rendered society highly attractive and agreeable.

That lightness and frivolity of character, unbecoming the gentleman and lady, and which is disgusting to an elevated and refined mind, was not to be met with in the higher and fashionable circles of society.

We have given the foregoing extract of a most valuable sermon, in order to give the reader some idea of what then constituted greatness of character; and would to God that the present age would labor to copy after such an example as is here held up to view.

If all the energies of the intellect, and all the treasures which have been expended in fostering malignant passions, and in promoting contentions and warfare, had been devoted to the great object of cultivating the principle of benevolence, and distributing happiness among men, the moral and physical aspect of our world would, long ago, have assumed a very different appearance from what it now wears.

GENEALOGY OF THE MALBORN AND BRINLEY FAMILIES.

The Malborn and Brinley families figured largely in the past history of Newport. Col. Godfrey Malborn was a native of Prince Anne county, Virginia, and his farm was near the city and borough of Norfolk. He came to Rhode Island about 1700. He was a man of sturdy frame and character. The tradition is, that he disliked school discipline, absconded from his friends, became a sailor boy, and that he was actually bound out as an apprentice to a ship-master, by the authority of the town of Bristol, then in the jurisdiction of Massachusetts. During his apprenticeship, by the death of one of his ancestors, he became entitled to a large property in Virginia. He settled in Newport, where he married Margaret Scott; became, as the reader has already seen, a distinguished merchant, and was eminently successful. In the war of 1740, with France and Spain, he fitted out several private armed vessels of war, which made many captures. He died at Newport, February 22d, 1768, and was buried in the vault under Trinity Church, of which he was one of the founders. He left two sons, Godfrey and John; Thomas, another son, a graduate of Cambridge, Massachusetts, having died at an early age, the victim, it has been said, of an over-devotion to study.

Godfrey, the eldest son, was educated at Queen's College, Oxford; returned to Rhode Island in 1774, and carried on business on a large scale, in company with his brother John. They were largely engaged in the Colonial Neutral trade, in the war of 1756–7, ending by the peace of 1763, and at first was uncommonly successful, but in the end suffered severely, by the application of the rule of 1756. Two large ships laden with sugar, bound for Hamburgh, having been captured, were condemned, after a long and expensive litigation in the English Courts of Admiralty. These, and other vexatious losses, induced Mr. Malborn to retire from business, to the calm retreat of his large estate, in Pomfret, Connecticut. Mr. Malborn built an Episcopal Church in Brooklyn, known as the "Malborn Church."

"This was the first church erected, and for a long period, the only church of that denomination in this country. It was erected before the Revolutionary war, by Godfrey Malborn, Jun., Esq., a gentleman from Newport, Rhode Island. On his removal to Connecticut, he brought with him fifty or sixty slaves, on his large estate on which he resided. A great proportion of the colored people in this part of the State are their descendants."—*Connecticut Historical Collections.*

The Rev. Mr. Fog, the first Rector of the church, was a gentleman of highly respectable attainments, and continued to officiate until his death.

Mr. Malborn married Miss Brinley, of Roxbury, sister of Francis Brinley, of Newport, and died without issue, 1785. His remains lay interred in the church-yard of the Episcopal Church in Brooklyn.

Godfrey Malborn, senior, had five daughters; one married the above Francis Brinley; another, the youngest, to Dr. William Hunter, father of the late Hon. William Hunter.

One married Major Fairchild, one Dr. Mac-Kay, and another Shubel Hutchinson.

Thomas Brinley, in the reign of Charles the First, held the office of Auditor-General. At the downfall of that sovereign, he adhered to the fortunes of Charles the Second, and followed him on his exile upon the Continent. Upon the restoration of the second Charles, he held the same office under him, and died one year after; he was buried in the middle aisle of Datchet church, near London; the slab over his remains, still records these facts.

His son, Francis, (the first of Newport,) left England, and arrived at Newport, Rhode Island, and there amassed a large fortune; he died in Newport. He had previously sent his eldest son, Thomas, to England, for his education; he married in London, and had three children, and died there with the small-pox. His son, William, died, aged 13. His eldest son, Francis, (the second,) and daughter Elizabeth, with their mother, came to America, and inherited the fortune of his grandfather. He built the house at Roxbury, after the model of the old family mansion at Datchet, in England.

Elizabeth, grand-daughter of Thomas Brinley, Auditor-General for King Charles First and Second, came over with her brother Frank and their mother, from England, and settled at Roxbury; she married a Mr. Hutchinson, father of Shrimpton Hutchinson, who married a Malborn. Mrs. Col. Putman, George Brinley's wife's mother, was, in 1840, the only one of the stock remaining, *id. est.* the Hutchinsons.

There was a branch of the Brinley's in New Jersey, as early as 1776; I know this from the following records in my office, (Surveyor-General's :)—

" Lib. 2, fols. 33 & 80 : } Warrt. Survey and Patent, from
8th March, 1677. } Sir George Carteret, Knt., &c. Proprietor of E. Jersey, to Simon Brinley, ' for a parcel of land about the towne of Piscataway.' "

Simon Brinley's will was recorded at Trenton, 5th January, 1724–5, in " Book A, of Wills, page 348." I can trace him no farther.

Frank W. Brinley, Esq., of Perth Amboy, N. J., General Surveyor, one of my old schoolfellows, has kindly furnished some interesting notes of his family, which are here subjoined, as standing in most intimate relation with the past events of Newport.

"Thomas Brinley, first son of Francis and Deborah, of Roxbury, Massachusetts, was a King's Counsellor, and went to England with the British troops. He married a Miss Leyed, received a compensation from the British government, and died in England ; he left no issue.

"Edward Brinley, third son, remained in Boston at the Revolution, and was much persecuted as a Loyalist ; he kept a grocery in Boston, and was very unfortunate. He was father of George Brinley, druggist, now of Hartford, Connecticut, and of Frank and William, who lived at Roxbury.

"Nathaniel Brinley, fourth son, lived at Tingsbury, a farmer of large estate : had one son, Robert, still alive, and resident at Tingsbury ; said to be one of the best of men.

"George Brinley, fifth son, (my father's idol.) He was Commissary in the British army, during the Revolution. In 1777, at the time of the action at Princeton, the British being in New Brunswick and Perth Amboy, on his way from New Brunswick to Perth Amboy, with one servant, he was fired upon by a party of Provincials, 'minute-men,' who had come down from Woodbridge, on the main road between Brunswick and Amboy, from what is now (1850,) known as the 'Old Tappan House,' in the village of Bonhamtown. He received five musket balls in various parts of his body ; but retained his seat on horseback. His servant, being somewhat behind, wheeled, and rode back to New Brunswick, reporting his master as killed. Each ball made a flesh wound, and did not touch a bone. George rode on, until he reached 'Hangman's Corner,' (the parting roads from Perth Amboy, to Bonhamtown and Woodbridge,) where he fell from his horse, from loss of blood, and was seen to fall by the sentinel at the 'King's barracks.' A party was sent out, who brought him in, with his horse, that remained by him. He laid many months at Amboy. My father, (Edward,) who came from Newport to attend him, says, 'that when he saw his uncle, he had lain so long, that the shoulder-bones were through the skin.' He finally recovered, and returned with the British troops; was appointed Commissary at Halifax, and afterwards Commissary-General of the British troops in America.

" He married a daughter of Governor Wentworth, of New Hampshire, had two sons, Thomas and William, and a daughter, Mary. William was a pay-master in the British army. Mary married a 'Moody,' in England, and one of her daughters was in Boston two or three years ago.

" Frank, my father's eldest brother, served his time with Dr. Hunter, who married Miss Malborn, (my grand-mother's sister.) Frank was Surgeon of the 'New-York Volunteers,' and went to Carolina with them,—afterwards died at my father's house, (Edward Brinley,) at Shelburne, in 1757–8.

" Commissary George's son, Tom, was a Colonel in the British army, and was with Sir John Moore, in Spain; was detached to the West Indies, and there died an Adjutant-General.

" Francis Brinley, my grand-father, lived at Newport, Rhode Island; married Aleph Malborn, daughter of Godfrey Malborn. My uncle, 'Frank,' died young; was at College, at Cambridge, Massachusetts, at the time the British troops marched to Lexington. My father, Edward, was there on a visit to his brother. On the retreat of the British, the Americans were in pursuit, and, from the circumstance of some of the British officers having been with Frank and my father, (Ned,) imagined that Frank had 'pilotted the troops.' The Americans, or some of them, were so exasperated, that my father and others were obliged to lower Frank, by sheets tied together, from one of the College windows; while the Americans battered the door of his room, and destroyed everything.

" Frank and Ned afterwards came together, got an old horse from a pasture, and went " ride and tie' to Newport, 'full of wrath.' They met the British troops and joined them, and were called 'Tories' ever afterwards. My father says, 'Had it not been for this circumstance, we would have been the best of Democrats.'

" Deborah, my aunt, married an Episcopal clergyman, Rev. Daniel Fogg, of Brooklyn, Connecticut. She died a few years ago; had Francis Brinley Fogg, who studied at Newport, under the late Hon. William Hunter, and removed to Nashville,

Tennessee, where he married, and is an eminent lawyer: Edward, who still lives with his sister, Aleph Brinley Fogg, at Brooklyn, and Godfrey Malborn Fogg, who is, I believe, still living.

" Elizabeth, my aunt, married Capt. William Littlefield, formerly of the United States army, stationed at Newport; Littlefield was aid-de-camp to Gen. Nathaniel Greene, who married his sister.

" Edward Brinley Littlefield, of Tennessee, who was highly esteemed there, William, of Newport, and John, a physician, who died some years since, at New Orleans.

" Thomas, my uncle, still resides at Newport, a very aged man, though remarkably vigorous for one of his years. (He has recently died, aged 87.)

" Catharine, my aunt, married a Dr. Field, a Surgeon in the British army, and died at Jamaica, on Long Island, without issue.

" Gertrude Aleph, my sister, married the Rev. Edward Gilpin, son of John Gilpin, long his Britannic Majesty's Consul at Newport.

" Elizabeth Parker, my sister, married the Rev. J .F. Halsey, son of Capt. Halsey, of the United States' army.

" My father married, in 1806, Mary, the daughter of Dr. Johnson, of Newport; had issue, Edward L. Brinley, now a merchant, of the firm of Furness, Brinley & Co., Philadelphia: he married Fanny, sister of Major Brown, now in Russia.

" My son, Edward, is an officer in the United States' navy.

" My father, Edward Brinley, resides with me; he is 94 years old, but will not use a cane. He was, when young, shot through the body, with an iron ramrod, still in my possession. The following is the copy of the record of the accident in his own hand-writing:

" ' RECORD.

" ' This ramrod was shot through my body, when I was about twenty-one years old. It was an accident, and happened thus; I was out shooting snipe, robins, and other small birds, in company with a young man of about my own age; his gun had an iron ramrod, and in the course of the morning's shooting got foul, and the ramrod stuck, and being stronger in the grip with my fingers, I had twice pulled it out for him, the third time it stuck so fast that I could not draw it. I proposed firing against a crib, about twenty-five yards distance, and, I suppose, I cocked the gun for that purpose. He objected, saying, that he would lose his sport for the remainder of the day. I then told him to take hold of the breech, and I took the end of the ramrod, and both pulled away. I think it probable his hand was before the guard of the trigger, and he must have touched it with his finger. Off went the gun, the ramrod through my body. It entered about two or two and a half inches above my navel, and came out about the same distance from the back-bone, going, as the doctors said, through the lower part of the liver. The ramrod was found at the foot of an apple-tree, in the same form that it is now, ⌒, about thirty yards off. My companion, half-frightened to death, ran off, leaving me to get to a house, not far distant, but with a five-rail fence to get over. An express was immediately sent off to town, about two miles distant, and my father, and mother, and sister, and three doctors, two of them skilful surgeons in the British army, who then were in Newport, to whose knowledge of similar cases, I am, probably, indebted for my life. In about three weeks I was taken to town in a litter, and in another three weeks quite well, except weakness.

" Given under my hand this Eighteenth day of October, A. D. 1848.

" EDWARD BRINLEY, aged 90 years."

" The pictures of my great-grand-father, and great-grand-mother, hanging up in my parlor, were painted by Simybert, who came over to this country with George Berkley, Lord Bishop of Cloyne, about 1700. The child in my great-grand-mother's arms is my grandfather, Francis Brinley, (second of Newport.) The back ground of the picture representing my great-grand-father, is a view of his meadows, &c., with the town in the distance. The pictures are in good preservation, (life size,) and have been pronounced ' chef-d'œuvres.'

" The house at Roxbury, Massachusetts, built by Francis Brinley, of Roxbury, was after the model of the old family mansion at Datchet, near London, and still is in good preservation."

1634. The record of the Brinley family, commences in America. It will be perceived by the reader, that the Brinley family were Loyalists. They may have thought, like Saul of Tarsus, when he was waging a war of extermination against Christians, that they did it all in good conscience. But "the sword of the Lord and of Gideon" prevailed against our enemies; and they and their descendants have reaped the blessings acquired by other hearts, and other hands, in the glorious enterprise.

I have the following information of an old family of Newport, taken from these Records, viz.:

"Book C, page 158, 1st August, 1694. } Deed from Sarah Reape, widow of William Reape, late of Rhode Island, deceased, to William Marsh, son of Jonathan Marsh, of Newport, mariner, for certain lands in Monmouth county, N. J."

William Brinley signs this deed as a witness; dated in Shrewsbury, Monmouth county, New-York.

It appears that this Sarah came from Newport, about the year 1676, and had one patent for land to her in Shrewsbury, of 2010 acres, and various other large patents; one of 500 acres, "in right of her deceased husband."

"Lib. B 2, fol. 165, 20 Sept. 1685. } Deed from Jonathan Marsh, of Newport, &c., merchant, to Sarah Reape, for a right of Propriety in East Jersey."

From the above documents, I find that her husband's (William Reape) will, was dated 1st August, 1670.

"Lib. A, of Wills, page 5, 7th of Jan. 1715. } Sarah Reape's Will;" (by which it appears she had a large estate in Weymouth, Dorsetshire, in Old England. She devises as follows):—"To my grandson, William Brinley, my house lot, that I bought of the town of Newport, on Rhode Island, with the *housings* thereon. And also all my land at Rack (Wreck) Pond; and unto his three sons, Francis, William, and Thomas, a silver spoon to each, and all my tract of land of about 400 acres, in freehold. To my grand-daughter, Sarah Brinley, feather-beds, &c.; to my grandson William Brinley, my great silver cup, and all my land that lyeth at Whale Point, and all my right of propriety; to my grand-daughter, Elizabeth Brinley, a silver spoon, &c.; to my grandson, William Brinley, youngest son of Reape Brinley, my lands in Weymouth, in Old England," &c.

By her will she must have been very rich.

My presumption is, that Francis Brinley, (first) of Newport, had first, Thomas, then a second son, who married a daughter of William and Sarah Reape, of Newport, and their son, William, emigrated about the year 1685, to Monmouth county, New Jersey, and settled with his grandmother; he was one of the executors to his grandmother's will.

This William became a man of large possessions, and of mnch note. He is first named on the Records as a yeoman, then esquire, gentleman, and judge. The first grant of lands to him was in 1718; and he had many extensive grants of land besides those devised to him by his grandmother, Sarah.

He died about the year 1765, in Shrewsbury.

John Brinley appears on the Records, from 1754 to 1774. He died during the Revolution.

Reape Brinley, heir of William Brinley, and the youngest son, (mentioned in Sarah Reape's will,) was alive, in Shrewsbury, the 10th August, 1801. His son, Joseph Brinley, lived near Eatontown, in Shrewsbury, a man of considerable property, and a member of our Legislature about 1840. He died about 1843, leaving one child, a daughter.

A LITERARY AND PHILOSOPHICAL SOCIETY ESTABLISHED AT NEWPORT.

The celebrated Dean, afterwards Bishop Berkley, who resided here at the time is thought to have suggested its formation. The society was select, and some of its members were men of great intellectual power, among whom were Judge Edward Scott, Hon. Daniel Updike, Governor Jonas Lyndon, Dr. John Brett, Hon. Thomas Ward, Hon. William Ellery, Rev. James Honeyman, Rev. James Searing, Rev. John Chickley, Jun., and the Rev. Jeremiah Condy, of Boston.

Among the occasional numbers, were Governor Stephen Hopkins, and Samuel Johnson, D.D., afterwards President of Columbia College, New-York, and to this distinguished array of talent the Rev. Elisha Callender also belonged.

As this was probably one of the earliest societies of the kind in this country, we have thought that it might prove interesting to the reader, to subjoin a few extracts from the "Rules and Regulations of the Society." The original is in the handwriting of Judge Scott.

"First Regulation.—The members of this society shall meet every Monday evening, at the house of one of the members, *seriatim*, and converse about, and debate, some useful qnestion in divinity, morality, philosophy, history, &c.

"Second.—The member who proposes the question, shall be moderator, *pro hac vice*, and see that order and decency be maintained in all the debates and conversation.

"Fifth.—No member shall divulge the opinions or arguments of any particular member, as to any subject debated in the society, on penalty of a perpetual exclusion. Nevertheless, any member may gratify the curiosity of any that may enquire the names, number, general design, method, and laws of the society, and the opinions, or conclusions of the major part, without discovering how any particular member voted.

"Newport, February 2d, 1735.'

One of the objects of this society, was the collection of valuable books. It was subsequently joined by Abraham Redwood, Esq., who gave the sum of five hundred pounds sterling, to increase its library, on condition that the society would build a suitable edifice.

The society obtained a charter from the Colony in 1747, by the name of "The Company of the Redwood Library."

Abraham Redwood, was the son of Abraham Redwood, formerly of Bristol, England, and Mehitable, his wife, daughter of Jonas Langford, of the island of Antigua. At what time they came to Rhode Island is unknown. Mr. Redwood died in Newport, in 1772. They belonged to the Society of Friends. Mr. Redwood, by the death of an elder brother, became sole heir of the large estate of his grandfather, Langford, in Antigua.

In 1748, the present classical building was commenced, from a design by Mr. Harrison, the assistant architect of Blenheim House, England. It is remarked by Dr. Waterhouse, that in architectural taste and costly structure, Newport stood preeminent. He says: " Where is there a structure now in New England, that surpasses the Redwood Library? We have only to lament its perishable material. If you say that it was copied from an Athenian temple, still there is some credit due to them in selecting, seventy years ago, and relishing so chaste a specimen of Grecian taste." At this period, Newport was the " Athens of America."

We would suggest that the entrance to the Library be restored, agreeably to its original design, which was a gate in the centre, leading direct to the steps. It is now in bad taste, and contrary to the rules of architecture.

Henry Collins, Esq., proved a noble coadjutor of Mr. Redwood, and presented, in June, 1748, to the Company, the lot of land then called Bowling-Green, on which the present edifice now stands.

The building was not completed until 1750; a tax of twelve hundred pounds was assessed on the members of the Company, to defray the expense of completing it. The principal library room occupies the whole of the main building, is thirty-seven feet long, twenty-six feet broad, and nineteen feet in height. The present number of volumes is 6,000. The King of England gave to Redwood Library eighty-four volumes, of which seventy-two are large folios, and twelve octavos, which is said to be the largest collection sent to this country. The entire set has been nearly thirty-five years in the course of publication, and from the great demand for the different works of which it is composed, many of them have become exceedingly scarce, and some of them are now out of print. They consist of Doom's-day Book, Statutes of the realm, Parliamentary Acts of both England, Scotland, &c.

The master builders of the library were, Wing Spooner, Samuel Greene, Thomas Melville, and Isaac Chapman.

Abraham Redwood, of Dorset-place, Mary-le-bone, London, England, gave the homestead place, situated in Newport, to the library. In 1837, Baron Hollinguer, a distinguished banker, of Paris, who was connected by marriage with the Redwood family, presented the Company one thousand francs, for the restoration of the building. Many other bequests have been made by the friends of literature.

A certain elegant writer, (Dr. Waterhouse,) asserts, "That the founders of Redwood Library, sowed the seeds of science among us, and rendered the inhabitants, if not a more learned, yet a better read, and more inquisitive people, than that of any other town in the then British Provinces."

The late Dr. W. E. Channing, in a discourse delivered in Newport, in 1836, alludes to the neglected condition of the Library, at the period during which he pursued his studies in the town. He says, "I had no Professor to guide me; but I had two noble places of study,—one was yonder beautiful edifice, now so frequented, and so useful as a public library, then so deserted, that I spent day after day, and sometimes week after week, amidst its dusty volumes, without interruption from a single visitor."

The other classical spot was Easton's Beach, then equally as retired, though now so much frequented. He remarks, in his usual glowing style: "No spot on earth has helped to form me so much as that beach. There I lifted up my voice in praise, amid the tempest; there, softened by beauty, I poured out my thanksgiving, and contrite confessions. There, in reverential sympathy with the mighty power around me, I became conscious of power within. There, struggling thoughts and emotions broke forth, as if moved to utterance by nature's eloquence of the winds and waves. There began a happiness surpassing all worldly pleasure, all gifts of fortune, the happiness of communing with the works of God."

As the name of Berkley has been introduced in this connection, it may not be amiss to dwell somewhat on his character, which, for moral purity, was unexampled. Berkley was endued with great powers of mind, and possessed vast stores of erudition. His intellectual and moral qualities, inspired to form in him a character of high and attractive excellence. The learned Bishop Atterbury said of him, " So much innocence, and such humility, I did not think had been the portion of any but angels, until I saw this gentleman." Pope, who as a friend knew him well, describes him as possessed of " every virtue under Heaven."

It was to such society, that Newport was indebted for the intelligence and refinement of manners, which characterized her past history. Berkley was highly prepossessed in favor of Newport, as his letters to his friends plainly show.

The following is an extract, from a letter, written by Dean Berkley, to Thomas Prior, Esq.

" NEWPORT, ON RHODE ISLAND,
April 24th, 1729.

" I can by this time say something to you, from my own experience, of this place and people. The inhabitants are of a mixed kind, consisting of many sects, and subdivisions of sects. Here are four sorts of Anabaptists, besides Presbyterians, Quakers, Independents, and many of no profession at all. Notwithstanding so many differences, here are fewer quarrels about religion than elsewhere, the people living peaceably with their neighbors of whatsoever persuasion. They all agree in one point, that the Church of England is the second best. This island is pleasantly laid out in hills and vales, and rising ground ; hath plenty of excellent springs, and fine rivulets, and many delightful landscapes of rocks, and promontories, and adjacent lands.

" The town of Newport is the most thriving place in all America, for business. It is very pretty, and pleasantly situated. I was never more agreeably surprised, than at the first sight of the town and harbor."

The following verses were written by Bishop Berkley, during his residence in Newport, which fact demands their insertion.

"ON THE PROSPECT OF PLANTING ARTS AND LEARNING IN AMERICA.

"The muse disgusted at an age and clime,
Barren of every glorious theme;
In distant lands, now waits a better time,
Producing subjects worthy fame.

In happy climes, where from the genial sun
And virgin earth, fresh scenes ensue,
The force of art by Nature seem outdone,
And fancied beauties by the true.

In happy climes, the seat of innocence,
Where Nature guides and virtue rules;
Where men shall not impose for truth and sense,
The pedantry of Courts and schools.

There shall be sung another golden age,
The rise of empire and of arts;
The good and great inspiring epic rage,
The wisest heads, and noblest hearts.

Not such as Europe breeds in her decay,
Such as she bred when fresh and young;
When heavenly flame did animate the clay,
By future ages shall be sung.

Westward the course of empire takes its way,
The four first acts already past;
A fifth shall close the drama with the day,
Time's noblest offspring is the last."

"*The Minute Philosopher*," which he penned while he was a resident of Newport, consists of a series of dialogues, involving most of the important topics in debate between Christians and Infidels, the principal arguments by which Christianity is defended, and the principal objections with which it has been opposed.

In treating on academical study, he remarks, "Academical study may be comprised in two points, reading and meditation. Their reading is chiefly employed on ancient authors, in dead languages; so that a great part of their time is spent in learning words, which, when they have mastered with infinite pain, what do they get by it? but old and obsolete notions, which are now quite exploded and out of use: then, as to their meditations, what can they possibly be good for? He that wants the proper materials of thought, may think and meditate for ever to no purpose. Those cobwebs, spun by scholars out of their own brains, being alike unserviceable, either for use or ornament. Proper ideas, or materials, are only to be got by frequenting good company. I know several gentlemen, who, since their appearance in the world, have spent as much time in rubbing off the rust and pedantry of a college education, as they had before in acquiring it."—*Minute Philosopher*, pp. 35, 36.

"The weather was so fine, we had a mind to spend the day abroad, and take a cold dinner under a shade in some pleasant part of the country. Whereupon, after breakfast, we went down to a beach, about half-a-mile off, where we walked on the smooth sand, with the ocean on one hand, and on the other, wild broken rocks, intermixed with shady trees and springs of water, till the sun began to be uneasy. We then withdrew into a hollow glade between two rocks.

"Here we felt that sort of joyful instinct which a rural scene inspires, and proposed no small pleasure in resuming and continuing our conference without interruption till dinner. But we had hardly seated ourselves, and looked about us, when we saw a fox running by the foot of our mound, in an adjacent thicket. A few moments after we heard a confused noise of the opening of hounds, the winding of horns, and the shouts of the country squires."—*Berkley*.

It must strike the mind of the reader with surprise now that the island is nearly cleared of wood, that such fine sport was enjoyed by the early inhabitants; but one hundred and twenty-five years have wrought great and surprising changes.

The spot which Berkley so graphically describes, is the Hanging Rocks, which was his favorite retreat; it is near Sachuest Beach, on which he often rambled. It was not far from Whitehall, his former place of residence. The scenery is highly romantic, and, to a mind like his, was justly appreciated.

Bishop Berkley, during his residence at Newport, augmented the library of Harvard College, by valuable donations of the Latin and Greek classics. To Yale College he presented eight hundred and eighty volumes; and, on his departure from

Newport, he gave the Whitehall estate, consisting of his mansion and one hundred acres of land, for three scholarships in Latin and Greek. He returned to England in 1733, and died suddenly and calmly at Oxford, January 14th, 1753, in the 73d year of his age.

Bishop Berkley, though an Episcopalian, was no sectarian, as his public gifts plainly show. He was far in advance of the age in which he lived, which is evident from the prophetic vision in his poem, "On the Prospect of Planting Arts and Learning in America."

This extraordinary prophecy may be considered only as the result of long foresight and uncommon sagacity; of a foresight and sagacity stimulated, nevertheless, by exciting feeling and high enthusiasm. So clear a vision of what America would become, was not founded on square miles, or on existing numbers, or on any vulgar laws of statistics. It was an intuitive glance into futurity; it was a grand conception, strong, ardent, glowing, embracing all time since the creation of the world, and all regions of which that world is composed; and, judging of the future by just analogy with the past. And the inimitable imagery and beauty with which the thought is expressed, joined to the conception itself, render it one of the most striking passages in the language.

Could he have lived to this day, to witness the rapid strides which have been made westward, until the Pacific Ocean has been reached, and cities planted by American enterprize, it would have rejoiced his benevolent heart. And it should be matter of exultation and pride to every American, that republican principles are destined to exert a moral, and political influence over this vast continent. Nothing short of the power of God, has wrought such stupendous changes, in so short a period of time.

The high encomium passed on the state of society in Newport, by Bishop Berkley, was highly honorable and commendatory, and should influence the inhabitants to cherish a spirit of mutual forbearance and kindness, toward one another. His mind was not circumscribed and limited to self; he took a broad and comprehensive view of things, and believed that good would ever spring up out of evil. He remarks that "men of narrow capacities, and short sight, being able to see no further than one link in a chain of consequences, are shocked at small evils, which attend upon vice. But those who can enlarge their views, and look through a long series of events, may behold happiness resulting from vice, and good springing out of evil, in a thousand instances."—*Minute Philosopher.*

"The Rev. George Berkley, D. D., was born and educated in Ireland, being of an English family, who had settled there in the time of the Stuarts. His native place was Kilcrin, in the county of Kilkenny, where he was born in 1684. In his youth, like his friend Oglethrope, he was patronized by the Earl of Peterborough, who had an instinct for discovering and bringing forward men of different orders of talent. Berkley was also the intimate friend and companion of Pope, Dean Swift, and Sir Richard Steele, for the latter of whom he wrote several pieces for his periodical, called "The Guardian."

"Displaying at an early age great literary abilities, Berkley soon gained a high reputation in the learned world, by several of those works which still entitle him to be classed among the most profound and original inquirers into the philosophy of mind and the first principles of knowledge. His first work, written before he was twenty years of age, was on mathematics. This was followed at various periods, among other writings, by his "Essay towards a new theory of Vision;" "Principles of Human Knowledge," and "Alciphron, or the Minute Philosopher," the latter of which was written dnring his residence in Newport, Rhode Island.

"This great public benefactor was promoted in 1734, through the patronage of Queen Caroline, to the Bishopric of Cloyne, and resided in that diocese until July, 1752, when he removed to Oxford, to superintend the education of his son.

"He had three sons and a daughter. In person he was stout, and well made, his face was benignant and expressive, and his manners elegant, engaging, and enthusiastic. In the latter part of his life he continued his literary labors, and published various of his writings. His "Minute Philosopher," written as we have mentioned during his residence at Newport, Rhode Island, was published in 1732.

"His remains were interred in Christ Church, Oxford, and an elegant monument was erected to his memory by his widow." —*New York Atlas.*

ELEGANT COUNTRY AND TOWN RESIDENCES.

As Newport increased in wealth and prosperity, many of her eminent citizens turned their attention to the erection of town and country residences; the most splendid of which, was that erected by Col. Godfrey Malborn, about one mile from the State House. It was commenced in 1744, and was some time in the course of completion. It was sixty-four feet front, and fifty-two in depth, and was pronounced the most splendid edifice in all the Colonies. The materials of which it was built was Connecticut stone. It was two stories high, with a double-pitched room, dormer windows, with a cupola, which commanded an extensive view of the ocean, and Narraganset Bay. In architectural style, it is said to have resembled the State House. The fifteen steps leading to the hall were spacious, and standing as the building did on elevated ground, gave to it an imposing appearance. The interior is said to have been equally as grand. The doors were of mahogany, as well as the elegant finished circular stair-way, which led to the attic. An aged gentleman, of Newport, remarked to the author, "that the cost of the stair-way alone, he had heard his father say, was equal to the expense of building the Brenton House, now owned and occupied by Simmons S. Coe, Esq., in Thames-street. The estimated expense of this palace, for it well deserves the appellation, was one hundred thousand dollars.

The farm consisted of upwards of six hundred acres, extending north to Coddington's Cove. The garden, which lay direct in front of the mansion, with natural embankments, embracing as it did ten acres, was enchantingly laid out, with graveled walks, and highly ornamented with box, fruits of the rarest and choicest kinds, flowers, and shrubbery of every description. Three artificial ponds, with the silver fish sporting in the water, gave to the place the most romantic appearance. We have often fancied to ourselves, in our youthful days, when seated on the high flight of steps which led to the spacious hall of this princely mansion, and which commanded an extensive view of the beautiful bay of Newport, of the magnificent state in which Col. Malborn must have lived, far beyond any thing of the present day. It is one thing to have wealth, and another to know how, and in what manner to appropriate it. There was, at this period, sublime conception and taste, which enabled the gentleman to beautify and adorn the island.

No situation could possibly exhibit a scene more diversified and pleasing than this ; here the eye wandered from one beauty, to another more enchanting, and when it seemed to have discovered a still more superior view, the slightest glance presented another, if possible more inviting and wonderful,—apparently raised by the power of magic to captivate the astonished beholder.

This seat was once the resort of all the gay, and great ones of the island, and has been the scene of many a splendid banquet and joyous festivals.

"Here, if some wand'ring wretch, the child of fate
Told his sad tale, and humbly ask'd relief,
No surly menial drove him from the gate,
Humanity beguiled the tear of grief.

The well-known bench the moss will over-creep,
And where each rose in gay luxuriance hung,—
Rude tangling weeds will proud dominion keep,
And nettles group the spot where blossoms sprung.

Wild berries clust'ring on its straggling thorn,
Will then remain, to mark the shrubb'ry's bound ;
O'er-grown with weeds, the solitary lawn,
To mem'ry scarce will prove its high renown.

The dreary thought my sinking heart appals,
And trembling I quit the fancied gloom
Alas ! like this, each human fabric falls,
And gradual sinks oblivious in the tomb.

Majestic ruin ! noble in decay,—
Thy fame shall live, when thou art sunk away."

On June 7th, 1766, this elegant dwelling was entirely consumed by fire. The Colonel had a large party at dinner. It was a calamity to be deplored. His name, however, has become immortalized by the erection of this magnificent structure, with the garden attached, which still bears the name of "Malborn's Garden," though but little remains beside the artificial ponds.

Saturday dinners were alternately given among the principal families, and continued until the death of Francis Brinley, Esq. One principal dish, which was served up on the occasion, was *dun-fish*, a very choice article. Thomas Brinley, Esq., informed the author, that they cost at that day, as high as ten dollars per quintal. The process of cooking them was quite different from the ordinary mode now pursued; they were placed in soak over night, then taken out and sewed up in a napkin, and simply simmered over the fire; they were then served up whole, with melted butter and boiled eggs. A variety of other dishes went to make up the entertainment.

It was on one of these occasions, that the blacks in the kitchen of Col. Malborn, through carelessness, permitted the wood-work above the fireplace to take fire, and being destitute of brains, did not at once throw on a bucket of water, which would have extinguished it. It spread so rapidly, that before the engines arrived from Newport, it was enveloped in a sheet of flame, and beyond their power to check its progress; its walls crumbled and fell.

It has been stated that the Colonel bore his loss with much sang-froid, but this tradition we do not believe. A ridiculous statement was made in a small work, published a few years since, that Mrs. Malborn, for fear that her rich and costly furniture would be injured, prohibited the firemen from entering the house. Now, the presumption is, that Mrs. Malborn, like all other ladies, was so much terrified, as not to dictate on this occasion, but to make her exit from the burning house with all possible dispatch, and hence save her life

The wealthy portion of Newport, in those days, lived in epicurean style; perhaps there was no place in the Colonies, that could vie with them in the magnificence of their public entertainments. It was Old-English hospitality,—when the wine was passed round after dinner, and then followed "the feast of reason, and the flow of soul."

The town-house of Col Malborn, which is yet standing in Newport, was a splendid habitation. It is an ancient brick building, and has an imposing appearance with its portico, double flight of lofty steps, and its heavy and highly ornamental iron gate and railings. On the gate-posts were placed stone pine-apples, and the iron railing around the portico, bore the initials G. M. in the centre. The interior also presented many vestiges of its former splendor, in its gilded cornices and panel-work, and its mantels of rich marble. A splendid hall, with a noble flight of circular stairs, reaching to the attic, displayed the fine taste of its owner. Does the reader ask, where is this building ? Alas ! the hand of modern vandalism has shorn it of its former splendor ; it is now but an ordinary building, and scarcely noticed.

Mr. Malborn added much to the interest of the place, and was generous in all his public acts. It is said that he once remarked, " What will not money buy ?"—being a man of ordinary appearance, a wag standing near, overheard the remark, and was disposed to have some sport. He penned the following lines, and stuck them up where they could be seen and read :

" All the money in the place,
Won't buy Old Malborn a handsome face."

This highly exasperated Col. Malborn, whereupon he offered a reward of ten guineas to find out the author. The real author came forward, and frankly acknowledged it. It is said, that the Colonel was so much amused with the joke, that he paid him the reward, and treated him in the bargain. Commerce expands the mind, and liberalizes the heart.

The site formerly occupied by Mr. Malborn's house, after a period of eighty-four years, has been improved by J. Prescott Hall, Esq., of New-York, who has erected a house for a summer residence, but the glory has departed.

Mr. Hall's mother was the daughter of Peter Mumford, Esq., of Newport, and his wife being a Rhode Island lady, daughter of the late Hon. James D'Wolf, of Bristol, has attached him to Newport.

FIRE-ENGINE, No. 1,—MILL-STREET.

Engine No. 1, was the gift of Col. Godfrey Malborn. It was manufactured by Newsham and Ragg, of London, in the year

173.6 With the exception of the box, it remains the same, and is pronounced as perfect a specimen of the kind, as is to be met with, even in this day of improvement.

Judge Bowler, like most of the wealthy merchants of that period, had his town and country residence. The former is now the Vernon Mansion, corner of Clarke and Mary-streets, and is certainly a beautiful specimen of architecture. And the latter, the farm, now occupied and belonging to the heirs of Isaac Chase, in Portsmouth, which then contained an elegant garden, filled with every description of fruits and flowers, with artificial ponds, &c., at present is nothing more than an ordinary place.

Mr. Bowler married, in 1750, Ann Fairchild, of Newport, and left a number of descendants.

Vaucluse, the residence of the late Samuel Elam, Esq., he inherited from his uncle, Jarvis Elam, who resided on the place for many years before his death. Samuel was an English gentleman of the old school, and the taste which he displayed in laying out, and embellishing his grounds, is evidence of the truth of the remark. His style of living was profuse, and he could well afford it, for his income was large, and fully adequate to keep up such an establishment. On occasions, when he gave large dinner parties to his friends, the choicest viands graced his table, as well as superior wines and liquors, of which he was a connoisseur. Many were the entertainments given at Vaucluse, in which the guests were treated with sumptuous hospitality.

His equipage was after the English style, with postillion and footman. He had his town as well as country residence ; and, on bank days, (for he was President of the Rhode Island Union Bank,) he uniformly took dinner at Newport. An old female domestic, Marcy Sambo, took charge of the house, and provided for the occasion. He was a Quaker, and wore the peculiar garb of that sect, and contributed to the society. He was a gentleman of strong prejudices, but whenever he took a fancy to an individual, he was most strongly devoted. Many an anecdote is related of him, which goes to corroborate the truth of the remark. His port and carriage was truly dignified and noble. His property fell to a nephew, residing in England, who came over to America, and disposed of his whole estate ;

and he immediately returned home, his taste being different from that of his uncle's. Vaucluse is now the property of Thomas R. Harard, Esq., and is certainly the most interesting spot on the island.

The garden contains seventeen acres, most elegantly laid out, including a labyrinth, with serpentine walks, a fit emblem of ancient Troy. The walks are spacious, and running in different directions, presents a charming and picturesque scenery, and such as a highly cultivated mind would justly appreciate. The farm consists of about one hundred and fifty acres, scientifically cultivated. Mr. Harard is a practical farmer; every thing indicates system and proper management, and a walk over his extensive grounds, would soon convince the reader, that we have not too highly colored the picture.

Many other beautiful residences were to be found on the island, in her palmy days; the Overing, Bannister, &c., which shows the taste of the inhabitants at that interesting period.

Many of the inhabitants were from the first families in England, and Newport was regarded not only for her commercial importance, but as the emporium of fashion, refinement, and taste. "This aristocratic trait of character has continued among her inhabitants to the present day." The writer from whom we have made this extract, says, "But the change of population, and the death, dispersion, and poverty of those families, has now reduced society more conformable to the general republican manners of the country, and has levelled those arbitrary distinctions, which once so generally prevailed." Now the views here entertained of the aristocracy of Newport, being based on wealth, and the loss of wealth levelling those distinctions, is not founded in fact. The aristocracy of Newport rested on a sub-stratum more durable. It was intellect, and refinement of manners, which made the broad distinction in society. The mere boor, with no other recommendation than money, his society was not courted; while many, whose pecuniary means were limited, were held in high estimation for their moral and intellectual acquirements. This was the peculiar characteristic which distinguished the age, and which outweighed every minor consideration.

"Worth then made the man,not money—the want of it the fellow;
The rest was all but leather or prunella."

We wage no crusade against wealth, provided it be justly acquired, and judiciously appropriated. But when it is made the idol, and used as an instrument of power, it then becomes a curse ; and induces many to obtain it in the most fraudulent manner, in order that their respectability may be secured. It is truly painful, when we reflect, that man can be so besotted with gold, which will perish with the using; and arrogate so much self-importance, when there is evidently a want of intellectual ballast, which renders them pitiful objects to contemplate.

> " There's not a day, but to the man of thought,
> Betrays some secret,—that throws new reproach
> On life, and makes him sick of seeing man."

In 1768, the ship Endeavor, commanded by Capt. James Cook, sailed from England for the South Seas, having on board Sir Joseph Banks, &c., for the purpose of observing the transit of Venus over the Sun's disk, which took place on the 4th of June, 1769. After making the observation at Otaheite, Capt. Cook proceeded south, and having made many discoveries, returned, by the way of the Cape of Good Hope, to England, in 1771. She was subsequently engaged in the whaling business, and put into Newport, in consequence of the war between England and France, where she was condemned. She was then sold for the benefit of the underwriters, to Capt. John Cahoone, and his brother, Stephen, (father of Benjamin J. Cahoone, Esq., of the United States' navy,) who were building a packet called the Concord, and the materials which were found suitable were worked in. For many years the lower part of her hull lay on Cahoone's shore, at the south part of the town. It has long since disappeared, having been manufactured into canes, boxes, &c., as curiosities. William Gilpin, Esq., has in his possession the crown, taken from her stern.

CUNDALL'S MILLS.

The fanciful name now employed is the " Glen." We prefer, however, the original name, as being associated with many interesting events. It is now the property of the Hon. Samuel

Clarke, who married Barbary, the daughter of the late Joseph Cundall, Esq., of Portsmouth. Judge Clarke furnished the author with the subjoined facts :

" The earliest notice of the Cundall family in my possession is, an indenture of apprenticeship of Joseph Cundall, son of widow Cundall, of Bruntloff, in the county of York, England ; said indenture is dated 'first day of ye first month, called March, in the fifth year of the reign of our Sovereign Lady Queen Anne, A. D. 1706.' As the term of time required to learn a trade was seven years at least, it may be supposed that said Joseph Cundall was born about 1692. Said Joseph Cundall erected, or purchased, a small fulling-mill, where a stone factory now stands, in which to dress woolen cloths, &c., and purchased a third of a dwelling-house, in the north-east corner of Hunting Swamp, (where sportsmen resorted for game) ; said house stood on the south side of the highway, nearly opposite the residence of what was then Abraham Anthony's, who was Town Clerk of the town of Portsmouth. At this house, the wife of said Joseph Cundall died, on the 3rd day of June, 1745. Said Joseph Cundall purchased, of James Sisson, the farm, long called Cundall's Homestead. It contained forty-six acres, with a fulling-mill, and other buildings thereon."

The farm at present consists of one hundred and forty acres. The descendants now living are Isaac Cundall, Samuel B., and Mary, the wife of Perrin Burdick, merchant, of Newport, and Barbary, the wife of Judge Clarke, who resides at the place.

On Christmas-eve, December 24th, ——, a violent snow storm occurred, in which Mr. Cundall, on leaving his mill for home, perished, having lost his way.

Cundall's Mills is one of the most romantic spots on the island, and has become a general resort of strangers, who visit Newport in summer, to enjoy the salubrity of its climate, and its picturesque scenery. The walk through the shady bower of trees, which opens to the east passage, with Tiverton and Little Compton in view, is a rural scene, at once grand and imposing, suited to convey a just appreciation of the enjoyment of retirement, over the busy whirlpool of fashion.

The stream of water, which propels the small fulling-mill, adds beauty and sublimity to the scene. It flows on uninterruptedly in its course, agreeably to the language of the poet :—

" How steadily thou murmurest on, thou tangled little stream,
That stealthily in this deep glen hides—from the day's broad beam;
Small birds are singing near thee, green branches wave on high,—
But neither breeze, nor bird's glad song, thy murm'ring may put by."

LAWTON'S VALLEY.

This valley, or gulley, as it was once called, is situated on the west side of the island, in the town of Portsmouth. This is a delightful retreat in summer; blooming wild weeds hang luxuriantly in waving wreaths from innumerable impending projections of rock. Many beautiful vagrant rills gently steal through various crevices, while some, impeded in their course by rude fragments of stone, impetuously break a passage, and precipitate the sparkling foam down the declivity, till it pauses in the many windings of a gentle stream. It is sublimely beautiful to contemplate this wild luxuriance of prolific nature. No spot furnishes more inviting rides and walks than the island of Rhode Island, and to the mind of perception and taste, is presented a wide field for contemplation on the beauties of nature.

The entrance to this rural retreat, is situated about midway of the road running west from the Union Meeting-house, near the bridge, known as Cuff's bridge. Cuff was an old family negro, belonging to the Lawton family. His residence was a small cottage at the base of the hill, near the bridge. The old cellar is all that remains to mark the spot. We well remember his coming to market, in his old-fashioned coat, with the produce of his small plantation. These reminiscences afford pleasure and delight, far beyond anything of the present day.

This portion of the island is very interesting, and to one who prefers solitude to the vortex of fashion, presents attractions of a highly interesting character.

COUNT SEGUIN'S VIEWS ON SEEING NEWPORT.

" Other parts of America were only beautiful by anticipation, but the prosperity of Rhode Island was already complete;

industry, cultivation, activity of trade, were all carried to great perfection.

" Newport, well and regularly built, contained a numerous population, whose happiness was indicated by its prosperity It offered delightful circles, composed of enlightened men and modest and handsome women, whose talents heightened their personal attractions. All the French officers who knew them, recollect the names and beauty of Miss Champlin, the two Misses Hunter, and several others.

" Like the remainder of my companions, I rendered them homage, to which they were justly entitled, but my longest visits were paid to an old man, very silent, who very seldom bared his thoughts, and never bared his head. His gravity and monosyllabic conversation announced at first that he was a Quaker. It must however be confessed, in spite of all the veneration I felt for his virtues, our first interview would probably have been our last, had not I seen the door of the drawing-room suddenly open, and a being which resembled a nymph rather than a woman, enter the apartment. So much beauty, so much simplicity, so much elegance, and so much modesty, were perhaps never combined in the same person. It was Polly Leighton, (the way it was then pronounced, but it was always spelt Lawton,) the daughter of my grave Quaker. Her gown was white, like herself, while her ample muslin neckerchief, and the envious cambric of her cap, which scarcely allowed me to see her light-colored hair, and the modest attire, in short, of a pious virgin, seemed vainly to endeavor to conceal the most graceful figure, and the most beautiful form imaginable. Her eyes appeared to reflect, as in a mirror, the meekness and purity of her mind, and the goodness of her heart; she received us with an open ingenuity which delighted me, and the use of the familiar word 'thou,' which the rules of her sect prescribed, gave to our acquaintance the appearance of an old friendship.

" In our conversation she excited my surprise, by the candor, full of originality, of her questions:

" 'Thou hast, then,' she said, 'neither wife nor children in Europe, since thou leavest thy country, and comest so far to engage in that cruel occupation, war?'

" 'But it is for your welfare,' I replied, 'that I quit all I held dear, and it is to defend your liberty that I come to fight the English.'

" 'The English,' she rejoined, 'have done thee no harm, and wherefore shouldst thou care about our liberty? We ought never to interfere in other people's business, unless it be to reconcile them together, and prevent the effusion of blood.'

" 'But,' said I, 'my king has ordered me to come here, and engage his enemies, and your own.'

" 'Thy king, then, orders thee to do a thing which is unjust, inhuman, and contrary to what thy God ordereth. Thou shouldst obey thy God and disobey thy king, for he is a king to preserve, and not to destroy. I am sure that thy wife, if she has a good heart, is of my opinion.'

" What could I reply to that angel? for, in truth, I was tempted to believe that she was a celestial being. Certain it is, that, if I had not been married and happy, I should, whilst coming to defend the liberty of the Americans, have lost my own, at the feet of Polly Leighton.

" The impression produced upon me by this charming girl, was so different from what is experienced in the gay vortex of the world, that, as a natural consequence, it diverted my mind, at least for a time, from all idea of concerts, fêtés, and balls.

" However, the ladies of Newport had acquired strong claims upon our gratitude, by the kind reception they had honored us with, and by the favorable opinion they expressed of our companions in arms, whose absence they deeply regretted; we resolved to give them a magnificent ball and supper, a step not dictated by absolute prudence, since we were only seven or eight officers, ten leagues distant from our army.

" Long Island, which was occupied by our enemies, was not far from Newport; and we were told that the English privateers sometimes made their appearance on the coast. Such being the case, and the report of our fêté having got abroad, they might have paid us a visit, and rather strangely disturbed our jovial party. This apprehension, however, appeared to us quite unfounded, and I quickly sent for some musicians belonging to the regiment of Soissonnais Desoteux. Desoteux, who since acquired some celebrity during our revolution, as a leader of 'Chouans,' under the name of Comartin, took upon himself, assisted by Vauban, to make the necessary preparations for the ball and supper, whilst we went about town, distributing our invitations.

"The little fêté was one of the prettiest I have ever witnessed; it was adorned by beauty, and cordiality presided over the reception and entertainment of the guests. But Polly Leighton could not be present, and I cannot deny that this circumstance occasionally cast a gloom over my spirits.

"Time glided on so agreeably at Newport, that we were not anxious to return to our tents, and, relying upon the indulgence of our General, we exceeded by a few days the leave of absence he had given us. But M. De Rochambeau, who knew all the importance of a strict adherence to discipline, dispatched positive orders for us to join immediately our respective regiments; we therefore reluctantly quitted Newport, and quickly returned to our head quarters, which were at Providence, and which, at that period, contained three thousand inhabitants."—*Count Seguin's Memoirs.*

Polly Leighton, or Lawton, lived in the house, corner of Spring and Washington-square, now Touro, changed in honor of Abraham Touro, Esq., for his noble bequest.

Count Seguin's vivid description of Newport, cannot fail to convince the reader, of the justness of the high-wrought encomiums which have been passed upon her, by those who well knew her past history. There were acknowledged leaders of the *ton*, and their elegant and polished manners, with minds intelligent and cultivated, combined to draw around them the *elite* of the capital, and to render their mansions a most attractive place of resort.

Entertainments of every description was the order of the day, and the prominent fashionables were emulous in gaiety. Newport gave the ton to the surrounding country, who looked to them for fashions and manners, previous to the revolution.

THE WARD FAMILY.

As this family held a high rank, and occupied an important position in the early history of Newport, we have felt called upon to chronicle the interesting part which they took in the political drama.

The first of this family who came to Rhode Island, was Thomas Ward, who came from Glo'ster, in England, to Newport, where he married and settled. His father, John Ward, afterwards came over, and died in 1693. Thomas Ward died the same year, aged 48 years.

Richard Ward, the son of Thomas, was born in April, 1689. He was elected, in 1714, General-Recorder, or Secretary of the Colony, and held the office till 1733. In 1740, he was elected Deputy-Governor; and, on the death of Governor Wanton, was appointed by the General-Assembly to the office of Governor for the remainder of the year. In 1741–2, he was re-elected by the people to the same office. He died at Newport, 21st August, 1763, leaving a numerous issue; among his sons were Samuel Ward, who was Governor of the Colony in 1762—65; Thomas Ward, who died in 1760, was fourteen years Secretary of the Colony, and Henry Ward, who was Secretary from 1750 until his death in the year 1797, a period of thirty-eight years.

Many of the descendants are now living in New-York, highly respectable;—R. R. Ward, Esq., John Ward, and Samuel Ward.

The year 1758 is rendered memorable in the history of Rhode Island, as opening the great political drama of Messrs. Samuel Ward and Stephen Hopkins.

Mr. Hopkins at the time filled the chair of the chief magistrate, and Mr. Ward entered the field to contend with him for that honor. The office, at this period, was held in high estimation in Rhode Island. Mr. Ward was the favorite candidate of the South, and received the almost undivided support of the mercantile interest; while Mr. Hopkins was as warmly supported by the yeomanry of the North; and was again re-elected the three succeeding years.

In 1762, Mr. Ward was elected, but was defeated the following year, and Mr. Hopkins elected. The strife of political party raged with increasing violence, until such was the heart-burning hostility of the belligerent parties, as very greatly to impair the enjoyment of domestic tranquillity, and interrupt the hospitalities of social life.

In 1763, the office of Deputy-Governor was vacated by the

death of the Hon. John Gardiner, who then filled that place. On the meeting of the General Assembly, Mr. Hopkins and friends proposed that Mr. Ward be invited to fill that office, and that he be elected by the Assembly, then in session. Accordingly, a committee waited on Mr. Ward with this propo sition, which was indignantly rejected, and a message returned, embracing the only conditions of peace, viz.: "that both rival candidates, at the ensuing election, relinquish their pretensions and retire from the field."

Another proposition was then submitted by the House of Assistants, to Mr. Ward, to induce him to accept that office; that five, or one-half of that body, would cheerfully resign their seats in favor of an equal number of his friends, and the division of the spoils of offices should be equally divided between the parties at the approaching election. This proposition was too humiliating for the Spartan spirit of Mr. Ward, consequently, it was as unpropitious as the former one; and he returned for answer, "that no peace could be expected, while Mr. Hopkins was in the chair;"—but repeated his willingness to relinquish his pretensions, on condition that Mr. Hopkins would do the same. Other overtures were made to Mr. Ward, but without success, and both parties prepared to enter the field, with fixed and settled resolution.

The friends of Mr. Hopkins triumphed, and he was again elected; but the following spring he suffered a defeat, and Mr. Ward and friends were covered with laurels of political glory, which they were permitted to wear the two succeeding years.

At the opening of the spring campaign, in 1667, Mr. Hopkins' party, having been recruited and drilled for the conflict, entered the field, with a firm determination to oust the incumbents; and achieved a victory, leaving Mr. Ward minus four hundred and fourteen. This was the last pitched battle between the belligerent parties.

At the October session of the General Assembly, overtures of peace were again made by Governor Hopkins to Mr. Ward, which were soon followed by a cessation of hostilities, and finally resulted in a reconciliation of the parties. This proposition, highly honorable to Mr. Hopkins, was as follows, viz.: that Mr. Ward and friends, should nominate a Governor from those in the interest of Mr. Hopkins; and these should nominate a Deputy-Governor from among the friends of Mr. Ward, and so forth, alternately, with the whole council; or if Mr. Ward and friends decline the nomination, his Honor, and those associated with him, will nominate a Governor from among the friends of Mr. Ward, and so on as before. Preliminaries were soon entered into by both parties at Providence, and a treaty of peace was finally concluded at Newport, March 29th, 1768.

Newport being the capital of the State, it is really gratifying to learn of the chivalry which she displayed in behalf of Mr. Ward, her favorite candidate. The venerable Moses Brown has said, "that the violent hostility between these rival candidates grew out of a private feud, which had long existed between William Wanton and R. Ward, and that to this cause alone was the political war waged for so long a period." At that day, however, a greater freedom of opinion was manifest; parties were not afraid to shew their colors; the chain had not then been forged to bind the human mind, and crush the intellectual power of man in the dust. There was a pride of character, then possessed by the inhabitants of Newport, which we would feign flatter ourselves may be revived.

These gentlemen were again soon called from the peaceful quiet of domestic retreat, to enter the field, as friends, to contend for the rights of the Colonies, against the encroachments of British power; and engaged in the cause of American freedom, when one soul animated each heart.

They were among the first who fearlessly stood forth in defence of the rights of their country. That they fully enjoyed the confidence of their fellow-citizens, both as patriots and statesmen, is demonstrated in their choice to represent them in the first Continental Congress. Mr. Hopkins' name, with that of William Ellery, stands inscribed on the proudest monument of fame—The Declaration of American Independence;—and, though Mr. Hopkins' hand trembled, owing to a paralytic stroke, his heart never.

The following inscription appears on his tombstone, which has a rich coat of arms emblazoned on its head:

This Monument is erected to the Memory of
THE HONORABLE RICHARD WARD, ESQ.,
LATE GOVERNOR OF THE COLONY.
He was early in life
Employed in the Public Service,
And for many years
Furnished some of the most Important Offices
For the Colony,
With great ability and reputation.
He was a Member of the Sabbatarian Church of the Town,
And adorned the doctrine of his Saviour,
By a sincere and steady practice
Of the various duties of life.
He died on the 21st day of August, 1763,
In the 75th year of his age.

THE HARARD FAMILY.

The Harards were descended from Thomas Harard, who emigrated from Wales, about the year 1639, to the Jerseys, and from thence to Rhode Island, and settled in Portsmouth in 1640. His son, Robert, at that time about four years old, came with him, and was the only son that did so, as far as can be ascertained. The eldest son of Robert was Thomas, who died in 1745, aged 92. His children were Robert, George, Jeremiah, Benjamin, Stephen, Jonathan, and Thomas. From these sons a numerous issue have descended, and many of them distinguished men.

George Harard, mentioned above in the record, was the son of Thomas, who was Lieutenant-Governor of the Colony in the years 1734, 5, 6, 7, and 8, and great-grandson of the first settlers, who died in South Kingston. George, the youngest, early settled in Newport, as a merchant, and was elected a representative to the General Assembly from that town, for many years. He was the only Mayor of Newport under the city charter, in 1784, and held other honorable and responsible offices in the State. He died at Newport, August 11th, 1797.

Nathaniel Harard, third son of Mayor George, was a representative in the General Assembly for several years, and was

Speaker of the House. In 1818, he was elected a representative to Congress. He died in Washington, and was interred in the Congressional burying-ground.

"The late Hon. Benjamin Harard was a profound lawyer, and represented his native town, Newport, in the General Assembly for thirty-one years, and, of course, was subjected to the ordeal of sixty-two popular elections, a singular proof of the enlightened stability of his constituents, of his general high desert, and his peculiar fitness for this important office. This fact, independent of all others, entitles him to claim rank as a distinguished man, and, as it were, demonstrates the possession of those impressive and useful qualities, whose combination render character at once eminent and enduring.

"His knowledge of the affairs of the State was far more extensive than that of any other man, and his attachment to her interest and prosperity was unbounded. Governor James Fenner once said, 'Mr. Harard, you are in every respect a Rhode Island man;' this was a high encomium, and well merited. Mr. Harard's course of reading and of study, operating upon a mind of genuine native strength, and confirming and justifying a native steadiness of will, (the germ and guarantee of greatness,) gave to all his literary efforts and political proceedings, an air and cast of originality. In the middle and latter periods of his professional career, he was employed in most of the important lawsuits of the day, both in the Courts of the State, and the United States."—*Updike's History of the Narragansett Church.*

A block of wood, from the house built by Governor William Coddington, was procured by W. A. Clarke, Esq., cashier of the bank of Rhode Island, and is now used to cancel notes.

In 1772, King, now Franklin, and Pelham-streets, were paved, from the proceeds of lotteries granted for that purpose.

On the 16th of July, a packet, from Newport to Providence, with a number of passengers, was captured near the north end of Prudence, by a refugee-boat, with eight men. On its being known at Newport, a packet was manned by volunteers, under Capt. Webster, who succeeded in recapturing the vessel, before she could be got to sea, and brought her in, together with five of the men belonging to the boat.

We presume that this was Capt. Nicholas Webster, who was

for many years a very successful packet-master; he was grandfather of the wife of James Atkinson, Esq., publisher of the "Advertiser."

On the 13th of July, a most distressing accident took place in Newport; a pleasure party, consisting of five young men, and thirteen young women, while on their way to Canonicut Island, in a two mast boat, were upset in a squall, and one of the young men, and six young women were drowned; the remainder of the party were rescued by a boat in sight. The names of those lost were John Stall, Betsy and Lydia Hockey, daughters of William Hockey, Polly Spooner, Betsy Allen, Nabby Stanton, and Suckey Hefferon.

Matthew Cozzens, an eminent merchant, built the house, commonly called the Dudley House, in Middletown.

FRANKLIN'S PRINTING PRESS.

The history of Franklin's press is this:—James Franklin, elder brother of Dr. Benjamin, imported, in 1720, a press and type, for the purpose of carrying on the "Art and business of Printing." He soon after issued the first number of the "New England Courant," the second paper published in America. His brother Benjamin became his apprentice, and was employed in distributing copies to his customers, after having assisted in composing and working them off. The publisher of the Courant having given offence to the Assembly, the paper was suppressed, and he removed his office to Newport. Here he first published the "Rhode Island Gazette," and shortly after (1758,) established the "Newport Mercury." The press was used as long as it was serviceable. It is now honored as the one on which Dr. Franklin worked, when learning his trade; and as giving to the world his first effusions, in the form of anonymous letters, printed in the "Courant." It still remains in the printing office of the "Newport Mercury."

Amidst the changes which have occurred in Newport, many of which are of a most painful character, there are, nevertheless, some estates, which have remained in the families from the early settlement of the Island, and some prior to the American Revolution. It may prove interesting to the reader to be informed on this subject. The Overing property has continued to the present period, in the hands of the heirs, Cahoone, Freebody, Hockey, Job Cornell, Webber, John Stephens, Martin Howard, corner of Malborough and Thames-street, Jonathan T. Almy, and the Marsh Estate, which deed was given by Governors Walter Clark, Bull, and Carr, from the early settlement.

In Portsmouth, the farm of Burrington Anthony, Esq., has been in the family from the period of the settlement, as well as the Mott, Coggeshall, Sisson, &c.

Caleb Carr was a native of Scotland, and came to Rhode Island, but the precise time is not known; he was a large owner of land in the towns of Newport and Jamestown, some of which is held by his descendants, together with the ferry, as originally granted to him, and have since remained in the family.

He held various offices in the Colony, and was Governor here in 1695, and died before the expiration of that political year. His tomb-stone is still legible, and lies in the Carr burial ground, in Newport, which ground was sequestered, and given by him for that use. It contains the following inscription:

Here lies the body of
CALEB CARR,
Governor of this Colony, who departed this life, the 17th day
of December, in the 73d year of his age,
in the year 1695.

He left three sons, John, Nicholas, and Samuel. John settled in Newport; Nicholas, in Jamestown; and Samuel, on Long Island. John, the eldest, died in Newport, 1717, leaving four sons, Samuel, Caleb, Robert, and Frances. Samuel, the oldest, settled and died in Newport, 1740, leaving four sons, Caleb, Samuel, Ebenezer, and John. Samuel, the second son, settled in Newport, afterwards removed to Jamestown, and died 1796, leaving two sons, Samuel and Ebenezer. Samuel, the oldest, settled in Newport, and died 1814, leaving four sons and one daughter, who owned the Ferry Estate, which descended to him, in a regular line, from Caleb Carr, to whom the first grant was given for a ferry between Newport and Jamestown, by an Act of the Assembly of Rhode Island. It is still in the possession of the grandchildren of Samuel Carr.

This account of the family was furnished the author by Robert R. Carr, Esq., of Newport, son of Samuel. The Carr burial ground is situated on the north side of what was once called the Ferry Wharf Lane, but now Mill-street. We would suggest the importance of having this ground renovated and improved.

THE ARTISTS OF NEWPORT.

The interest which accumulates as we proceed in the history of Newport, admonishes us of the necessity of being brief. No spot presents more attractive materials than Newport. Before the Revolution, she had attained to a high degree of celebrity, and stood unrivalled by any city or town in the Colonies. Doctor Benjamin Waterhouse, himself a native of Newport, says:

"The island of Rhode Island, from its salubrity, and surprising beauty, before the Revolutionary war so sadly defaced it, was the chosen resort of the rich and philosophical, from nearly all parts of the civilized world. In no spot of the thirteen, or rather twelve Colonies, was there concentrated more individual opulence, learning, and liberal leisure."

It was no doubt owing to the highly cultivated taste of her inhabitants, why so many of her youth indulged in poetry and painting. Newport has been fertile in producing artists, some of whom have been highly distinguished in their profession. Edward G. Malborn, son of Col. John Malborn, has left an imperishable fame as a miniature painter. It is said that when Mr. Malborn, who went to Europe for the purpose of improvement in his profession, was introduced to Mr. West, and produced specimens of his work, after examining them, that distinguished and celebrated artist, inquired for what purpose he had come to England? Mr. Malborn answered, to perfect himself in the art of painting. Mr. West replied, "Sir, you can go home again, for a man who can paint such a picture as this, need not come to England for instruction." His picture of the "Past, Present, and Future," now belonging to his brother-in-law, John G. Whitehorne, Esq., is one of the most chaste and splendid things of the kind in existence. It represents three female figures. The Past has an air of dejection, the Present seems all life and animation, the Future buoyant with hope, and anticipating unalloyed pleasure.

> "Earth's perfection, angel graces
> In each feature fair."

We fondly hope that this valuable relic will never be taken from Newport.

Washington Allston received his first instructions as a painter, from Mr. Samuel King, late of Newport, who displayed a fine taste in the art, and his propensity for painting was probably cultivated by his residence during his boyish days, amid the scenery of Newport, whence he had come from South Carolina to attend the classical school in this place, kept by the late Robert Rogers, Esq.

Charles B. King, now resident in Washington city, where as a painter, he is much patronized, is also a native of Newport. It has been said that Mr. King wishes to bestow his valuable collection of paintings on his native town, on condition that a suitable place be provided for their reception. It is highly desirable that a chaste building should at once be erected, for the Southern Department, in which to place whatever is valuable in a historical point of view. And many others, who have not engaged in this employment as a profession, in their early days have sketched, and drawn, and painted, until immersed in the business of life, they have dropped the pencil, but still retain the taste.

Gilbert Stewart is claimed as being a native of Newport, though Mr. Updike says he was born in Narragansett. We have no wish to claim for Newport more than she deserves, but will merely state the discrepancies of the two accounts of his birth-place, and leave the reader to judge.

The following is extracted from a letter of Miss Anne Stewart, the daughter of Gilbert Stewart, addressed to Mr. Updike. She states in reply to the questions asked, in relation to what family of Anthony's her great-grandmother was, that she "was the daughter of Captain John Anthony, who was from Wales, and had a farm on the Island, near Newport, which he sold to Bishop Berkley. It was on this farm that my mother was born, and was married in Narragansett to my grandfather, Gilbert Stewart, who was from Perth in Scotland. They had but three children, James, Anne, and Gilbert. *As to their birthplace, you are much better informed than myself.* My father was educated in the grammar-school in Newport, and then sent to Scotland, to Sir George Chambers, for the purpose of finishing his education at Glasgow, after which he returned to Newport, where he remained for a time, and was then sent to England to study with Benjamin West, the great historical painter of that day."—*Updike's History.*

It seems from this letter that Mr. Stewart was educated in Newport, and after going abroad, on his return comes to Newport, and here tarries, but not one word of his being at Narragansett. Miss Anne Stewart seems to be quite ignorant of her father's birth-place; she refers the matter entirely to Mr. Updike, which is most certainly strange and unaccountable. We have conversed with Miss Jane Stewart, and she appeared to be ignorant of his birth-place being in Narragansett. She remarked that her father's associations and attachments were all in Newport, and she expresses a strong wish that the remains of her father which lie buried in Boston, might be removed here and placed by the side of his wife, which repose in the common burial ground in Newport.

Without attempting to invalidate the statement made by Wilbour Hammond, of the conversation *said* to have passed between him and Mr. Stewart, on his last visit to Narragansett, as every one is liable to mistakes and misapprehensions; it becomes us to offer such evidence as is furnished of the birthplace of this distinguished man.

An aged and highly respectable citizen of Newport, in a conversation with him on his last visit to Newport, and before crossing the ferries to visit the old snuff mill, which his father had formerly carried on, he asked him the question, where he was born; standing near the spot, he pointed to the story and half house, at the head of Bannister wharf, on the south side, and said: "there I have been told that I was born." This statement is confirmed by other aged citizens, which has given the impression that Stewart was a native of Newport. It is certain that the name of Gilbert Stewart appears in the census taken by John Bannister in 1770, and he is there found in the very spot where he stated that he was born. The building has since been taken down and another erected in its place. It is also said that he derived his first impression of painting from witnessing Neptune Thurston, a slave, who was employed in his master's cooper-shop, sketch likenesses on the head of casks, and remarked that if he had an instructor, he would make quite a celebrated artist.

Stewart has been pronounced to have been the greatest painter of the human head, that the age in which he lived produced, and perhaps of any other age. The form and features of the father of his country, the immortal Washington, from his pencil, will be transmitted to posterity, not only with truth and accuracy, but in a style of execution, worthy of the subject, and that, too, by a son of our own favored isle. The likeness of Washington, in the State House at Newport, was pronounced by Stewart as his greatest effort. And it is said he wished his native town to have it.

THE NEWPORT BAR.

1771. Henry Bull was the grandson of Henry Bull, one of the eighteen associates who first came to Rhode Island. He was born 23d of November, 1687. Being a man of strong powers of mind, he studied, and soon acquired a knowledge of the law, and became distinguished as a practitioner in the courts. He was occasionally a member of the House of Representatives from Newport, elected Attorney-General, in 1721, re-elected in 1722, but declined serving. He was elected Speaker of the House of Representatives in 1728–9; was one of the Committee to conduct and manage the controversy between the Colonies of Rhode Island and Massachusetts, respecting the eastern boundary. He was Chief Justice of the Court of Common Pleas for Newport county, at its first establishment in 1749.

"I have heard," says Major Bull, "the aged who had been acquainted with him, relate what he had told about his law education. When he had made up his mind to practice law, he went into the garden to exercise his talents in addressing the Court and Jury. He then selected five aabbages, in one row, for Judges, and twelve in another row for Jurors. After trying his hand there awhile, he went boldly into court and took upon himself the duties of an advocate, and a little observation and experience there, convinced him that the same cabbages were in the court house which he thought he had left in the garden; five in one row and twelve in another."

The conclusion to which he arrived proves him to have been a man of common sense, and a strict observer of human nature. But by whatever means he acquired a knowledge of the law, he certainly rose to the height of his profession, as a practitioner in the courts of law and admiralty; as the profession stood in his day.

He partook liberally of the enjoyments of life, was of an amiable and engaging disposition, and lived to a great age; having been born November 23d, 1687, and dying December 24th, 1771, aged 84.

James Honyman was the son of Rev. James Honyman, Rector of Trinity church, Newport. As a speaker, Mr. Honyman was elaborate, but his industry, talents, and faithfulness, commanded an extensive and profitable practice at Newport, and on the circuit. In deportment he was dignified—always dressed in the best fashions of the times—scrupulously formal in manners—domestic, yet social in his habits. In person, he was tall, broad-shouldered, and muscular, but not fleshy.

Mr. Honyman married Elizabeth, the daughter of George Golding, a merchant of Newport, and left two sons and six daughters. Most of his daughters and granddaughters having married British officers, or Americans adhering to the cause of the Crown, departed with the enemy, when the British evacuated Newport; and the estates devised to them by Mr. Honyman were confiscated. They were afterwards restored by an Act of Assembly.

Daniel Updike having applied himself to the study of the law, and being duly admitted to the bar, opened an office in Newport, and married Sarah, the daughter of Gov. Benedict Arnold Mr. Updike in person was about five feet ten inches in height, with prominent features. As an advocate, he sustained a high reputation; and among other personal advantages, possessed a clear, full, and musical voice. Dr. Bradford used to speak of him as being a "fine speaker, with great pathos and piercing irony." Mr. Updike possessed a large library of classical and general literature, a considerable portion of which is now extant.

Mr. Updike and Dean Berkley were intimate friends. In testimony of the friendship and esteem which the Dean entertained for Mr. Updike, he presented him on his departure for Europe, an elegantly wrought silver coffee pot, and after his arrival, sent him his "Minute Philosopher," which now remains in the family as remembrancers of this distinguished divine.

Augustus Johnson. He came to Rhode Island, when quite young, studied law with Matthew Robinson, Esq., who was his step-father, and settled at Newport. After a few years' practice he was considered one of the best lawyers in the State. With an acute and penetrating mind, he could unravel the most intricate cases with apparent ease, but his great *forte* was in sifting and reconciling discordant testimony.

Mr. Johnson was a loyalist, and the stand which he took in favor of the Crown, brought down the ire of the whole populace against him. This was on account of his acceptance of the office of Stamp-Master. He was constantly hissed at and insulted in the streets, but it had little or no effect on his determinations. In 1765, his house was surrounded by an infuriated collection of men, who by their unusual tumult and rage, first led him to feel that his person was in danger. He was afterwards seized, and after suffering many indignities, a promise was extorted from him, to resign the office, with which he reluctantly complied.

On the repeal of the Stamp Act, in 1766, as soon as the news was received, the people of Newport erected a gallows, near the State House, and had the effigies of Mr. Johnson, Martin Howard, jun., and Dr. Moffat, the stamp-masters, conveyed through the streets, in a cart, with halters about their necks. They were carried to the gallows and hanged, and shortly after cut down and burnt, amid the shouts and acclamations of the assembly. The contents of their houses and cellars were destroyed by a mob at night. Howard died Chief Justice of South Carolina; a fine portrait of him is in the Boston Court House. The popular indignation made it necessary for Mr. Johnson to seek protection on board of a British armed vessel then lying in the harbor. In the year 1779, he accompanied the enemy's forces to New-York. His property in Newport was confiscated, and as remuneration for his persecutions, he received a pension from the British Government as long as he lived, and after him the same was continued to his widow, who survived him many years.

Major Matthew Robinson Johnson, was the son of Augustus Johnson, who was a native of New Jersey; he was born in Newport, in 1761, and entered the British army at an early age, and served under the Duke of York and General Abercromby, at the siege of Dunkirk, and was in the various battles during the campaign in Holland; he afterwards served in the West Indies, and in all sustained the reputation of an accomplished and brave officer.

After the peace of 1800, feeling a longing desire to revisit his native place, he sold his commission, and came to Newport, where he married, and resided, except for a few years, on a farm in Portsmouth, until his death, which took place on the 5th of May, 1818, in the 56th year of his age. He was a high-minded and honorable man, and enjoyed the respect of all who knew him. His former residence, in Portsmouth, is now the Asylum for the Poor of that town.

Henry Marchant, was another highly distinguished counsellor. His father was Hexford Marchant, of Martha's Vineyard, a captain in the merchant service. His wife was a Butler, who died when the subject of this memoir was four years old, a short time after the removal of the family to Newport. Capt. Marchant married, for his second wife, the daughter of the first, and sister of the second General Ward.

The connection which the father had formed with the Ward family, had a happy effect upon the future destiny of the son. Having completed his studies under every favorable advantage, he came to Newport, and commenced practise. He was the only dissenting, or "liberty lawyer," in the Colony. His acquirements, industry, and forensic talent, soon raised him to the head of his profession. In 1766, Mr. Marchant wrote and prepared the deed from William Read, to William Ellery, John Collins, Robert Cooke, and Samuel Fowler, of "Liberty Tree lot," (a large buttonwood tree standing on it, at the north end of Thames-street, Newport.) Said lot and tree thereon, were conveyed to the grantees "in trust, and forever thereafter to be known by the name of the 'Tree of Liberty,' to be set apart to, and for the use of, the sons of liberty; and that the same stand as a monument of the spirited and noble opposition to the

Stamp Act, in the year 1765, by the sons of liberty in Newport, and throughout the continent of North America, and to be considered as emblematical of 'public liberty taking deep root in English America, of her strength and spreading protection, of her benign influences, refreshing her sons in all their just struggles against the attempts of tyranny and oppression.' And furthermore, the said tree of liberty is destined and set apart for exposing to public ignominy and reproach, all offenders against the liberties of the country, and the abettors and approvers of such as would enslave her. And, in general, said tree is hereby set apart, for such other purposes as they, the true born sons of liberty, shall, from time to time, from age to age, and in all times and ages hereafter, apprehend, judge, and resolve, may subserve the glorious cause of Public Liberty." The deed is witnessed by thirty-one of the most respectable and influential Whigs in Newport.

When the island was afterwards possessed by the enemy, the tree, thus dedicated, was destroyed; but after the evacuation, in 1783, it was replaced by another, which is still standing. The names, engraved on copper, and placed on the tree, are nearly covered over by the tree's enlargement. Let the inhabitants of Newport be reminded of their liberties, when they look on this tree, and guard against every attempt to undermine their glorious privileges.

THE

HON. HENRY MARCHANT,

Member of the Revolutionary Congress, and

United States' Judge for the District of Rhode Island,

Died August 30th, 1796,

ÆTATIS 56.

William Channing was another distinguished counsellor, of Newport. In early life he sustained many honorable offices by legislative appointment, and at the annual State election in 1777, he was, by his fellow-citizens, elected Attorney-General, without opposition; his predecessor, Mr. Marchant, having been, at the same period, chosen delegate to the Confederated Congress.

Mr. Channing was grandson of John Channing, of Dorsetshire, England; the first of the name who came to America, and who arrived in Boston about 1715. He was born in Newport, May 31st, 1751, and was educated at Aashua Hall, (Princeton College,) where he graduated in 1769. He was the father of the late W. E. Channing, D. D., who ranks as one of the most eminent divines the world has ever produced, as also Walter Channing, M. D., of Boston, who is distinguished as a philanthropist.

Matthew Robinson, the only son of Robert Robinson, was appointed Searcher of the Customs in Newport, by Queen Anne, and assumed the duties of the office about the year 1706. Matthew was born in Newport, in tho year 1709. He was well educated, and was an apt and ready Latin and Greek scholar, but whether he graduated from any public institution, cannot now be ascertained. He established an office in Newport, about forty years before the Revolution, and practised law with reputation, and his business was considerable on the circuits. He was a great collector of amazing incidents, trite sayings, and conundrums, which he preserved in a book kept for that purpose. One was, " that it was difficult to drive a black hog in the dark."

Robert Lightfoot was born in London, in 1716. His family were wealthy, and of high respectability. He graduated from the University of Oxford, studied law in the Inner Temple, and was appointed Judge of the Vice Admiralty, in the Southern District of the United States, in the reign of George II, with a salary of £6,000 a year. He entered upon the duties of his office, but the climate enfeebling his health, he came to Newport, which was then, as now, celebrated for its restorative influence to renovate his impaired constitution. Finding the island and its scenery as delightful as his fancy could sketch, and its society refined and attractive, he was disinclined to return, and resigned his office.

The venerable Dr. Waterhouse, in his letter, observes, " I knew Judge Lightfoot very well; he was a well-educated man, and first taught me to value and study Lord Bacon, and from him I learnt to value Locke, and Newton, and Boerhaave. He was the oracle of literary men in Newport; was a very able and learned man, and appeared, at Rhode Island, I thought—

* * * 'Condemn'd to trudge,
Without an equal, and without a judge.'

"He was a great epicure, a perfect encyclopædia, and welcome to the tables of the first characters, and constantly dined from home." (In those days Grahamism was unknown, and to enjoy life seemed to be the wish and desire of all.) "He was not a buffoon or mimic, but a fine relator of apt anecdotes. He informed every body, and contradicted no one, but had a happy Socratic method of teaching. He honored me with his notice, and I gained more knowledge from him than any other man in the choice of books." These were the palmy days of Newport, when the island was the intellectual constellation of this Western hemisphere.

MEDICAL FACULTY.

The names of Hunter, Halliburton, Brett, Moffat, Hooper, &c., rank high among the most eminent physicians of that or any other age. Dr. Waterhouse says:

"About the year 1756, Dr. William Hunter gave at Newport, R. I., the first anatomical and surgical lectures ever delivered in the twelve Colonies. They were delivered in the Court House, two seasons in succession, by cards of invitation, and to great satisfaction. His collection of instruments was much larger than any professor exhibits at this day. Dr. Hunter was a man of talents, well-educated at Edinburgh, and a gentleman of taste in the fine arts."

He further says, alluding to Dr. Hunter and Halliburton: "We doubt whether Boston, New-York, or Philadelphia, ever had, at one and the same time, two practitioners of physic and surgery, better educated and more skillful than these two gentlemen."

Dr. Hunter's daughters were said to have been beautiful and accomplished women. Soon after the peace of 1783, they went with their mother to Europe, for the purpese of procuring medical aid for one of the daughters. The youngest was married on the Continent, to Mr. Falconer, a celebrated banker in Naples, and the other to Count de Callender.

Dr Hunter was the father of the late Hon. William Hunter, who was Minister to Brazil, South America. Of his distinguished talents we are fully acquainted. He was one of nature's noblemen, and his native town of Newport felt justly proud of him, and highly appreciated his commanding talents, in their electing him to the various offices of importance in the State, and in the national councils. In the Senate of the United States none held a higher rank. His eloquence was listened to with the profoundest attention. He showed himself a man; one who was every way qualified to discharge the high and important trust committed to him by his constituents. His form and carriage indicated the finished gentleman. Those who remember him in his palmy days, will be ready to respond to the view here given of him.

Mr. Hunter was an independent man; he acknowledged no superior in the sense as to lead him to abandon his own private opinion, to gratify some would-be lordling. He planted his feet on the broad principle of right, and maintained the honor and dignity of the country which gave him birth. He enjoyed the friendship and esteem of James Madison and Andrew Jackson, which we conceived to be no small honor. Mr. Hunter was of the old school. He never followed in the track of the modern pigmies and dwarfs, whose pedantry lead them to think that all knowledge will die with them. His was a higher standard of moral excellence, derived from an age when firmness and stability of character were the characteristics of the times.

Dr. Isaac Center, who succeeded the distinguished names already, was a native of Londonderry, N. H., and was born about the year 1753. He received his medical education in Newport, R. I., that place being famed at the time for the number of its distinguished physicians. While pursuing his studies, the news of the battle of Lexington, April 1775, arrived, and filled with patriotic ardor, he immediately joined the Rhode Island troops, whom he accompanied to the camp at Cambridge, as a surgeon. On the organization of the army, he received a confirmation of his appointment, and was sent with the expedition of Gen. Arnold to Quebec. The road was up the Kennebec river, through the untried wilderness, which occupied thirty-two days, in the inclement months of November and December, before they reached the settlement on the Chaudiere; the whole march was made on foot, during which he, with the rest of the army, suffered almost incredible hardships. In the assault on Quebec, all of Arnold's division were either killed or made prisoners of war;

among the latter was young Center, who after being detained some time to attend to the sick and wounded, was released and suffered to return home. In 1779, he quitted the army, and served as a physician, in the town of Cranston, R. I., and was soon after elected one of the Representatives to the General Assembly, from that town. In 1784 he was chosen Surgeon and Physician-General of the State and Army, and removed to Newport, where he commenced the practice of physic, under the most favorable auspices, nearly all the old physicans having either died or emigrated during the war.

The Rev. William E. Channing, D. D., in speaking of Dr. Isaac Center, says: "He was a physician of extensive practice, who was thought to unite with great experience, a rare genius in his profession, and whose commanding figure rises before me, at the distance of forty-five years, as a specimen of manly beauty, worthy of the chisel of a Grecian sculptor."

He contributed to several papers, and also to the medical publications of the day, which acquired him a reputation not only in his own country, but in Europe. He died in 1799. He left two sons and three daughters. Dr. Horace Center, was educated in England, and was a practising physician of Newport, a gentleman highly distinguished in his profession. He was killed near Savannah, Geo., in a duel with the Hon. John Rutledge, of South Carolina. Nathaniel Greene Center died at sea, having been in the East India service. Edward Gilbon, the youngest son, was a young man of fine genius and elegant appearance. His eldest daughter, Eliza, married Rev. N. B. Crocker, D. D., Rector of St. John's church, Providence. For forty-eight years he has continued to minister to this church and congregation, with acceptance. Having devoted the energies of his nature in proclaiming the Gospel of Christ, avoiding questions which gender strife, rather "than godly edifying, which is in faith"—a long life has not alienated, but increased and strengthened the affections of his people towards him, and evidences the preponderance of good sense over ignorance, which distinguishes the society. It is no flattery to say of him, that he is a man of "blameless life and godly conversation," and entitled to the respect and confidence of the community among whom he has lived for nearly half a century.

Sarah married Clement S. Hunt, Purser in the U. S. Navy.

A Charter was granted to the Artillery Company in 1741. The first officers elected were:

Jahleel Brenton, Capt.	John Channing, Samuel Freebody, Walter Cranston, Josiah Brown, } Sergeants.
John Brown, 1st Lieut.	
William Mamford, 2d "	
John Tillinghast, Ensign.	Job Bennett, Peter Freby, } Drummers.
Josias Lyndon, Clerk.	

This company has always held a high rank, and embraced the most distinguished citizens of Newport. And for the honor of the town, and out of respect to the memory of the first officers, may it never lose its hold on the hearts of the people.

A List of Fish brought to Newport in 1779, *as reported by Edward Thurston, Esq.*

A

Alewives
Anchovies

B

Bass, Sea and Striped
Blue Fish
Brill
Bonnetta
Bull Fish
Bull's Eyes

C

Cod
Cusk
Cochogset
Cravalleys
Clams, Mud
" Beach
Cockles
Crabs, Green
' Sand
" Spider
" King
" Sea
" Running
" Fiddler
Cat Fish

D

Dace
Drum

E

Egg Fish
Eels, Sea
" Lamper
" Conger
" Common
" Sand

F

Flounders
Frost Fish
Flying Fish

G

Grunters

H

Haddock
Hake
Holibut
Herrings, English

L

Lancets
Lobsters
Limpets

M

Mackerel, Round
" Small ditto
" Large Horse
" Small ditto
" Spanish
Menhaden
Mussels
Millets
Mummy Chogs
Maids
Minnums

O

Oysters

P

Perch, Sea
" Fresh-water
Polluck, Whiting
Plaice
Pouts
Pike
Pumpkin Fish
Porpoise

Q

Quahog

R

Razor Fish
Rudder Fish

S

Ship Jack
Scuppague
Sheep's Head
Sneateague
Sturgeon
Skate
Shad
Smelts
Sucking Fish
Salmon
Slice Fish
Sole
Scollops
Squirt
Shrimps
Sea Mails
Sagars
Sword Fish
Shiners
Sun Fish
Sharks

T

Thrasher
Tarpum
Tautogue
Tom-Cod
Trout
Toad Fish
Tortoise
" Sea

W

Whale, Right
" Humpback
" Striped
" Bone

Newport has long been justly celebrated, for having the best fish market in the world, both for variety and quality. The choicest kinds, and the most sought after, are the Tautogue Sea Bass, Striped Bass, Horse Mackerel, and Blue Fish. The Tautogue, as served up in Newport style, is esteemed a very great luxury by the epicure: cooked as they are, immediately after taken from the sea, render them greatly superior to those obtained elsewhere. It is one great inducement for strangers to visit Newport, in connection with other attractions which are to be met within this highly interesting town.

It is delightful to ascend the cliff where the fishermen resort, and enjoy the healthy breezes of the ocean, and contemplate the restless wave, dashing its starry foam along the rock-bound shore; while at a distance the inflated white sails of passing vessels, burnished by the meridian sun, glide on the bosom of the ocean, and dazzle with its brightness the attentive eye that watches the beautiful sight.

Fishing, to the gentleman of leisure, is a pleasant pastime; nothing is more exciting and animating, than to hook a fine white chin tautogue, and draw him up on the rocks, in connection with anticipating the moment when he is placed on the gridiron, well-smothered with onions, &c. Why the mere thought makes the mouth water for such a repast.

It has been a question whether the facilities for fishing, which are enjoyed to so high a degree in Newport, is of advantage or not to the place. We have no hesitation in saying, that situated as Newport is, it proves a great blessing to the inhabitants, affording employment to many who would otherwise have nothing to do; and it is also a laudable occupation and conducive to health and longevity. It is one of God's blessings to his creatures, and as such, should be highly appreciated and valued by the inhabitants.

The Point—the northern part of Newport—is a highly interesting and beautiful portion, already beginning to be appreciated by strangers. In this section of the town, many of the inhabitants procure a livelihood by following the business of fishing. They own their boats, and go outside as far as Beaver-tail; occasionally they obtain a job to pilot some vessel to Providence, Fall River, &c. The Youngs, Gladdings, Huddys, &c., have been an easy and clever set of fellows, and they have well performed their part in securing varieties from the briny deep.

An old fisherman, Samuel Maxson, has kindly furnished the author with the most noted spots which have long been the resort of the inhabitants of Newport, to take fish. They are to be found at the south part of the island, about two miles from the town, viz: Taylor's Point, Ellison's Rocks, Shelf Rock, Stanton Rock, Coggeshall's Ledge, Bass Rock, Rough Point, Cluster Island Rocks, Gulley, near the boat-house, Spouting Rock, a little to the west of south, Jeffries' Point, or Rock Farm Point, Gooseberry Island, a short distance from Rhode Island. This was a favorite place of resort of Col. John Malborn, and his associates, who were often in the habit of spending a week on the island, taking fish and adhering strictly to the old maxim of having their swim three times. They used to have a jolly time of it, and often indulged to excess. Cherry Neck, Price's Neck, Seal Rock, Brenton's Reef, Castle Hill, so named from an old fort remaining on the farm, Isle Rock, Church's Beach, Kettle-bottom Rock, Almy's Pond, and Lily Pond, where perch were occasionally taken; the salt water fish being preferred, on account of their superior flavor, not many are taken. These are the most important places in Coggeshall and Brenton's Neck; and no sight is more pleasing than to witness the fishermen returning with a fine supply of fish, to furnish Newport market.

Every day in the year some kinds of fish may be found at the head of Banister's Wharf, Ferry Wharf, and the Granary or Brick Market, the three principal depots. Here stand the wheel-barrows, with their choice contents, an object of interest to the inhabitants. This is one of the old land-marks, like the blue eggs and egg-nog, which continue to be sold on the day of general election, and may these relics of antiquity forever distinguish the town.

Wild fowl are at certain seasons quite abundant, and are esteemed a great luxury by many. Captain Jeremiah Bliss, the son of the late Elder Bliss, who has attained to the advanced age of fourscore years, was considered the best shot on the Island; he has been known in former days to load a horse with sea-fowl.

To the man of leisure, it is fine sport to shoot the fowl which hover around the shores, and still more gratifying, to partake of a fine stew, made of them

Having alluded to the Boat-house, we would subjoin a few remarks. It has existed from a very early period, and was intended as an accommodation to the inhabitants of Newport. Captain Jeremiah Bliss says: "I have known it for more than sixty years, and helped to build the one which was destroyed in the September gale." The Malborn's, &c., were in the habit of resorting there before this period, and had partitioned off a room to keep their guns and ammunition. In the transfer of the farm, which has been frequent, this privilege to the land has always been granted, as being a public benefit in which each citizen of the town had a right to participate. There was one attempt made to question the propriety of having this site occupied for the above purpose, but public opinion put the matter to rest.

Sir Granville Temple's daughter died of small pox, and was buried on the Harrison Farm, S. S. W. of the Lime Rocks.

Dark Day, 1780. The Dark Day was distinguished by the phenomenon of a remarkable darkness in the North part of America, and is still called the Dark Day.

The following is an account of its appearance at Newport, as given at the time:

"There fell here a singular and remarkable darkness, which overspread the hemisphere for about five hours. In the morning were showers attended with distant thunder; about 10 o'clock A. M., a darkness came on, which by 11 o'clock, was perceived to be very unusual and extraordinary, and in half an hour after was considered as what was never before seen in these northern climates in America. The darkness was so intense, from a little before noon to two o'clock, as that persons could not read, and it became necessary to light up candles. Even the fowls, it is said, went to roost. Many of the inhabitants were thereupon thrown into the greatest consternation, as if the appearance was supernatural, and believed that the Day of Judgment was about to come. A little after 2, P. M., it became somewhat lighter, but the darkness soon returned. About 3 o'clock it began to go off, and at 4, P. M., the heavens resumed their usual light, as in a cloudy day, although the cloudiness continued all the rest of the afternoon."

Various were the speculations on the event, but no fixed conclusions were ever arrived at.

GREAT SNOW STORMS AND INTENSE COLD.

In 1717, two great snow storms took place, on the 20th and 24th of February, which covered the ground so deep with snow, that people for some days could not pass from one house to another. Old Indians said, their fathers had never told them of such a snow. It was from ten to twenty feet deep, and generally covered the lower stories, so that people dug paths from one house to another, under the snow. Soon after, a slight rain fell, and the frost crusted it over, so that the people went out of their chamber windows, and walked over it. Many of the farmers lost their sheep, and most of the sheep and swine which were saved, lived from one to two weeks without food.

Great damage was done to the orchards, by the snow freezing to the branches, and splitting them from the trees by its great weight.

This fall of snow formed a remarkable era in New England, and old people in relating an event would say, that it happened so many years before, or after, the great snow.

About the first of January, 1780, a period of steady cold commenced; during forty days, even on the south and sunny side of the buildings in warm situations, there was no indication of a thaw. The light and dry snow drifted and eddied with the incessant motion of the wind; paths opened, were immediately filled up, and communication was entirely interrupted. Narragansett Bay remained frozen over for six weeks, and the ice extended from the shore as far as the eye could see.

The inhabitants of Newport experienced the greatest distress for fuel; wood could not be had, and they were obliged to resort to wharf logs, old buildings, fences, and every other expedient to keep themselves from freezing. Wood was sold at the enormous price of $20 per cord. Provisions were equally scarce. Corn was sold at four silver dollars per bushel, and potatoes at two dollars per bushel; and other articles in like proportion.

In 1756, a look-out house was built on the top of the stone mill, which then belonged to John Banister, Esq. Benedict Arnold's daughter married Edward Pelham, who inherited his estate. Mr. Pelham left two daughters, one of whom married John Banister, and the other John Cowley, to whom his estate descended, consisting of Banister's Wharf, and the one known as Stephens' Wharf, which extended from Pelham-street to what is now called Bellevue-street.

The Banister family once filled a large place in Newport. The farm of the late George Irish, Esq., was the country seat of the Banisters. They lived in a style of affluence, and the choice viands which graced their table, would satisfy an epicurean palate. But one of the name is now left in Newport, of this once distinguished family. We have in our view at this very moment, Mrs. Banister, one of the older branches of the family, who resembled a lady dowager in the dignity of her appearance, and the courteousness of her manners.

THE STONE MILL.

" Fancy spreads her wing
Around thy time-scathed brow, and deeply tints
Her fairy scroll, while hoar antiquity
In silence frowns upon the aimless flight.

And whatsoever bears
The stamp of hoary time, and hath not been
The minister of evil, claims from us
Some tribute of respect."

In dimensions this mill is nearly twenty-five feet in height, its diameter on the outside is twenty-three feet, and inside is eighteen feet nine inches. It is circular, and supported upon eight arches, resting on thick columns, about ten feet high; the height of the centre of the arches from the ground is twelve feet six inches, and the foundation extends to the depth of four or five feet.

There has been much speculation, in relation to this structure, within the last twenty years; strangers, visiting Newport, have attempted to make it out as being erected by the labor of Northmen, whom they supposed to have discovered this continent, anterior to Columbus in the twelfth century.

These Northmen were the descendants of the Scandinavians, who, it is thought, sprang from the Thracians, mentioned by Homer, a nation now extinct. The Danes, Swedes, Norwegians, and Icelanders, all come under the name of Northmen, or Norsemen. Their literature has been compared, in extent, to the literary remains of Greece and Latium. This opens a new fountain of research, where the scholar may often

"Return and linger, linger and return."

In a work recently published in Denmark, the author has attempted to show that the old Stone Mill was built by Northmen. The Rev. Mr. Kipp, of Albany, tells me he saw at the residence of the Duke of Tuscany, a Swedish Count, who spoke of this building as the work of Northmen. He was perfectly familiar with the discoveries of those whom he proudly called "his people."

"The active mind of man instinctively surveys the dark regions of the past, and would gladly break the unfathomable silence of the nations of the dead, and raise the veil where their beauty and glory have slept for ages. The strong desire to learn something of those who lived when time was young, leads the antiquarian to often adopt groundless theories."—*Antiquities of America*, by A. Davis.

We have made this extract, for the purpose of preparing the mind of the reader, to draw his own inferences from the views entertained by antiquarians, with those which are held by the people of Newport, especially those of David Melville, Esq., who has devoted much time and attention to the investigation of the subject.

The most ridiculous views have been entertained of the nature and object of this structure, and also of the period when it was erected. These visionary ideas are of recent origin, and are not founded in fact, but the mere workings of a fanciful imagination which aims to surround the structure with a kind of romance, in order to gratify a morbid appetite which delights in the marvellous. We shall offer extracts from the will of Governor Benedict Arnold, and of Edward Pelham, who married his daughter, and then present the arguments which have been ably employed by one of our most respectable citizens, David Melville, Esq:

"My body I desire and appoint to be buried at ye northeast corner of a parcel of ground containing three rods square, being of, and lying in, my land, in or near the line or path from my dwelling-house, leading to my stone-built wind-mill, in ye town of Newport abovementioned."—*A True Copy from the Records of the Town Clerk's Office in the Town of Newport, Page* 348. *No.* 5 *Probate Records.*

What language could possibly have been employed, more significant, to convey to the mind the object for which this structure was reared, "my stone-built wind-mill, in the town of Newport." He does not say, "my *so-called* mill," as though he was ignorant of the origin or the design of the structure, but speaks in the most explicit manner, no doubt being entertained in his mind, of the nature and design of the building. We have asked the opinion of legal men, in what light they understood the language of Governor Arnold, and they have at once admitted that it was to be understood in its most literal signification, as a mill built by Governor Arnold, for a useful purpose, viz.: to grind corn for the early settlers.

Extract from Edward Pelham's will, dated May 21, 1741. Bequest to his daughter Hermæoine, the wife of John Banister, after others previously made:

"Also one other piece or parcel of land situated, lying and being in Newport aforesaid, containing eight acres or thereabouts, with an old stone wind-mill thereon standing, and being and commonly called and known by the name of the mill field, or upper field."

The butts and bounds shew this to be part of the lot mentioned in Benedict Arnold's will, on which he says "standeth my dwelling, or mansion-house," &c., "as also my stone-built wind-mill."

This property remained in the Banister family until the American Revolution. Here we have additional testimony of the nature and object of this structure, which has called forth such frequent discussions in the public prints. It is here clearly implied, if language can be understood, that it was built for a wind-mill, and this has been the opinion of the inhabitants of Newport, who have given the least attention to the subject.

Mr. Pelham does not attempt to make out in his will, that it was anything else than what had been before so lucidly and clearly described by Governor Benedict Arnold, but says, " an old stone wind-mill thereon standing." No instrument ever written could have been plainer or more to the point; and it shows a very great weakness in the human mind, to attempt to prove that it was built anterior to the discovery of this Continent by Columbus.

Those who settled the Island of Aquedneck, were not ignorant men, they had a knowledge of architecture, acquired in Europe, and the abundance of stone at their hand, induced them to erect the wind-mill, of this material, as being more permanent and lasting. There is nothing very remarkable in its construction. It is built of rough stone, placed without order, though in a communication made to the Antiquarian Society of Copenhagen, by Dr. Webb, he has made a statement so entirely incorrect as to deceive the Society into the idea that it could not have been erected by the early settlers of the island. He represents it as "built of stone, and laid in *regular* courses," which is not the fact, and had a tendency to mislead the mind of those to whom the statement was sent.

To our mind, the construction of this mill for an important and useful purpose, viz., to prepare food for the inhabitants, is a rational conclusion to arrive at, and one infinitely preferable to the vague notion embraced by many minds living at a distance, that it was erected as a fortress to defend a race who occupied the Island in the twelfth century. The former is the only sensible view which can be taken of the subject, while the latter is replete with the most egregious folly.

Nicholas Easton, who built the first house in Newport, makes no mention of the mill, which, if it had then been standing, would no doubt have been made matter of record by him or others of the early settlers.

A gentleman procured a quantity of the cement or mortar, from the wall of the old stone house in Spring-street, which was built by Henry Bull, one of the first purchasers of the Island, and immediately after the first settlement of the town, in 1638, and specimens from several other ancient buildings and stone chimneys, and some from the tombs of Governor Arnold and his wife, and from the stone mill, and analyzed and compared them, and found them of the same quality, and composed of shell lime, sand, and gravel; and considered it very strong evidence that they were built not far from the same time—all probably within a period of thirty or forty years from each other. It will be borne in mind by the reader, that we noticed the making of shell-lime at a very early period of the settlement of the town.

It may appear strange to the reader that this discovery has so recently been made. But when it is considered that public attention has never been called to the investigation of the subject until of late, their surprise and astonishment should cease. Many things are taken for granted, which may not in fact be true. It was currently reported and believed in olden times, that the celebrated spot known as Purgatory, at the second beach, had no bottom, and that frequent attempts had been made to sound it, but without effect. Now, so far from this being the truth, the tide ebbs and flows into it, and at low water it is quite shallow. Superstition has ever had its votaries, down to the period of spiritual knockings.

We will now subjoin a portion of the correspondence, held through the *Newport Herald* and *The Rhode Islander*, on this recently mooted subject, feeling satisfied in our own mind that our venerable townsman, David Melville, Esq., has done ample justice to the subject, and confounded the idle theories of his opponents, and shown to the world that it is nothing more or less than an old stone mill.

"Mr. Eastman,

"Your readers will recollect the controversy published some months since in relation to this ancient structure, which originated from the inquiry of a 'Visitor,' published in the Mercury, as to its origin and object, which was answered by a writer in the Newport Daily News, under the signature of 'Antiquarian, Brown University, Providence, Rhode Island.' The correctness of which was disputed, and pronounced false and groundless by the writer, under the signature of 'One of the Oldest Inhabitants,' published in the Herald of the Times and Rhode Islander. The publication of his last article on the subject, in the Herald of August 5th, 1847, silenced 'Antiquarian,' by showing conclusively that his whole statement was a base fabrication, without the least foundation in truth, and undoubtedly intended for deception; the object of which appeared to be to fix the date of its structure to remote antiquity, and that it was the works of the North-men, (the ancient Scandinavians,) who visited the eastern portion of this continent as early as the tenth century, and as evidence that they visited, and established themselves on this island at that period; from what sinister motives this was undertaken, the writer will not attempt to decide, but leaves that to the public.

"In conformity to the declared intention of the writer to represent the facts to the Royal Society of Antiquarians at Copenhagen, he forwarded to the President of the Institution, by the favor of the Honorable George Bancroft, our Minister in England, through the Danish Legation in London, a copy of the Herald of the Times and Rhode Islander, of August 5, 1847, which contained the full report attributed to Professor Scrobien, as published by 'Antiquarian, Brown University, Providence, Rhode Island,' with a letter, calling the attention of the Royal College to the subject, (which is too lengthy and quite unnecessary to be published,) asking the favor of an answer, if such a report had ever been made to the Society, and acted upon as stated in the report.

"To this communication, the writer has just received the following answer:

"'COPENHAGEN, January 4th, 1848.

"'SIR,

"'Your letter of the 12th of August, with the Herald of the Times and Rhode Islander, of August 5th, 1847, I duly received a few days ago.

"'I beg to return you my thanks for the communication transmitted, and deem it my duty to inform you that the article which lately appeared in your journals, on the subject of the ancient structure in Newport is, from beginning to end, a downright fabrication, no such having ever been made to the Royal Society of Northern Antiquities as the one alluded to. The persons mentioned in the article, too, Bishop Oelrischer, Professors Scrobien, Graety, &c., are all fictitious characters, there never having existed here individuals bearing those names. Thus the entire notice is nothing more than a fiction, the object of which is to mystify the public.

" 'It were to be wished, that such of the American journals as have admitted the article in question into their columns, would apprize the public of its entire falsity.

" 'In 1837 I published, on behalf of our Society, the Old Northern Sources to the Ante-Columbian History of America in the work entitled, ANTIQUITATES AMERICANÆ. Taking the astronomical, nautical, and geographical evidences contained in the ancient records themselves for a groundwork, I have endeavored to prove that our Scandinavian forefathers in the tenth century discovered a portion of the eastern coast of North America, and in particular visited Massachusetts and Rhode Island.

" 'Inquirers of the greatest celebrity here in Europe, have looked upon the arguments used by me as conclusive, among whom I may mention Alexander Humboldt, in his recently published KOSMOS, vol. 11, pages 269–272, where he considers the results of my investigations as historical facts fully demonstrated.

" 'At the time when I published the work above alluded to, I was not aware of the ancient structure in Newport, which, consequently, cannot have led in the remotest degree to the results deduced, nor is there a single word said about it in my work, which, moreover, is to be met with in most of the larger libraries in America, as well as in Europe; and thus opens an easier access to the study of the original written sources themselves.

" 'The right interpretation of the accounts in the ancient parchment copies, clearly proves that it was precisely Massachusetts and Rhode Island which the ancient Scandinavians visited, and where they established themselves. The agreement of the astronomical, nautical, and geographical evidences, leads in this respect to so certain a result, that doubtless nothing further is required.

" 'The early monuments which are met with in those regions, unquestionably merit the attention of the investigator, but we must be cautious in regard to the inferences to be drawn from them.

" 'Concerning the ancient structure in Newport, (of which we had no previous knowledge whatever,) we first received a communication on the 22d of May, 1839, from Thomas H.

Webb, M. D., (now of Boston, formerly of Providence,) which is inserted in our Memories des Antiquaires du Nord, 1836—1839, page 361, and I feel assured, that whoever reads that article, will therein discern all the caution which a scientific investigation demands, and all the respect due to an institution which has acquired confidence in and out of Europe.

"'From the drawings transmitted to us by a trust-worthy hand, our ablest judges skilled in the history of architecture, have pronounced the architectural style of the building to be that of the twelfth century, from which period a structure exactly corresponding has been pointed out, along with others in the same style. It is difficult, however, without being on the spot, to offer any decided opinion as to the period to which the structure itself is to be referred, nor has any one here ventured to do so. Here, in the North, no wind-mills occur of this construction, and a gentleman distinguished for his knowledge in the progressive history of the arts, and who has traveled much in Europe, has declared, that he never met with any such.* It would seem better, therefore, to leave the matter undecided, until further information can be obtained. But, even supposing that the origin of this and other monuments cannot be ascertained with precision, this in no way affects the stability of the historical facts deduced from the ancient manuscripts; that the Scandinavians in the tenth century, discovered and established themselves in Rhode Island and Massachusetts, in proof of which no other testimony is required than what is afforded by the ancient records themselves.

"'Our Society would be glad to receive trust-worthy

* In the "Penny Magazine of the Society for the diffusion of Useful Knowledge, for November, 1836," p. 480, there is an engraving of a Wind-mill at Chesterton, Warwickshire, England, erected after a design of Inigo Jones, which. without the roof and vanes, shew an exact fac-simile of the Old Mill at Newport. An aged ship-master, late of this town, of the first respectability and of undoubted integrity, who has been many voyages to the North of Europe, informs me that he has seen there more than forty wind-mills, of the same material and construction as the old wind-mill here; and he had curiosity once to ask, at one of them, why they were built on pillars and open between them? and was informed that on this construction the wind having a free passage through, there was no eddy wind caused to make a back sail and lessen the power. Other authorities might be quoted, but we think it wholly unnecessary, for every sensible mind after reading the evidence adduced, must be convinced of the object for which the structure was intended.—*Note by the Author.*

communications on the subject of Ante-Columbian Monuments of America, to be preserved in the American section of the Society's Historico-Archæological Archives, and also for insertion in their Memories, in as far as they may be suited for the purpose. Such articles as the one you have made known to us, merits no place within the pale of science, and we are glad to observe that by you also, they are estimated according to their deserts.

" ' I have the honor to be, sir,

" ' Your obedient servant,

" ' Charles C. Rafn,

" ' Sec'y, R. S. N. A."

" ' David Melville, Esq., Newport, R. I.'

" It appears by the foregoing letter that the Royal College received a communication on the 22d of May, 1839, from Thomas H. Webb, M. D., (now of Boston, formerly of Providence,) which is inserted in their Memoirs des Antiquaries du Nort, of 1836—1839, page 361, in which Doctor Webb gives a description of the architectural construction of the ruin, and they received also drawings of the same, transmitted to them by trust-worthy hands, from which description, and the drawings referred to, their 'ablest judges,' skilled in the history of architecture, have pronounced the architectural style of the building to be that of the twelfth century. Upon this it is barely necessary to remark, that the description given by Dr. Webb, as well as the drawings which were transmitted, though in their general contour correct, are in their minutiæ visibly incorrect, so decidedly so, as to mislead the judgment of those best skilled in the history of architecture, and to render it impossible for them to determine with any reliable precision, the period to which the structure may be referred; there is no reliance, therefore, upon the opinions pronounced by the ablest judges skilled in the history of architecture, founded on date so incorrect as that submitted to their inspection.

" The Royal Society of Antiquarians, at Copenhagen, which is universally considered as the source of correct information, on facts relating to subjects of antiquity, have been imposed upon by unprincipled miscreants in this country. As an instance of their success in their attempts at deception, I would refer to the following: The inscription on the *Dighton Rock*, which is undoubtedly an Indian inscription in commemoration of some great battle, and was so pronounced by General Washington, when a copy of it was shown to him at Cambridge, during the Revolutionary War, he having seen many similar to it in the Indian country; and is so considered by Henry R. Schoolcraft, Esq., Professor of Geology in the service of the United States, who visited the Rock the last summer, and who has seen many of the same description in various parts of the country, from Maine to the source of the Mississippi, and is acquainted with the meaning of many of the characters in the inscription. This inscription has been copied by some designing wretch, and forwarded to the Royal Society of Antiquarians, at Copenhagen, undoubtedly for deception, and published in the work alluded to by Prof. Rafn, entitled *Antiquitates Americanæ.* The version of the inscription published in that work, and distributed throughout Europe and America, was altered so as to make it appear to have been the work of the Scandinavians, by altering the characters, and adding in the body of the inscription, the characters, O R I N X, which is said to be the name of one of their early navigators; such unwarrantable conduct is disgraceful to the authors, an imposition on that highly respectable institution and the world, and ought to be discountenanced and exposed by every admirer of the correctness of facts relating to ages past. The Society has, (from misrepresentations made to them in regard to the 'Newport Ruins,' as it has of late been called,) been drawn into an error in supposing that their Scandinavian forefathers visited in the 10th century the island of Rhode Island. At the remote period referred to, in the letter of Professor Rafn, they may have visited Massachusetts, and reported it by its true Indian name, and if they had visited this Island, it is reasonable to suppose they would have called it by the name it was called by the native inhabitants, which was *Acquethneck.* It was not called Rhode Island until 1644, as appears from the following extracts from the Old Colony Records, 'at a General Court held at Newport on the 15th day of the 1st month, 1644.'

"'It is ordered by this Court that ye island commonly called Acquethneck, shall be from henceforth called ye Isle of Rhodes, or Rhode Island.'

"There is no doubt that the Northmen discovered in the tenth century, the eastern coast of this Continent, and visited that part called by the Indian inhabitants, Massachusetts, but it is doubtful if they visited at that period the Island of Acquethneck, now Rhode Island. There does not appear from any history or tradition from our ancestors, that there was any tradition among the Indians of Acquethneck, ever having been visited by white men before the settlement of the country by our British ancestors. When the first white inhabitants settled on the Elizabeth Islands, there was a tradition among the Indians, that the Vineyard had been visited many ages before by a colony of white men, who came there in a vessel from the North, and remained there for a season, and returned to the North in the winter, with an intention of returning there again the next year, but never came back, and were supposed to have been lost, and the same tradition was rife among the Indians on the main, and remains to this day. It is very probable that these were the Northmen from the borders of the St. Lawrence, and that the Vineyard Island was the extent of their progress westward along the coast. From this circumstance, and from sinister motives, it has been endeavored to be shown that the Northmen visited this Island in the tenth or eleventh century, and called the island 'Vinelant,' &c., and the Newport Ruin has been endeavored to be palmed upon the world through the Royal Society of Antiquarians at Copenhagen, as evidence of the fact of the visit of the Northmen, and the work of their hands,* but

"Let Antiquarians say what they will,
It is nothing but an Old Stone Mill.
"ONE OF THE OLDEST INHABITANTS."

What better traditionary evidence than that of Gov. Arnold's grandson, Josiah Arnold, who died long since the Revolutionary war, and that of his great-grandson, Sanford Arnold, who has been deceased but a few years, who both spoke of it as the old Stone Mill, built by their ancestor Benedict Arnold, as has been heretofore stated, but disregarded? Why then dispute its origin, and the use for which it was erected, except it be for interested and unholy purposes?

In 1784, the harbor with the rivers, were all closed with ice, from Castle Hill to Providence; so that people crossed there from the Island to the main.

* The author of this imposition, as well as the report attributed to Scrobien, is supposed to be a *foreigner*, a few years since a resident of this town.

THE DESCENDANTS OF ABRAHAM.

1763. This year the Jewish Synagogue, in Newport, which was erected the year before, was dedicated to the God of Abraham, with great pomp and magnificence, according to the custom of the Hebrews. At this time the town of Newport contained upwards of sixty families of Jews; among them were many merchants of wealth and enterprise. Mr. Aaron Lopez was a man of eminent probity and benevolence, his bounties were widely diffused, and not confined to creed and sect, and the people of Newport, notwithstanding the lapse of time, still consecrate his memory. Mr. Lopez was afterwards drowned in his carriage in Scott's Pond, a few miles north of Providence.

Rev. Mr. Touro, married, in Newport, a sister of the late Moses Hays, of Boston, and left two sons and one daughter. Mr. Hays removed from Newport soon after the peace, taking with him his family. One of the sons was the late Abraham Touro, who died in Boston in 1822, leaving a large estate; by his will a fund of $10,000 was left for the support of the synagogue and burial-place in Newport, and $5,000 for keeping Touro-street in repair, on which they front. This fund is under the direction of the Town Council of Newport, and the interest is judiciously applied for the purposes above-mentioned.

The other son is Judah Touro, Esq., of New-Orleans, a gentleman distinguished for his many acts of munificence. He went to New-Orleans previous to the cession of Louisiana, where in mercantile pursuits, he has acquired a princely estate, and is universally esteemed by the inhabitants of the city of New-Orleans. Such is the attachment of the Jews for Newport, and the sepulchre of their fathers, that their remains are brought here for interment.

A gentleman who settled in Newport, about twenty years since, and erected a tasteful mansion in Bellevue-street, near the Jewish burial-ground, in a conversation had with a personal friend of Mr. Judah Touro, suggested that it would be a commendable act on the part of Mr. Touro, were he to enclose the burial ground with a noble wall of granite, as the then present brick wall was in a decayed state, having been slightly built. He gave an assurance that he would address him on the subject, which he accordingly did; and Mr. Touro, with a liberality which has uniformly distinguished him, authorized his friend to apply to some eminent architect for a suitable plan. The work was commenced, and completed in 1842, and a more chaste and beautiful enclosure, with the ornamental gateway, is not to be found in the country. The whole cost was $11,000. The architect was Isaiah Rogers, Esq., of Boston.

A few years since, he gave $1000 to repair Redwood Library. His adopted city has experienced his noble benefactions, irrespective of denominational distinctions, in which he has set an example worthy to be imitated by Gentiles. Such an individual is a blessing to society, and throws into the shade many, whose niggardly spirit renders them a burden to themselves and to the world at large.

Abraham Rod. Riviera, a highly respected Jew, was an importer of dry goods, in connection with other business. In early life Abraham was called "the honest man," which title he merited as long as he lived. He was extensively engaged in commerce, and met with many losses; and at that date there were no Insurance Companies, consequently, the risks in navigation were very great. Although a man of wealth, frequent losses at sea, forced him to assign his property, which, when divided, cancelled but a part of his liabilities. As soon as the failure was known in England, the merchants with whom he had traded, offered him any amount of dry goods; and, that he might avail himself of their generous offer, took the benefit of the Insolvent Act, clearing himself from old claims, and opening a way to the renewal of business. He was prosperous, and at the end of a few years, gave his old creditors a dinner party, placing under the plate of each guest a check, for the amount due him, with interest. He died worth $120,000. Such was the honesty of the past.

There is now in the Town-Clerk's office, the copy of a deed, (certified by William Coddington, Town-Clerk, Oct. 19th, 1677,) in book No. 3, page 11, of Land Evidences, of a certain lot of land, thirty feet square, sold by Nathaniel Dickens, to Mordecai Campannall and Moses Packeckoe, for a burial-place for the Jews. This deed is dated February 28th, 1677, which shows that some of the descendants of Abraham found an asylum of rest, from oppression and persecution, on this island of the sea, at an early period of the settlement. It has been said that it was as early as 1657.

How long prior to the purchase of the burial-ground, we have no accurate means of ascertaining. The first Jews who settled in Newport were of Dutch extraction, from Curraso, and were not possessed of the wealth, intelligence, or enterprise, which so eminently distinguished those who subsequently settled in this town, which, with the smallness of their number, accounts for the lapse of time from the first Jewish settlement in Newport, to the erection of the synagogue.

It is not probable, however, that during all this time they maintained no regular form of public worship, and there is a tradition amongst the most ancient people of Newport, now living, that from the earliest settlement here, public religious worship was regularly maintained in private houses.

Between the years 1750–60, many families of wealth and distinction came to this country from Spain and Portugal, and settled in Newport, which contributed largely to the intelligence and commercial prosperity of the town.

The synagogue was thronged with worshippers, from its erection until the war commenced, and the scriptures were publicly read, and the God of Abraham worshipped in the Hebrew language, in Newport, by more than three hundred of the dispersed house of Israel, up to that time.

About 1763, and long after, flourished the distinguished families of Lopez, Riviera, Pollock, Levi, Hart, Seixas, and their late respected priest, Isaac Touro. The north side of what is now the Mall, was once covered with Jewish residences, which were destroyed by fire. The Revolutionary war, so disastrous to the commercial interest and prosperity of Newport, induced the greater part of them to leave the town ; and after the conclusion of the war, the remnant that was left gradually declined, until not an individual now remains. Moses Lopez, nephew of the celebrated Aaron Lopez, was the last resident Jew in Newport. A few years previous to his death, he removed to New-York ; his remains were brought to Newport, and interred by the side of his brother Jacob, in the burial-place of their fathers. Moses Lopez was a man of no common abilities ; he was an honorable merchant, deeply versed in mathematics, and of uncommon mechanical skill. He was pleasant and interesting in conversation, and an ingenious defender of his religious belief. The Society of Jews, generally, who settled in this town, have left a reputation for integrity and uprightness, which should perpetuate their memory from generation to generation.

After the long interval of sixty years, in which the synagogue had been closed, in the year 1850 it was thrown open again, and services were performed on Saturday (the Jewish sabbath,) by an eminent Rabbi from New-York. It was an important era, and calculated to revive in the mind the great and important events, which had taken place in the history of this distinguished people.

Emery's Corner, at the south side of Bridge-street, was a general resort in olden time for young men, residing in that section of the town. Hence we meet with it very frequently in the old records of the town, as we do that of the Granary, or Brick-market, where the inhabitants assembled, and still continue to assemble. We like to retain antique names, as they remind us of the past, and the inhabitants of Newport have been more tenacious than most places, of innovation. But the recent resort of strangers to Newport, has led to an attempt to remove the ancient land-marks, which should not be countenanced for a moment by the original inhabitants. It is the remains of antiquity in Newport, which invests it with so much interest, and makes the spot more deeply interesting to the Antiquarian.

Hog Hole, before the hand of modern vandalism despoiled it of its pristine beauty, was the scene of many a joyous festival. Purgatory, at Sachuest Beach, is invested with a high degree of romance, from the traditionary account of two lovers, who met at the brink of this dangerous chasm. The lady, to test the strength of his affections towards her, as the condition of the nuptial celebration, required that he should leap across it. Dangerous as was the experiment, he quickly sprung; she caught the skirt of his coat, which instantly rent, while he landed safe on the opposite side to the terror and dismay of the fair one. The Devil's foot-print is strongly impressed on the rocks, near to this chasm, with other singular marks, which has made it a place of interest to those visiting the island.

It affords pleasure and delight to ramble amid those joyous scenes, and listen to the ærial choristers warbling their orisons. The inhabitants of this charming retreat, seem the only undelighted enjoyers of the scene, because to them it exhibits no novelty, consequently but little allurement; the eye of the stranger alone beholds it with admiration and wonder, and the heart of sensibility could alone feel the exquisite sensation of delight its contemplation inspires. In the words of the poet, we would say:

"There's not a brook I have not leapt,
Anear my native town—
Nor field nor hill where man has stept,
I have not wandered down:
And these as freshly haunt me still,
And still their forms I know—
The brook, the field, the high peaked hill,
That charmed me long ago!"

In 1772, the first equestrian performances on Rhode Island, and probably in America, took place in Newport. The name of the manager was Bates.

Two of the guns of the sloop Tartar, were placed at the foot of the Parade, where they remained until within a few years, when they were removed, and placed in front of the fountain, at the end of the Mall.

THE REV. MARMADUKE BROWN.

As Newport has been the birthplace of many distinguished personages, as well as the residence of others who have occupied important positions in society, we have been induced to notice such parties, believing that it would prove highly interesting to the reader.

In 1760, on the resignation of the Rev. Mr. Pollen, the Rev. Marmaduke Brown, a native of Ireland, was unanimously chosen to officiate as Minister of Trinity Church, Newport, and was appointed a Missionary by the Home Society.

Mr. Brown continued his connection with Trinity Church until his death, which took place on the 19th of March, 1771.

He left an only son, who, in 1795, caused a marble tablet, with a raised profile likeness of his father, to be erected on the walls of Trinity Church, in memory of his parents. It bears the following inscription :

To the Memory of

THE REV. MARMADUKE BROWN,

Formerly Rector of this Parish,

A Man eminent for Talents, Learning, and Religion,

Who departed this Life on the 19th of March, 1771,

AND OF ANN, HIS WIFE,

A Lady of Uncommon Piety, and Suavity of Manners,

Who died the 6th of January, 1767.

This Monument was Erected by their Son,

ARTHUR BROWN, ESQ.,

Now Senior Fellow of Trinity College,

Dublin, Ireland,

And Representative in Parliament for the same ;

In Token of his Gratitude and Affection

To the best and tenderest of Parents,

And his Respect and Love for a Congregation,

Among whom, and for a Place where,

He spent the Earliest and Happiest of His Days.

Heu! Quanto minus est,

Cum allis Versari,

Quam tui Memisse.

M.D.CCXCV.

His above-mentioned son is the subject of the following notice :

Hon. Arthur Brown, LL. D.,was at an early age sent from Newport to the care of a relative in Ireland, for education. He was a man gifted with extraordinary mental powers, which he improved by almost incessant study, and by an intercourse with the most able scholars and politicians of the day. He soon rose to eminence—was Senior Fellow, and Senior Proctor of Trinity College, a Doctor of Civil Laws, King's Professor of Greek, &c., &c. For a length of time he held the Vicar-Generalship of the

Diocese of Kildare, and also practised in the courts, as an eminent, though not a leading barrister,

For many years no person in the University enjoyed greater popularity. They gave him their best and most honorable gifts —they appointed him their representative in the National Legislature, and the Irish House of Commons for many years listened with surprise and admiration, to his bold and powerful eloquence.

On questions of great national importance, Dr. Brown could speak with surprising effect. With little subjects he seldom interfered. If with the opposition it was his desire or chance to associate—he supported all their leading measures—on the Place and Pension bills, Catholic Emancipation, the Suspension of the Habeas Corpus, &c., he brought all his talents into action. He was a strong advocate of Parliamentary reform, an enemy to the abuse of power, and always stood forward as the champion of the people.

On the great question of the Union of Great Britain and Ireland, he took part with the ministry, and his support and example greatly contributed to that event.

Shortly after the Union, Dr. Brown was appointed Prime Sergeant, and it is supposed, had he survived, he would have obtained a situation on the bench.

Beside various political pamphlets, Dr. Brown was the author of two volumes of miscellaneous essays and dissertations, in which many questions of literature and criticism were ably discussed. These volumes are now out of print, which is the more to be regretted, as one of the essays was devoted to a picture of Colonial manners and habits, especially as exhibited by the society of Newpnrt, Rhode Island.

In a note he referred to many of the families with whom he was intimate—the Brentons, Malborns, Redwoods, &c. His great work, however, is that on the Civil Law, which has passed through various editions, and is considered by the profession as a standard.

This celebrated man died in Dublin, in the summer of 1805, of a dropsical complaint, leaving a large property, which he acquired from his situations in the College, and his exertions as a lawyer.

The late Baron Kinsale, of Ireland, was also a native of

Newport. The following notice of the Baron De Courcy, is taken from the *Newport Mercury*, 1832:

"On the 1st of February last, died at Kinsale, the Right Honorable Thomas De Courcy, Lord Kinsale, Baron De Courcy, and Ringrone. His lordship was Premier Baron of Ireland, and enjoyed the hereditary privilege of wearing his hat in the royal presence, granted to John De Courcy, Earl of Ulster, by King John, and lately exercised by Lord John De Courcy, at a court held in Dublin Castle, by George IV., in 1821."

We transcribe this obituary notice from a London paper of February 20th, 1832, because we of Rhode Island, feel a peculiar interest with regard to this family, of which the present branch sprung from the town of Newport, Rhode Island.

It was probably about the years 1720 and 1725, that the younger, and we presume the only brother of the Baron of Kinsale, for some reasons of discontent, emigrated to North America, and selected Newport, Rhode Island, as the place of his residence.

William Rogers, D. D., Professor of English Oratory in the University of Pennsylvania, was born in Newport, Rhode Island, July 22d, 1751. A graduate of Brown University in 1769. He received his license to preach in 1771, and in May of the following year was ordained pastor of the Baptist church, Philadelphia, where he continued till the commencement of the Revolution, in 1775, when he was appointed Chaplain of the Pennsylvanian forces, and not long after, of the Continental Army, and remained in the service till 1781.

In 1789, he was elected Professor of English Oratory in the College of Philadelphia, and afterwards was appointed to the same office in the University of Pennsylvania, and held it till 1812, when he resigned. His death took place April 7th, 1824, in the 74th year of his age.

He held a highly respectable rank in talents and learning, and was greatly esteemed for his ability and faithfulness as a preacher.

His daughter, a very estimable lady, is the wife of William Henry De Wolf, Esq., of Bristol, Rhode Island.

THE AUCHMUTY FAMILY.

Robert Auchmuty was the first of the American family of that name. He was the descendant of an ancient Scotch family, holding a barony in the north of that country. His father settled in England, early in the eighteenth century. Robert came to this country and settled in Boston; he was considered a profound lawyer, and possessed remarkable talents, shrewdness, and wit. Anecdotes of him have been handed down from generation to generation, to this day. He was greatly respected and beloved, both in public and private life. His memory is held in high veneration by the bar in Massachusetts, and his opinions are still respected by the profession. He has many descendants still left there. He was Judge of Admiralty many years before his death.

Rev. Samuel Auchmuty, son of the elder Robert, was born in Boston, in 1725, graduated at Harvard University in 1742, and was taken by his father to England, where he was ordained a minister of the Episcopal Church, and was appointed by the Society for the Propagation of the Gospel, an assistant minister of Trinity Church, New-York. He married in 1749, a daughter of Robert Nichols, Governor of that Province in 1764. At the death of the Rector, he was appointed to succeed him, and took charge of all the churches in the city, performing his arduous duties with faithfulness until the Revolution.

The children of Rev. Dr. Auchmuty were, 1st, Mary Juliana, born 1750, married General Mulcaster, of the Royal Engineers, and left two sons and two daughters; 2d, married, died young; 3d, Isabella, born 1753, married a Mr. Burton, of Kent, in England, and left no children; 4th, Robert Nichols, born in 1758, married Henrietta, daughter of Henry John Overing, of Newport, his second cousin. He died at Newport, Rhode Island, and was interred in Trinity churchyard, leaving eight children, Samuel O. Auchmuty, Harriet, who married Major Heileman of the U. S. Army, a most accomplished gentleman and superior officer, Maria, widow of Capt. Wainwright of the Marine Corps, Robert, Richard of the U. S. Navy, Joanna, Isabella, and John of the U. S. Navy.

Samuel, afterwards Sir Samuel, born 1758, graduated at Columbia College, served in England, under Sir Ralph Abercrombie, was a Brigadier-General, and K. C. B., in 1807, and commanded the expedition against Montevideo, which he took. He was promoted to be Lieutenant-General, received the thanks of Parliament and a service of plate. He was afterwards entrusted with a very important command in the Channel, at the time of Napoleon's threatened invasion; was the Governor of Madras, and commander of an expedition against the Island of Java, which he took, in 1800. On returning to England, he again received the thanks of Parliament, and a service of plate from the East India Company. He retired for a while to his estate in Kent, which he left on being appointed commander of the forces in Ireland, where he died, August 11th, 1822.

The inscription on his tomb-stone is:

Sacred to the Memory of

THE RIGHT HON. SIR SAMUEL AUCHMUTY, G. C. B.

Of His Majesty's Seventy-eight of Foot, who died on the 11th of August, aged sixty-four, while commanding his Majesty's forces in Ireland. He was a brave, experienced, and successful officer, and victorious whenever he had the command. He twice received the thanks of Parliament for his services. The capture of Montevideo, in South America, and the Island of Java, in the East Indies, added both to his fame and fortune.

THIS MONUMENT WAS ERECTED BY HIS RELATIVES, AS A TRIBUTE TO HIS PRIVATE AS WELL AS HIS PUBLIC WORTH.

He left in his will a princely fortune to the children of his brother, Robert Nichols Auchmuty, of Newport, Rhode Island.

We have dwelt thus long on the history of this family, from the fact of their intimate connection with Newport. Of the two surviving children of Robert N. Auchmuty, Esq., Maria and Joanna, it is no flattery to speak of them in the highest terms, as illustrating the female attractions of the past. Maria was tall, and of exquisite proportions, her complexion beautifully transparent, the roseate bloom of health diffused its beauties on her cheek, and the benignant softness that beamed from her blue eye, gave her the appearance of a celestial divinity. Col. George

Gibbs expressed his admiration of her charms, on witnessing her appearance at the ball-room in Newport, with the splendid head-dress on, the gift of Sir Samuel, K. C. B. Her sister Joanna, was equally as graceful and captivating in form and manners. Her complexion clear, her teeth beautifully white and regular, a sweet expression played around her coral lips, her eyes were expressive, her voice exquisitely melodious, and her genius lively and expanded. In the science of music she took delight, and touched the harpsicord to perfection. In the dance she was the sprightly ærial of the scene, when her inimitable attitude and grace captivated every beholder.

Those who recollect Monsieur Carpentier's dancing-room, which was graced with the elite and fashion of Newport, will be ready to respond to the description here given of this lovely person. And now that the season of youth and gayety has passed away, her mind has been profitably and usefully employed in the cultivation of the morals of the nieces and nephews of her widowed sister. From a gentleman of the first rank in the United States Army, we have received the most flattering account of her amiable qualities, which we could justly appreciate, from a long acquaintance with her and her family.

"When heaven's harbinger shall claim his prize,
And waft her purest soul to purer skies,
Then shall recording angels trace her fame,
And pity weep when memory breathes her name.'

THE MINTURN FAMILY.

The ancestor of the Minturn family in this country, was a native of England, and was one of the early settlers of Narragansett. Jonas Minturn married Penelope Brown, of South Kingston, and died on his own farm in Narragansett. He left three children, William, Hannah, and John, the latter of whom died at an early age. Hannah remained unmarried, and died at an advanced age, in Newport. William early exhibited that energy and decision of character, which was so conspicuous during his life. Being of an enterprising disposition, and wishing to see more of the world than his circumstances permitted, he made several voyages from Newport, in a ship of which he soon became mate; during one of these voyages to a port in England, the vessel in which he sailed had the misfortune to be captured and taken into France, England being at that time at war with that country.

The voyage was thus in danger of being broken up, threatening great loss to those who were concerned in its success. The French commander offered to accept a ransom for the vessel, which though ardently desired by the American captain, was deemed by him to be entirely out of his power to accomplish at this juncture. Mr. Minturn, seeing how vitally important was the measure, presented himself before the master of the ship: "Captain," said he, "land me on the coast of England—I will go to London; I am certain that I can effect this desirable result to a commercial house in that city." It was done; dressed as he was, in his sailor's clothes, he proceeded on foot to London, found out the firm he was in search of, and by his intelligence and perseverance, was able to convince them of the importance and feasibility of the object. He then re-crossed the channel, paid the ransom money, and arrived safely with the vessel at Newport.

In testimony of the high opinion which the owners of the ship entertained towards him, by this signal service, he was immediately made captain of the same vessel; and so fortunate was he, that he was soon able to become himself a shipowner, and to establish himself at Newport, where, becoming a successful merchant, he was greatly distinguished for benevolence and public spirit. Mr. Minturn removed from Newport to Hudson, in 1788, but finding, however, the branch of mercantile business in which he was more especially engaged, that of commerce and navigation, could be prosecuted with more success at a point less remote from the sea, he concluded upon a change of location, and finally fixed upon the city of New-York, as possessing those superior commercial advantages which have since been accredited to it by the world. Hither he removed in 1791, continuing his successful career, and realizing all the advantages which he had anticipated from this new abode. Having amassed a large estate for the times in which he lived, he retired from the active duties of commercial life, enjoying the respect, the esteem, and affection of his fellow-citizens.

In 1799, Mr. Minturn's health so rapidly declined, that he ardently longed to breathe once more his native air; confidently believing that it would bring with it healing on its wings. He was also anxious to consult with Dr. Center, of Newport, the physician of his early life. In this desire he was warmly encouraged by his friend and former partner in business, George Gibbs, Esq., who kindly procured a commodious house for his reception; but his cherished hopes, and those of his attached family, were destined to be soon destroyed. His disease increased in severity, and he died in August of that year, universally lamented. Justice, firmness, and charity, were the distinguishing traits of his character.

William Minturn married Penelope, daughter of Benjamin Greene; she was a near relative of Major Nathaniel Greene, of the Revolution, with whom she spent a considerable part of her early life, at Patawamut. After her husband's decease, Mrs. Minturn returned to New-York, where she resided till her death, in 1821; dying in that humility and faith which her Christian life had so pre-eminently exemplified.

William Minturn left ten children; 1st, Penelope, married to John T. Champlain; 2d, Benjamin Greene, married to Mary, daughter of Robert Bowne; 3d, Hannah, who died in 1817; 4th, William, also married to a daughter of Robert Bowne; 5th, Jonas, married to Esther, daughter of William T. Robinson; 6th, Mary, married to Henry Post; 7th, Deborah, msrried to Robert Abbot, jun.; 8th, Nathaniel G., married to Lydia, daughter of Samuel Coates, of Philadelphia; 9th, Niobe, who resides in New-York; and 10th, John, who in 1817, removed to New-Orleans—he married Lydia, daughter of James Clements, of Philadelphia. The descendants of William Minturn have numbered one hundred and forty-six persons. Some of his descendants are now extensive merchants in New-York.

SIR CHARLES WAGER.

" NEWPORT, 2 Mo. 1, 1853.

" The following is an extract from a letter I received from Rowland T. Robinson, dated Ferrisburgh, Vermont, 1 Mo. 22d, 1848, and, I presume, will convey the information you request

" Your friend,

" T. R. HAZARD.

" To Edward Peterson.

" ' I have obtained the following genealogical information from my father, whose recollections are clear on the matter; and I also find they are confirmed by " W. Updike's History," page 249.

" ' William Hazard, the father of Lydia Hazard, who married John Field, was the son of Caleb Hazard. William had two brothers, Dr. Robert, and Caleb.

" ' Caleb Hazard, the father of William, married Abigail Gardiner, daughter of William Gardiner; she was the sister of Dr. Sylvester Gardiner, of Boston.

" ' After Caleb Hazard's death, his widow, Abigail, married Wm. Robinson, called Governor Robinson, who was my great-grandfather. They had six sons and two daughters, Christopher, William, Thomas (my grandfather), Sylvester, James, and John. The daughters were Mary, who married a Dockray, and Abigail.

" ' Phœbe Hull, who married William Hazard, was daughter of Captain Hull, who brought up Admiral Wager, of the British navy; Charles Wager was taken by Capt. John Hull, when a poor boy, from Newport, and trained to the sea. In consequence of an advertisement which appeared in the public papers, Capt. Hull took Wager to England, and assisted him in obtaining a large estate, and he became an Admiral.

" ' I have often heard my father relate the following anecdote, which may be somewhat amusing to thy New-York correspondent. Capt. Hull was a plain Friend, and in the pursuit of his calling, he was at one time in some part of the West Indies, and learning that his ward, now Admiral Wager, was lying in the same port, he took his long boat, and went on board the Admiral's ship. He enquired for the Admiral, stating he wished to see him. His appearance being rough, he was met by a sprig of the navy, and denied admittance; but watching his opportunity, he stepped into the cabin, knowing he would be safe when once recognized, which proved to be the case. He was received with great kindness by the Admiral, greatly to the confusion of the officer who had denied him an audience. An intimacy was long afterwards maintained, and the Admiral used to make an annual demonstration of his remembrance of his old master, by sending him a quarter-cask of wine.' "

" New-York, March 2, 1853.

" Dear Sir,

" Hearing you were about publishing a history of Newport, and the events of the past, so highly important and interesting, connected with its early settlement, I beg leave to hand you an anecdote or two of the celebrated Admiral, Sir Charles Wager, who was bound apprentice to a Quaker sea captain, of the name of John Hull, of Newport. It was of Capt. Hull that Sir Charles first learned his skill as a captain, and by whom he was brought up in the straight ways of industry, perseverance, and honesty, which appear to have distinguished him through life.

" ' Your sincere friend and servant,

" Oliver Hull.

" Mr. Peterson.

" It is perhaps not generally known, even by the reading public, that the celebrated Admiral Wager, of the British navy, when a boy, was bound apprentice to a Quaker, of the name of John Hull, who sailed a vessel between Newport, (Rhode Island,) and London; and in whose service he probably learned the rudiments of that nautical skill, as well as that upright honor and integrity, for which he is so much lauded by his biographer. The circumstance of running his master's vessel over a privateer, first recommended him to an advantageous place in the British navy. The facts of this encounter, as near as I can gather them, are these: the privateer was a small schooner, full of men, and was about boarding the ship of Capt. Hull, whose religious scruples prevented him from taking any measures of a hostile nature. After much persuasion from young Wager, the peaceable captain retired to his cabin, and gave the command of his ship to his apprentice. His anxiety, however, induced him to look out from the companion way, and occasionally give directions to the boy, who, he perceived, designed to run over the privateer, saying to him, 'Charles, if thee intends to run over that schooner, thou must put the helm a little more to the starboard.' The ship passed directly over the schooner, which instantly sunk, with every soul on board.

"On one occasion, when the Admiral was in Newport, Capt. Hull called at the coffee-house to see his former apprentice, and seeing a Lieutenant there, asked him, 'Where is Charles?' at which the Lieutenant took umbrage, and threatened to chastise the old Quaker for his insolence, in not speaking more respectfully of his Admiral. When Wager heard of it, he took occasion to reprove the Lieutenant before Capt. Hull, saying, 'Mr. Hull, sir, is my honored master.'

"The certificate of marriage of John Hull, which is of parchment, among the witnesses, bears the signature of the mother of Admiral Wager, thus, 'Prudence Wager.'

"John Hull died at Conanicut, on the 1st day of December, 1732, aged seventy-eight years.

"The following inscription is on the monument, erected to the memory of Admiral Wager, in Westminster Abbey, London, England:

"'To the Memory of
SIR CHARLES WAGER, KNT.,
Admiral of the White,
First Commissioner of the Admiralty, and
A Privy Councillor;
A man of great natural talents, improved by Industry,
and long Experience;
Who bore the highest commands, and passed through the greatest Employments,
With Credit to himself, and Honor to his Country.
He was in his Private Life, Humane, Temperate, Just, and Bountiful;
In Public Station, Prudent, Wise, and Honest;
Easy of access to all; steady and resolute in his conduct;
So remarkably happy in his presence of mind, that no danger
Ever discomposed him.
Esteemed and favored by his King, Beloved and honored by his Country.
He died the Twenty-fourth of May, 1743
Aged 79 years.

EVENTS OF THE REVOLUTION.

We have been pleasantly employed in presenting to the mind of the reader, the growth and prosperity of Newport, with the highly cultivated state of manners, which characterized her early history. And it would afford unspeakable gratification, could we continue the prosecution of a theme, so deeply interesting to the human mind; but every thing earthly is mutable, and subject to change. The prosperous to-day, may be in adversity to-morrow; so with States and Empires,—but the events so painful in themselves, are not without their uses, for out of the discordant materials good will ultimately arise.

No town in the British Colonies flourished to the degree of Newport, and while her canvass whitened every sea, and the products of every clime came freighted to her shores, it did not render her supremely selfish, as is too apt to be the case, but her influence was directed to the cultivation of the arts and sciences, which rendered her highly distinguished. The society of Newport was polished and refined; this was owing in a great degree to the intimate relationship which subsisted between them and the mother country. The officers under the Crown were educated gentlemen, and this exerted a powerful influence on the minds of the inhabitants, and but for the Revolution, no one could possibly have predicted the extent of prosperity to which Newport would have arrived. But the oppression of the British Parliament towards her Colonies became insupportable, until forbearance ceased to be a virtue. Every remonstrance on the part of the Colonists, only tended the more highly to exasperate Great Britain towards them. Now it was never the intention of the Colonies to sunder the ties which so closely linked them to the mother country, but simply to obtain a redress of grievances. They had stood by England in storm as well as sunshine. When she had been engaged in conflict with other nations, the Colonies had furnished their quota of men and money to overcome her enemies.

This loyalty on the part of the Colonies, could never have been alienated, but for the continual aggressions on the part of the Crown, disregarding the most solemn appeals, and setting at defiance every remonstrance made of the injustice of their policy towards the Colonies. They were aware of their great inferiority, to attempt to cope with so gigantic a power as that of Great Britain, celebrated for her military and naval prowess, with her immense resources; hence any measure which wisdom and prudence could dictate to effect a reconciliation was resorted to, but without effect. Great Britain was determined to overawe her Colonies, to submit to her arbitrary and despotic measures. But the principle of liberty was lodged deep in the hearts of the Colonists, and they could not tamely acquiesce in British misrule and oppression.

The first act of the British Parliament to tax the Colonies, passed that body in September, 1764; the avowed object of which was to raise a revenue for the better protection of his Majesty's Colonies in New England, by a duty paid the British Crown, on certain articles of commerce sold in the Colonies. This was to test the fidelity of their subjects, and to open the way for bolder developments. Accordingly, by the next spring, the famous, or rather IN-famous Stamp Act, passed both Houses of Parliament.

This Act required that all deeds, notes, bonds, &c., in the Colonies, should be null and void, unless executed on stamp paper, for which a duty must be paid the Crown. The former Act the Colonies could not approve, because it was arbitrary and unjust, levying a tax without their consent, not being represented in that body. But such was their attachment to the honor of their fathers, that they acquiesced in the measure, however oppressive and unjust.

On the subject of the right of the British Parliament to tax the Colonies, it was asserted, in the Mother Country, "to be essential to the unity, and of course prosperity, of the Empire, that the British Parliament should have right of taxation over every part of the Royal dominions." In the Colonies it was contended, "that taxation and representation were inseparable, and that they could not be safe, if their property might be taken from them without their consent." This claim of the right of taxation on the one side, and the denial of it on the other, was the very hinge on which the Revolution turned.

Mr. Pitt, the invariable friend of the Colonies, delivered his famous speech on American Liberty, in which he declared it to be his opinion, that the kingdom has no right to tax the

Colonies; that he rejoiced that they had resisted, and he hoped that they would resist to the last drop of their blood."

These sentiments proved Mr. Pitt to have been a man of principle, and the sworn enemy to oppression.

When this bill was brought in, the Ministers, and particularly Charles Townshild, exclaimed:

"These Americans, our own children, planted by our care, nourished by our indulgence, &c., will they now turn their backs upon us, and grudge to contribute their mite to relieve us from the heavy load which overwhelms us?"

Col. Barre caught the words, and with a vehemency becoming a soldier, rose and said:

"*Planted by your care!* No! Your oppression planted them in America! They fled from your tyranny into a then uncultivated land, where they were exposed to almost all the hardships to which human nature is liable; and among others, to the savage cruelty of the enemy of the country—a people the most subtle, and I take upon me to say, the most truly terrible of any people that ever inhabited any part of God's earth. And yet, actuated by principles of true English liberty, they met all these hardships with pleasure, compared with those they suffered in their own country, from the hands of those that should have been their friends."

The night after this Act passed, Dr. Franklin, who was then in London, wrote to Charles Thompson, afterwards Secretary of the Continental Congress: "The sun of liberty is set; the Americans must light the lamps of industry and economy." To which Mr. Thompson answered: "Be assured, *we shall light torches, quite of another sort.*" Thus predicting the convulsions which were about to follow.

On the arrival of the news of the Stamp Act, in America, a general indignation spread through the country, and resolutions were passed against the Act, by most of the Colonial Assemblies.

It will not be necessary, in a history like this, to go into a recapitulation of all the preliminary steps which occurred, before actual hostilities commenced; but merely to show that a cause existed, of vital importance to the interest of the Colonies, why they should oppose British aggressions. They could not conscientiously succumb to the unjust laws, attempted to be exercised over them by a foreign power, without fearlessly showing a spirit of resistance toward such high-handed measures. The spirit of liberty which burnt brightly on the altar of the heart, could not tamely brook such outrages, without showing that independence of character which had invariably characterized their history.

No people had greater cause to fear a rupture between the Colonies and Great Britain, than those of Newport. Her commercial prosperity was identified with her union with the mother country. Her exposed situation was fraught with imminent peril, and without the means of defence, she must be rendered desolate; but no selfish consideration could for a moment deter her from embarking in the glorious struggle for liberty and independence. They never flinched, as we shall have occasion to notice as we proceed to show the events of the American Revolution. Some have been heard to say, that the causes which brought about the struggle, were not of sufficient magnitude to have involved the nation in all the horrors of war. But such reasoning is highly preposterous and absurd. Had the Colonies tamely submitted to the first attempt of aggression, it would have been followed up, and like Rehoboam, they would have "put men to the yoke," and attempted to chastise us with "scorpions." Had no resistance been made to British misrule, the condition of this Western Continent would have been equally as distressing as that of England, where the many would have been the slaves of the few; and those who opposed the action of the Colonies, and cast in their influence on the side of tyranny, were unworthy of the name of freemen, and their names have been justly handed down as traitors to their country, and the stigma of reproach has rested upon them.

Associations were formed, and resolutions were passed, into the spirit of which, the *female sex* entered with patriotic ardor, not to import or use goods imported from Great Britain, until this obnoxious and oppressive Act be repealed. So universal and determined were the Colonies in their opposition to this Act, that Parliament had no alternative but to repeal it. This, however, was followed by another infamous Act, which struck at the last hope of freedom, and assumed the right and power, "in all cases whatsoever, to bind the Colonies." Accordingly, a new tax was laid on glass, paper, tea, &c., &c. This, in addition with other acts equally arbitrary and oppressive, kindled up anew the spirit of opposition to the British ministry, which had in some degree subsided on the repeal of the Stamp Act.

On the meeting of Parliament in February, 1769, both Houses of that body, in an address to the King, recommended that the Royal Governor of Massachusetts, be directed to notice all such as manifested a spirit of disloyalty to His Majesty's edicts, that they might be sent to England and tried as traitors.

Such intolerance and oppression could not any longer be endured, it would have evinced a weak and pusilanimous spirit, unbecoming freemen, and they came forward in their majesty, and on the altar of liberty pledged their lives, their fortunes, and sacred honor, in defence of the Colonies.

The first overt act in the great drama which separated the Colonies from Great Britain, and which finally resulted in the American Independence, although claimed by, and awarded to others, was made at Newport, in 1769, in the destruction of his Britannic Majesty's armed sloop, Liberty. And when it is considered that the principle of liberty had been more generally diffused among the inhabitants of the Island, it should be no surprise that they were the *first* to strike the blow in the cause of freedom. And however unwilling other sections of the country may be to award to them the praise, we shall claim it as an act of justice of which they are deserving.

The sloop was fitted out by the King's officers at Boston, to enforce the revenue laws on the inhabitants of this Colony; and were directed to examine and detain all vessels suspected of evading or violating these laws. Two vessels, a sloop and a brig, belonging to Connecticut, had been seized and brought into Newport. A few days subsequently, the captain of the brig went on board his vessel, when on inquiring for his wearing apparel, he was informed they had been removed on board of His Majesty's sloop Liberty. Missing also his sword, he made inquiry for that, when he was told that a man belonging to the Liberty was lying on it in the cabin. As he descended the cabin, he was met with a volley of savage and cowardly oaths. He seized his sword, which the men of the Liberty endeavored in vain to wrest from his hands, sprang into his boat with two of his men, and made for the shore; on which the officer of the Liberty ordered his men to fire on the captain of the brig, and a musket and brace of pistols were fired at the boat.

This unprovoked attack upon the life of Captain Packwood, so enraged the populace of Newport, that the following evening a large number of citizens met Captain Reid, of the sloop Liberty, on the Long Wharf, and demanded that the man should be sent on shore, who fired on Captain Packwood. Accordingly, a man was sent for, but they asserted he was not the man, and another, and another, until all the men on board, except the mate, were on shore. A number then went on board the Liberty and cut away her cables, when she drifted over to a wharf on the Point, where she grounded.

Here they cut away her mast, and threw overboard all her armament and stores of war, scuttled her, and left her to the mercy of the elements. Her boats were dragged by the insulted and enthusiastic multitude, up the Long Wharf, thence up the Parade, through Broad-street, at the head of which, on the Common, they were burned.

Tradition says, that owing to the keel of the boats being shod with iron, such was the velocity of their locomotion, as they passed up the Parade, that a stream of fire was left in the rear of several feet in length.

The fate of His Majesty's sloop Liberty, may be learned from the *Newport Mercury*, July 31st, of that year:

"Last Saturday the sloop Liberty was floated by a high tide, and drifted over to Goat Island, and is grounded at the north end, near the place where the pirates were buried. What this prognosticates we leave to the determination of astrologers."

August 7th, the same paper observes:

"Last Monday evening, just after the storm of rain, hail, and lightning, the sloop Liberty, which we mentioned in our last as having drifted to Goat Island, was discovered to be on fire, and continued burning several days, until almost entirely consumed."

This was the *first* motion given to the Revolutionary ball, which continued to roll until independence was acquired by the Colonies. The Gasper was destroyed three years after, and the people of Boston destroyed the cargo of tea, in 1773. These popular resistances to British oppression was taking the *bull* by the horns, and showed plainly what would be the final result in the great struggle.

In consequence of the associations and resolutions of the Colonies to suspend the importation and use of tea, a vast quantity of nearly twenty million pounds, accumulated on the hands of the East India Company, when Parliament granted them permission to export the same to any part of the world, free from duty. Confident that under these circumstances, they should find a ready market in America, they shipped large quantities to the Colonies. But it was *too late.* The resolutions of the Americans were fixed, and the market for tea was closed. That destined for Boston was consigned to the friends and relatives of the Royal Governor; but the populace was so enraged, that instead of its being landed on the wharf, it was thrown into the sea as an oblation to "the watery god."

On the first intelligence of this in England, the Boston Port Bill was passed by the British Parliament, by which its commerce was entirely destroyed, and many of its inhabitants reduced to the greatest distress. Expressions of sympathy, and resolutions of united resistance to these arbitrary and unjust measures of the British throne, were forwarded from every part of the country, to the suffering inhabitants of Boston.

The people of Newport, in Town Meeting, Jan. 12, 1774, passed the following resolutions:

"*Whereas,* The East India Company, notwithstanding the resolutions of the Colonies not to import tea while it remains subject to a duty in America, have attempted to force large quantities thereof, into some of our sister Colonies, without their consent, in order to be sold in this country; and Whereas, they may attempt to introduce it into this Colony, we, the inhabitants of Newport, legally convened in Town Meeting, do firmly resolve:

"1. That the disposal of their own property is the inherent right of freemen; that there can be no property in that which another can, of right, take from them without their consent; that the claim of Parliament to tax America, is a claim of right to levy contributions upon us at their pleasure.

"2. That the duty imposed by Parliament on tea, is taxing the Americans, or levying contributions on them, without their consent.

"3. That a virtuous and inflexible opposition to the ministerial plan of governing America, is absolutely necessary, to preserve even the shadow of liberty,—and is a duty which every freeman in America owes to his country, to himself, and to his posterity.

"4. That the resolution lately entered into by the East-India Company, to send out their tea to America, subject to the payment of a duty on being landed here, is an open attempt to force the ministerial plan, and a violent attack upon the liberties of the Americans.

"5. That it is the duty of every American to oppose this attempt. That whoever shall, directly or indirectly, countenance this attempt, or in any wise aid or abet in unloading, receiving, or vending the tea sent out by the East-India Company, or by any other person, while it remains subject to the payment of a duty in America, is an enemy to his country."

At a subsequent Town Meeting, they passed the following expression of sympathy, for the suffering inhabitants of Boston :

"Resolved,—That we have the deepest sense of the injuries done the town of Boston, by the Act of Parliament lately passed, for putting an end to their trade, and destroying their port : And that we consider this attack upon them, as utterly subversive of American liberty ; for the same power may, at pleasure, destroy the trade, and shut up the ports of every other Colony, so that there will be a total end of all prosperity.

"Resolved,—That we will heartily unite with the other Colonies, in all reasonable and proper measures to procure the establishment of the rights of the Colonies ; and particularly in case the other Colonies shall, upon this most alarming occasion, put a stop to their trade with Great Britain and the West Indies, we will heartily join with them in the measure."

An exciting and animated paper was circulated in Newport, with this motto, "JOIN OR DIE." The state of Boston was represented as a regular siege, and this was a direct and hostile invasion of all the Colonies. "The Generals of despotism," it says, "are now drawing the lines of circumvallation around our bulwarks of liberty, and nothing but unity, resolution, and perseverance, can save ourselves and posterity, from what is worse than death, slavery."

In 1769, the manifestation of liberty in Newport, exceeded that of many places, which laid claim to great patriotism.

The country were resolved, with the Virginia orator, on "liberty or death." The boldness of Patrick Henry, and the great influence which he exerted, caused him to be presented to the British Government in a bill of attainder. His name, with that of Thomas Jefferson, Peyton Randolph, John Adams, Samuel Adams, John Hancock, and several others, were on the black list, and had the Colonies not succeeded, they would undoubtedly have been hung on the gibbet, as the most prominent rebels.

At this day we find a class of apologists for Great Britain, who contend, that her feelings towards America is purely pacific, and disposed to rejoice at our prosperity. Such fallacious reasoning will never be countenanced by the patriot who has learnt experience by the past. The mind has evidently deteriorated under the light and culture of science ; it has lost its elasticity and force, by being cradled in the lap of ease, secure from the rude storms which spent its fury against the veterans of the Revolution, whose towering heads received the shock undismayed. They were men of iron frame, and giant intellect, and not to be diverted from their purpose by threats or flattery.

The harbor of Newport was occupied by his Majesty's ships, for several years previous to actual hostilities, for the purpose of enforcing the revenue laws, and sustaining the authority of the King over his rebellious subjects. But after the destruction of the sloop Liberty, in the harbor of Newport, and as the the hostility of the Colonies to the acts of the British ministry, began manfully to develope itself, their number was increased until a whole squadron of ships of war, under the command of Admiral Wallace, were stationed in the bay, to watch over his Majesty's subjects in Rhode Island. This Admiral, (Wallace,) was a most miserable poltroon, and incurred the hatred of the people of the island, for his mean and despicable acts.

On the 19th of April, 1775, the dark elements of strife, which had been so long gathering, portentous of the storm of blood and carnage, burst upon the Colonies in the battle of Lexington, where eight Americans were shot by the wanton cruelty of the British commander, Major Pitcairn, without the least provocation. This fired the Americans with indignation, and the battle of Bunker Hill, and the surrender of Ticonderoga to the American arms, under the command of Col. Ethan Allen, followed each other in quick succession.

Ticonderoga, on Lake Champlain, was the key to the northern entrance into Canada, and was under the command of La Place, an old friend of Allen's. Colonel Ethan Allen, with only eighty-three men, approached the fortress in the grey of the morning, being conducted by a boy whom he met in the neighborhood, to the door of La Place's bed-chamber, who, at the moment, appeared half-dressed, and demanded the cause of the tumult. The rough and well-known voice of Col. Allen bade him surrender the fort. " By what authority do you make the demand ?" asked La Place. " By the Great Jehovah, and the Continental Congress," thundered Allen. The commander found it useless to parley, and at once surrendered.

They secured one hundred and twenty brass cannon, twenty-four pounders, several howitzers, balls, bombs, and ammunition. A party was immediately sent to sieze Crown-Point, which was easily effected, and more than a hundred pieces of artillery were secured.

Such were the master spirits which achieved our glorious Independence.

" Long years have pass'd away, and all dismantled and alone,
Thou standest there, thy blacken'd walls with weeds and grass o'ergrown;
Amid thy trenched bound, which once the clang of war could wake,
Is heard no sound, save insects' hum, or bugle's from the lake,"

A REGIMENT RAISED.

In May, of this year, a regiment was raised in the county of Newport, commanded by Col. Church, of Little Compton. Newport raised three companies of sixty men each, commanded by John Topham, William Tew, and Ebenezer Flagg. One company was raised in Portsmouth, commanded by Jonathan Browning. This regiment marched to Boston, and joined the American army at that place, during this and the following month, when this island was guarded by the militia and minute-men.

Sept.—Admiral Wallace, who commanded the British fleet in the harbor at this time, exciting the suspicions of the inhabitants, that he intended to remove from the south part of the Island (called the Neck) a quantity of stock, several persons during the night went down, and brought off about fifty head of cattle, and one thousand sheep. A few days after this, Wallace removed some stock from the two lower farms on the Island, where it was supposed they had been collected for supplying his Majesty's troops at Boston. But the arrival of three hundred minute-men, who marched to the place and drove off the remaining cattle, prevented any more from being removed by the enemy. But this so enraged the British lion, that he threatened destruction to everything around him, both by sea and land. He laid the town under contribution to supply the fleet with provisions, and urged his rigorous demands by cutting off all supplies of fuel and provisions from the main, and by continued threats of cannonading the town. The menacing attitude of Wallace against the place, threw the inhabitants into the greatest agitation and distress, and about one-half of the inhabitants left the town, and many the Island. It is stated that "Wallace would place lanterns in the shrouds of the shipping, as the signal for firing on the town," which so alarmed and terrified the female portion of the inhabitants, that many died through fright. It cannot well be conceived, at this late period, the sufferings which were endured by the inhabitants of Newport. And it has been said that many who sought shelter on the main did not improve their condition, owing to the want of the *friend in the pocket*. Nearly all the principal merchants left, with their families and effects.

A treaty was finally concluded between Wallace and the town of Newport, by consent of the State government, and concurrence of the Continental Congress, then in session; who unanimously recommended that, in the present exigency, Newport should supply the fleet with beer and fresh provisions, as usual, and also the removal of the troops from the town. Such being the condition of the treaty, Wallace agreed to remove his restrictions.

Many were of the opinion that Wallace *dared* not burn the town, and that his only object was to awe the inhabitants into a compliance with his demands. But there was no other alternative in the then present position of affairs, but to acquiesce in his requirements. On the 7th of October, he sailed up the river to Bristol, where he demanded three hundred sheep in sacrifice to his sacred Majesty, King George III. But the inhabitants of that town, not being satisfied of the divine right of his Majesty to make the demand, refused the sacrifice. That evening, about eight o'clock, Wallace commenced a heavy cannonading of the town, and Governor Bradford's house, with seventeen others, was burnt; also the Episcopal church, and Congregational meeting-house. The inhabitants were plundered of everything valuable they could lay their hands on. "The females, even, had their clothes taken, all that were deemed of sufficient value to carry away, and their rings forced from their fingers."

Nothing could surpass the consternation of Bristol, when surprised by the entrance of the British. Whether they did not expect their return at all, or whether they expected them to reëmbark at Papoose Squaw Neck, is not known; but they seemed to be taken by surprise, and women and children were flying in every direction. From Bristol, they proceeded to Warren, burning a windmill on their way, and plundering and destroying at every step.

Wallace captured all American vessels that came into port, and sent them to Boston with their crews, and many of them never returned. About the last of November he sailed out of the harbor, passed over to Connanicut, landing about two hundred marines, and burnt all the buildings at and in the neighborhood of the ferry. This wanton outrage in the destruction of property, was aggravated by the death of one of the inhabitants, a Mr. Martin, grandfather of T. Prescott Hall, Esq., the owner of the Malborn garden seat, who was shot while standing at his own door. He was a *loyalist*, and it was supposed to have been done through mistake.

It is a well known fact in the history of those times, that little was effected by the blockading squadron of Wallace, except keeping the inhabitants in constant alarm, by threats and petty depredations on the adjacent islands and neighborhoods. He effected the landing of three hundred troops on Prudence Island, and laid in ruins every building, with their contents. One of the inhabitants of the island was shot by a British soldier, in attempting to escape. Mr. Pierce, the father of the late Hon. Dexter T. Pierce, received a letter from Governor Wanton, of Newport, whose tenant he was, informing him the fleet would appear off Prudence next day, and that he would be able to dispose of his stock at good prices. But he, being a patriot of the first water, was determined not to gratify Wanton, or the British for whom he appeared so deeply interested. As the wind did not favor the ships, he was able to get off his stock and provisions before they took possession of the Island. A glance at the Wanton family may be interesting to the reader.

"Edward Wanton emigrated from London to Boston, before 1658. He assisted in the execution of the Quakers in 1659. Convinced of the injustice of their persecution, and won by the fortitude and resignation with which they suffered, he became a convert to them. He removed to Scituate, Mass., in 1661, where he had previously purchased an estate. He became a Quaker preacher, and was a popular propagator of their doctrines. He died at Scituate, aged 85.

His eldest son, Joseph, settled at Tiverton, R. I., in 1688, and both he and his wife were speakers in the Society of Friends. William Wanton (son of Edward) left Scituate and settled in Newport. Before his removal, he married Ruth, the daughter of Deacon Bryant; she was a Congregationalist, and he a Quaker. Religious objections were made against the match on both sides. He said: 'Friend Ruth, let us break from this unreasonable bondage—I will give up *my* religion, and *thou* shalt *thine*, and we will go over to the Church of England, *and go to the Devil together*.' They fulfilled this resolution so far as to go to the Church of England, and marrying, and adhering to the Church of England during life. He sustained many offices. In 1732, he was elected Governor of the State, and was reëlected in 1733. He died in December of that year. John Wanton, brother of William, from success in trade, had become one of the most wealthy citizens of Newport. He adhered to the faith of the Quakers. To heal party divisions, which ran high at this period, he was induced to permit himself to be voted for, and was elected Governor in 1734, and was successively reëlected for six years. He died in office, July 5th, 1740. Gideon Wanton, son of Philip, and nephew of William and John, was an enterprising merchant of Newport, and in addition to other offices, was elected Governor of Rhode Island in 1745, and 1747. He died in September, 1767, aged 74.

Joseph Wanton was the son of William, who died governor in 1733, and grand-son of the first Edward. He was an opulent merchant in Newport, and connected by blood and affinity with the wealthiest and most popular families in the Colony. In 1764 and 1767, he was elected Lieutenant-Governor through the Hopkins' influence. In 1769 he succeeded Governor Lyndon as Governor of the Colony, and was annually reëlected, until the political troubles of 1775, when the office was declared vacant."—*Updike.*

American blood had been shed at Lexington, and the Colony of Rhode Island was aroused. The Legislature then in session, April 1775, passed a resolution to raise and embody 1,500 men, to repel any insult or violence that may be offered to the inhabitants, &c. Governor Wanton sent in his protest against the measures of that body, which, in the present excited state of the public mind, rendered his conduct highly obnoxious to the people. The General Assembly declared the seat vacant, and Nicholas Cook, then Lieutenant-Governor, was elected to fill his place.

Extract of a letter addressed to the northern part of the Colony, by Stephen Hopkins, in 1764, in justification of the character of Mr. Wanton, who was Deputy-Governor under him:

"I hear it said he is but a boy, is a proud, foppish fellow, wears ruffles and laced clothes, and will not take any notice of or speak to a poor man. As to the first, he is about thirty-four years old. He has been genteelly bred, and received a liberal education, which was matured and polished, a sound understanding and enterprising genius. His haughty carriage and despising of the poor, is nothing more than an unworthy calumny of his enemies; and this I can safely affirm, that in General Assembly, where I have been chiefly acquainted with him, he remarkably and invariably appeared to be the poor man's friend, as all can testify who have served there with him. Perhaps many of you are desirous that the northern part of the

Colony should have its equal share in the administration of government. If this be the case, you may be fully assured that nothing can tend so directly to weaken and destroy that intention, as the placing both Governor and Deputy-Governor in one town in the northern part of the Colony.

STEPHEN HOPKINS.

Providence, April 16th, 1764."

The family of Wantons, from having occupied a high position in the Colony, by their subsequent conduct, in opposing all measures of resistance against the invaders of their country, and also in favoring the British interest at the expense of the rights and liberties of the Colonies, died a political death. Governor Wanton is said to have been a man "of amiable disposition, elegant manners, handsome person, and splendid appearance. He dressed in the finest style of the times, with a large white wig, with three curls, one falling down his back, and one forward of each shoulder." His likeness is placed in the Redwood Library. He died at Newport, July 19, 1780, aged 75 years, and was interred in the family vault in the Clifton burial place. The name has become extinct in Newport. His former residence in Thames-street, is now owned by the heirs of the late Captain Robert Lawton.

"We hear from Newport that Joseph Wanton, Esq., finding the British were about to evacuate that place, loaded a vessel with his effects, in order to take his departure with them, but the master being on shore, and the mate having a fair gale for putting off, slipped out of the harbor, and instead of taking the desired course, carried the vessel and effects to Providence, where they were cheerfully received."

It would have been far more gratifying could we have enrolled his name as a patriot in the war of the Revolution, instead of favoring the enemies of his country.

About this period a regiment was raised for this station, commanded by Col. Babcock. General Lee was also sent from Boston, to our assistance, by General Washington, with several companies of riflemen. He arrested all the Tories he could find, imposed upon them the most severe restrictions, and soon after returned to Boston.

In the autumn of this year, a large number of the Rhode

Island troops stationed at Boston, embarked in Montgomery's expedition against Quebec, under command of General Arnold. No expedition during the war, was attended with greater difficulties, or displayed a more unconquerable spirit of perseverance, than this. Their march through a trackless, unexplored wilderness, for more than three hundred miles, rendered their progress slow and difficult. To support life, they were compelled to eat their dogs, shoes, &c., and when at one hundred miles from a human habitation, they divided their last morsel of bread. And yet such was their unconquerable spirit of patriotism, that their fortitude remained unshaken. On the 1st of December, a siege was commenced upon Quebec, by the united forces of Arnold and Montgomery. The attempt proved unsuccessful, and fatal to the brave Montgomery, who fell at the onset, with two distinguished officers at his side.

General Arnold was wounded in the action, and carried from the field, when the command devolved on, and the fort was taken by Col. Morgan, a gallant and intrepid officer.

General Arnold remained encamped during the winter, a few miles from Quebec, but the following spring, not being reinforced, and his own forces being insufficient to attempt the reduction of the place, he retired, and by the middle of June, the Americans had wholly evacuated Canada. We could almost have wished the wound of Arnold had proved mortal, and he not have been left to disgrace his country, and involve a valuable officer in obloquy and ruin.

The fate of Major Andre, who was a most highly accomplished and meritorious officer, has continued to be a subject of universal regret; and could Washington, consistently with the usages of war, have pardoned the unfortunate man, it would most cheerfully have been done. But the decision of the Court Martial, of which Gen. Greene was President, adjudged him worthy of *death*, and it was not within the province of the Commander-in-Chief to reverse that decision, without subjecting himself to censure and reproach.

Major Andre, it is said, was strongly attached to a lady in England, and while *in prison*, penned the following striking and significant lines:

"Return, enraptured hours,
When Delia's heart was mine,
When she with wreaths of flowers
My temples did entwine.

No jealousy or care
Corroded o'er my breast;
No visions, light as air,
Presided o'er my rest.

Since I'm removed from state,
And bid adieu to time,
At my unhappy fate
Let Delia not repine.

Oh, may the mighty Jove
Crown her with happiness;
Grant! grant! ye powers above,
To take her home to rest."

Wallace maintained the possession of the harbor until the spring of 1776.

A newspaper called "*The Newport Gazette*," was established under the patronage of the British authorities at Newport. It was published by John Howe, in 1777.

On the 6th of April, troops having arrived from Providence to our assistance, with two row galleys of two eighteen pounders each, and while the fleet lay at anchor about a mile from Newport, Col. Babcock directed that two eighteen pounders be placed on an eminence near the shore, in open view of the enemy, and without any works to protect them. Here the intrepid Col. Elliot, together with the galleys, under command of Commodore Grimes, soon rendered the situation of the cowardly Wallace extremely uncomfortable, and he abandoned the harbor with the whole squadron. The Glasgow, of twenty guns, commanded by Captain Snow, returned to Newport, and came to anchor near Fort Island, having fallen in with, and received a severe chastisement from, Admiral Hopkins, off Block Island. The same evening, Col. Richmond ordered several pieces of heavy artillery to be brought and placed on Brenton's Point, where a slight breastwork was thrown up during the night. The following morning he opened so vigorous and well directed a fire upon her and the transport ship Snow, that they hastily cut their cables and went out to sea. A few days subsequently the British ship of war Scarborough, of twenty guns, and two hundred and twenty-five men, with the Cimetar, of eighteen guns and one hundred and forty men, having with them two prize ships, put into Newport harbor, and came to anchor a little to the south of Rose Island. A resolution was at once formed to attempt the rescue of the prizes. The plan adopted was for Captain Hyers, of the Washington galley, to attack and hold the Scarborough at bay, while Captain Grimes, of the Spitfire galley, was to board and bring off the prizes. Col. Babcock had also made preparations, in case either of the ships should approach sufficiently near the North Battery at Brenton's Point, to give them at these places a warm reception. About 11 o'clock at night, Capt. Grimes came along-side, and boarded and took the prize brig from under the stern of the man-of-war. The Scarborough immediately prepared to give chase, but was so annoyed and embarrassed in her course by Captain Hyers, that the brig was brought safely to harbor, and the Scarborough brought within reach of the North Battery, when Col. Babcock poured upon her such an incessant shower of balls, together with the well-directed and galling fire of the Washington galley, as entirely to arrest her progress and prevent further pursuit. At that moment the prize sloop was sailing with the intention of getting under the protecting wing of the Scarborough, but was disappointed by the intrepidity of Capt. Grimes, who cut her off, boarded, and sent her to Providence.

The British ships having both received a severe chastisement, the Scarborough from the North Battery, and the Washington galley, and the Cimetar from the battery at Brenton's Point and the Spitfire galley, Capt. Grimes, came to anchor between Connanicut and Rose Island. But this position was as unpropitious as the former, for a battery was opened and the storm of death soon came down upon them from the shores of Connanicut, so that finding no safety in the harbor, and danger threatening them whichever way they flew, they deemed it the better part of valor to abandon their position, by a hasty and inglorious retreat. But in leaving the harbor they had another fiery ordeal to pass, both at Brenton's Point and Castle Hill, where they received a severe and vigorous cannonade from the American batteries at these places. The ships returned the fire with great rage, and departed in mortification and disgrace. During these eight or ten days of almost incessant and successful struggles, the Americans had only one man slightly wounded.

During this season a number of privateers were fitted out at Newport and Providence, which captured from fifty to one hundred valuable prizes, which were sent to Providence, New-London, &c.

Early in the fall, intelligence was received that a large British fleet and army were soon expected to arrive, to take possession of the Island. All the cattle the American commander could collect, probably one-half on the Island, were driven to Howland's Ferry, and swam over the river, to prevent their falling into the hands of the enemy.

In December the British fleet and army arrived, under the command of Sir Peter Parker. The American force being altogether insufficient to make any effectual resistance, retreated from the Island, and many of the inhabitants left at the same time.

The consternation is said to have been dreadful. Many of the inhabitants could not procure vehicles, as everything of the kind was in requisition, and they were obliged to travel on foot to Howland's Ferry, and on arriving there, were compelled to wait before they could be ferried over, as the crowd assembled was so numerous. The fleet ran up the west side of Connanicut, crossed over from the north point of that Island, and landed their troops in Middletown, about four and a half miles from Newport.

The British army consisted of about eight or ten thousand men, English and Hessians, of each about an equal number, commanded by General Clinton and Lord Percy. They marched up and encamped on Gould's and Weaver's Hill, except a few who landed at Coddington's Cove, and marched into Newport. The Hessians who accompanied the British, were hired for a small sum, and were made to believe that the people they were about to subdue were weak and inefficient. And so sanguine were they of success, that it is said many had prepared themselves with milking pails and other apparatus to cultivate the land.

When the fleet arrived here, there were two new Rhode Island frigates, called the Warren, and the Providence, lying in the harbor of Newport, with eight or ten privateers, which all got under weigh, and ran up the river. Both frigates and privateers, however, during the winter, taking advantage of the north-east wind, made their escape and went to sea, notwithstanding the utmost vigilance and care with which each passage was guarded by the British fleet; demonstrating the importance of the bay, and proving the impossibility of its being blockaded.

In 1778, in the month of November, there was collected in the harbor of Newport, twelve British ships of the line, and two frigates.

As soon as the army landed, they commenced plundering the inhabitants; sheep, fowls, stacks of hay, and every thing else they could lay their hands on, went off as by magic, the first night. This was their intention at the outset, and as they could not unjustly tax the Colonies, and rob them of their earnings with impunity, they had recourse to powder and ball, in order more effectually to carry out their diabolical plans, and compel them to yield obedience to their arbitrary mandates.

After having remained in camp for one week, the barrack officer went through the neighborhood, surveying every house, and unceremoniously quartering in each, from ten to forty, and even forty-five men, according to the size and convenience of the house. They remained quartered on the inhabitants until the following May, when they again returned to camp. The female portion of the inhabitants of the town, who were accustomed to the needle, made clothing for the soldiers, and in this way obtained a living, while the place was a British garrison. It has been said, that the people who remained at Newport, fared much better than many who left, and went on the main. It was undoubtedly a time of trial, and no place suffered more severely than did Newport.

About this time, several thousands of the British troops left Rhode Island for New-York, under the command of General Clinton, and Lord Percy. The command then devolved upon General Prescott. This officer was a haughty, tyrannical, and despicable character; and actuated by principles and habits purely aristocratical, founded on his position as commander, he was poorly qualified to gain the friendship and esteem of his enemies, or strengthen the confidence of his friends.

His constant habit while walking the streets, if he saw any of the inhabitants conversing together, was to shake his cane at them, and say, "Disperse, ye rebels." During one of his perambulations about the streets, he chanced to meet with one Elisha Anthony, a member of the Society of Friends, and one asking Friend Anthony, in passing, "why he did not take his hat off?" Anthony said, "It was against his principles to shew those signs of respect to man." Prescott hearing the observation, ordered his servant to knock off his hat, which he did; and they passed on, leaving the Friend, who very coolly picked up his broad-brim, and passed on.

This Mr. Anthony's residence was on the corner of King and Thames-street, formerly the old Crown Coffee-house. He possessed a span of the finest horses on the island, and he attended and caressed them with almost as much tenderness as he would have bestowed upon human beings, and the very next day after the hat transaction, Prescott sent for these horses, saying he wanted them to carry an express to Boston.

What he did with one of them is not known; but Mr. Anthony, having occasion to go out on the island next day, found one of them rode to death, on the road side. The poor horse was dying, and as his master came up to him, he recognized him, and lifting his head from the ground, gave him such a pitiful and reproachful look as penetrated his heart. He said he could never get over the feeling it gave him. Warned by this instance of malice, Mr. Anthony secreted his cow, and other domestic animals, in his kitchen.

No wonder Prescott was sent back to Newport, after his exchange. He was a worthy minion of arbitrary power, though if he had had the feelings of a man, he would rather have been hanged than have appeared there again.

July 10, 1777, Colonel Barton, of Providence, conceived and executed one of the most bold and hazardous enterprises recorded in the history of the Revolution. General Prescott was quartered at this time about five miles from Newport, on the west road, leading to the ferry, at the seat of Mr. Overing. Barton's design was to pass over to Rhode Island from the main, seize Prescott at his quarters, and carry him to the American camp.

This enterprise, though hazardous in the extreme, was planned with cool deliberation and consummate prudence. Having chosen several officers in whom he could repose unlimited confidence, he selected about forty men, whom he knew well understood rowing, and on whose tried valor he could rely in the most perilous exigency.

David P. Hall, Esq., of New-York, stated, "that Quako Honyman, formerly a servant of the Rev. James Honyman, who was at this time a waiter of General Prescott, communicated to Col. Barton his exact position, and accompanied him on the enterprise."

At this time there were three British frigates, the Lark, the Diamond, and the Juno, lying with their guard-boats out, on the east side of Prudence. On the 10th of the month, at about nine o'clock in the evening, the Colonel, with his company, embarked on board their boats, from Warwick Neck, and with muffled oars passed over to Rhode Island, between Prudence and Patience. As they passed the south end of Prudence, they heard from the guard-boats of the enemy, the sentinel's cry, "All's well." As they landed, Barton divided his men into several divisions, assigning to each their station, when they advanced toward the house, preserving the strictest order, and the most profound silence. They passed the British guard-house from eighty to one hundred rods on the left, and a company of light horse at about an equal distance on the right, and a little left of that was the Redwood seat, where General Smith, second in command, was stationed. (The house is now the property of Elbert J. Anderson, Esq., of New-York, who married a descendant of Mr. Redwood.)

One of the divisions was directed by a circuitous course to advance upon the house in the rear, and secure the doors, while Barton, with the other division, was to advance up in front of the house, through the gate. As they approached the gate, the sentinel, who stood a few yards from them, cried out, "Who comes there?" Not readily receiving an answer, he hailed the second time, and demanded the countersign, when Barton sternly replied, "We have no countersign to give; have you seen any deserters to-night?" This had the intended effect. They continued to advance upon him, Barton still demanding with greater vehemence, "Have you seen any deserters?" so that he never suspected them as foes, until his musket was seized, and he was told that if he made the least noise, he was a dead man.

The other division had already taken possession of, and secured the doors, so that egress from it by its inmates was impossible. General Prescott was not alarmed, till his captors were at the door of his bed-chamber, which was fast closed. The negro before mentioned, Quako Honyman, instantly thrust his beetle-head through the panel-door and secured his victim.

In the mean time, Major Barrington, aid-de-camp to General Prescott, finding the house attacked, leaped out of a window, intending to seek security in flight; but when he reached the ground, was secured a prisoner.

Colonel Barton, placing his hand on Prescott's shoulder, told him he was his prisoner, and that silence was his only safety. General Prescott requested permission to dress, but was told by Barton that their business required haste, and that he could only have time to wrap his cloak around him.

For security, and in order that the General might keep time with the light hearts and quick step of the Colonel's party, he was compelled to walk between two officers, one arm resting on the shoulder of each, while Major Barrington and the sentinel, were stationed in the centre of the party.

They passed through a barley-field, a few rods north of where Mr. Peleg Coggeshall's barn now stands, and but a short distance from the guard-house. When they arrived at the boats, General Prescott was permitted to dress; when he was seated in the boat commanded by Col. Barton, Gen. Prescott implicitly obeyed the injunction of silence, until they had passed for some distance the British ships. As they landed at Warwick Neck, he turned to Colonel Barton, and said, "Sir, you have made a bold push to-night." Barton replied, "We have been fortunate." Colonel Elliot was found waiting there, with a coach, to receive and convey him to Providence, where himself, with Col. Barton and prisoner, arrived early in the morning.

Prescott was subsequently taken to Pomfret, in Connecticut, where he remained a short time. It is said that the landlord of the house where he stopped, brought him a dish of beans and corn, at which he was so highly exasperated, that he threw them into the face of the landlord, who very deliberately wiped his face with his shirt sleeve, and left the room. He, however, soon returned, with a cow-hide, and the manner in which he applied it to his back, was a striking caution.

Quako, the black, who piloted the enterprise, and who was rewarded for his services, lived for many years in Pomfret, Connecticut; he afterwards removed to Munson, Massachusetts, where he died. It is stated that the British were so incensed against him, that if they could have caught him, he would have been hung, drawn, and quartered.

General Prescott was afterwards exchanged for General Lee, who had fallen into the hands of the enemy, and, at the close of the same year, or the beginning of the next, he again took command of the British forces on Rhode Island, where he remained until its final evacuation.

The imprisonment of Colonel Barton, for the term of fourteen years, in Vermont, was a blot on the national escutcheon. A man who had rendered such essential service to his country, should have received the aid of the nation. But not until General La Fayette came to this country on a visit, was his liberation effected. He, like a noble patriot, enquired after his old friend and companion in arms, and on being informed of his imprisonment, went out of his way to meet him, (and it was a joyful meeting,) the prison doors were opened instanter, and the captive set at liberty.

On the 27th, Congress voted Colonel Barton an elegant sword, in acknowledgment of his capture of General Prescott, and sent him a vote of thanks, for that important service. Important it was on many accounts. It had a tendency to excite in a high degree the enthusiasm of the people, to convince them that their foes in this quarter were not invincible, and to humble the arrogance of the enemy.

Colonel Barton was quite an amusing man, and whether the countenance is the true index of the heart or not, he had the happy faculty of always appearing pleasant. It was a familiar saying of his—

> "To die and be forgot, is the lot of all mankind,
> But to be forgot before you are dead is hard."

He would then break forth from his reverie, and sing most amusingly these words,—

> "But while we're here, with friends so dear,
> Let's drive dull care away."

In September, 1777, a secret expedition against Rhode Island was concerted by General Spencer, the commander-in-chief of the American forces in Rhode Island. The Americans were stationed at Tiverton, near where the stone bridge now is. By some means, however, the British commander was apprised of Spencer's intention, and made preparations for his reception. He directed several dams to be thrown across the brook, running from the north, through the land of the late William Bailey, southward to Easton's Pond, which raised the water to the depth of three or four feet, all through that valley. It is said, the British intended to permit them to land, and march up without opposition, then destroy their boats, and cut off their retreat.

The expedition was, however, abandoned, even after the troops had embarked on board their boats. The certain cause of its failure is yet unknown. It has been suggested, that it was designed as a feint, to divert the attention of the enemy, and thereby succeed in dislodging them from other and more important points.

General Burgoyne's surrender immediately followed this event, and but little regard was paid to the course of policy adopted by General Spencer, while in command of the troops on the Island.

General Spencer, on leaving his quarters one morning, found the following doggerel verse, written in large letters, placed in full view of the public :

" Israel wanted bread,
The Lord sent them manna ;
Rhode Island wants a head,
And Congress sends—a granny !"

After this, the Major-General was called by the sobriquet of " Granny Spencer," as long as he remained in Rhode Island.

On October 17, 1777, a flag arrived at Newport from Providence, bearing intelligence of the surrender of General Burgoyne and army to the American forces. A knowledge of this event had reached the Island, and was known by certain individuals two days previous to its public announcement by the arrival of the flag. During the whole time the British had possession of the island, a correspondence was maintained between certain individuals of the island and the main, at Little Compton, so that the American officers were constantly apprized of the general movements of the enemy, while in possession of Rhode Island.

The correspondence was maintained by signals given on the Island, indicating a clear coast, and that a messenger could pass over in safety, after dark. The first signal was the leaving down of a certain pair of bars, which, with the spy-glass, could be distinctly seen from the main. Afterward, for fear of exciting the suspicion of the enemy, the signal was changed—when an open window of Mr. Peleg Peckham's barn answered the same purpose.

A small vault in the ground, near the shore, and at no great distance from Mr. Peckham's, covered with a flat stone, served as a depository of communication. There, letters and papers were regularly deposited and removed, by the respective individuals engaged in the correspondence. It was through this medium of communication that the intelligence of Burgoyne's surrender first reached the Island. It is said that the papers bringing this intelligence, and which were found safely deposited in the vault, are still preserved in the family of a Mr. Barker, on the Island. This noted spot is in Middletown, on the east side of the Island, in sight of Little Compton.

That part of the British army now in possession of the Island, consisted of the 22d regiment, commanded by Colonel Campbell; the 43d, by Colonel Marsh; the 54th, by Col. Bruce; and the 63d, by Major Sill. The artillery was commanded by Colonel Ennis. The Hessian regiments were, the Heno, the Beno, the Dedford, and Lanscraft, deriving their names from their respective commanders. There was also a company of light horse attached to the army, with a regiment of refugees, commanded by Colonel Fanning. There were also a few companies attached to the army, called Soushears and Anspaks; these were Germans.

In the spring of 1778, General Sullivan having been appointed to the command of the American troops in Rhode Island, the British commander at Newport, anticipating an attempt upon the Island by the Americans, sent a detachment of five hundred men up the river to destroy their boats, and by this means frustrate the anticipated expedition. They landed on the morning of May 25, at daylight, between Warren and Bristol, and proceeded in two divisions, one for Warren, and the other for the head of Kickemuet river, "when they destroyed about seventy flat-bottom boats, and set fire to one of the State galleys." They also burnt a large quantity of pitch, tar, plank, and other property belonging to the Americans at that place. The party which proceeded to Warren, after having burnt the meeting-house and a number of dwelling houses, plundered and robbed the inhabitants, not even the females excepted, who were robbed of their shoe buckles, gold rings, handkerchiefs, &c. A few days subsequently, a body of one hundred and fifty men were sent to burn the mill, and other buildings around it, at Tiverton. They burnt the old mill, and another building at the landing; but in proceeding to the town, the place of their intended plunder, their progress was arrested at the bridge by a Spartan band of twenty-five men, who had planted themselves there, and disputed their passage. Nor were they able to carry the bridge, although frequently attempted, and were compelled to return without effecting the object of their expedition.

In July, 1778, the French fleet of eleven sail of line ships, besides frigates and transports, under the command of Count D'Estaing, appeared off the harbor, to the great joy of the inhabitants, and anchored near to Brenton's Reef. One of the ships of the fleet ran up the west side of Connanicut, and anchored at the north point of the Island. The three British frigates above mentioned, lay at anchor on the east side of Prudence. A few mornings after, they weighed anchor and sailed, with the design of getting under protection of the battery at Tammany Hill. The French ship, aware of their intention, got under way at the same time, and cut them off.

The frigates then stood in for the shore, and were run aground about five or six miles from Newport, on the west side of Rhode Island. Before they grounded, they cut away the masts, for the purpose of driving them nearer the shore; and as soon as they struck, they set them on fire, and made for the shore in their boats. During this time, the French ship was sufficiently near to have thrown grape shot over them, yet when she saw them fire and abandon their vessels, she retired and took her former position, without firing a gun. A number of British vessels, lying at Coddington Cove, were also set on fire as soon as the burning of the frigates was discovered. The Grand Duke, lying a little to the north of Long Wharf, with several other vessels, was burnt. The Falcon and the Flora, frigates, were sunk; the latter at Fort Walcott Wharf, and they were never afterward able to float her. About a year after the British evacuated the Island, and the Americans took possession, the Flora was floated, fitted for sea, and sent to France. About the same time the frigates were burnt in the harbor and along the shore, the King Fisher, a man-of-war, was burnt in the East Passage.

The French fleet, after lying at anchor for several days, ran up the middle passage, and anchored under Gould Island. They ran up under three topsails, and received the fire of the British batteries as they passed, but returned it with such warmth that they soon silenced the forts. Several shots from the French fleet were unintentionally thrown into the town. As soon as the fleet approached the harbor, the British troops commenced burning the houses about two miles from Newport, commencing at the house formerly owned by the late Geo. Irish, Esq.; they burnt every house on the West road, for the distance of a mile; on the East road about half that distance; and from the West road to the shore. At the same time a party, principally refugees, was employed and sent out through the Island, headed by one William Crosson, who cut and destroyed cart-wheels, wagons, and carriages of all descriptions, grindstones, scythes, axes, hatchets, and every other edged tool they could find, and filled up many of the wells. Crosson's deeds of darkness were perpetrated during the night, and were not confined to the limits of the Island, but often extended as far as Swanzey Neck, Little Compton, and Fall River, plundering the inhabitants of everything he could bring off in his boats, and frequently not even sparing the citizens themselves. In one of his midnight excursions, he seized and brought off a worthy and respectable citizen of Swanzey Neck, by the name of Slade, who died of the small pox on board of the British prison ship in the harbor of Newport. Many others, who had the misfortune to fall into his hands, were never after permitted to return.

Crosson's character had become so notorious, and public indignation so excited, that measures were taken for his apprehension. But securely sheltered under the protecting wing of British power by day, no prospect of his capture appeared, unless it could be effected when engaged in his depredations at night. Accordingly a boat was fitted out at Little Compton called a shaving mill, commanded by Lemuel Bayley of that town, for his capture. Nor was it long before he found himself a prisoner. He was conveyed to Providence under a strong guard, but when he arrived there, such was the public feeling of indignation against him, that with great difficulty the guard could protect him from popular violence. After having been in prison for several months in that town, by some means, supposed to be by the influence of a *bribe*, he escaped from jail and appeared again in Newport. When the British evacuated the Island, Crossons went off with them, and probably considered it safe to remain with them, as he never afterward returned to Newport. Dollars and cents, it seems, have always had an unbounded influence with some in the Plantations.—Among the reckless associates of Crosson, was a man by the name of Gouldsborough. He landed his party at Little Compton one evening, near the place where a lad by the name of Taggart, son of Judge William Taggart, senior, and brother of the late Judge Taggart, of Middletown, was stationed as a sentinel. The inhuman Gouldsborough seized and murdered young Taggart on the spot.

A few days previous to this, the British commander had seized and drove within the lines all the stock, cows, oxen, &c., he could find on the Island. Sheep there were none, having all been previously stolen.

The same day (at night) on which the French fleet came in, the British withdrew their troops from the north end of the island, and took up their position on the heights, about two miles from Newport. Their line extended from Coddington's Cove to Easton's Beach; the whole distance being defended by breastworks and redoubts; besides which, they had a line still nearer the town, running from the West of the north mill down to the Gills' farm, formerly the property of Nicholas Easton. On the following morning, the American army landed on the north end of the Island, without opposition, and took possession of the neighboring heights. The army was composed of militia, continental troops, and volunteers, commanded by Generals Sullivan, Green, Glover, and the Marquis de Lafayette, supposed to number from ten to fifteen thousand men.

On the afternoon of the same day that the Americans landed on the Island, the British fleet of twenty-five sail was discovered standing in for Newport. They came too off Point Judith for the night, but a sudden change of wind favoring the Count the following morning, he stood out to sea with his whole squadron. Lord Howe, after some unsuccessful manœuvering to get the weather guage of the French fleet, put to sea, followed by Count D'Estaing, and both fleets were soon lost sight of in the distance. The storm which had already commenced, continued to rage with increasing violence for several days, so that no general action was obtained between the fleets. Both, however, were greatly damaged by the storm.

The Languedoc, of ninety guns, commanded by Count D'Estaing, had neither mast nor bowsprit standing, and several others were in a similar situation. The American troops encamped on the north part of the Island, sufferred not less than the ships. Such was the violence of the tempest, attended with a powerful rain, that by the night of the 12th, not a tent or marquee remained standing. Many horses and several of the soldiers perished by the severity of the storm, and the whole army was in the most wretched and deplorable condition. And in addition to their own personal sufferings, the greater part of their ammunition was either destroyed or greatly damaged by the storm. The 14th, the storm having subsided, and the day being serene and warm, the American army spent in drying their clothes, &c., and in making ready for their future operations. On the following morning, they took up their line of march in three several divisions; one on the East road, one on the West, and the third through the centre of the Island, and possessed themselves of the heights, about one and a half miles from the British lines. General Sullivan quartered about five miles from Newport, at what is now called the Gibbs Farm. General Lafayette quartered on the East side of the Island, at what was then called the Bowler Garden Farm, about the same distance from Newport. General Green quartered on the farm now owned by the heirs of the late Colonel Richard K. Randolph, of Newport.

The British had thrown up a large fort, the remains of which are still visible, a little to the north and east of the residence of the late George Irish, Esq., and directly opposite on Honyman's Hill. At a distance of little more than a mile, the Americans had thrown up a fort and other works, and by the 20th, they had opened two four-gun batteries, and by the 23d had mounted seventeen pieces of heavy artillery, two ten-inch mortars, and three five and a half inch howitzers.

From these works, on either side, was kept up a continual cannonading by day, and throwing of bombs by night, by which many were killed on both sides. An amusing circumstance is related of the discharge of a cannon from the battery at Honyman's Hill. A large dinner party had assembled at the Dudley Farm, now occupied by Edward Van Zandt, Esq., when just as the guests were about to seat themselves at the table, a ball passed through the hall, and the company fled precipitately out of the house, with the loss of their dinner.

GREAT SNOW STORM.

On the night of the 22d of December, 1778, a snow storm commenced with a severity never before experienced by the oldest inhabitants, for the quantity of snow which fell, as also for the severity of the cold.

In Newport, all the sentinels of the British army who were stationed in the exterior lines, that were not called in before night, were found after the storm, frozen to death at their posts; many soldiers perished in buildings where they had no fire, and many perished in endeavoring to find their quarters during the snow storm. The storm was afterwards known as the "Hessian storm," from the great number of soldiers of that nation who perished.

No tidings were received, and nothing was known of the disabled and wrecked condition of the fleets, until about a week after the storm, when the French fleet were seen at a distance, standing for Newport.

At 7 o'clock, P. M., the Marquis de Lafayette, and other

officers, went on board to consult with the French officers, on measures for the vigorous and successful prosecution of the expedition, and prevail with them immediately to enter the harbor. But their efforts were without success, and about 12 at night they left the ships and returned on shore. The conduct of the Count, in refusing a compliance with the request of the American officers, when conquest appeared so easy, and victory so sure, was most severely censured. But when it is considered that his instructions were positive from the Court of France, in case of disaster, and that his officers unanimously signed a protest against entering the harbor in their disabled condition, this censure at least in a very great degree, must appear to be unmerited and severe.

We have never been able to discover that any very important aid was furnished by the French fleet, while in the waters of Newport. There was, we grant, a *show* of resistance, but the efficiency in prosecuting the line of defence, failed. Far be it from us, however, to undervalue the aid received from the French. It decided the contest. "It cost her more than three hundred millions of dollars," and hurried her into a revolution, more exhausting than any other state in the tide of time.

The chief object of the treaties of 1778, was the establisment of the Liberty, Sovereignty, and Independence of the United States in the war of the Revolution. It was a dark and gloomy period with the Colonies, when France offered her assistance. The hopes which had been kindled by early successes, were almost extinguished by recent and successive disasters. It was at this painful moment that allied armies, fresh, vigorous, and well-appointed, coöperating with a gallant fleet, met the invader, and his surrender at Yorktown, opened the way to peace, sovereignty, and independence.

The militia raised for this expedition, were drafted only for three weeks; one-half of which were on service, and the remainder were to hold themselves in readiness, to succeed them at the expiration of that time, if called for. Within twenty-four hours after the French fleet sailed for Boston, between two and three thousand volunteers from Boston and other parts of New-England, left the army and returned home. And many of the militia whose term of service had now expired, returned, while those who were to succeed them, came on with reluctance, and not more than half their number was ever supplied, so that the American army was greatly reduced.

In this situation, without a naval force to protect or succor them, the possibility of a successful retreat was the only alternative. But it was deemed prudent not hastily to abandon their present position, lest they should thus encourage the pursuit of their foes, and hazard the honor of a successful retreat. They still maintained their post until the night of the 28th, when about 12th o'clock, the army began to move toward the north end of the Island, secure a communication with the main, and wait until information should be received from the French fleet in Boston.

Gen. de Lafayette was despatched with a message to Count D'Estaing, to ascertain whether the assistance and coöperation of the fleet could be expected, and to solicit its speedy return. The Count could not consent that the fleet should return, but promptly offered to march his troops from Boston, to the assistance of the American forces on Rhode Island, if requested. At daylight, the retreat having been discovered by the British, they took up their march in pursuit.

The French have never been distinguished on the ocean ; in the battle-field they have never had their superiors. If the fleet had been possessed of sufficient nerve they might at this exigency have rendered essential service to our troops, but as it was, they displayed a very great weakness, and gave the enemy the advantage. About six miles from Newport, the regiment in advance, commanded by Col. Campbell, was separated in two divisions, and pressed forward in pursuit ; one division retaining the road, the other the open field to the left. They advanced without opposition or obstruction, until they approached a wall running from the west a little to the north of Sampson Sherman's house. Here the Americans had lying in ambush, under the wall, a piquet guard of between three and four hundred men, who were not discovered by the enemy, and who were ordered not to fire until the word was given by the commander ; again to load and fire, and then continue their retreat.

The orders were strictly obeyed, and the command to fire was not given until the enemy were within half gun shot, when they poured upon them such a flood of death, as not only to check the advancing foe, but throw them into the greatest confusion, giving the guard sufficient time again to fire and make good their retreat, with but very little loss.

Col. Campbell had several balls pass through his clothes, and his horse killed under him. At one of the field pieces every man was shot down at the first fire. In the rear, and at a distance of not more than half a mile, the Fifty-fourth and two Hessian regiments were advancing, but so unexpected and fatal had been the work of that moment, and so rapid the retreat of the assailants, that they arrived too late to render their dying companions the least assistance.

The main body of the American army had gained and taken possession of Butt's Hill, on the northern part of the Island. It has generally been supposed, even at this time, had General Green's advice been taken, a most signal victory might have been gained over the pursuing enemy. His advice was overruled, however, and the enemy pressed onward toward the American lines. They advanced near the left wing of the American army, but were repulsed and driven back by General Glover, when they retired and took possession of Quaker Hill, about a mile from the position occupied by the Americans. A continued skirmishing was kept up between the two armies, during this and the following day, and frequently whole regiments were engaged in the deadly strife at once, and the same spot of ground was taken possession of and abandoned by both the belligerent parties. The last and most severe skirmish during the action, was an attempt made by the British on a redoubt in possession of the Americans. A reinforcement was sent to its relief, who arrived just in time to prevent the success of the enemy, and just as they were making a third and desperate effort to carry the redoubt; they were repulsed with considerable loss, and in great confusion precipitately retreated, leaving many of their slain and wounded on the field of battle. After this action, the firing of the musketry ceased, but the roar of the artillery still continued on both sides.

One grand object of the American commander in planting himself on these heights, and maintaining so long the sanguinary conflict, was to secure the removal of the baggage and heavy artillery with the stores of war, which was briskly going on in the rear, while the roar of cannon and the storm of death were raging in the front. The sentinels of both armies were stationed at a distance of not more than seventy rods from each other, so that it required no small degree of generalship to cover the design of retreat from the suspicion of a watchful enemy, and render that retreat triumphant and successful. On the 30th of the month, a number of tents were erected in full view of the enemy, and the whole army were apparently engaged in fortifying and strengthening their present position; after the going down of the sun, they built a large number of fires, extending nearly across the Island, to lull the enemy into security, and cover from suspicion their intended retreat.

As soon as the surrounding darkness favored the design, the tents were struck, and the troops with the artillery and baggage, moved to the north, embarked in their flat-bottomed boats, and were all safely landed on the main before the dawn of day. The brave and generous de Lafayette, who returned from Boston at the moment our troops were landing, was very greatly disappointed in not having been permitted to share in the perils of the action. Anticipating such an event, he had rode the distance of seventy miles in about six hours. Nor could he be prevented from passing over to bring off the piquet and other parties who covered the American retreat. This he effected with such consummate prudence and self-possession, that not a man was left behind, nor the slightest loss sustained. This retreat, notwithstanding the failure of the expedition, reflected the highest honor on the American commanders, and the wisdom and skill by which it was executed, was applauded even by the British officers themselves.

The loss of the Americans, as stated by General Sullivan, was,—

Killed	30
Wounded	137
Missing	44
Total	211

Nearly 1200 Americans were engaged in the action, and they are said to have shown great firmness. The day after the action, a cannonade was kept up by both armies.

A letter was received from General Washington, informing him (General Sullivan,) that a large body of troops had sailed from New-York, most probably for the relief of Newport; and a resolution was immediately formed to evacuate the island. The delay of a single day would, probably, have been fatal to the Americans; for Sir Henry Clinton, who had been delayed by adverse winds, arrived with a reinforcement of 4000 men, on the very next day, when a retreat, it is presumed, would have been impracticable.

The troops on Rhode Island, under the command of General Sullivan, on the 4th of August, were arranged as follows:—

Varnum's brigade,	including officers	..	1,037
Glover's	do.	ditto	1,131
Cornell's	do.	ditto	1,719
Green's	do.	ditto	1,626
Lovell's	do.	ditto	1,158
Titcomb's	do.	ditto	959
Livingstone's advance,		ditto	659
West's reserve,		ditto	1,025
Artillery		ditto	810
	Total amount		10,124

On November 28th, 1776, the day of General Washington's retreat over the Delaware, the British took possession of Rhode Island.

The scenes which have been enacted on the island, invests it with peculiar interest, and should remind us, of the present day, of the sufferings which our fathers endured, to bequeath to their children the rich legacy of liberty and independence. The island has been consecrated by the blood of our patriot sires; and when we walk over the fields of carnage, may we be reminded of the value of the American Union, and discountenance every attempt made by fanatics, to weaken the ties which hold us together as one people.

The British held position of the island, until the autumn of 1779, when Sir Henry Clinton, at New-York, anticipating an attack upon that place by the combined forces of America and France, dispatched a number of transports to bring off the troops from Rhode Island, to strengthen his forces at New-York; they embarked on the 25th of October, at the south end of the island, and arrived at New-York on the 27th.

On the day the island was evacuated, orders were issued by the British commander, that the inhabitants of Newport should keep within their houses during the time the royal troops were passing through Thames-street, the route which they took to the Neck, the place of their embarkation, on pain of death. This injunction was strictly complied with, so that those who had the curiosity to see the invaders of their peaceful shores march through their streets, stole a glance at them through the crevices of their windows and doors.

The British burnt all the barracks at Fort Adams, and the light-house at Beaver Tail, and carried off with them the Town Records, consisting of the books of Registry of Deeds, the Records of the Town Council, the Court of Probate, &c., which, in their passage to New-York, were unfortunately sunk with the vessel which carried them away, near Hell Gate, and were under water for several hours before they were recovered. They were detained in New-York about three years, and when they were afterwards returned to Newport, they were in a damaged condition. Had they been copied immediately on their recovery, many valuable documents might have been preserved, but having been neglected so long, they are now in a dilapidated state, and of little use.

On the arrival of Sir Henry Clinton, the last William Coddington, an aged and respectable gentleman, who held the office of Town Clerk, not willing to remain in prison, left the island, and went to Providence, there to reside until the army had abandoned the enterprise, and left the State. It is to be regretted that he had not taken with him the Records of the town, instead of placing them in the hands of his friend, Walter Chaloner, who took them to New-York, and their fate has been described above.

In 1782, the Town Council of Newport, having made application to General Carlton, the British Commander at New-York, for the return of the Town Records, which had been taken away at the evacuation of the town; they, in December, received by a flag of truce, the books and papers, General Carlton expressing his sorrow, " for the damage they had sustained, from the sinking of the transport in Hell Gate, and the long time they had lain (three years,) without examination."

The possession of the island for three years, by a strong and powerful foe, who treated its inhabitants as rebels against the authority of their King, and consequently claiming the divine right of his Majesty to whatever the royal troops should please to possess, reduced the inhabitants to the greatest poverty and distress. At this distant period, it is impossible to form the least conception of the wretchedness and misery endured by the inhabitants of the island at that trying period ; and nothing but the providence of God sustained them in the hour of peril ; they were, however, delivered from their enemies, and ultimately achieved their freedom from the galling yoke of British tyranny.

During the period of their stay, they had cut down and consumed all the flourishing groves of forest trees, with many of the most valuable orchards, and numerous ornamental trees, which beautified and adorned the island, so that the inhabitants were entirely destitute of fuel. The wells at Portsmouth were filled up, the houses on the heights of Middletown were set on fire by the General's order, and even the wharves, in Newport, which at that period were built of timber, were torn up for fuel, as the weather was so extremely severe in 1779–80.

It is estimated that nine hundred dwellings, besides warehouses, were destroyed, while the British had possession of Newport. The town presented a wide scene of desolation after the evacuation, and it should be no surprise to the reader that Newport has never recovered her former prosperity, when the ravages committed by a lawless and infuriated nation are duly considered.

Rhode Island was one of the principal points, and her spacious harbor, capable of containing the whole British fleet, rendered it a key of great importance, in pushing forward their schemes, in the subjugation of the rebellious Colonies.

During the possession of the island by the British, the freemen of Newport had held their Town Meetings, for choice of representatives in the General Assembly in Providence, the "hornet's nest," as the British called it, agreeably to an Act of that body, granting them permission to do so.

Middletown and Portsmonth held Town Meetings in Tiverton, for the election of representatives to the General Assembly; but after the evacuation of the island by the enemy, that body passed an act, empowering the town of Newport to resume their corporate powers, and choose Town officers, providing every person should be excluded from voting, who had in any-wise aided the enemy. The first meeting of the freemen for the choice of officers, was held at the Friends' Meeting-House, in November, 1779.

In January, 1779, the sum of five hundred pounds of lawful money, was granted by the General Assembly, for the relief of the distressed inhabitants of Newport; and large contributions continued to be made for the same object, in this, and the adjoining States.

The General Assembly, at their June session, in 1780, banished thirty-six persons from the State, and confiscated their estates, for adhering to the enemy.

On the 10th July, 1780, the French fleet, of seven sail of the line and five frigates, with a large number of transports, and an army of six thousand men, arrived at Newport, to the great joy of the inhabitants. The fleet was commanded by the Chevalier de Tournay, and the army by Count de Rochambeau. The town was illuminated, and the arrival of the fleet and army greeted with the fullest demonstrations of gratitude and joy. Complimentary addresses were made by a committee of the General Assembly, then in session, both to Admiral de Tourney and Count de Rochambeau, to which they gave the most spirited and patriotic replies.

In July, it having been ascertained that a large naval and land force were destined against Newport, the inhabitants associated, and formed themselves into companies, both for the common defence, and also that the disaffected might be known. The town was divided into four districts, and by a vote of the freemen, the inhabitants were required to meet, and sign articles of association; and those who should not appear at the place designated in the several districts, were to be deemed as enemies of their country; and all persons refusing to take up arms against the enemy, were to be banished from the place. It was voted that a copy of the list of disaffected persons, ordered to be forwarded to the Council of War, be also sent to General Heath, that if the British fleet and army arrive, before any return is received from the Council, he may know what persons the town requests should be removed from the island. The list sent to the Council of War, was called the "black list," embracing the votes of the town, that such persons be sent instanter from the island, as inimical to the United States.

The militia from Connecticut and Massachusetts, were ordered to the defence of Rhode Island. The expedition was, however, abandoned by Sir Henry Clinton, even after having sailed from New-York with a large fleet, and an army of eight thousand men, as far as Huntington Bay, on Long Island, much to the disappointment and grief of our magnanimous allies, who were prepared to give him a most warm and hearty reception.

It is painful to be called upon to notice a class of men, who rendered themselves so obnoxious in the war of the Revolution. They were traitors to their country, and had no just claim on the sympathies of the people; they had flattered themselves with the idea of the final triumph of the British arms, and, consequently, sided in with what they conceived to be the strongest party. But they were deceived, and highly disappointed, and the name of traitor was affixed to their character, and by that appellation they have ever been known. The course pursued towards them by the town was just, and highly commendatory. As patriots, warring for liberty, they could give no quarter to traitors.

On the 20th of August, nineteen warriors of the Oneida Indians, arrived in Newport, and dined with General Rochambeau and Admiral de Tourney; they also dined with General Heath, from all of whom they received presents.

Admiral de Tourney died soon after his arrival at Newport, and was buried with military honors, in Trinity church-yard, where a slab was afterwards erected to his memory, on the north side of the church. The funeral procession is said to have been grand and imposing, extending from his residence on the Point, at the Hunter House, to the church-yard, one dense mass of living beings, with the bands of music from the fleet, playing the most solemn strains, was a scene of deep interest to contemplate.

In March, 1781, General Washington, the saviour of his country, arrived at Newport. He passed over from the main by Conanicut Ferry, and landed from his barge at the head of Long Wharf. As he passed, the French fleet, lying at the back of the fort, fired a salute, and the army was drawn up in order for his reception at the Long Wharf. Washington, the immortal commander-in-chief of the French and American armies, never appeared to greater advantage than when he passed over to Newport to review the French forces under Count Rochambeau. He was received at the head of Long Wharf by the French officers, at the head of 7,000 men, who lined the streets from thence to the State House.

"I never," says a bystander now living, "felt the solid earth tremble under me before. The firing from the French ships that lined the harbor, was tremendous; it was one continued roar, and looked as though the very Bay was on fire. Washington, as you know, was a Marshal of France; he could not command the French army without being invested with that title. He wore, on this day, the insignia of his office, and was received with all the honors due to one in that capacity. It is known that many of the flower of the French nobility were numbered in the army that acted in our defence. Never," said the aged narrator, "will that scene be erased from my memory. The attitudes of the nobles, their deep obeisance, the lifting of hats and caps, the waving of standards, the sea of plumes, the long line of French soldiers and the general disposition of their arms, unique to us, separating to the right and left, the Chief, with Count Rochambeau on his left, unbonneted, walked through. The French nobles, commanders, and their under officers, followed in the rear. Count Rochambeau was a small, keen looking man, not handsome as was his son, afterwards Governor of Martinique. Count Noailles looked like what he was—a great man. But the resplendent beauty of the two Viosminels eclipsed all the rest. They were brothers, and one of them a General in the army, who bore the title of Count too. Newport never saw anything so handsome as these two young brothers.

"But we, the populace, were the only ones that looked at them, for the eye of every Frenchman was directed to Washington. Calm and unmoved by all the honors that surrounded him, the voice of adulation nor the din of battle had ever disturbed the equanimity of his deportment. Ever dignified, he wore on this day the same saint-like expression that always characterized him. They proceeded from the State House to the lodgings of Count Rochambeau, the present residence of the heirs of the late Samuel Verner, corner of Clark and Mary streets. It was a proud day for Newport, to be honored with the presence of Washington, a name dear to every American heart."

A committee of citizens waited upon him on his arrival, and presented him with an address, to which he politely replied.

Committee's Address to his Excellency, George Washington, Esq., General and Commander-in-Chief of the Armies of the Thirteen United States of America.

SIR—The inhabitants of the ancient town of Newport, warmed with the purest sentiments of esteem and respect, beg leave, through their Committee, to congratulate your Excellency upon your arrival at this town, the capital of the State of Rhode Island and Providence Plantations; permit us to assure your Excellency that words are inadequate to express the joy which your presence has infused into the hearts of our fellow-citizens. Happily guided by the Supreme Director of the American Councils, your Excellency was placed at the head of the armies; our gratitude is greatly due to Heaven for the protection of your Excellency's person through all those scenes of danger and enterprise incident to war, and which your Excellency has sustained with patriotism and fortitude unparalleled in the page of history.

We will not cloud the festivity of this day by enumerating the scenes of lawless rapine and devastation, which have so peculiarly marked the steps of a tyrannical and rapacious enemy in this town. The thought merely occurs, as it deprives us of affording your Excellency some further manifestations of our sincere regard.

Suffer us here, Sir, because we know it must give your Excellency a most sensible pleasure, to express the happiness this town has enjoyed with the army and fleet of our illustrious ally, who have, by the wisdom and prudence of their commanders, as well as their own most zealous inclinations, allied themselves to us, not as soldiers only, but as friends and citizens; armed with a most righteous cause, engaged for all that men hold most dear, what blessings may not America, under the auspices of a kind and overruling Providence, be led to expect from the future exertions of your Excellency, the military ardor of the

American troops, and an army and fleet of a most generous and magnanimous ally, thirsting for glory, and eager to bleed in the cause of liberty and mankind.

We congratulate your Excellency upon the late signal successes of the American arms by land, and those of our allies by sea. May the succeeding campaign be productive of the end of all our efforts—liberty, peace, and independence to the United States of America, and happiness to all mankind.

CHRISTOPHER ELLERY,
WILLIAM CHANNING,
WILLIAM TAGGART,
SOLOMON SOUTHWICK,
} *Committee.*

To which Gen. Washington returned the following answer:

To Christopher Ellery, William Channing, William Taggart, and Solomon Southwick, Esqrs.:

Gentlemen—Among the distinguished honors which have a claim to my gratitude since my arrival, I have seen with peculiar satisfaction those expressions of esteem and attachment which have manifested themselves in the citizens of this ancient town.

My happiness is complete in the moment that unites the expressions of their sentiments for me with their suffrages in favor of our allies. The conduct of the French army and fleet, of which the inhabitants testify in so grateful and so affectionate a sense, at the same time that it evinces the wisdom of the commanders and the discipline of the troops, is a new proof of the magnanimity of the nation. It is a further demonstration of that generous zeal and concern for the happiness of America which brought them to our assistance, a happy presage of future harmony—a pleasing evidence that an intercourse between the two nations will more and more cement the union by the solid and lasting ties of mutual affection.

I sincerely sympathize with you, gentlemen, in lamenting the depredations suffered by the town while in possession of the enemy, and heartily join you in those liberal wishes, the accomplishment of which would soon more than restore it to its former flourishing condition.

Accept my acknowledgments for the polite and obliging manner in which you have been pleased to communicate to me the sentiments of your fellow-citizens, and the assurance of my warmest esteem for them and for you personally.

Newport, March 8th, 1781. G. WASHINGTON.

The town was illuminated, the evening after his arrival at Newport. Count de Rochambeau gave a splendid ball to Gen. Washington, which was attended by the most fashionable families in Newport. This was the first interview Washington enjoyed with the French officers, and it is said that he and the Count de Rochambeau laid their plans for an attack upon New York, which was disconcerted by the arrival of a large fleet and army to the assistance of Sir Henry Clinton, under the command of Admiral Rodney. About this time, Admiral D'Barras arrived at Boston, and succeeded to the command of the French squadron at Newport. It was soon after decided in a council of war, held at Wethersfield, Conn., by General Washington, Count de Rochambeau, and other distinguished officers, that the troops on Rhode Island (with the exception of about five hundred to guard the works), should immediately march to the North River, to join the American army. During the whole period the French army was quartered in Newport, such was their strict regard to the rights and property of the inhabitants, that the whole amount of damage done by them would not exceed one hundred dollars.

The pleasure which the French officers derived in mingling with the polished society of Newport, has been already alluded to, in the description given by Count Seguin in relation to the fancy ball, which was given on the 3d of January, by the officers of the regiments of Royal Duex Ponts. In was an elegant *fete*, composed of the first rank in the society of the ancient metropolis.

EXECUTION.

On the 1st of June, 1781, a sergeant of the French artillery was executed at the south part of Newport, a little back from what was then called Huddy's Lane, now the Bowery near the Ocean House, in presence of the whole army, who were drawn up in a hollow square for the occasion. The criminal on being brought to the place of execution, had his right hand cut off and burnt by the executioner, and he was then hanged. His crime was attempting to murder his officer. It appeared that in a fit of jealousy he had in the night waylaid the Captain of his Company, and after stabbing him repeatedly, had thrown him into an old cellar at the corner of Denison and Spring-streets, where the Barker House now stands. The officer was found in his wounded state and conveyed to his quarters, and afterwards recovered.

The Frenchmen were very much smitten by the Newport ladies, and many of them, it is said, *lost their hearts*. It is not to be wondered at, when we consider the elegance of person, and the refinement of manners which preëminently distinguished the fair sex in the past. Many romantic events have transpired on the island, which if we should allude to them all, would increase our volume beyond the ordinary limit which was designed.

The Chevalier de Fayelle, Aid-de Camp to the Marquis de Lafayette, died very suddenly at Newport, as he was going on board the French frigate Hermoine. He was buried with military honors in Trinity church-yard.

The surrender of Lord Cornwallis and army, to the united forces of America and France, on the 19th of October, 1781, decided the fate of the Revolution, and was virtually the termination of the war; for although several places of importance were still in possession of the enemy, yet their days were numbered, and their destiny sealed.

On the 4th of March, 1782, the British Parliament, in the House of Commons, passed a resolution declaring all as enemies to His Majesty, and His Majesty's Kingdom, who should advise to the longer continuance of the war in America. Preliminaries of peace were entered into at Paris, in November, 1782, and a definite treaty, in which Great Britain acknowledged the Sovereignty and Independence of the United States, was signed in September, 1783.

In 1783, the British frigate Mercy, Capt. Stanhope, arrived at Newport, on the 19th of July, from Halifax. While at Newport he married Miss Peggy Malborn, daughter of Francis Malborn, sen., Esq. Capt. Stanhope was afterward Admiral, and Knight of the Bath, and one of the Lords of Admiralty. We again shall have occasion to allude to this distinguished individual.

Francis Malborn, senior, was a native of Prince Anna county, Virginia, and came to Rhode Island about 1758. He was a ship-master in the employ of Godfrey Malborn; he then engaged in mercantile pursuits, and was a partner of the house of E. & F. Malborn, well known as enterprising and successful merchants in Newport, previous to the Revolution. He left two sons and three daughters; one of his sons was the Hon. Francis Malborn, who was representative and subsequently a Senator in the Congress of the United States. He was a finished gentleman of the old school, and universally respected by all classes of the community.

During the war of the Revolution, although Newport, being in possession of the enemy, had but few privateers engaged in the deadly strife, still she furnished a number of distinguished naval commanders, and a greater number of marines, perhaps, than any other town in New-England, in proportion to her size and population. It is supposed by those who lived in times that "tried men's souls," that Newport probably furnished a thousand men for the naval service in that war, and that one-half of these fell into the hands of the enemy, and died on board a man-of-war, the Forton prison, in England, or the old Jersey prison-ship, which for the loathsomeness and terror of its dungeons, compared with the Black Hole of Calcutta.

A certain elegant writer, has said: "Happy, indeed, and thrice happy, were Warren, Montgomery, and Mercer; happy those other gallant spirits who fell with glory in the heat of battle, distinguished by their country and covered with her applause. Every soul sensible to honor, envies rather than compassionates their fates. It was in the dungeons of our inhuman invaders—it was in their pestiferous prison-ships that the wretchedness of our countrymen still makes the heart bleed. It was there that hunger, and thirst, and disease, and all the contumely cold-hearted cruelty could bestow, sharpened every pang of death. Misery there rung every fibre that could feel, before she gave the blow of grace which sent the sufferer to eternity. It is said that poison was employed! No! there was no such mercy there. There nothing was employed which could blunt the susceptibility to anguish, or which, by hastening death, could rob its agonies of a single pang. On board one only of these floating hells, above *eleven thousand* of our brave countrymen are said to have perished! *She was called the Jersey Deep and dreadful as the coloring of this picture may appear, it is but a faint and imperfect sketch of the original. You must remember a thousand unutterable calamities, a thousand instances of domestic as well as national anxiety and distress, which mock description. You ought to remember them; you ought to hand them down in tradition to your posterity, that they may know the awful price their fathers paid for freedom."

The naval commanders in that war were John Grimes, Benj. Pierce, Joseph Gardiner, William Dennis, James Godfrey, Remembrance Simmons, Thomas Stacy, Oliver Read, Capt. Bently, Samuel Jeffers, John Coggeshall, William Finch, Capt. Jaquays, James Phillips, Ezekiel Burroughs, Isaac Freeborn, William Ladd, Joseph Sheffield, Capt. Gazzee, and John Murphy. These either sailed from Newport previous to its possession by the enemy, or subsequently from other ports of New-England, West Indies, &c. The privateers, though small in numerical power and force, yet they constantly annoyed the enemy, took many valuable prizes, and achieved some splendid victories.

An anecdote is related of John Murphy, one of the commanders, which is too good to be lost. A Mrs. Webber, who kept a boarding-house at the head of Stephens' Wharf, was a remarkable neat woman, which was one of the characteristics of the females of Newport in the past. It was her constant practice to scour her floor every week, and sand it in diamond form. Paint was not generally in vogue at that period. She had on that very day completed her task, which proved to be rainy, and the streets of course muddy. Murphy, knowing the fact, and designing to play off a joke, sallied forth to the lower market, and announced with much earnestness to the countrymen who had collected there, that there was a great curiosity to be seen at Mrs. Webber's, viz., a "Whistling Pig;" the crowd instanter rushed to her house, and bolted into the room, inquiring at the top of their voices, for the "pig," which brought forward the lady, who on discovering the condition of her floor, covered with mud, as may well be imagined, threw her into the greatest rage, and the *green-horns* had to make their exit with all possible haste, while Murphy amused himself with the joke, which he had so adroitly played off. He was the father of the late Capt. John Murphy, long an enterprising shipmaster from Newport.

Capt. Oliver Read of Newport, justly deserves a place in the history of these times. No sooner was intelligence received that the invaders of his country had commenced the work of destruction in the environs of Boston, than he left the quiet retirement of home, and hastened to the rescue. He offered his services to his country as a volunteer, and joined the American troops in the vicinity of Boston. But the dull monotony of the camp was neither suited to the character or habits of Capt. Read. He soon left the army and sailed as the commander of a privateer. His bold, adventurous spirit exposed him to great dangers, and during the continuance of the war, he was often in the power of his foes; but the same merciful Providence which watched over and directed the destiny of that event, watched over and preserved this bold and fearless patriot. After having been several times taken prisoner, and suffered some ungentlemanly treatment from his enemies, he solemnly protested, if ever he commanded another vessel, to make atonement for the insults received. He was no sooner released from his confinement, than his friends purchased and fitted for him a new and well-built brig, called the Rochambeau. In this brig Capt. Read achieved several victories, and took many rich and valuable prizes; but he was destined to see his favorite brig in the possession of his foes, and himself again a prisoner of war, by the chicanery of one of his youthful companions, who was a Loyalist, or, in common *parlance* of that age, a Tory. Capt. Read and his companions were taken to New-York, and from thence transferred to the Jersey prison-ship. He resolved, however, not to remain without attempting his escape, if he perished in the attempt. He communicated his design to several of his companions, Capt. Isaiah Cahoone, and Capt. John Tower, of Providence, with one or two others, who, with the same bold, daring intrepidity, resolved to share the fate of Capt. Read. The only plan of escape which afforded the least hope of success, was to seize the boat of the prison-ship, and effect their escape under the guns of the vessel.

This plan, hazardous in the extreme, and full of danger, was finally agreed upon, and they waited only for a fit opportunity to present itself, when, at a concerted signal, they were to attempt its execution. After waiting with impatience for several days, Providence seemed to favor their design, and to grant them a favorable opportunity for attempting their escape. Just before night, the boat of the prison-ship returned from shore, and discharged her stores of provisions, when, at the given signal of Captain Read, his companions leaped after him into the boat, cut away her painter, and made for the shore, amidst a volley of balls. The darkness of the night, accompanied with a driving snow-storm, which at that moment commenced, prevented the pursuit of their enemies, and they fortunately landed on Long Island during the night. Captain Read soon returned to Newport, with a heart burning with revenge, especially against his old school-fellow, Crandall, the notorious tory. It is said that when Read was delivered up by Crandall, to the officers of the Jersey prison-ship, he cast a withering look at that reckless being, and said, "A short life to one of us! If we meet again, and meet again we shall, one of us dies."

Capt. Read was soon in command of another vessel, of about an equal force with the Rochambeau, which was now commanded by the infamous Crandall. It was not long before she was descried, although newly painted, and disguised. Read prepared for action, and, as he approached her, hoisted American colors; being hailed, he answered by a broadside, and at the same time showed himself to the astonished Crandall, who supposed him safely lodged in the Jersey prison-ship. The conflict lasted for several hours, until almost every man on board the Rochambeau was either slain or wounded. And when taken possession of, the lion heart of even Captain Read was deeply affected. There lay the headless trunk of the treacherous Crandall, surrounded by his fallen companions, while the deck was literally covered with human gore. Captain Read again entered his native port, accompanied by his favorite Rochambeau. The brig was immediately repaired and fitted for sea, when her bold commander again sailed on another cruise. Captain Read, having learnt off Sandy Hook that the brig Spy of Providence had been taken by his Majesty's ship Lyon, of sixty-four guns, and ordered to New York, resolved if possible to recapture her. Accordingly, he moored his vessel in safety, and kept on the look out, near the Hook. The Spy soon came in sight under British colors, cast anchor, and waited for a pilot. Captain Read, with a few brave fellows to man his boat, came alongside and offered his services as a pilot, to take her to New York. His services were readily accepted, and he took his position at the helm.

The wind favoring his design, he put her head for his native town, and let her drive; nor was the trick discovered until it was too late. For as they were approaching near the place of destination, the prize-master said to the pilot, "Sir, we are going to New York, are we?" The pilot, bowing very respectfully, answered laconically, "No, Sir; no. We are going to Newport."

George W. Babcock, of Narragansett, who sailed from Newport, was another distinguished hero, and was engaged in some of the most obstinate battles during the war. In the spring of 1779, he sailed from Boston, and on the 16th of May he fell in with, and succeeded in capturing after an obstinate engagement, a British privateer called the Tartar, a few days from Cork. The Tartar mounted twenty-six guns, with a complement of one hundred and fifty men; but having previously taken and manned several prizes, the actual number in the engagement could not have exceeded one hundred and twenty men. The crew of the Mifflin were principally from Newport and Narragansett. Her first lieutenant, Mr. Timothy Coggeshall, was an inhabitant of the Island. The battle raged with increasing violence for several hours, at a very short distance, and before the deadly conflict was hushed, the vessels were so near each other that they could readily leap from one to the other. But the British flag finally came down, and Capt. Babcock took possession of the Tartar.

Two days previous to this engagement, he had fallen in with and captured the British store-ship Elephant, which was conveying to England a large number of invalids, both officers and privates. When Captain Babcock approached the Elephant, and demanded that her colors be struck to an American privateer, her proud and haughty commander, although he knew he could make no effectual resistance, refused to comply.

It is said that Babcock reasoned with him, and remonstrated against the unnecessary effusion of blood his obstinacy would inevitably involve, for several minutes before he ordered his men to fire. The engagement lasted but a few moments, before the flag of the Elephant was struck; but those moments proved fatal to her commander, who fell, with six of his crew by his side. The success of Captain Babcock and his brave crew had nearly proved fatal to them. The number of their prisoners had now so increased, as to render their situation far more hazardous than the roar of the British cannon. The only alternative of safety that presented itself, was the dismissal of a large number of them. Accordingly, after having received a bill from the British officer, acknowledging the receipt of so many prisoners of war, Captain Babcock put them on board a prize-ship, and left them to pursue their voyage. The Mifflin, after the engagement, sailed for France, and the Tartar was sent to Boston, where she subsequently arrived in safety.

It was not Newport and the Island merely, that suffered from the British depredators; but Tiverton, and Seconnet river, also experienced the horrors of war. The English vessels that guarded the entrance of the Seconnet river, and occasionally came up nearly where the Stone Bridge now is, were a great annoyance. Sometimes, however, they would get aground on the Tiverton or Little Compton side, where the water is very shoal, and occasion much trouble to themselves; and, at one time, a large privateer of the enemy was run aground on the shore at Little Compton, just below the farm of Deacon Brownell, when the enemy were obliged to burn her and make their escape. Tiverton witnessed much suffering of a domestic nature during the time the enemy were in possession of Rhode Island. The people were often called to share their morsel with the suffering inhabitants, who from time to time came over, and who came off at the surrender of the town of Newport, and lingered about the opposite shore in hopes their stay might be short, and they be permitted to go back and collect the remnant of their property. A venerable and respected citizen of Portsmouth, who had held many important offices, remarked, "I was but seven years old when the British entered Newport; yet I distinctly recollect the state of alarm and constant excitement during that period. My father occupied a small house, built on his own land, about three miles equal distance from Bristol and Howland's ferry. I have but little recollection of what took place, particularly, until one day when the Americans under Sullivan were retreating from Rhode Island. A party of the enemy came up to the house of an aged man, and commanded him to draw water for them; and while the venerable man tottered to the well, they barbarously shot him in the back."

The Cory family seemed peculiarly a patriotic one; two of the brothers, Samuel and Pardon, were among the capturers of Prescott. His son, Thomas Corey, married a daughter of Lieutenant Wilcox, one of those who went ahead in the enterprise of taking Prescott.

Fogland Ferry, at the period of the Revolution, had a house of entertainment near the end of the point, kept by Mrs. Sarah Gray. Exposed as they were, the house was often the resort of the British officers and soldiers, and their insolence was such that Mrs. Gray often had occasion to exercise her authority to keep them in subjection. She was a woman of uncommon nerve, and never daunted by the threats of the enemy. A Hessian soldier, on one occasion, inquired for West India rum. He was told they had none, but they could furnish him with some *East India*. He replied that he would have a glass.

The East River was often the scene of conflict. The Amercan troops stationed at Little Compton brought two cannon to bear, one twelve and one eighteen-pounder, and poured so destructive a fire on the British frigate Cerberus, which was then at anchor there, as to compel her to slip her cables and to make her escape.

On the return of peace, the town of Newport was in ruins. The storm of war had beat heavily upon her, and in the language of Dr. Waterhouse, "she resembled an old battered shield, long held up against the common enemy." According to the estimate of a committee appointed by the General Assembly for that purpose, it appears that the loss sustained by the inhabitants of Newport, in the destruction of dwelling houses, warehouses, &c., amounted to £124,798 13s. 5d., silver money. This estimate includes only the loss of private property sustained by individuals. By an estimate of the number of inhabitants in Newport, taken by order of the General Assembly in 1782, there were at that time 4,912 whites, and 618 colored, including 69 Indians—making the whole population 5,530.

This estimate, compared with that made by order of the General Government in 1774, shows a decrease during the war of 3,679. That estimate gave to Newport a population of 7,917 whites, 1,246 blacks, and 46 Indians—making the sum total of 9,209. And this was supposed to fall considerably below the actual number, being underrated for the purpose of escaping greater requisitions for men and money. If, as is supposed, Newport once numbered 12,000 inhabitants, about one-half that number was dispersed by the Revolution.

No town had greater occasion of indignation towards the British Government, than Newport. When she surveyed the desolations brought on her once prosperous town by modern vandals, it was not to be supposed that she should give the least countenance to a class of men who had deserted her in the hour of peril, and given their influence in support of the enemy. It is a matter of pain to the patriot, that so many traitors to the cause of liberty were found in Newport. They had vainly indulged the idea that victory would yet dawn on the British arms, and their prosperity follow as a necessary consequence. But happily, they were disappointed, and their names cast out as evil. After the peace, and when business began to resume its former prospects, these refugees, who had fled their country when their services were required, manifested an anxiety to return to Newport and resume their former position in society. John Goodrich, sen., an American refugee, arrived at Newport soon after the peace, and solicited liberty to settle there with his family, and become an inhabitant of the town—offering, in case permission was granted, to bring twenty sail of vessels, and establish himself in mercantile business. But Goodrich having taken an active part during the war, by fitting out privateers, and other obnoxious acts against his countrymen, the town voted by a large majority, that he should not be allowed to settle in the place. He afterwards settled in Bermuda.

Many at this day would be ready to condemn the action of the freemen of Newport, when the principle which governs man in all his acts is founded on dollars and cents. But higher and weightier considerations influenced their conduct; they had been engaged in a righteous cause, in defending their firesides from the ruthless invaders of their peace, and they could not readily forget the aid and comfort which had been furnished the enemy, by a band of traitors, who were legally and constitutionally bound to put forth their efforts in the cause of liberty and human rights.

It was no trifling matter which urged our fathers forward, in resisting British oppression, as every one must be sensible, who has taken pains to investigate the subject. An able writer has well remarked, " But these were not the beggarly and servile conflicts between a red rose and a white one; not whether a weak and inglorious bigot, or a wanton and abandoned debauchee, should be king; they were not these temporary bursts of misery, which now and then agitate the wretched inhabitants of Constantinople, and which an execution will allay without exhibiting any evidence of its justice. They sprung from that unbroken spirit, that wild and unfettered boldness, that restless, that uncontrollable, that sublime love of liberty, which sometimes, indeed, mistakes its means, but never loses sight of its object, which, while it seems to endanger, often secures that object, and which burns with undiminished force, while one generous sentiment lingers in the human breast to support it."

The part which the inhabitants of Newport took in the great struggle for liberty and independence, renders their character worthy of all praise. They had been early instructed in the principles of liberty; the minds that had colonized this island, were imbued with the spirit of freedom, and labored to impress it indelibly on the hearts of the people. They could not passively submit to political outrages; they felt that they possessed inherent rights, which could not be trampled on with impunity, and in the majesty of their strength they resolved to conquer or to die. It was a noble resolution, worthy the name of Rhode Islanders; and by their zeal and devotion, aided by Omnipotent power, they triumphed. And it is now the " land of the free, and the home of the brave."

The return of peace, once more, gave promise of prosperity; the inhabitants of Newport had the satisfaction of knowing that they were free and independent, and that a motive now existed for them to put forth their energies in endeavoring to recover their former prosperity. Commerce once more resumed its former activity, and the wharfs, which had been deserted, were again in requisition; the sound of the hammer was now heard, giving encouragement to labor. But so heavy had been the blow which had fallen on the ancient town, that the inhabitants could not well flatter themselves of being able to arrive to that commercial distinction, which she had once enjoyed.

In 1784, Newport was incorporated as a city, and on the first day of June, of that year, the first choice of city officers was had; the following gentlemen having been chosen on that occasion, viz.:—

George Hazard, for Mayor.

George Champlin,
Samuel Fowler,
Peleg Clarke,
Oliver King Warner, } Aldermen.

Henry Bliss,
Samuel Freebody,
John Slocum,
Robert Stephens,
George Sears,
Nich. P. Tillinghast, } Common Council.

Peleg Barker, City Clerk.

This form of government being found more expensive, was soon abandoned, and the old form of town government again resumed, in March, 1787, which was a highly sensible and judicions move.

An attempt was made a few years since, to revive the charter form of government, but the freemen of the town, in Town Meeting assembled, settled the question, and we would hope, for ever.

It now became necessary to form a system of government, embracing the great interest and common welfare of the several Colonies. But in order to this, it became requisite for each State to surrender a portion of their power to the general government; and this must ever be the case, in a confederated form of government.

In conformity to a resolution of the General Congress, all the Colonies, except Rhode Island, chose delegates, to meet in Philadelphia, in General Convention, for the purpose of deliberating upon, and framing a Constitution.

It was owing to the state of party feeling in Rhode Island, that she was not represented in that body. The motion made in the General Assembly, for the appointment of delegates to meet in General Convention, having been lost, by a majority of twenty-three against it. The opposition lay principally in the northern part of the State.

The course pursued by Rhode Island, in her refusing to come into the Union, is a gross reflection on her character; and we would hope, for the honor of Newport, that none of her citizens aided in so rebellious an act, having given such convincing evidence of her patriotism and love of country.

Unhappily for the State, a certain class have been found, opposing liberal principles, setting up a standard of their own, which was in direct conflict with the spirit of republican institutions, and which, they flattered themselves, would ultimately triumph. Hence, a want of co-operation has been remarkably illustrated, in the various attempts at political reform, which have so highly distinguished the age, and which God grant may never cease, until the rights and liberties of every American citizen are secured.

At a meeting of the freemen of Newport, held agreeably to the Act of the Assembly, on the fourth Monday in March, 1778, the day appointed for the several towns in the State to hold town meetings, to consider the proposed Constitution, the business of the meeting was prefaced by the Moderator, by reciting the Acts of Government which were referred to the decision of the people.

The Constitution was then read; and the Moderator stated the proceedings of the General Assembly upon it, since it had been transmitted to them. He also informed the town of the uniform conduct of their representatives, in endeavoring to obtain the appointment of a Convention.

Several gentlemen entered into an investigation of the Act of Assembly; altering the mode of decision from that recommended by the General Convention to Congress, and while they paid all possible respect to the Legislature who passed the act, most unqualified terms. The meeting appointed a Committee to draft instructions to our representatives, to endeavor to have a Convention called. The meeting was composed of be- the principle on which it was founded was reprobated in the tween three and four hundred freemen, yet eleven persons only voted on the question, TEN against, and only ONE in favor of the Constitution.

In Providence, only one person voted, and he in the negative.

In Warwick, and Greenwich, the Federalists, or friends of the Constitution, entered a protest against the alteration of the mode of decision, as illegal and unprecedented. In Bristol and Little Compton, there was a majority in favor of the Constitution. The other towns generally gave their voice against it; and not until compelled by the action of the General Government, did Rhode Island come into the Union.

The union was not effected until 1790, and until, by Acts of Congress, the commercial relations of Rhode Island were placed on a footing with foreign commerce, exacting foreign duties and tonnage from our vessels.

In January, 1790, an Act passed in General Assembly, for calling a Convention of the State, which met in Newport the following March, when the Constitution was agreed to, and the State came into the Confederacy.

The paper money system was formerly, if not now, a matter of party controversy. Governors were elected or turned out of office, as the different interests happened to prevail. The commercial interest was invariably opposed to the system, as it tended greatly to embarrass trade, and by its depreciation, and constant fluctuation, great injustice grew out of the system. Many took advantage of the laws, making it a tender at par, to pay debts in depreciated money; and creditors, who had parted with their gold and silver, were compelled to receive these shin-plasters, in return for their debts.

In 1710, the Colony of Rhode Island commenced the issue of paper money, to defray the public expenditure of the war, for that year, and after that period, new emissions were made from time to time, as circumstances required. Sometimes paper was issued to replenish the treasury, sometimes to loan the people on mortgage, until the increasing amount issued, caused it almost constantly to depreciate in current value; and as the money depreciated in value, the emissions were increased, until about 1749, when the General Assembly were restricted by Parliament from making any more, except under certain limitations.

The various emissions, from time to time, were, at the time for which they were issued expired, called in and sunk, they generally being made redeemable in some given time. It has been estimated that in 1748, there was in circulation in this State, in what was called old tenor, £500,000. By a report of a Committee to the General Assembly, in 1749, they made the outstanding bills, at that time, £320,444 2s. 3 1-2d. By a report of a Committee to the General Assembly, in 1764, in answer to the inquiry of the Lords Commissioners of Trade, it appears there was then in circulation, £30,000, in bills issued to carry on the war, equal to £30,000 sterling; about two-thirds of which sum must be called in and sunk in a year from that time, after which, they say, £13,000 only of the bills issued to defray the expense of the war, will be in circulation, and these, with the small remainder of old tenor bills that shall be outstanding, will come to a final end in 1767.

By an Act of Assembly, Sept. 1770, the circulation of the old tenor bills was prohibited. They were to be brought into the treasury and exchanged for treasury notes, at the rate of £8, old tenor, for one dollar. In May, 1775, the State having voted to raise troops, issued £20,000, in bills, on interest, at two-and-a-half per cent, and made them a tender for all debts, 6s. 9d, to the silver ounce.

In August of this year, the continental bills, of which there were beginning to be large emissions by Congress, were made a tender at 6s. per dollar. Emissions of paper were now frequently made by the Colony, and those persons who should undervalue the bills, were declared enemies to the public weal, and every possible exertion was made during the Revolutionary war, to sustain their credit and keep up their value.

In 1776, a Committee of the New-England States recommended them to emit no more bills of credit, unless absolutely necessary; but to tax or borrow, and if they did emit money, to issue bills on interest at four per cent. The General Assembly approved this plan, and ordered £40,000 to be hired, in notes payable in two years. In 1777, they ordered £50,000 lawful money to be hired, and notes given on interest for the same at four per cent.

These notes were at first made a legal tender, but was subsequently repealed, and all contracts were to be made in specie. In 1778 and 1782, acts were passed for consolidating the paper money, and ordering all notes and bills to be brought into the treasury, and interest calculated at six per cent from June, 1778, when they were struck out of circulation, and new notes given on interest.

On the return of peace in 1783, there was very little gold and silver in circulation, and nothing to supply its place as a circulating medium. It was customary for the merchants to pay the mechanics and laborers in their employ, in tea, sugar, coffee, &c., which they were obliged to take to market, and exchange with the farmers for provisions. And so difficult was it to raise money, that the farmers suffered greatly in having cattle taken from them and sold for payment of taxes.

This State, from its local situation, was exposed, during the war, to the frequent incursions of the enemy. These incursions were repelled chiefly by the military of Rhode Island, under the direction, and at the expense, (in the first instance,) of the State; by reason of which, Rhode Island incurred a much larger debt than perhaps any of her sister States, in proportion to her estimated rate in the valuation of the United States.

A Committee appointed by the General Assembly, to inquire into the state of the public securities, due from the State, reported a debt of £153,047 15s. 9½d., of which £106,976 11s. 3½d., was on interest at 6 per cent., for treasury notes issued for soldiers' wages, depreciation of soldiers' wages, debts due for confiscated estates, for money loaned, &c., &c.; £46,071 4s. 6d. of which was on interest at 4 per cent., and was for debts due from Government, in 1777.

In May, 1786, the paper money party having prevailed, and chosen their candidate for Governor, &c., an act was passed for emitting £100,000, lawful money, in bills of credit, and making the same a legal tender at par, for the payment of debts. The 6 per cent. debt was consolidated by a scale of depreciation to real money, at 6s. per dollar, and by an act of Assembly was to be paid in the paper emission of 1786, at its nominal value, although that had already depreciated to 48s. for a dollar. It was proposed to consolidate the 4 per cent. debt, at 40s. for one dollar, and payable in the same emission at its nominal value.

In October, 1789, the value of bills emitted in 1786, was made fifteen paper dollars for one of silver. But gold and silver being very scarce, and considering the impracticability of discharging debts in specie, it was enacted that real estate of not less value than £40, and personal property within the State, might be substituted, in the payment of debts, under certain restrictions. The Governor in his Message to the General Assembly, in October, 1791, speaking of the State debt, says:

"This debt was wholly incurred during the late war, in the common defence of the nation."

After peace took place, as it was found by experience impracticable to discharge it in the ordinary mode of taxes, in gold and silver, recourse was had to paper money; this was issued in 1786. The holders of State securities were required to receive it in payment on penalty of forfeiting the whole amount of their respective demands. Owing to the unhappy divisions that prevailed, it suffered an unusual depreciation, but payments in paper were made to nearly the amount of £79,000, and securities to the amount of about £48,000, were lodged in the General Treasury, in consequence of the requisition of the Legislature from bringing them in for the paper money. The specie value of the payments thus made in paper, was only about one-sixth part, or perhaps less, of the nominal value, from the great depreciation of the paper money. And finally, at the rate of about 15 for 1, it became indispensably necessary for the Legislature to interpose; and as an appreciation of the paper at par, in the greatly depreciated state, would have been productive of as much, or perhaps more injustice, than its depreciation, the Legislature had no alternative but to arrest it as it was; to repeal the tender, and declare that it should finally be redeemed at the rate of 15 for 1. And an act for this purpose, was passed October, 1789.

In August, last year, Congress assumed $21,500,000 of the debt of the several States, including in the assumption $200,000 of the debt of this State; and as the sum assumed is charged by the United States to the State from which it is assumed, if the Legislature had not interposed, those who did not comply with the requisition for receiving the paper money, would have received the whole benefit of this assumption, and a realization of the greatest part of their securities; while those who did comply would not only lose five-sixths of their demands, but must have contributed their full proportion to the paying the whole amount of the securities, which had been confiscated as before mentioned.

In obedience to acts of the General Assembly of this State, of January and June of 1795, making provision for the transfer of the stock of the United States, belonging to this State, to the individual creditors thereof, the General Treasurer reported as due for certificates issued for various kinds of debts incurred during the revolution, and for consolidating the paper money, and securities issued for paper money, and for sinking the 4 per cent. notes, and including notes issued previous to the Revolution, &c., the sum of £503,594 76, of which five-sixths, or $419,662 30, was issuable in certificates for funded stock of the United States, and one-sixth, or $83,932 46, in State certificates unprovided for.

In February, 1803, the General Treasurer reported the above $83,932 46, together with additional claims brought in, and allowed by the State from time to time, making in all a registered State debt of $163,163 71, which debt was afterward from time to time reduced, until June, 1804. By his report it appeared there was a balance of principal and interest then due of $120,949 04, and in a subsequent report in 1807, he reported $10,680 14 more of said balance as paid. But a large proportion of said balance remains to this day unpaid.

The debt we conceive to be a just one, and the payment should no longer be delayed to lawful claimants. These securities were received in good faith, and a portion of the demand paid, which was a virtual acknowledgment of the debt; and no apology can be offered in thus withholding the balance from the heirs of those who labored and toiled in their country's service. The idea of repudiation, which in later years has become far too common, both with the General and State Governments, should receive the withering rebuke of every friend of his country. It is unjust and cruel, and has no other justification than that might overcomes right.

In 1784, the General Assembly passed an act, authorizing the manumission of negroes, mulattoes, &c., and provided that no persons, negroes or mulattoes, born in the State after the 1st day of the year 1784, shall be slaves for life. The Assembly also repealed the clause contained in an act passed in 1774, permitting slaves brought from Africa to the West Indies, on board any vessel belonging to this their Colony, and that could not be disposed of in the West Indies, to be brought to this State; and provided that in future no negro or mulatto be brought into this State, to be sold or disposed of as a slave.

In 1787, the Legislature of Rhode Island passed an act to prevent the slave-trade from being carried on from this State, and for the encouragement of the abolition of slavery altogether within its jurisdiction.

We have already alluded to this subject in another part of this work, and have shown that the motive for manumitting the slaves of Rhode Island, was simply that their owners had become convinced that they were no longer profitable, but a burden upon them. It was not that there existed more moral purity in Rhode Island, a greater disregard of pecuniary advantage, than was to be found in slaveholding States, that influenced them to this course, but rather that it would be for their interest to do away with a system which entailed far more misery than good.

To the honor of Newport, it has never joined in a crusade against the South, but admitted that the institutions of the South was a matter which belonged exclusively to themselves; and any interference with their domestic concerns, was illegal, unconstitutional, and subversive of that Union, which it should be the bounden duty of every American to sustain and to perpetuate.

A class of men have lately sprung up who have made the discovery, that the laws of Congress conflict with the "*higher law*," and that this being the case the former should be trampled under foot, while the latter should govern man, (only, however, in this particular.) Now, who are these "Simon-pures?" Will it be found on examination that their general conduct is shaped after the moral law of God? In this one point they make use of the "higher law," to effect their own selfish purposes, without the least regard to the principles involved in that law, which if rightfully understood and faithfully executed, would afford scope sufficient for the exercise of their philanthropy, in relieving the wretched and the oppressed at their own doors, without turning aside to hunt out evils existing in slaveholding States. That is a question which exclusively belongs to themselves, and with which we of the North have no right to interfere.

The prophetic warning of the "Father of his Country," the immortal Washington, should be regarded with the deepest interest by every true patriot at the present critical moment, when attempts are making by a class of reckless, unprincipled men, to distract, and divide the Union, the labor of ages:

"The unity of government, which constitutes you one people,

is also dear to you. It is justly so; for it is a main pillar in the edifice of your real independence—the support of your tranquillity at home, your peace abroad, of your prosperity, of that very liberty which you so highly prize. But as it is easy to foresee that, from different causes and from different quarters, much pains will be taken, many artifices employed, to weaken in your minds the conviction of this truth, as this is the point in your political fortress against which the batteries of internal and external enemies, will be most constantly and actively, though often covertly and insidiously directed, it is of infinite moment that you should properly estimate the immense value of your National Union, to your collective and individual happiness; that you should cherish a cordial, habitual, and immoveable attachment to it; accustoming yourselves to think and speak of it as of the palladium of your political safety and prosperity, watching for its preservation with jealous anxiety, discountenancing whatever may suggest even a suspicion that it can in any event be abandoned; and indignantly frowning upon the first dawning of every attempt to alienate any portion of our country from the rest, and to enfeeble the sacred ties which now link together the various parts."

After the reader has reflected calmly on the sentiments so feelingly uttered by the sainted Washington, he must be horror-struck on witnessing the gross outrages, the intrigue, and the duplicity which is practised by political demagogues to effect some sinister purpose. With a self-complacency "from the sublime to the ridiculous," they will justify their acts of abomination, and still boast of their patriotism and love of country, even while the blush of conscious guilt should mantle their cheek But with an effrontery which defies any appeal to reason or justice, they will arrogantly lay claim to honesty of intention, when it is self-evident that not a particle of generosity, nobleness, or patriotism, is to be found in the elements which go to make up their character. When such sentiments are unblushingly made, so repugnant to liberty and the rights of the Confederacy, viz., let the Union be dissolved, they should meet with a simultaneous burst of indignation from every patriot's bosom.

Newport, after having recovered in some degree from the losses incurred in the Revolution, began to push her foreign and domestic commerce. She still had many enterprising merchants left, of whom were Gibbs & Channing, who were large ship-owners. The Mount Hope, of 600 tons, which at that day was one of the largest class of ships, followed the East India trade, and made many successful voyages.

The East India, West India, and Russia trade, were prosecuted with vigor, and the docks and wharves indicated a degree of commercial prosperity highly gratifying to the inhabitants. Now was again heard the music of the "ye-heave-ho," from the active tars who were loading and unloading the numerous vessels at the wharves.

Christopher and George Champlin, were merchants of distinction, as were also Peleg Clarke, Caleb Gardner, Thomas Dennis, on the Point, Stephen T. Northum, who at one period owned ten sail, Audley Clarke, Christopher Fowler, Price & Easton, Earle & Allston, Robert Robinson, Rhodes & Cahoone, Bowen & Ennis, Simon Newton, John Coggeshall, and Gov. Simeon Martin. These were all engaged in foreign commerce, with many others whom we have not enumerated. There was as much enterprise in Newport, at this period, considering her capital, as that of any commercial place in the country. In 1820, the tonnage was estimated at 10,950 tons.

There was also a sugar-refinery, and seven distilleries in full blast, which gave constant employment to mechanics and laborers, many of whom were enabled from their savings to build houses, and at the same time to live comfortable.

There was also a line of New York packets, with splendid cabins, handsomely furnished for that day, which did a very profitable business. Commanders and owners—Edward Peterson, Nicholas Webster, Stephen Cahoone, two Blisses, Adams, John Cahoone (afterwards commander of the Revenue Cutter Vigilant,) &c. Bannister's Wharf, which was then their depôt, exhibited a degree of activity which some now living can remember with satisfaction and pleasure.

There were some five or six packets which ran daily between Newport and Providence. Commanders—Gardner, Heath, Bliven, Northup, Pratt, &c. The honor of bringing the Governor to election, when a Federalist or Whig, devolved on Captain James Gardner, who took great pride in rendering every attention to his passengers. Bannister's Wharf was also the head-quarters of these packets. At the head of the wharf was

Godfrey Wenwood's bake-house, noted for the superior quality of bread and butter-biscuit with which it supplied the numerous packets, and many of the families of the town.

In Thames-street, fronting the wharf, was the Coffee-House, then kept by "Uncle Tom Townsend," as he was familiarly called, which was liberally patronized. On the south side there was a brick walk, enclosed with a light fence, which was a fine promenade; here merchants, masters of vessels, &c., resorted to hear the news, and discuss the affairs of the nation.

The Misses Duncan, from Scotland, kept a toy shop, the only one in the place. It was considered quite a curiosity at that day. It stood where Brownell's tin-shop now stands. Forts Adams, Wolcott, and Rose Island, were garrisoned, and the officers, when in town, assembled at Townsend's Corner, for by that cognomen was it known, until superseded by the name of Pelham-street. Then was heard from Fort Wolcott the beat of the reveille, warbling its sweetest notes along the shore, by those inimitable and graceful performers, the Hoopers, Mulligin, &c.

The town at this period was on the increase; many houses were built on the hill and in other sections of the town; and old English hospitality seemed about to revive. The female portion, at this period, were highly beautiful and accomplished. The celebration of Washington's birth-day by a ball in the evening, was then got up in taste, and was graced by the élite and fashion of Newport, which exhibited traces of the elegance of person and the refinement of manners which preëminently characterized the past. But alas, those days of splendor have fled —fled. In olden time, one of the most pleasant and gratifying amusements was a ride on the Island to Congdon's or Cornell's, speak for coffee, take a turn round the Square or to the Bridge, and return back in time to enjoy the splendid repast furnished by "mine host." It was no unusual thing to meet there a company of twenty or thirty carriages from Newport, including Sam Place's hack, which was in constant requisition in summer; and even at this late period, we remember with delight Aunt Hannah Cornell's "shovel cakes," floating with new made butter, plum-cake, dried beef, etc., sufficient to satisfy the most delicate appetite, all furnished for the small sum of twenty-five cents. Mr. Congdon amassed a sufficiency to purchase him a farm in Connecticut, where he afterwards removed. The house formerly kept by him has been taken down, and a new one now supplies its place. Moses Lawton, Esq., is the present proprietor, but the old associations have nearly vanished by the change.

"Our early days! How often back
We turn on life's bewildering track,
To where o'er hill and valley plays
The sunlight of our early days."

The Spanish brig Minerva, Angel Cifuenter master, bound to Bristol, R. I., was wrecked on Brenton's Reef, on the night of the 24th of December, 1810. The vessel was totally lost. Three pipes of rum and eight casks of Catalonia wine were saved, as appears from the Custom House entries.

This event occurred in one of the most violent storms on record. It blew a perfect hurricane, accompanied with a driving snow-storm, which rendered it impossible to afford the brig and crew the least assistance. It was truly solemn to hear the minute guns, which continued their mournful sound as long as the brig held together. Soon, however, the sound ceased, and the crew were submerged in the briny deep. Ten perished, including every officer, and nine were saved. The shore was covered with the fragments of the wreck, and its contents. There was a large amount of specie on board, which was never recovered, though attempts were made with the diving bell, but without success. Three of the bodies of those who perished were recovered, viz., Captain, mate, and cook, and were buried near by, on the Castle Hill farm.

But no sooner had Newport begun to prosper than the political horizon began to be darkened, and war with Great Britain seemed inevitable. Not being satisfied with having received some severe chastisement, she was determined to invade our rights by impressing American seamen, and by this and other acts of hostility to drive us to take up arms in defence of our sacred liberties, which our forefathers had fought, bled, and died to acquire. These acts were done in violation of treaties entered into by the respective governments. Great Britain has been justly chargeable with aiming to subvert and to overthrow every government which was founded on the principles of liberty and the rights of man. This country stood forth, a beacon light, to shame and confound the principles of monarchical forms of government, and she vainly flattered herself that by dividing the North and South, she might yet effect the subjugation of these United States. But if, when we were short of three millions of people, and without military resources, we could drive them from our shores, what possibility existed of their success? Only, as has been before observed, by dividing the Union. Let Great Britain not imagine, for a moment, that the elements of character which go to make up this confederacy can ever be divided, when a foreign enemy attempts to invade our shores. There may be differences of opinion among ourselves, but when the third party attempts to use their influence, it will be like the quarrels of man and wife—both will fall upon her, and drive her to destruction.

There are redeeming traits of character in this nation, which do not exist elsewhere; and the nations of Europe do not perfectly understand our political institutions. Hence, when controversy—it may be, angry controversy—exists in our national councils, as has been the case of late, they stand ready to believe that the speedy overthrow of this Union is at hand. When we consider, however, that the principles of our republic originated with men of sterling virtue, of noble patriotism, we have reason to believe that the God of heaven will preserve it from every unhallowed touch, and render this nation an instrument in His hands in the accomplishment of His purposes, in the redemption of the world from a despotism which now holds so large a portion of the great brotherhood of mankind, in its iron grasp.

In 1812, the American government formally declared war with Great Britain, when Newport was again exposed to all the apprehensions of being visited by a hostile foe, whose ships of war were frequently seen during its continuance, hovering round her shores. A memorial was sent from Newport to the General Government, setting forth her exposed and defenceless condition in case of an invasion. But little regard was paid to it, for we had hardly a corporal's guard from the General Government. But fortunately, Newport was not much annoyed by the enemy. Our militia and independent companies were all that Newport had to depend upon for protection, for some time after war was declared, the Government having drawn away the United States troops stationed in the forts of her harbor. But notwithstanding this impolitic measure, the inhabitants were resolved to repel any attempts made by the enemy, and their forces were ever ready to repair to their posts, on any alarm. One day, towards evening, the British fleet, which lay but a short distance south of the Island, made demonstrations as though it was their design to enter the harbor. The telegraph, which was erected on high land in the neck, gave the concerted signal, and the inhabitants of the town were thrown into great consternation. The military were instantly mustered, and with beat of drum, and swords flourishing, and bayonets glistening, they marched by the 2d Baptist Church, who that evening had a lecture, which so terrified the congregation that they immediately broke up. It was quite a busy night, but nobody was hurt. The ships wore about, and stood off to their usual place of rendezvous. The British ships obtained all the provisions they required from the farmers who resided near the shore; it was impossible for them, in their defenceless state, to prevent it. And if they had not sold it to them, they would have taken it by force. Fishing boats from Newport were compelled to sell their fish, or have them taken from them by the enemy. It is said that they procured the newspapers wet from the press, by which they obtained the weekly intelligence. The principal seat of war lay South, while the North escaped the horrors of war in a great degree.

On the 6th of December, the inhabitants of Newport had the pleasure of seeing the British frigate Macedonian arrive in the harbor, a prize to the American frigate United States, Captain Stephen Decatur. Her wounded were landed at Coaster's Harbor, and conveyed to the hospital on the Island; they received every attention their situation demanded. At the commencement of hostilities, the British blockaded the coast of America—at first the southern coast, but afterwards it extended as far north as the east end of Long Island Sound. This gave the ports of Massachusetts and Rhode Island the advantage of the neutral trade, until the blockade of the whole American coast.

Newport for a while enjoyed a large share of the trade, and the arrival and clearances of the neutral vessels, the sale of their cargoes, &c., gave employment to many of her citizens. The inhabitants of Newport took the precaution to send from the Island the records of the town, made since the revolution. They were deposited with the town of South Kingston, for safe keeping, where they remained until peace was again proclaimed. The Banks of Newport also removed their specie from the town.

The late Commodore Oliver H. Perry, was a descendant of Thomas Hazard, the first settler, in the sixth degree. Raymond, father of the Commodore, was the son of Judge Freeman Perry, who married the daughter of Oliver Hazard, of South Kingston. The Commodore was named after his maternal great-grandfather, Oliver Hazard.

Commodore Perry had a most expressive and charming countenance, which, added to his graceful form, rendered him an object of admiration. He possessed a noble spirit, a generous expansion of soul, and an understanding chaste and refined; while liberality, gratitude, and generosity, were the aspiring virtues of his heart. He took the most lively interest in the welfare and prosperity of Newport, and through his influence, many natives of the town were elevated to posts of honor and distinction.

The present Commodore, M. C. Perry, brother of the late naval hero, was born in Newport, Rhode Island. This gallant officer has distinguished himself in the Mexican war, and he alone of the five brothers, Oliver H., Raymond, Alexander, and Nathaniel, all of the United States' navy, survives.

We have alluded to the pedigree of Commodore Perry, before adverting to his naval career, which so highly distinguished him, and added fresh laurels to his country's glory. In 1813, he left Newport, with a detachment of seamen from the gunboats in the harbor, to take the command of the American squadron on Lake Erie. On the arrival of Capt. Perry at the lake, there was no squadron there, and it was found that measures must be immediately taken to construct a fleet, which should be able to grapple with the British lion. Capt. Perry had taken with him some ship carpenters from Newport, and such was the rapidity in felling trees, and preparing the requisite materials, that the work was soon completed, and the vessels ready for service.

As this was a battle fought, and a victory won, principally by natives of Newport, it requires a more particular notice. It was on the 10th of September, 1813, when the struggle between the British and American squadrons for the victory, took place. It was a moment of painful anxiety, as, on the issue, very much depended. The American squadron consisted of nine vessels, carrying 54 guns; that of the British, of six vessels, and 63 guns.

There was in all, five hundred and two men in the British squadron, and deducting those on the sick list, we know for certainty that there were four hundred and fifty in health when it went into action. The Americans numbered by the muster-roll, four hundred and fifty, of whom one hundred and sixteen were sick on the morning of the action. Say that sixteen of these sick Americans came on deck and took part in the battle, it would leave us with one hundred fighting men less than the British.

The circumstances under which the battle was fought, gave to the British the full benefit of their substitution of length of gun for calibre.

Perry, before the battle commenced, went round the deck, carefully examining his battery gun by gun, to see that every thing was in order, stopping at each, and exchanging words with the captains. For all he had some pleasant joke, or some expression of encouragement. Seeing some of the Constitution's, he said to them, "Well, boys! are you ready?" "All ready, your honor," was the brief reply, with a general touch of the hat. "But I need not say anything to you," he added, "you know how to beat those fellows!" Passing on, with a smile of recognition, he exclaimed, "Ah, here are the Newport boys! they will do their duty, I warrant." Having mounted on a gun slide, and calling his crew about him, he thus briefly addressed them: "My brave lads," at the same time unfurling a flag, "this flag contains the last words of Capt. Lawrence! Shall I hoist it?" "Ay! ay! sir!" resounded from every voice in the ship, and the flag was briskly run up to the main-royal-mast-head of the Lawrence.

The line of battle was formed at eleven, and at a quarter before twelve, the enemy's flag-ship, Queen Charlotte, opened a tremendous fire upon the Lawrence, the flag-ship of Commodore Perry, which was stationed by the latter full ten minutes before she could bring her carronades to bear. At length she bore up and engaged the enemy, making signals to the remainder of the squadron, to hasten to her support. Unfortunately, the wind was too light to admit of a compliance to the order, and she was compelled to contend, for two hours, with two ships of equal force. By this time the brig had become unmanageable, and her crew, excepting four or five, were either killed or wounded.

While thus surrounded with death, and destruction still pouring in upon him, Perry left the brig, now only a wreck, in an open boat, and heroically waving his sword, passed unhurt to the Niagara, of twenty guns. The wind now rose, and ordering every canvass to be spread, he bore down upon the enemy, passing the enemy's vessels, Detroit, Queen Charlotte, and Lady Prevost on the one side, and the Chippewa and Little Belt on the other, into each of which he poured a broadside ; he at length engaged the Lady Prevost, which received so heavy a fire, as to compel her men to retire below. The remainder of the American squadron, now, one after another, arrived, and following the example of their intrepid leader, now closed in with the enemy, and the battle became general. Three hours finished the contest, and enabled Perry to announce to General Harrison the capture of the whole squadron, which he did in this modest, laconic, and emphatic style, " We have met the enemy, and they are ours." The loss in the contest was great, in proportion to the numbers engaged. The Americans had twenty-seven killed, and ninety-six wounded ; but the British loss was still greater, being about two hundred in killed and wounded.

The following persons, belonging to Newport, were engaged in the battle, viz. :—

OFFICERS :

Commodore Oliver H. Perry,

A. Perry,	Thomas Almy,
Daniel Turner,	Thomas Breeze,
William V. Taylor,	Peleg Dunham,
Thomas Brownell,	Stephen Champlin.

PETTY OFFICERS AND SEAMEN:

George Cornell, Carpenter,	— Allen,
Wilson Mays, ditto's mate,	John Coddington,
Lemuel Palmer,	Isaac Peckham,
George Southwick,	J. Phillips,
Joseph Southwick,	Hannibal Colins, colored,
John Lawton,	

And many others, not recollected at this distant period.

The above list was furnished the author by Capt. Thomas Brownell, who, with the others, highly distinguished himself in that memorable battle.

There was one individual who kept at a respectful distance in the battle, and that was Commodore Elliott. While Perry was engaged in the hottest of the fight, and had to abandon the Lawrence, she having become unmanageable, and all of the crew but four or five either killed or wounded, Elliott labored to pluck the laurels from the victor's brow, to grace his own; but his ungentlemanlike course of conduct, only tended to throw him further into the shade, and exalt Commodore Perry in the estimation of his countrymen.

To show that Commodore Perry was not deceived in the high opinion which he had formed of the "Newport boys," we will give an anecdote, taken from the "Life of Commodore O. H. Perry, by Alex. Slidell Mackenzie, U.S.N." "There was a young man from Newport, named Wilson Mays, and rated a carpenter's mate. He was much reduced by the lake sickness, and entirely unfit for duty: but, while the crew were going to quarters he came on deck. He was directed to go below, as being too sick to render service; but he remarked, that the vessel was short of men, and that he could supply the place of a well-man, by sitting on the pumps, where he was stationed, and using the sounding rod. The poor fellow was killed in that situation."

On the 4th of October, 1813, a small British privateer, called the Dart, which had been hovering about the harbor of Newport, was seen, having in company a ship, a brig, and schooner, which she had detained. The revenue cutter, Vigilant, Capt.

John Cahoone, was manned with volunteers from Newport, and seamen from the gun-boats, and went out in pursuit of her. They soon came up with and carried her, after a slight resistance, and brought her into Newport. The first lieutenant of the Dart was killed. The capture of this privateer was unquestionably the means of saving a large amount of property from being captured.

The sloop Providence, a privateer of eight guns, and manned principally by citizens from Newport, viz.: John Trevett, lieutenant, Peleg Hull, sailing master, Edward Clanning, Henry Clanning, John Scranton, &c. In the course of the war, she captured many valuable prizes; and, in one of her cruizes, she entered the harbor of New Providence, when a detachment of men, under the command of Lieutenant Trevett surprised the fort, and there being but few men in the garrison, resistance was useless. Scranton at once climbed the flag-staff, and flung out the American banner to the breeze. They then dispatched an order to the Governor, to furnish instanter a dinner for thirty officers, or, otherwise, they would turn the guns and batter down the town. The order was quickly complied with, and turtle-soup was one of the dishes provided for the occasion, when the officers regaled themselves to their hearts' content. After remaining in quiet possession of the fort three days, they then spiked the cannon, returned on board, and soon sailed out of the harbor. It was an adroit and gallant movement, considering there were but twenty-eight men, all told, engaged in the enterprise.

In the War of the Revolution, Rhode Island furnished more men, in proportion to her ability, than any of the thirteen Colonies.

A vessel, called the Wampoa, loaded with French brandy, was driven on the Narragansett shore by a British armed vessel; the inhabitants turned out to defend her from the British boats, who were attempting to destroy her. The militia of Narragansett succeeded in saving the cargo, which was brought round to Newport, and sold.

A wealthy gentleman purchased a pipe of it, on account of its superior quality. The society of which he was a member, had long considered that he was in the too frequent practice of using alcoholic drinks; a committee was accordingly appointed to wait on him, and labor to persuade him to cease from the evil and pernicious habit. He received them with all that courtesy which distinguished the gentleman, and as the day was unusually cold, and they had rode quite a distance, he very soon ordered his servant to bring in some of the "Wampoa." They partook of it very lightly, but soon the effect was quite visible, and they forgot entirely the object of their mission. At the next annual meeting there was a gift of $100, which acted as a quietus, and the gentleman died in full fellowship with the society.

In December, the President of the United States, in a message to Congress, says, "The tendency of our commercial and navigation laws, in their present state, to favor the enemy, and thereby prolong the war, is more and more developed by experience. Supplies of the most essential kind find their way, not only to British ports and British armies at a distance, but the armies in our neighborhood, with which our own are contending, derive from our ports and outlets, a subsistence attainable with difficulty, if attainable at all from other sources. Even the fleets and troops infesting our coasts and waters, are by like supplies accommodated, and encouraged in their pedatory and incursive warfare."

Much of this was to be attributed to the want of action, on the part of the Federal Government, in not placing the coast in a proper state of defence. It has been already remarked, that if the people had not disposed of their produce, for a proper equivalent, that the enemy would have taken it by force. An embargo was immediately laid by Congress on all vessels, except neutrals, which were permitted to depart, provided they carried nothing with them but sea stores.

The embargo at once suspended all business, and the streets of Newport wore a sad and gloomy appearance.

On the 30th of May, 1814, a Swedish brig, from St. Barts, attempting to violate the blockade, was chased on shore by the British armed brig, Nimrod, in the East Passage, on Smith's Beach. The next morning the Nimrod came to anchor about a mile from the shore, and sent a barge to set fire to the brig, which they effectually accomplished. Whether they sustained any loss of life, was not exactly known. Every exertion was made by the militia of Middletown, the artillery company of

Newport, under the command of Colonel Fry, and a detachment of seamen from the United States flotilla, to prevent it; but having nothing but small arms with them, their efforts were ineffectual. It would have been far more politic to have taken the brass field-piece belonging to the Artillery Company, the night previous, and thrown up a breast-work which would have prevented the success of the enemy. The Nimrod fired about 200 cannon-balls, one of which killed Mr. John Smith of the Middletown militia, took off the leg of Isaac Basset, a seaman belonging to the flotilla, and knocked down Oliver Wood.

The skill and nerve of Doctor William Turner, was displayed on this occasion, when the *chicken-heart* of another had failed. He in a very few moments amputated and dressed the leg of Basset, proving his superiority as a surgeon. The boys who had assembled on the beach would, the very moment the shot struck, commence digging them out of the sand, and some made a profitable day's work of it, for Greene Burroughs was ready to cash them.

A few days previous to this, the barges of the Nimrod had chased two sloops on shore in the east passage; but the militia of Little Compton having assembled in considerable numbers, they were prevented from taking possession of them. The sloops were got off, and proceeded up the river.

In June, 1814, the General Assembly passed an act authorizing the Town Councils of the several seaport towns to cause the shipping to be removed from their wharves and harbors, whenever by them it should be thought advisable. The Town Council of Newport accordingly, ordered the shipping to be removed, lest it should be an inducement for the enemy to visit Newport.

In July, 1814, the Artillery Company of the town of Newport, under command of Col. Benjamin Fry, took possession of Fort Green, at the north end of Washington-street, on the Point, by order of the United States Government. The company, rank and file, numbered about one hundred and fifty men. Col. Fry was to have the entire command of the fort, and the company to be under the control of the Governor of the State. While the company were in possession of the fort, they kept it in fine order; the parade ground was gravelled, &c., by the labor of the company, and they were ready to defend the town in case of invasion.

DARTMOOR PRISON.

In the course of the war of 1812, one of the sons of Capt. Evan Malborn, was taken prisoner by the British and confined in Dartmoor prison. He wished the keeper to take a note to Lord Stanhope; the keeper seemed greatly surprised at his presumed acquaintance with so illustrious a personage; without condescending to enter into particulars, he urged the forwarding of the note, which was complied with, and on its reception Lord Stanhope repaired to the prison with all possible haste, in his State carriage, attended by his servants in livery, when orders were instantly issued for the liberation of Mr. Malborn from confinement.

Having lost his all, he stood in need of pecuniary aid, which was quickly furnished by Lord Stanhope, who placed at his disposal fifty guineas, in order that he might clothe himself in a manner becoming his rank and as a relative of his wife. He was then taken to his princely mansion, where he tarried for a few weeks, enjoying the munificent hospitality of the noble Lord. When the period for his leaving had arrived, funds were furnished, and a free passport granted him to America. They were chased by a British man-of-war, and in the confusion he forgot his passport, the vessel was run on shore, and he at last arrived home, having, however, again lost his all, which a moment's thought might have prevented. Lord Stanhope's bust still occupies a place over the mantle-piece in the Malborn house, now owned and occupied by James R. Newton, Esq.

The entrance to the harbor was also garrisoned about this time, by the enlisted State Corps, under command of Col. John Wood, father of Dr. Wood of the U. S. Army. These posts were occupied until the proclamation of peace.

Provisions, in the time of the war, were extravagantly high; flour sold for $15 00 per barrel, meal $2 00 per bushel, molasses $2 00 per gallon, sugar and coffee 2s. per lb., and so in proportion with all articles of merchandize. The difficulty of obtaining every kind of articles, owing to the coast being so completely blockaded, was one great cause of the high price of provisions. As there was little or nothing doing in Newport, during a great part of the war, it rendered the condition of the laboring classes very trying. Newport had every reason to wish for the termination of a war so injurious to her commercial prosperity. On the 14th of February, 1815, the joyful news of peace was proclaimed by the merry peal of bells, the roar of cannon, and the display of the military. In the evening, a most splendid and general illumination of the town took place, and a display of paper lanterns with emblematic devices, suspended in the streets, which, notwithstanding the great quantity of snow that had fallen, were thoroughly promenaded by nearly all the inhabitants of the place.

This war, though of short duration, was signalized by many splendid victories, both by land and sea, and proved that Great Britain was not invincible. Having been so long mistress of the ocean, she felt an assurance that she should be able to sweep the ocean of everything that floated, and capture our vessels of war, whenever fortune should throw them in her way. But in this she was most egregiously disappointed. The victories of Hull, Decatur, Porter, and Jones, on the ocean, and Perry and Lawrence on the lakes, evidenced to the British, that they had an enemy to compete with, who proved themselves their superiors. The arrogance of the English nation has never been equalled; assuming to control the destinies of the world, she looked on this growing republic with jealousy, and flattered herself that she might yet be able to humble her pride, and subject her to British domination.

At a meeting of the merchants, manufacturers, ship-owners, and underwriters, in the city of Glasgow, in 1814, it was declared by them: "There is reason to believe, in the short space of twenty-four months, above eight hundred vessels have been captured by a power whose maritime strength we have hitherto held in contempt. The number of privateers that infest our coast, and the audacity with which they approach our shores, and their success, is humiliating to our pride." And they further say: "Our nation have declared the whole coast of America in blockade, and it is mortifying that our ships cannot traverse our own channels in safety. Insurance cannot be effected, but at an excessive premium."

The war of 1812, demonstrated to the British Government our maritime power, and that it was a fruitless attempt to labor to overcome us, and we trust that England will learn a wise lesson from the past, and never again attempt to come in collision with America, whose power is gigantic, and whose overthrow is impossible.

Rhode Island can justly boast of having furnished a Greene for her country, in the war of the Revolution, who in rank and generalship, was second to none, save the immortal Washington himself. And the war of 1812, brought forth and contributed to her country's glory, the mighty energies of her gallant Perry.

Mr. Hunter, who was then Senator to Congress from Rhode Island, in a speech in the Senate of the United States, on the resolutions complimentary of Commodore Perry's victory, said: "While I hold in my hand this resolution expressive of a nation's gratitude toward this youthful Rhode Island hero, for his deliverance of the West, I can point the other to the likeness of that illustrious Rhode Island veteran, (alluding to the likeness of Gen. Greene, in the Senate,) who in the sacred war of the Revolution, saved the South, and accelerated and ascertained the independence of his country."

The sentiments expressed by Mr. Hunter were truly patriotic, evincing his love of country, and that he gloried in the success of the American arms over a foreign enemy.

The brilliant career of Commodore Perry was short. He died in the 34th year of his age, August 23d, A. D., 1819, on board the U. S. schooner, Nonsuch, at the moment the schooner was entering the harbor of Port Spain, in the island of Trinidad. He died of the yellow fever, contracted at Angostura, where he had been transacting business for our Government. His remains were interred on the 24th, at Port Spain, with every mark of respect from Sir Ralph Woodford, Governor of Trinidad, and the inhabitants of the place.

The body was landed from the John Adams, where it had been removed from the schooner, under a salute of minute guns from that ship. When it reached the shore, the Fort of St. Andrews continued the ceremony, until the long procession, accompanied by the band of the 3d West India regiment, playing the dead march in Saul, reached the burial place. After the funeral, the following card was published by the American officers:

"The officers of the United States vessels, John Adams and

Nonsuch, tender their grateful acknowledgments to the inhabitants of Port Spain, for their kind and respectful attention to the funeral rites bestowed on the body of their late Commander, Commodore Perry."

The disposition manifested by all classes, was highly in unison with their feelings, and merited their warmest thanks.

Commodore Perry, at the time of his death, was engaged in executing the duties of a "highly flattering command, involving diplomatic and naval functions of critical nicety and importance." President Monroe, in his message to Congress in December following, referring to several acts and orders for the protection of our commerce, and the suppression of the slave trade, says, "In the execution of the duty imposed by these acts, and of high trust connected with it, it is with deep regret I have to state the loss which has been sustained by the death of Commodore Perry. His gallantry in a brilliant exploit in the late war, added to the renown of his country; his death is deplored as a national misfortune."

The remains of Commodore Perry arrived at Newport from Trinidad, in the sloop of war Lexington, and were landed on Overing's Wharf, on Monday, Nov. 27, 1826, and on the following Monday, Dec. 4th, were interred in the common burial place, with the honors due to his rank and character. The military companies of Providence, Pawtucket, and Bristol, attended the procession with the companies of Newport. The Governor, and other officers of the State, with several distinguished naval and military officers, were present, and the vast assemblage of citizens testified their respect to the character of their fellow-townsman. The State of Rhode Island has since erected a monument in honor of the memory of this lamented and gallant officer.

The 23d of September, 1815, was rendered memorable by a most awful and destructive gale, which swept away and laid prostrate almost everything in its course. The Newport Mercury says: "The gale commenced early in the morning, at northeast, and continued increasing in violence, the wind varying from northeast to southeast, and southwest, until about eleven o'clock, when it began to abate, and about one o'clock the danger from the wind and tide was over." At Newport, the tide rose three feet and a half higher than it had ever been known before

Two dwelling houses, and nine stores and workshops, on the Long Wharf, were swept away by the violence of the wind and tumult of the waves; and those that withstood the power of this desolating scourge, were rendered almost untenable, by vessels, lumber, &c., driving against them. Several of the stores carried away, contained a considerable amount of property, nearly the whole of which was lost.

In one of the buildings carried away on the Long Wharf, five persons perished. The wharves on the Point, and most of the stores with them, were swept away. The wharves in other parts of the town, also, with the stores on them, sustained considerable injury, and everything moveable on the wharves was swept away. In some of the stores, the water was four feet deep.

A large three-story store, containing hemp, flour, &c., was lifted from its foundation, and floated into the harbor. The steeples of the 1st and 2nd Congregational churches were partially blown down, and the roofs of the Episcopal and First Congregational churches were partly carried away. At the Beach, the storm was sublimely awful; the sea broke sixty feet, extending to Easton's pond. Mr. John Irish, who had repaired to the beach to secure his boats and seines, was swept away and perished.

The stone bridge, connecting the Island with Tiverton on the main, was damaged to the amount of $20,000, and rendered wholly impassable. The draw and toll-house were carried away; a new channel, about three hundred feet wide, was made at the West end of the bridge, and where the toll-house had stood, the water was thirty feet deep at low tide. The light-house on Point Judith was swept away, with several other houses in its vicinity. The Rhode Island Republican says: "So great and general has been the devastation of property, that it is found impossible to give a correct account of the extent of the damage."

After the storm, it was found that the outside of windows were covered with a fine salt, conveyed from the ocean through the air. This was also noticed for many miles inland, after the gale. The shipping in the harbor were driven from their anchorage, and went ashore. Some lying at the wharves, were lifted on them by the violence of the wind and tide, and left there. Four sloops were thrown on the Long Wharf, and a sloop loaded with wood went over the wharf into the cove. No one, unless they had been a spectator of the scene, could form an adequate conception of its wide-spread desolations. If the tide had not turned as it did, it would have swept everything before it.

INSTITUTIONS HIGHLY CREDITABLE TO THE TOWN.

There have been many improvements made in and about Newport, of late years, and there are several flourishing institutions, highly creditable to the town. Among them the Savings' Bank, the Asylum for the Poor, and the Public Schools stand the most prominent. The Savings' Bank of Newport was incorporated by Charter granted by the General Assembly at the June session, 1819, and went into operation soon after. It is a singular circumstance that the success of similar establishments in other places, induced a philanthropic citizen to procure every information necessary for the establishment of a Savings' Bank in Newport; when, by an article published in one of the newspapers of the town, he invited those who were inclined to favor the undertaking, to meet at the State House, and take the subject into consideration. At this meeting, ten or twelve persons only assembled; they chose a chairman and secretary, and the information that had been received was communicated. A committee of correspondence was appointed to obtain further information from similar establishments, and the meeting adjourned. There were several subsequent meetings, at which not more than six or seven persons, including the chairman and clerk, attended. At these meetings, the committee of correspondence reported progress, and the meeting was adjourned from time to time, until the charters, by-laws, &c., of several institutions of the kind had been received, and every necessary information obtained and reported by the committee of correspondence. A committee of three was then appointed to draft a charter for the Savings' Bank of Newport, and a petition to the General Assembly to pass an act granting it, and a committee was appointed to obtain signatures to the petition, and present it to General Assembly. Notice was given in the papers when the next meeting would be held, and the object of it ; and all who were favorable to the project were invited to attend. This caused a meeting of a considerable number of citizens who were favorable to the undertaking, but who had not before attended the meetings. They were pleased with the plan, and the progress made in the establishment, and joined heartily in its support. At this period, a number of the Directors of the Banks in Newport came forward, and used every argument in their power to persuade those who originated the project, and those who had united with them, to abandon it—assigning as a reason, that there would not be sufficient deposited to render it profitable. The charter was granted, and at the first meeting of the Corporation, twenty-four Directors were chosen, all of whom, except one, accepted the appointment. At a subsequent meeting of the Directors, they elected a President, and appointed a Treasurer and Secretary, and the Savings' Bank of Newport went into operation. At the first meeting of the Board, more than $1,000 had been deposited. Since its establishment, hundreds of thousands of dollars have been deposited, and occasionally withdrawn with interest, by depositors. At this time, September, 1850, the number of deposits are near one thousand (nine hundred and eighty-six), and the amount in deposits is $163,395. The depositors are chiefly minors, girls out at service, laborers, seamen, and operatives in the manufactories, saved from their earnings. The money deposited is invested in bonds and mortgage on real estate, and in bank stock. The interest on the sum now in deposit amounts, at 6 per cent., to over $9,800 per year. The institution, since its establishment, has never paid less than 5 per cent. interest per annum, to the depositors. At this time, and for some time past, a semi-annual dividend is declared, of 3 per cent on all sums that have been in three months after a dividend has been declared; that which is not called for is, at the end of three months, added to the sum deposited by each depositor. The institution is well managed, and has attained a high reputation The philanthropic citizen who first proposed its establishment, is a descendant from one of the ancient families of Newport, born before the Revolution, being now near eighty years of age.

He was chosen as one of the first Directors of the Bank, and has been annually reëlected from that time to the present.

THE ASYLUM FOR THE POOR.

This is an establishment worthy of commendation and praise, as a humane institution, highly creditable to the town. The former Poor establishment was, for many years, an alms-house and work-house connected. It was located on the west side of the common burying ground, where the abject poor, the lame, the blind, and the insane were sent by the overseers of the poor. Those who were able to do something towards their support, were employed (by the keeper appointed by the town) in the work-house, in spinning, picking oakum, &c. To those whose feelings of humanity induced them occasionally to visit the establishment, the inmates always complained of ill fare, and of not having sufficient food. Be this as it may, they were meanly clad, and all who were sent there went stricken with the idea that their next removal would be to the adjacent burial ground. A part of those who were able to hobble out, were allowed daily, except Sundays, to roam the streets in their rags, and the town was constantly, to its disgrace, infested with beggars, to the great annoyance of the citizens and visiting strangers. Those poor who could partly support themselves by their labor, were allowed pensions by the town, of from fifty cents to a dollar a week, to aid them in their support, which, together with the alms-house expenses, occasioned a heavy tax on the people, of which they complained, but knew not how to remedy. It was for many years in contemplation to alter and improve the plan of the establishment for the poor, and the mode of their support. Many plans were suggested from time to time, but none that met with general approbation; they were generally objected to, as being more expensive in their erection and support than the town could afford. At length, the same philanthropic and humane citizen who first proposed the establishment of the Savings' Bank, and who by his perseverance had got it into successful operation, encouraged by the favor with which it had been received by the public, after obtaining information in regard to the establishments for the poor, and the manner and expense of their support, in various places, communicated the information obtained to those acquaintances who were favorable to an improvement in the condition of the poor, and proposed a plan which was approved. It was proposed that a new house should be built for the accommodation of the poor, in a suitable location, with land attached, on which those who were able to work might be profitably employed; to do away with the odious idea of an alms-house; to call it "The Newport Asylum for the Poor"; to abolish the pension system, and oblige all who required aid from the town to go to the Asylum for their support.

This plan being arranged, a Town Meeting was called, at which it was submitted for the consideration of the freemen; the meeting was numerously attended, and the plan was generally approved, and a committee appointed to visit several lots belonging to the town, and also Coaster's Harbor Island, and to recommend such a location as they should think most suitable for the establishment.

The committee, at the suggestion of the projector of the plan, first visited Coaster's Harbor Island, and after considering the advantages and disadvantages of the place, unanimously recommended it, on every account, as the most suitable place for its location.

At a subsequent Town Meeting, the report of the committee was received and approved, and a building committee appointed to draw a plan of said building, and estimate the expense. The edifice was to be built of stone, of which there was abundance on the spot. The projector of the plan was one of that committee, and drew the plan and elevation of the Asylum, which the Town adopted, and according to which it was erected, with the exception of the cupola, which was objected to as an unnecessary expense, but has since been added. The plan of the building is considered admirably calculated for the purpose for which it was intended, containing every necessary apartment for the accommodation of the poor, as well as the family of the keeper, and ample room for the whole.

Coaster's Harbor Island, on which the Newport Asylum is erected, belonged to the Town; it contains about ninety acres of upland, and the shore affords an abundance of sea manure.

Those who are able to labor are employed upon the farm, which is in a good state of cultivation, and the products go far towards the support of the establishment.

The island is situated about one mile north of the compact part of the town, and separated from it by water, which is not fordable, about ten rods wide, which prevents the inmates of the Asylum from visiting the town without permission.

The Asylum was completed, and ready for the reception of the poor in 1822 ; before their removal to their new habitation, they were well cleaned, and clad, and left their dirt at the old establishment. The pension system was abolished, and all those pensioners, who chose to avail themselves of the support offered them, were removed to the new establishment. The citizens of Newport have the pleasure to enjoy the complete success of the new system, as an amelioration of the condition of the poor, as well as a great saving of expense in their support; and to see them well supplied with wholesome food, comfortably lodged and clothed, and the town relieved from the disgrace of having the streets infested with beggars, as formerly, to the great scandal of the citizens and annoyance to strangers.

No spot can be more charmingly situated than the one selected ; it rather resembles the country-seat of a gentleman, than an Asylum for the poor. Let the interior resemble the exterior.

As this Asylum was established expressly for the improvement of the condition of the virtuous poor, the vicious and the unprincipled should be kept separate, and not suffered to associate with them, or to eat at the same table. Let the Commissioners labor to make this institution a model, worthy of imitation by every city and town in the country.

The whole establishment, including land, is worth about $15,000. The Overseer of the Poor distributes the rent of a lot of land, containing about seven acres, left by Mr. Freebody, and also the interest of the "Derby Fund," to such persons as he may think proper. And, the Commissioners of the Asylum distribute, in the same way, the dividends of one share in the New England Commercial Bank, left by the late Mrs. Sarah Redwood.

PUBLIC SCHOOLS.

We have already alluded to the interest which was taken by the town of Newport, in the promotion of education, as early as 1640 ; and private schools have ranked as high in this place as that of any section of the country.

The Newport Academy, Col. Levi Tower, Principal, had a very extensive popularity. Students from the South, as well as the New England States, were to be found under his instruction and guidance. The higher, as well as the common branches of education were taught. In penmanship the pupils excelled. Many of them are occupying places in counting-houses, banks, &c., in the various cities in the Union. Once a week, the older male scholars engaged in declamation, at which their parents, and other spectators were present, and who were both highly amused and gratified. It is no flattery to say of Col. Tower, that the school under his supervision, has never been excelled, if equalled, by any other in the State. It was the *ne plus ultra !*

In March, 1825, the freemen of Newport decided, by vote, to establish free schools in the town ; and a Committee, in May following, recommended to erect two school houses, to obtain the Church school house, and thus establish three free schools in the town.

In 1820, a Committee of the town reported on a resolution of the General Assembly of this State, calling on the several towns for information on the subject of free schools, and recommended that the town instruct their representatives in General Assembly, to unite their efforts, to procure an act for such a general system of public schools, as in their wisdom they may devise.

On the 14th of July, 1826, the corner stone of the town school house, No. 1, was laid by Lieutenant-Governor Charles Collins. The Rev. Mr. Gammell offered an appropriate prayer on the occasion.

A Committee was appointed in April, 1826, to investigate and enquire into money, said to be due from the town, for or on account of school lands. In their report they say, " The undersigned, a Committee of said town, appointed on the 3d of

September, 1825, to inquire into the evidence of the title of the town of Newport to the Newtown, or school lands, on the subject of which lands a former Committee reported on the 16th of May last, from which report, and other representations then made, some of the freemen were induced to believe that the town received the aforesaid land as a gift, on condition to apply the whole income to the education of the youth of said town, and that the town was, in law and equity, bound for the faithful performance of the same; and as the town had sold most of the lands in question soon after the Revolutionary War, to pay the debts of the town, they must now make good by taxation the trust committed to them by the donor. It was also reported by that Committee, that the town was indebted to said education fund, in the sum of $51,283 34." The Committee, after detailing sundry acts and resolutions of the town, relative to said Newtown or school lands, gleaned from the old mutilated records of the town, among which is a report of a Committee made to the town in 1763, which Committee say, "Upon examining the town records, we found that the said land was purchased by the town of one Bartholomew Hunt, the 17th day of December, 1661, for which they gave him in exchange a lot of one hundred acres, now lying in Middletown." They say, "Thus it appears that the town, in the year 1661, exchanged one hundred acres for the tract since called Newtown, or school land, being the property in question. If your Committee were allowed in any conjecture respecting the hundred acres exchanged, they submit the subjoined extract, from 'Callender's Centenary Sermon,' acknowledging at the same time, that it is but a connection of remote and detached circumstances, resting as much on possibilities as probabilities." The extract from Callender's Sermon has been already noticed, in a former part of this work, showing that the town appropriated one hundred acres of land, for a school, for the encouragement of the poorer sort to train up their youth in learning, &c., at an early period of the settlement.

In March, 1827, the town passed an act to establish a School Fund, and appointed three Commissioners of said fund; one to go out every year, and a new one to be chosen in his place, who are to receive all donations and bequests thereafter given for public schools, as also the bequest of the late Constant

Taber; likewise all moneys received for licenses, auction tax, and estates taken by the town for want of known heirs; and directed that the remainder of the said Newtown lot be sold, and the proceeds placed in the fund.

During the January session of 1829, the General Assembly of Rhode Island, appropriated $10,000 per ann., for the support of public schools, to be paid over to the several towns, according to their respective population, under the age of sixteen years; and authorizing the several towns to raise by tax, in each year, as the majority of the freemen in Town Meeting shall judge proper, a sum not exceeding double the amount to be received out of the general Treasury. The number of schools have since been increased.

On July 4th, 1826, Major John Handy read the Declaration of Independence, from the steps of the State House, in Newport, that being the place where, fifty years before, it was read to the people by the same gentleman. The steps were decorated with an arch of flowers. Major Handy addressed the multitude as follows: "My respected fellow-citizens,—at your united request, I appear before you in this public station, at an age when it would seem advisable that I should remain a silent spectator of the performances of this day, a day which, half a century past, secured to us our independence and prosperity; and no nation more prosperous! My own feelings on this occasion I have sacrificed, to gratify your wishes. The recollection of past scenes of the last fifty years, rushes in succession on my mind, with a hope and belief that the mantle of charity will be thrown over my imperfections; and under that impression I shall proceed to the performance of the part required of me." After the Declaration was read, a hymn was sung in the tune of "Old Hundred," the whole multitude uniting their voices, with a fervency and zeal which gave it a most sublime and happy effect.

It is a most painful truth, and one from which the heart recoils with horror, that the course which has been pursued for a few years by a certain class, calling themselves Philanthropists, has had an indirect tendency to nearly, or quite, obliterate from the mind of the rising generation, all remembrance of the glorious events connected with American Independence. Such profess to have the entire monopoly of all the benevolence, but which is rather the product of ambition, a desire of self-aggrandizement even at the expense of the liberties of the Union. The roar of cannon, accompanied with the soul-stirring sound of martial music, animating the heart of every true patriot, who loves liberty in preference to slavery, and the free exercise of his mind to all the vain honors and distinctions which wealth confers, if purchased by the relinquishment of his inalienable rights, dearer by far to him than even life itself—has no charms for such stoical minds.

We have no hesitation in saying that the abolition of the Christian Sabbath, would not more effectively efface from the heart all regard to the precepts of Jesus Christ, and render the land a waste howling wilderness, and the people mere heathens, than the forgetfulness and neglect of observing the national jubilee, would go to the overthrow of the liberties of this country. It is by a recurrence to the event that the flame of liberty is fanned and made to burn more brightly on the altar of the heart. Auspicious day! let the mind of every American ascend to heaven in triumphant songs of praise! Let the bugle sound loud and long, through the vallies and reverberate over the hills of our dear native Isle: "Independence now! and Independence forever!"

No day in the calendar ever gave us such intense delight, as the Fourth of July, when party spirit becomes merged in the one glorious event. It was the social meeting of the American brotherhood on the broad platform of universal liberty and the rights of man. But in some sections how changed the scene! Shall the political horizon continue to be dimmed by one cloud to mar the festivities of the day? Rather let us regard the views entertained by the elder Adams, the Colossus of American liberty, and not suffer his prophetic language to fail of its accomplishment:

"When we are in our graves, our children will honor it. They will celebrate it with thanksgiving, with festivity, with bonfires, and illuminations. On its annual return they will shed tears, copious, gushing tears, not of subjection and slavery, not of agony and distress, but of exultation, of gratitude, and of joy."

Let us prize this bulwark of constitutional liberty, and discountenance every attempt to undermine its foundation, in which consists our glory, our happiness and our independence.

Major John Handy was a merchant of Newport. He was the son of Charles Handy, Esq., a distinguished citizen of Newport. He entered the Revolutionary army, to defend the honor of his country, and was promoted to the rank of Major. He died in Newport in 1828, aged 72 years.

The late Thomas Handy, Esq., brother of the Major, was a gentleman of dignified and courteous manners. He married Mary, the daughter of John Henry Overing, an eminent merchant of Newport. Mrs. Handy was truly a most estimable lady, endowed with those rare virtues and accomplishments which rendered her an ornament to society. Of a large and highly interesting family of children, but four survive her. Mary, who married her cousin, James Overing, of Westchester, N. Y.; Matilda, widow of Mr. Levi of Philadelphia; Robert, of the U. S. Navy; and Augustus, the wife of Mr. Sinclair of the city of New-York, a Counsellor at Law.

These reminiscences, though highly interesting in their character, yet nevertheless recall to mind solemn and affecting thoughts on the ravages produced by time, in the domestic circle, and should teach a salutary lesson of the fading and transitory nature of all earthly glory. As the Handy family held an important position in society, and was highly regarded, a mere glance at their history we view as important in a work of this kind.

General Charles T. James, whose recent election to the Senate of the United States has created such an unusual degree of interest in the public mind, stands intimately and prominently connected with Newport, and we have felt called upon to notice his origin.

His grandfather John James, and his maternal grandfather, Charles Tillinghast, settled in Newport at an early period. His grandfather Tillinghast, was a devoted patriot; he was in Sullivan's expedition on Rhode Island, and was subsequently seized in his house at night by a band of British soldiers, and carried off. His sad fate was never satisfactorily known; it was, however, reported that he had died of the small pox.

Silas James, the father of the General, was born in Newport, and although a lad, was also in the expedition with his grandfather; he afterwards removed to West Greenwich, where he improved a farm, and was repeatedly elected to represent that town in General Assembly, and was also chosen Judge of the Court of Common Pleas, which office he held for many years.

There were six of the name of James, engaged in Sullivan's expedition, which proves them to have been men of the right stamp, and eminently fitted for that stormy period.

In 1827, the Newport Association of Mechanics and Manufacturers, appointed a committee to receive donations in books, or otherwise, for the purpose of establishing a library for the use of the members, and the apprentices of members. For more than thirty years the funds of this Society, although never extensive, have been invariably and zealously devoted to the most beneficial purposes. This Association, as far as its resources would permit, has clothed the naked, fed the hungry, and instructed the ignorant. It has ever been rich in disposition to do good, given to hospitality, and distributing to the necessities of the indigent.

THE ASIATIC CHOLERA.

The Asiatic Cholera made its first appearance in August, at Jessore, a considerable city about one hundred miles north of Calcutta. After desolating some of the fairest portions of Asia, it penetrated the northern part of Europe, and sweeping over a great part of that continent, reached the British Isles. It has mastered every variety of climate, has passed mountains and swept over seas, proving equally fatal amid the burning sands of Arabia, and on the frozen shores of the White sea; and in the space of less than fifteen years has swept off more than fifty millions of the human race!

This dreadful disorder, two or three years previous to its appearance on this continent, was scarcely known to exist by a great portion of the American people. It first began to attract attention here, when it was known to have reached England, and its destructive ravages in Paris created alarm; but the hope was entertained that the Atlantic would prove a barrier to its approach. But when that barrier was passed, and it was known that this destroying angel had begun its march of death on this continent, a general consternation prevailed through the land.

It soon reached Albany and New-York, from Canada, and shortly spread dismay and death among the inhabitants of many of our cities.

At the June Session of the General Assembly of Rhode Island of that year, they recommended a public fast. The preamble of the act says:

" *Whereas*, That scourge to the human race, the Asiatic Cholera, has made its appearance on this continent, and as no human exertions can effectually resist the approach of this threatening pestilence which 'walketh in darkness and wasteth at noon day,' it becometh us humbly and devoutly to acknowledge our dependence upon, and to implore the aid of Him in whose hand our breath is, and whose mercies endureth forever; therefore,

" Resolved, that Thursday, the 5th day of July next, be, and is hereby set apart, as a day of humiliation and prayer to Almighty God, that he would stay this plague, and avert the appalling visitations of his judgments."

Newport was remarkably favored; but few deaths occurred, and those originated from imprudence. And it was remarked that the health of our cities, other than this disorder, was better than what is usually the case at the same season of the year.

In 1849, when this disease again made its appearance in this country, sweeping off very many in our larger cities, not one instance of death from the disease occurred at Newport. And when it is considered that there were some four thousand strangers visiting at Newport, which, added to her own population, made the aggregate of 13,000, it is most certainly an evidence of the remarkable healthiness of the climate.

The present population of the Island, according to the census of 1850, is 12,228, viz.: Newport, 9,963; Middletown, 832, and Portsmouth, 1,833. The fertility of the Island is, perhaps, unexampled; this is owing, in a great measure, to the facilities for obtaining manure, which consists of Menhaden fish and sea-weed, which are abundant, and which seem particularly adapted to the soil. The exports have consisted of potatoes, onions, apples, pork, &c. Farms distant from Newport, are usually from one hundred to one hundred and fifty dollars per acre, according to their location and the quality of the soil.

The farms generally are small, having been cut up and

divided from time to time. This, however, is preferable, as a few acres, well cultivated, will yield far more than a larger quantity, partially cultivated. It was the saying of Virgil, "great farms to look at, and small farms for profit." As an illustration of this truth, it may be found in the proceeds of the model farm of the late Judge Child, of Portsmouth, which contains about forty acres of land. It was stated to the author, that he had realized $1000 per annum, independent of his living. Farming is a most honorable employment, and the most independent which can possibly be followed. It is said that when the early Romans praised a good man, they called him an agriculturist and a good husbandman; and that on a certain occasion, when a distinguished citizen of Rome was visited by a foreign ambassador, he was found cooking his repast of vegetables raised by his own hand from his seven acre farm.

It must appear obvious to the mind which has given the least attention to the subject, that more land is held in possession than is scientifically cultivated, and which is rather an expense than a profit to the owner. If the farms on the Island were still subdivided and parcelled out, it would not only increase the population, but also be far more productive, as there would be less land to manure, and a greater attention bestowed on the subject.

Those seeking a country-place, may take for their creed, that

Man wants but little land below,
Nor wants that little dear.

The town of Portsmouth, a few years since, purchased a farm containing about sixty acres of land, as an Asylum for the Poor. It is most delightfully located, and every necessary comfort is furnished the inmates, which their condition requires. It was an act highly creditable to the town, as it went to ameliorate the evils of poverty, to which all are exposed in this world of vicissitude and change. Dyre's Island lays nearly opposite the Asylum.

Since penning these thoughts, we have met with the Report of Thomas R. Hazard, Esq., on "The Condition of the Poor and Insane in Rhode Island," in which he has presented a most melancholy picture of the treatment of the poor in the Portsmouth Asylum. For the honor of the town, if such be the painful fact disclosed, we would indulge the hope that an amelioration of their condition may at once be effected.

Let it not be said, that in the nineteenth century, and more especially on the island of Rhode Island, where toleration has been so highly enjoyed, that a want of principle exists towards a class of unfortunate beings, who have such strong claims on our sympathy and compassion. All are liable to misfortune in this changing world, and the prosperous to-day may be in adversity to-morrow. This shows the necessity for those having the supervision of the poor, to treat them with that degree of kindness which they themselves would expect, were they in the same unhappy condition. And none can lay claim to the character of a Christian, who do not feel called upon to soothe and mitigate the evils of poverty, so far as in them lie, which we conceive to be the test of Christian character, agreeable to the teachings of the Saviour, recorded in the 25th chapter of Matthew.

Mr. Hazard has shown a commendable spirit, in thus devoting his time and attention to the investigation of this most important subject; which has already led to an improvement in the condition of the poor, in many of the towns in our State. God speed the day, when Rhode Island shall be found foremost in every good work to advance the happiness of man. We take pleasure in being able to state that a marked improvement has taken place in the Portsmouth Asylum, since the publication of Mr. Hazard's Report, and to him belongs the credit.

In 1808, a deposit of coal was discovered in Portsmouth, by Doct. Case, of Newport. It was worked for a time, and then abandoned. It was subsequently renewed by a company from Boston, but being impregnated with iron, it was found difficult to ignite. One of the proprietors called on a lawyer of New-York, who was rather of an eccentric character, to recommend the article, which he cordially did. But the certificate proved to be such a one as would not be likely to advance the sale of the article. It was as follows: "At the general conflagration of the universe, the most secure place to be found, would be the coal mine at Portsmouth, R. I."

More recently a company from Providence have taken it in hand, and have succeeded in finding a better quality of coal. For manufacturing purposes it is said to answer as well as the anthracite, and at far less expense. The excavations are very extensive. Many families in the neighborhood now burn it. Since the mining operations were first commenced, a large amount of capital has been sunk in the enterprise.

RECORDS OF FIRE DEPARTMENT.

Heart Fire Club was established about 1790. The number of members was limited to fifty; one captain, one lieutenant, a treasurer, and clerk. The object of this Association was to aid in the preservation of property in time of fire. An annual dinner was provided for the Association, and the expenses were defrayed by an equal assessment upon the members. No member was to be excused, unless by a vote of the Club. The return of the anniversary was looked forward to with great interest, when all participated in the good things which a kind Providence had furnished. The evening was spent in the relation of anecdotes and recitations, occasionally interspersed with songs, and was the means of strengthening the bond of union among the fraternity.

Perhaps there is no town of equal size where the inhabitants are so careful of fire as Newport, and where the firemen are more vigilant and active in suppressing it, whenever it occurs. The estimate of losses for the last hundred years, is comparatively trifling, and when it is considered that Newport has been settled for more than two hundred years, that not a building was ever consumed in Thames-street, may well be looked upon as almost miraculous. We question whether another such instance can be found on record.

Insurance Companies may feel quite safe in taking riskes on property in Newport. We would suggest, that it would be good policy for the town to establish an Insurance Office, and hence retain the premiums, which now go to build up other places.

John W. Davis, Esq., Foreman of Engine Company, No. 1, has kindly furnished the following valuable information, being a statement, from the books of the Company, of all the Fires, of any consequence, which have occurred in Newport, for one hundred years, viz. :—

FIRES FROM 1749 TO 1848.

1749. December, Ellery house, on the Hill.
1759. December, Goddard's house, on the Point.
1762. February, Fire on Long Wharf.
1763. September, Dillingham's shop.
1764. October 26th, Dr. Stiles' Meeting House, (the Central now,) and Trinity Church, both struck by lightning.
1766. June 7, Colonel Malborn's mansion, on the site of J. Prescott Hall's new house.
October 1st, Green's sugar house.
1769. June 28th, Malborn house.
1770. June 21st, Green's sugar house.
December 28th, Rodman and Dennis' houses.
1771. January 18th, Lyon's coopers' shop, Green's sugar house, and sundry other buildings consumed.
August 1st, Cole's tanyard.
1763. February, Nicholas Easton's house.
1774. January 9th, Moore and Anthony's shop consumed.
1780. September 7th, Samuel Gardner's stock and fodder.
1781. July 13th, House of John Handy, in New lane, (now Mary-street.)
1784. September 21st, Larken's barn, with five tons of hay and one horse burnt.
1786. March 24th, M. Hookey's house, in Cannon-street.
1787. December 11th, John Hadwin's store, on Long Wharf.
June 29th, David Melville's pewterer's shop, slight damage.
1788. October 15th, Ebenezer Richardson's house, slight damage to the roof.
1789. December 2d, Noah White's blacksmith's shop burnt down.
1791. April 16th, John Hadwin's and J. Richardson's.
1792. January 21st, Tanyard and bark-house of William Tripp, and store of Governor Collin's consumed.
1795. November 17th, Jonathan Southwick's boat-builder's shop burnt down.
November 24th, John Frazier's school house, slight damage.

1797. August 7th, Francis Brinley's ropewalk.
December 22d, Job Cahoone's house, in Thames-street, slight damage.

1798. December 6th, Blacksmith's shop on Long Wharf consumed, and a man named Lewis was burnt up; also houses owned by Capt. George and John Shaw; Mr. Southwick's boat builder's shop torn down.

1800. October 25th, Mr. Delano's house and shed destroyed; also a negro man, belonging to Mr. Delano.

1803. April 22d, Nicholas Hart's barn burned down, corner of Church and Spring-streets.

1810. March 11th, Captain Thomas White's house, in Church-street, damaged.
October 14th, Jas. Westgate's bakehouse, slight damage.
December 17th, Mr. Wilson's house on the Point, slight damage.

1811. April 13th, Stable in Broad-street, owned by Mrs. Pitman, occupied by Edward Simmons, burnt down.

1819. February 7th, W. S. N. Allan's bakehouse, on Long Wharf, slight damage.
October 6th, Daniel W. Barker's house, in south part of Spring-street, burnt down.

1822. April 7th, Peleg Battle's house, on the Point, slight damage.
August 16th, John C. Almy's barn and dwelling house, belonging to A. Robbins, on Long Wharf, consumed.

1826. November 21st, Boat builder's shop, and house of Jon. Southwick, on Long Wharf, consumed.

1827. July 7th, Henry Ruggles' distillery, considerable damage.

1829. January 3d, Joseph Joslen's school house, Church street, slight damage.

1834. January 8th, Dr. B. W. Case's house, foot of Parade, slight damage.
March 22d, House belonging to the Seventh-day Baptist Society, in Thames-street, slight damage.

1835. August 8th, Dry goods store, occupied by William P. Hall, and owned by heirs of William Langley, and now occupied by Anderson's barber's shop, slight damage.
October 1st, Newport steam factory, slight damage.

1836. June 28th, Dry goods store of H. E. Brewster, (now occupied by W. H. Peek,) goods damaged.

1838. February 23d, Carpenter's shop on Beach-street, owned by Josiah Tew, consumed.

February 28th, Dwelling house in South Touro-street, owned by the heirs of Anthony Dixon, consumed.

August 2d, Thomas R. Hazard's factory; damage about $10,000.

1840. January 1st, House in Elm-street, occupied by William Greenman; damage $350.

February 17th, Store of D. S. Halloway, Ferry Wharf, damage $100.

1841. April 7th, Benjamin Chase's carpenter's shop, damage $200.

November 11th, Silas H. Cottrell's workshop, Thames-street, damage $300.

1842. February 17th, John H. Gilliat's new house, Touro-street, damage $1000.

May 27th, E. W. Lawton's wood-house, nearly destroyed.

September 2d, Elder Henry Burdick's stable destroyed.

September 6th, Thomas Townsend's barn destroyed, damage $600.

September 23d, Tower's school house, rear of Clarke-street.

September 24th, Building near Bath road, destroyed.

December 16th, John Bigley's house, Bridge-street, damage $200.

1844. February 26th, Drying house, on Woolen Mill Wharf, damage $250.

March 21st, Same building, damage $300.

1845. March 13th, Woolen factory, damage $600.

August 3d, Ocean House destroyed; loss $60.000. One life lost.

1846. January 9th, Woolen factory, damage $200.

1847. December 26th, First Baptist Meeting-house, damaged $200.

1848. April 17th, Store on Ferry Wharf, owned by Samuel Carr, damaged $250.

May 19th, Store on Long Wharf, occupied as a boat-builder's shop, damaged $650.

1848. July 25th, Four boat builder's shops, and one dwelling-house, on Long Wharf, destroyed ; loss $5,500.

October 4th, William A. Handy's house in Fair-street, damaged $200.

THE NARRAGANSETT TRIBES.

We have in this work labored to present the most interesting events connected with the history of this Island. Undoubtedly the lapse of time has buried much of value in oblivion. This was to be expected ; but sufficient has been recorded to show the reader the distinguished position which Newport occupied in the past, and of which there are some traces still remaining. When it is considered that little more than two centuries have elapsed since this Island was the residence of the red man, when the war-whoop rang through the valleys and reverberated over the hills, when he stood erect in his own native dignity, with the bow and arrow, the weapon of his defence, and felt himself to be the rightful owner of the soil; we ask, where now are the original inhabitants, the native "lords of the soil?" Is the feeble remnant of the Narragansetts, now under the protection of the State, all that remains of this once noble race of men? But where are they? Where are the villages, and warriors, and youths? the sachems, and the tribes? the hunters and their families? They have perished. They are consumed.

The wasting pestilence has not alone done the mighty work. No—nor famine, nor war. There has been a mightier power, a moral canker, which has eaten into their hearts' cores—a plague, which the touch of the white man communicated—a poison, which betrayed them into a lingering ruin. They know and feel that there is for them still one remove farther, not distant, nor unseen. It is the general burial-ground of their race.

The colonizing of America at the expense of the sufferings and final extermination of the aborigines of this country, is painful and humiliating to consider, and detracts from that pleasure and satisfaction which would otherwise be enjoyed.

From the report of a committee on Indian affairs in Rhode Island, made to the General Assembly in 1833, "it appears that the whole number of all grades and conditions of the once numerous and warlike tribes of Narragansetts (the only tribe now existing in the State), was one hundred and fifty-eight. Of this number, only seven were of genuine Narragansett blood, and several of these have since died; fourteen were half-blood, and one hundred and fifty-eight of different grades, less than half-blood, with twenty foreigners, who have no connection with the tribe, except by marriage and other promiscuous intercourse." Three thousand acres of land in Charlestown, now in their possession, is all that is left to them of their ancient domain.

"Canonicus, Miantonomu! friends and benefactors of the colony, thy nation is no more. Simple sons of the forest, the lands of thy fathers have passed into the possession of the descendants of those men, whom, when weak, defenceless and distressed, ye clothed, fed, and protected. And thou too, mighty Philip, who fell fighting for thy native soil, the graves of thy fathers, thy wives and children, and thy own loved Mount Haup,—the white man's foot now presses the soil once trodden by thee."

The scene is too painful to dwell upon. We turn away from it in sorrow, deeply regretting their sad fate.

We have already alluded to the principles which influenced the minds of the early settlers of the Island. As Mr. Callender properly observes, "they fled not from religion, order, or good government, but to have liberty to worship God, and enjoy their own religious opinions and belief." Our fathers professed to believe that

> "There is in man an individual sovereignty,
> Which none created might unpunished bind or touch,
> A sovereignty unbound, save by the eternal laws of God,
> And unamenable to all below."

And in matters relating to civil liberty, this great principle was recognized and practiced. They admitted in their State sovereignty, that the true and legitimate source of power, from whence those in authority and places of trust derived theirs, to legislate for the common good of all, was derived from the people; and by *people*, they understood not the mere appendages of wealth, which are possessed but by few, as giving an exclusive privilege to act, to the exclusion of the masses, but rather that moral and intellectual possessions were the true characteristics which went to make up the people. Incidental differences in men's circumstances and conditions were not regarded as constituting a qualification, or disqualification, to act in the concerns of the government; and this view of the case rendered the form of government purely democratic.

We are aware that the idea has become prevalent in the minds of a certain class, that the masses are unfit to govern; but we apprehend no danger, where the people are intelligent, and educated to believe that they are men—not merely in form, but intellectually and morally so—and bound to love the institutions of their beloved country, and to aid in their preservation. Deny to them this right, and you at once generate a band of villains, the counterparts of the Ishmaelites, "who will be against every man, and every man against them." It behooves us, then, to see to it that education is imparted to all, irrespective of rank or condition, and to be careful that honest poverty, where all the other requisite qualifications are possessed, is not overlooked, and that wealth be not allowed a complete monopoly in all things.

The notion of the incompetency of the people to govern themselves, has had its origin on the other side of the water; and its baneful influence and demoralizing effects have been severely felt, sufficient to alarm every true patriot and friend of human rights, and should act as an incentive to vigilance in guarding our liberties—the birth-right of high heaven—and never, never suffer them to be wrested from us by the rapacious cruelty and injustice of designing men, who take delight in lording it over the consciences of men.

Oppression is contrary to the very nature of man's being. God created the mind originally free; and it is an act of usurpation which should be frowned down most indignantly, whenever our natural rights are invaded.

The original settlers of the Island possessed, in a very high degree, the principles of civil and religious liberty, and to their precept and example we may trace some of the same spirit which exists among the people at the present day. Our forefathers had not only felt the hand of oppression in the mother country; but they had also experienced it from their lordly brethren in Massachusetts, and hence they felt constrained to flee to a spot where the standard of liberty could be unfurled, and under its broad shelter an asylum found for the persecuted and the oppressed of every clime. We trust that we shall not be chargeable with vanity or prejudice, in reasserting that the people of the Island were the most truly republican in their manners, of any portion of the maritime towns of New England. In this, we have the concurrence of enlightened minds, whose extensive observation of the world has given weight to their opinions.

Among the earliest records of legislation in Rhode Island, we find an act guarding the right of private opinion, and free discussion. In the preamble, they say, "That to suffer the civil magistrate to intrude his power into the field of opinions, and restrain the profession or propagation of principles, on the supposition of their ill tendency, is a dangerous fallacy, which at once destroys all religious liberty; because he, being judge of that tendency, will make his own opinions the rule of judgment, and approve or condemn the sentiments of others, only as they shall square with or differ from his own; that it is time enough for the rightful purposes of civil government, for its officers to interfere when principles break forth into overt acts against peace and good order; and finally, that truth is great and will prevail, if left to herself; that she is the proper and sufficient antagonist of error, and has nothing to fear from the conflict, unless by human power disarmed of her natural weapons, free argument and debate."

Such sentiments are worthy to be inscribed, in letters of gold, on our halls of legislation, showing the principles of liberty which were ingrained in the hearts of the early settlers of this Island. God grant that we, their descendants, may cherish and perpetuate the same glorious principles, and never prove recreant to the sacred trust committed to our care.

Nor were these rights, nor any part of them, relinquished by our venerable predecessors, when they entered the confederacy. They surrendered no inalienable rights; they made no compromise of the liberty "to know, utter, and argue freely," any of the great principles of civil and religious freedom on which the colony was founded. And when Rhode Island subscribed to and adopted the Constitution of the United States, the voice of freedom echoed from the halls of her convention, proclaiming, with trumpet tongue, "that there are certain natural righrs of which men, when they form a social compact, cannot deprive their posterity, among which are the enjoyment of life and liberty, with the means of acquiring, possessing, and protecting property, and pursuing and obtaining happiness and safety. That all men have an equal, natural, and inalienable right to the exercise of religion according to the dictates of their own consciences. That the people have a right to freedom of speech and of writing, and publishing their sentiments; that freedom of the press is one of the great bulwarks of liberty, and ought not to be violated.

"Under these impressions," say they, "and declaring that the rights aforesaid cannot be abridged, and that these declarations are consistent with the Constitution, we, the said delegates, in the name and in the behalf of the people of the State of Rhode Island and Providence Plantations, do by these presents assent to and ratify the said Constitution."

Such sentiments as these are democratic in the highest sense of the term, and should admonish those who would seek to curtail in the least the liberties of the people, that they have forgotten their sires, and the sacred principles which they promulgated. Their names should be inscribed high on the roll of fame, to be admired and esteemed by their descendants. As so little has been said of Clark and Coddington, by writers who have undertaken to dwell on the history of Rhode Island, we have indulged more at length on their characters, in order to place their names in the front rank instead of in the rear.

It is a most singular fact that the grave of Roger Williams, the founder of the Plantations, is unknown to this day.

In reviewing the past mercies of God towards our fathers, we have abundant cause of gratitude, thanksgiving, and praise. They came to this Island to rear the temple of civil and religious liberty. No selfish purpose actuated them in leaving the fatherland; it was not to increase their worldly honors that they sacrificed home, with all its endearments. Higher and nobler considerations influenced them. It was to establish an asylum where liberty, the birth-right of man, might be more fully enjoyed than it was in the land of their birth.

And the principles which they cherished in their own bosoms, and which they scattered broadcast among the people, have been transmitted down to the present generation. Reflections, however, have been cast on the want of intelligence among the people, as well as the looseness of our religious principles, by a class of bigots and sectarians. But the moral virtues which guided the inhabitants of the Island were as pure and as unmixed as those of any section of the country.

Dr. Mather, a little more than a century ago, said, "Rhode Island was occupied by Antinomians, Anabaptists, Quakers, Ranters, and everything else, but Roman Catholics and Christians; and if any man has lost his religion, he may find it in this general muster of opinions—in this Gawzzim of New England, this receptacle of the convicts of Jerusalem, and the outcasts of the land."

Now, to us of the present day, such intolerant and abusive language, from a professed believer in Christ, sounds strangely in our ears; yet the age in which he lived is some apology for his singular and unaccountable conduct. But no apology can now be offered for the sensorious remarks which have often been made in relation to our civil and religious institutions, by a class of unprincipled bigots, who view everything through a distorted medium.

Considering her geographical extent, with the number of her inhabitants, Rhode Island can justly lay claim to having produced as many distinguished minds as that of any section of the Union. Call it arrogance, if you please to indulge such a thought. We feel called upon to frown down with the most sovereign contempt, the interlopers who dare cast aspersions on her fair fame, whether they be agents of religious bodies, or school teachers whose pride has been elated by receiving the patronage of the people.

Ignorance at home, where they are best known, is profound knowledge when the soil of Rhode Island is pressed; and it is owing to this cause alone, of strangers having been preferred to enlighten the *dark* minds of Rhode Islanders, that the false impression has been given.

We trust, for the honor of the State, this disgrace will soon be remedied, and the stigma of reproach wiped from our escutcheon. We have no wish to deny that we had our birth and education on the Island of Rhode Island, where the glorious principles of liberty were first taught, and where none is accounted a delinquent in matters of religion. Happy, thrice happy spot! we will cherish in fond remembrance those sainted patriots, whose mouldering ashes now repose in the fairest gem of the ocean. The hallowed influence of their principles has leavened this mighty nation, and neutralized, if not subdued, the dark malignant spirit of bigotry and superstition, religious intolerance and persecution.

Our fathers understood the true principles of government—they acknowledged the sovereignty of the people. This is the basis of a republican form of government, and should be guarded with the most scrupulous care, as on this hinge turns our political freedom. Abandon this vital principle, and our glorious temple of liberty, reared by the hands and cemented by the blood of our patriot fathers, would crumble to pieces, and its funeral dirge be chanted throughout the world.

This is an admirable feature in our Constitution, that a redress of grievances lays with the people. Deny this position, and you at once hurl us back to the dark period, when the land was governed by a sovereign tyrant, at whose dictation the people must bow and do fealty; and the conclusion to which we unavoidably arrive by admitting this political dogma, is, that our Revolutionary forefathers were a body of insurgents, and throughout every step in the great moral and physical enterprise of attempting to break the fetters which bound us to Great Britain, were wholly unauthorized by every principle of justice and equity—and as an act of atonement for past wrongs, should lead the nation at once to recognize the supremacy of Queen Victoria, as the legitimate and rightful sovereign of the land, and thereby wipe from our escutcheon the infinite wrongs of which we have been guilty.

In the view of enlightened and liberal minds, they can never tolerate the idea, that absolute power should be vested in any one man, or body of men, to be exercised according to their discretion, over the rights and liberties of others. It is an assumption of power, which the light of science wherever enjoyed, will not for a moment sanction. It must, however, be admitted that there is a want of moral courage prevalent at this day, more especially in the New-England States, which often gives to minorities the complete ascendency. We feel called upon to enter our solemn protest against such imbecility and weakness, derogatory to the character of man, which threatens the overthrow of our social, political, and religious liberties, which have been purchased at the expense of the blood of our fathers.

It is far better to suffer nobly the "pangs of outrageous fortune," with a mind free and untrammelled, than to bask in the sunshine of worldly prosperity, a mere slave; for slavery of the mind is far more to be deprecated than that of the body. We are legally and constitutionally bound to respect our rulers, whenever their acts are in accordance with the letter and spirit of the Constitution. But when the principles embodied in the Magna Charta, are not complied with, that moment they transcend the power lodged in their hands, and disregard the wishes of their constituents, and render their acts obnoxious to the people, and *vox populi* should be raised that their places may be filled with better men, who will labor to promote the interest of the whole people, and not legislate merely for the few.

DISTRIBUTION OF PUBLIC LANDS.

This age is distinguished in some measure by endeavoring to grant facilities to the poorer classes, to enable them to subsist more comfortably than they do at present; hence the distribution of the public lands to actual settlers is now strongly advocated by many whose patriotism extends beyond their own selfish interest. And it behoves the Legislatures of each of the respective States of the Confederacy to authorize their representatives in Congress to use their influence in bringing about this highly important and meritorious object, and not permit the waste land to be monopolized by speculators. Many of the States, to their praise be it said, have also passed the Homestead Exemption Law, where the value does not exceed from five hundred to a thousand dollars. This is a humane and charitable act, and should be followed by every state in the Union. It is for the people to straighten what is now crooked, and to right what is at present wrong. These should be made the test questions in our future elections, as being of infinitely more importance to the interest of the people, than the *tweedle-dum* and *tweedle-dee.* Let not a craven spirit continue to influence the minds of the people of Rhode Island, for it is too humiliating to witness man, elevated as he is above all the works of God, fearful of acting out the sentiments of his heart, for fear of the opinion which some worm of the dust may entertain of him, which may possibly endanger his temporary interest. Let the language of David to his son Solomon, be regarded and practised, "show thyself a man!"

In bringing this work to a close, let me urge on the minds of the inhabitants of the island, the value and importance of cultivating a spirit of enlarged liberality. Suffer not the mind to be influenced by merely selfish considerations, which are opposed in their nature to the principles advocated by the early settlers. Keep their example in full view, which will act as a stimulus in urging you forward in the sacred cause of justice. The spot which you occupy has been properly called the "Paradise of America," in a physical point of view, and in the past it was so in a moral and intellectual point of view. But, alas! "the gold has become dim, and the most find gold changed." The venerable Dr. Waterhouse has remarked: "Newport will be—must be—the Bath of the United States, to which rich invalids will retire for lost health. I often wish that I had some pleasant spot or farm on my native Island, to which, if not myself, my invalid posterity might resort to enjoy peace, health, and liberty."

Such were the views entertained by the venerable Doctor, and which have subsequently been realized in the vast crowds which now resort to Newport, to spend a few weeks during the sultry heat of summer. Here the gentleman of leisure can find exemption from the evils which exist in crowded cities, while a rich treat is furnished the lovers of pleasure which can no where else be enjoyed in the same degree.

This has turned the attention of the inhabitants to the building of large and spacious hotels, for the accommodation of the numerous strangers who resort here, until it has in a very great degree excluded every other kind of business from the place. Such precarious business should not, however, be the sole reliance of the inhabitants, but secondary in importance. Newport, with her spacious and commodious harbor, should enjoy an extensive commerce. Her situation is admirably adapted to the whaling and fishery business, and it should be remembered that commerce was the means of her former prosperity and glory, and its decay her downfall.

We are aware that great and important changes have been wrought in the country-places. Those once insignificant have sprung into being, as by magic; still it does not necessarily follow, that Newport must remain forever in *statu quo*, satisfied with having the town a mere resort of strangers for a few weeks. If this be the manifest destiny, why of course, the people must passively submit.

It must, however, appear obvious to the mind that has given the least attention to the subject, that the great depth of water at Easton's Point, the northern extremity of the town, presents facilities which are not enjoyed elsewhere. In many of the maritime cities, they often meet with obstacles which cause delay, owing to the want of sufficient water to float the larger class of ships, while here, at low tide, from eighteen to twenty feet of water is found.

In this age of progress there appears to be a demand for a still larger class of steamships, and it has been suggested that in the lapse of time Newport may become one of the principal depôts for steam navigation. But this view of the subject is highly improbable, as there is no market to be found here, and merchants would not be at the expense of freighting their merchandize to New-York, Boston, &c. The idea is too preposterous to be indulged in for a moment. If these natural advantages, which are possessed in so high a degree, are to be made subservient to the prosperity of the place, it must be effected by the enterprise of the inhabitants alone, and all Quixotic schemes abandoned forever.

We have not, in this work, attempted to draw comparisons between the past and the present, but have rather preferred to let the intelligent reader draw his own inferences; for it must be confessed that the moral, intellectual, and physical condition of the place is so wholly and entirely changed, as to render it painful to contemplate. We can hardly realize that it is the same place; and many, who after years of absence have returned, have found so sad a deterioration, that they have preferred a residence elsewhere. In fact, it is only in the past that Newport appears interesting to a reflective mind.

The houseless, wandering descendant looks at the mansion of his fathers and exclaims:

——"Now thou standest
In faded majesty, as if to mourn
The desolation of an ancient race.'

We flatter ourselves that the work will be read with interest, more especially by the inhabitants of the Island, as well as those who are in the habit of resorting there to admire the romantic and picturesque scenery, which is the great attraction of the place. It will assist the reader to while away his leisure hours in its perusal, and carry the mind back to the interesting period, when the highly eminent characters which we have presented figured on life's busy stage, who have long since retired to make room for others.

A List of the Presidents of the Colony of Rhode Island and Providence Plantations, under the first Patent; and the Governors under the second Charter. Collected from the State Records.

PRESIDENTS UNDER THE FIRST PATENT.

From the year 1647 to 1648, John Coggeshall,
" " 1648 to 1649, Jeremiah Clarke,
" " 1649 to 1650, John Smith,
" " 1650 to 1652, Nicholas Easton.

GOVERNORS UNDER THE FIRST CHARTER.

From the year 1654 to 1657, Roger Williams,
" " 1657 to 1660, Benedict Arnold,
" " 1660 to 1662, William Brenton,
" " 1662 to 1663, Benedict Arnold.

GOVERNORS UNDER THE SECOND CHARTER.

From the year 1663 to 1666, Benedict Arnold,
" " 1666 to 1669, William Brenton,
" " 1669 to 1672, Benedict Arnold
" " 1672 to 1674, Nicholas Easton,
" " 1674 to 1676, William Coddington.

From the year 1676 to 1677, Walter Clarke,
" " 1677 to 1679, Benedict Arnold,
" " 1670 to 1680, John Cranston,
" " 1680 to 1683, Peleg Sanford,
" " 1683 to 1685, William Coddington,
" " 1685 to 1686, Henry Bull,
" " 1686 to ——, Walter Clarke.

The Charter was at this period superseded by Sir Edmund Andross, but it was again restored in 1689.

GOVERNORS AFTER THE RESTORATION.

From the year 1689 to 1690, Henry Bull,
" " 1690 to 1695, John Easton,
" " 1695 to 1696, Caleb Carr,
" " 1696 to 1698, Walter Clarke,
" " 1698 to 1727, Samuel Cranston,
" " 1732 to 1734, William Wanton,
" " 1734 to 1741, John Wanton,
" " 1741 to 1743, Richard Ward,
" " 1745 to 1746, Gideon Wanton,
" " 1747 to 1748, Gideon Wanton,
" " 1762 to 1763, Samuel Ward,
" " 1765 to 1767, Samuel Ward,
" " 1768 to 1769, Josias Lyndon,
" " 1769 to 1775, Joseph Wanton.

APPENDIX

TO THE

HISTORY OF THE CHURCHES

IN

RHODE ISLAND.

APPENDIX.

TRINITY CHURCH NEWPORT.

The following account is compiled from the Records of Henry Bull, Esq., with Notes by the Rev. Francis Vinton, and additional remarks.

Until nearly the close of the seventeenth century, there were but two orders of Christians in the town of Newport, who were organized, and regularly met together for the purpose of worship, and those were of the denomination of Baptists and Friends, or Quakers.

The original founder, and first principal patron of Trinity Church, in Newport, was Sir Francis Nicholson. He was by profession a soldier; was Lieutenant-Governor of New-York, under Sir Edmund Andros, and at the head of the Administration of that Colony from 1687 to 1690, at which time he was appointed Governor of Virginia, and so continued for two years.

From 1694 to 1699, he was Governor of Maryland, after which time he was again Governor of Virginia. He commanded the British forces sent to Canada, in 1710, and took the important fortress of Port Royal. In 1713 he became Governor of Nova Scotia, and in 1720, Governor of Carolina. He returned to England in June, 1725, and died in London in 1728.

Mr. Lockyer, an Episcopal clergyman, commenced preaching in Newport about the close of 1698; and by that means a Church was gathered. He was doubtless procured by the instrumentality of Sir Francis Nicholson, who was then Governor of Maryland; for the Records of Trinity Church fully sustain the fact, that Sir Francis was its founder. The people, and more especially the leading gentlemen of the town, were well disposed towards this new undertaking, and a considerable society was soon established, with sufficient strength and zeal, aided by their generous patron, to build a handsome Church, which was completed in or before 1702. "Handsomely," as they say, "finished all on the outside, and the inside pewed well, but not beautiful."

Thus far the Church had made its way without any aid from the mother country. In the year 1702, when the Society for Propagating the Gospel in Foreign Parts, was established and incorporated in England, the Wardens of Trinity Church applied to the Bishop of London, soliciting the aid of the Society; on which application the Rev. James Honyman was appointed Missionary, in 1704, and sent over to this station. The Society, as a further encouragement, sent also as a present to the Church, a valuable library of the best theological works of that day, consisting of seventy-five volumes, mostly folio. Many of these books are still in the possession of the Church.

Queen Anne presented the Church with the bell, which was received here in 1709; about which time the Minister, Wardens, and Vestry, wrote to the Governor of Massachusetts, and to the Rev. Samuel Miles, Minister of Boston, requesting each of them to forward money, left in their hands for the Church, by Sir Francis Nicholson, stating their present want of money, to enable them to prepare for and hang the bell but recently received.

Mr. Honeyman was a gentleman well calculated to unite his own society, which grew and flourished exceedingly under his charge, as well as to conciliate those of other religious denominations, all of whom he "embraced with the arms of charity."

In the year 1713, the Minister, Churchwardens, and Vestry, petitioned the Queen for the establishment of Bishops in America, setting forth the great benefit that would result to the church from such a measure. Mr. Nathaniel Kay, the Collector of the Queen's revenues in Rhode Island, who afterwards liberally endowed the school connected with this Church, was among the signers of this petition.

In the year 1724, Mr. Honyman writes to the Society in England, as follows: "That there was properly belonging to his church in Newport, above fifty communicants, who live in that place, exclusive of strangers. The church people grow now too numerous to be accommodated with seats in the old church, and many more offered to join themselves to the church communion." Mr. Honyman proposed to the church members, the building of a new church, and subscribed £30 himself for that purpose. The people heartily concurred, and he soon after obtained subscriptions amounting to £1000 of the currency of the country; but it was estimated the building would cost twice that amount. However, a sufficient sum was raised, and, in the year 1726, the church was completed, and Mr. Honyman held the service in it. The body of the building was seventy feet long, and forty-six wide. It had two tiers of windows, was full of pews, and had galleries all round to the east end. It was acknowledged by the people of that day to be the most beautiful timber structure in America. The old building was given to the people of Warwick, who had no church of their own.

We have every reason for believing that the new building was erected on the site of the old one, for the old one appears to have been disposed of by gift, to make room for the new, which would not otherwise have been done in a town rapidly increasing in population, and in want of more buildings. At the time of which we are writing, 1724 to 1726, there were Quakers and two sorts of Anabaptists in Newport, yet the members of the Church of England increased daily; and although there was not to be found alive at that time, four of the original promoters of church worship in this place, yet there was then above four times the number of all the first. Mr. Honyman had under his care at this time, the towns of Newport, Freetown, Tiverton, and Little Compton.

The history of this Church has been, thus far, principally derived from the publications of the Society for Propagating the Gospel in Foreign Parts, and from Letters from the Minister, Wardens, and Vestry, to Queen Anne, to the Bishop of London, and to Sir Francis Nicholson, copies of which have been preserved in the first parish records of the Church. The first book of the corporation records having been lost, is a circumstance much to be regretted. The second book commences with the date 1731.

A letter, written in Newport, and published in the "New England Journal," Boston, September 3d, 1729, says, "Yesterday, arrived here, Dean Berkley, of Londonderry, in a pretty large ship. He is a gentleman of middle stature, of an agreeable, pleasant, and erect aspect. He was ushered into the town with a great number of gentlemen, to whom he behaved himself after a very complaisant manner. 'Tis said he proposes to tarry here with his family about three months."

The connection of Dean Berkley with Trinity Church, calls for a passing notice of his sojourn in Newport, where he arrived by a circumstance purely incidental. He, with other gentlemen, his associates, were bound to Bermuda, with the intention of establishing there a college, for the education of the Indian youth of this country; a plan, however, which wholly failed. The captain of the ship in which he sailed could not find the island of Bermuda, and having given up the search after it, steered northward, until they discovered land unknown to them, and which they supposed to be inhabited only by savages. On making a signal, however, two men came on board from Block Island, in the character of pilots, who, on inquiry, informed them the harbor and town of Newport were near; that in the town there was an Episcopal Church, the Minister of which was Mr. James Honyman, on which they proceeded for Newport, but an adverse wind caused them to run into the west passage, where the ship came to anchor. The Dean wrote a letter to Mr. Honyman, which the pilots took on shore at Conanicut Island, and called on a Mr. Gardner and Mr. Martin, two members of Mr. Honyman's Church, informing them that a great dignitary of the Church of England, called a Dean, was on board the ship, together with other gentlemen passengers. They handed them the letter from the Dean, which Messrs. Gardner and Martin brought to Newport, in a small boat, with all possible dispatch. On their arrival they found Mr. Honyman was at church, it being a holyday, on which divine service was held then. They then sent the letter by a servant, who delivered it to Mr. Honyman in his pulpit. He opened it, and read it to the congregation, from the contents of which it appeared the Dean might be expected to land in

Newport, every moment. The church was dismissed with the blessing, and Mr. Honyman, with the wardens, vestry, church, and congregation, male and female, repaired immediately to the ferry wharf, where they arrived a little before the Dean, his family and friends. The foregoing tradition we have given as we received it, but other traditions vary a little from that; some of which say that "the ship made no land until she arrived in the East or Sachuest river, from which she came round the north end of Rhode Island to Newport." It has also been stated that Col. Godfrey Malborn, being out in his pleasure yacht, on discovering the ship, made towards her, and on being informed that the Dean and suit were on board, he took them to his magnificent country-seat, now the property of Prescott Hall, Esq., where they tarried until morning, and then started for Newport. The Dean purchased a farm of about one hundred acres in the town of Newport, adjoining one of about the same extent belonging to the Rev. James Honyman, on which Mr. Honyman resided. The Dean built him a house on his farm for his residence, which he called White Hall, which name it still retains. The house is still standing. It is situated in what is now the town of Middletown, about three miles from the State House in Newport, and a little back of the road which runs eastward from the town, near a beautiful little water course, which runs southward towards Sachuest Beach. This White Hall estate he gave to Yale College, in Connecticut, which still owns the fee.

The White Hall estate was sold soon after it came in possession of Yale College, on a lease of nine hundred and ninety-nine years, at a rent of one hundred ounces of silver per annum. The mansion house is still standing, and is in the occupation of Mr. Abraham Brown, the present owner of the lease. It remains the same as when Bishop Berkley occupied it. We would suggest the importance of repairing the front, &c. He continued here about two years, perhaps a little longer. He was certainly here as late as September, 1731, as appears by a supplementary inscription on the tomb-stone of Nathaniel Kay, Esq., which is as follows: "Joining to the south of this tomb, lies Lucia Berkley, daughter of Dean Berkley, Obit. the 5th of September, 1731."

His preaching was eloquent and forcible, and attracted large congregations to Trinity church. When he was called to a sphere of greater usefulness in his native country, he was not forgetful of a residence which was endeared to him by many pleasing recollections; and which, moreover, possessed for him a melancholy interest, from the circumstance of its containing the ashes of his infant daughters, who had died during his sojourn in Newport.

After his return to England, he sent as a donation to Trinity Church, in the year 1733, a magnificent organ. This organ is surmounted by a crown in the centre, supported by two mitres, one on each side.

Mr. Nathaniel Kay, who came from England to Rhode Island as collector of the King's customs for the colony of Rhode Island, was the most liberal patron, as to the amount of his pecuniary aid, that the church has ever had. His house stood on the site now occupied by the dwelling-house of the heirs of the late George Engs, Esq., on the hill, near the head of Touro-street. It was, when built, one of the most spacious and elegant private dwellings in town.

No apology can be offered for the neglect of the church, in suffering it to be destroyed. It was a piece of modern vandalism, which we can never cease to regret. Since the revolution, it was occupied by a Mrs. Pollock, a lady from South Carolina, who kept her carriage, and lived in a style of affluence, befitting her rank and station. At the time of the embargo, when business was suspended, and no employment was to be had for the laboring classes, she, like a true philanthropist, opened a *soup-house*, and daily supplied the poor inhabitants throughout the winter. At his death, he devised and bequeathed to the church as follows: "I give and bequeath my dwelling house and coach house to my wife, during the term of her natural life; after which I give and bequeath both, with my lots of land in Rhode Island, and £400 in the currency of New England, to build a school house, to the minister of the church of England (Mr. Honyman), and the church wardens and vestry for the time being—that is to say, upon trust and confidence, and to the interest and purpose, benefit and use of a school to teach *ten poor boys* their grammar and the mathematics, gratis; and to appoint a master at all times, as occasion or vacancy may happen, who shall be Episcopally ordained, and assist the minister (Episcopal) of the town of Newport, in some proper office, as they shall think most useful." Mr. Updike, in his history, has attempted an apology for the loss of the estate thus kindly bequeathed by Mr. Kay to Trinity church. It only proves that property disposed of in this way, fails to be carried out according to the wish of the donor. The Rev. Theodore Deher took charge of the parish, as minister, in 1797. His gentlemanly deportment and conciliatory manners, his pulpit eloquence, his mild disposition, and his sound piety, soon brought back the wandering sheep to the common fold. The church was again filled with a numerous congregation, earnestly engaged in social worship.

In 1762, the edifice was greatly enlarged, by moving the easterly part about thirty feet, and adding as much in the middle. This was done at the expense of forty-six gentlemen, who took the pews they added in full satisfaction for the expense of said enlargement. In the same year that the organ was presented (1733), Jahleel Brenton, Esq., presented the clock in the tower —and we would suggest that, in memory of the donor, it should be put in repair.

In 1740, the bell presented by Queen Anne was cracked; it was taken down and sent to London to be recast. In 1741, the first school house was built, and Mr. Cornelius Bennett appointed schoolmaster.

In 1750, the Rev. Mr. Honyman died at an advanced age. He was buried at the expense of the church, on the south side of the passage from the gate to the church, where his tombstone now lies. His salary was £70 per annum.

In July, 1751, the Church agreed to ask the Society to send them Mr. Beach as minister. On the 27th of August, 1752, a committee was appointed to collect, by subscription, a sum sufficient to purchase a parsonage. Their success was such, that in December the house was purchased for the purpose aforesaid.

Mr. Thomas Potter arrived in 1754, having been sent by the Venerable Society as missionary. In November, Mr. Potter left. The church, being destitute of a minister, called the Rev. Marmaduke Brown, of Portsmouth. He accepted the call, and arrived in December.

In 1768, the old tower was taken down, and a new one built, eighteen feet square, and sixty feet high. In 1769, Mr. Brown went to England on a visit. During his absence, Mr. Bisset supplied his place as minister.

Oct. 27, 1770, there was a severe gale of wind, in which the spindle on the steeple was broken off below the ball.

The Easter-Monday after the death of Mr. Brown, the congregation chose Mr. Bisset their minister, until the Venerable Society should be heard from. On Sunday, the 8th of December, 1776, the British fleet and army took possession of the Island of Rhode Island, which event gave a new character to everything here of a local nature. Mr. Bisset continued with the church until the evacuation of the Island, which took place October 25th, 1779.

Many of the leading members of Trinity Church were of the royal party, who went with them to New York; and among the number was the minister, Mr. Bisset, who left his wife and child behind, in the most destitute circumstances. His furniture was seized by the State of Rhode Island ; but afterwards, upon the petition of his wife to the General Assembly, it was restored to her, and she, with her child, was permitted to go to her husband in New York.

A few days after the British left Newport, some young men of the town, and among them two American officers, entered the church, and despoiled it of the altar-piece, consisting of the King's arms, the Lion and the Unicorn. They were highly ornamented, and were placed against the great east window. After trampling them under foot, they were carried to the north battery, and set up for a target to fire at. The other emblems of royalty, being out of reach, were allowed to remain. They consist of one royal crown on the spire, and another on the top of the organ. This structure has never been subjected to the hand of modern vandalism, and we trust that the inhabitants of the ancient town will guard it with the most scrupulous care. The interior is now the same as when Dean Berkley preached in it, and the pulpit is now the only one in America ever graced by the occupancy of that distinguished prelate. The church was, at the time of which we are speaking, without a minister. As it had been nursed by the high church party in England, it was unpopular with the mass of the people, who were writhing under the scourge inflicted by that very party. The church edifice, too, had been spared by those ruthless invaders who had worshipped in it, while they had desecrated the other places of worship in the town, by converting them into hospitals, etc.; and every part of them but the shells, they had demolished.

There was no service in the church immediately after Mr. Bisset left, and the minister of the "Sixth principal Baptist Society" of this town, the Rev. Gardner Thurston, was allowed to occupy the church, with his numerous congregation, until their own place of worship was repaired—from 1781 to 1786—at which period the Rev. James Sayre was engaged and settled as minister.

He took upon him the duties of that office on the 1st of October. In 1787, the pews built in the west aisle of the church were taken down, and the passage from the north to the south doors again laid open.

In 1788, Mr. Bours and a majority of the congregation came to an open rupture with Mr. Sayre. They charged him with "refusing to put a vote in the vestry, which he had previously agreed to do."

It appears Mr. Sayre soon left the church; but by what means they got rid of him—whether through the means of Bishop Seabury, whose mediation had been requested by a portion of the congregation, by his voluntary relinquishment of his charge, or by compulsion, the records do not inform us.

By a vote of May 5th, 1789, the Rev. William Smith, of St. Paul's Church, Narragansett, was invited to visit the church every other week, which invitation he accepted, with the consent of his own church; and in December following, he was called to become the minister of Trinity church, which he accepted.

The Rev. Mr. Smith was not agreeably settled, inasmuch as the society were divided. The feuds which had originated between Mr. Sayre and Mr. Bours had not been healed, and many of the minority refused to attend church under the preaching of Mr. Smith, but preferred holding meetings of worship in their private houses. Mr. Smith received a call from the church at Norwalk, Conn., which he accepted, and embarked for his new station April 12, 1797.

The church, on the 14th of May, invited the Rev. John S. J. Gardner, assistant minister of Trinity church, Boston, to come to Newport, and spend a few Sundays. In Mr. Gardner's answer to the church, dated September 17th, he calls it "a scattered church, and a divided people." For these reasons, and because his own church, rather than part with him, had raised his salary to $800, he declined the invitation, but recommended to the church, a young man named Theodore Dehor. On the 8th of October, 1797, Mr. Dehor was chosen minister, and requested to obtain orders. November 19th, his salary was fixed at $700 per annum, with the use of the parsonage and lot, and other perquisites of said office. On the 7th of January, 1798, he entered upon the duties of his ministry. Mr. Dehor proved very acceptable to the society, which again united in the bonds of harmony and Christian fellowship, flourished and increased to an overflowing congregation. In 1798, a vestry was built in the north east corner of the church; in this spot a full length portrait of Mr. Honyman hangs. In 1799, a new school-house was erected on the lot where the old one formerly stood. The old one had been pulled down, as we have reason to believe, in the hard winter of 1780, and given to the poor of the church for fuel.

In 1804, the church bell which had been in use sixty-three years cracked, and was again cast over. In November of the same year, the new bell cracked and was still again re-cast. The affairs of the church having been settled under the pastoral care of Rev. Mr. Dehor, but little worthy of notice took place until 1809. For about ten years previous to that time, many members of the corporation had been anxious the church should possess a fund, to be invested, and the interest arising to be exclusively appropriated to the minister's salary. This year they set themselves to work in earnest to accomplish the desirable purpose. On the 2d of June, the vestry appointed a committee to report a plan to raise a permanent fund, and in August the said committee made a report which was not adopted.

A new committee was appointed, which reported in December, 1810, whose report being adopted, measures were taken for carrying it into effect. The members of the congregation were solicited to subscribe such sums as they were willing to contribute towards the fund; no one being obliged to pay until the whole sum subscribed should amount to six thousand dollars. In a short time a list of six thousand and fifty dollars was obtained. The subscribers being thus held for the amounts subscribed, agreeably to the terms of their subscriptions, the money was collected and invested in bank stock—the dividends on which were to be regularly invested until the capital should amount to ten thousand dollars. After which the yearly income was to be applied to the payment of the minister's salary, and for no other purpose. This was fully accomplished in due time, and one thousand dollars added by the bequest of Mr. Samuel Brown, of Boston, a native of Newport, making the permanent fund eleven thousand dollars, at the original cost of the stock.

In February, 1810, the Rev. Theodore Dehor resigned the rectorship of the church, but tendered his services until the ensuing autumn. On the 28th of October, he preached his last sermon to the congregation, and proceeded to exercise the Episcopal offices of Rector of St. Michael's, Charleston, and Bishop of South Carolina.

When Mr. Dehor retired, the Rev. Samuel Wheaton, who married the sister of Mr. Dehor, and who had been previously engaged to preside over the church, arrived here from New-Haven, and took charge of the parish. The Rev. Mr. Wheaton presided over the church for thirty years, when he resigned, and the Rev. Francis Vinton was chosen Rector, and entered on his duties at Easter, 1840, and was instituted Rector April 14th, 1841.

It is a subject of regret that Mr. Wheaton could not have continued to preside over the parish until his removal by death, for he was a devoted servant of Christ, and endeared himself to the people of Newport by a blameless life and godly conversation. His resignation was not voluntary but compulsory, and continued to be a source of bitterness to his mind, until his removal to higher honors in the church triumphant in heaven.

The present officiating minister is the Rev. Mr. Brewer. It has been intimated that there is an organ in Brooklyn, New-York, which bears the inscription as being the gift of Bishop Berkley; now Bishop Berkley never presented but one organ, and that was to Trinity church in Newport. If the *old pipes*, which were removed when the organ was repaired, were taken to Brooklyn, and worked into an organ, this does not make it the gift of Bishop Berkley. The reader can draw his own inferences.

Mr. Kay, of whom particular mention has been made as a benefactor to Trinity church, also made a liberal bequest to St. Michael's church, Bristol, of 160 acres of land on Pappoose Squaw Neck, to sustain a grammar school. What disposition has been made of the income, we are not properly apprized, but would hope that the wishes of the donor have been complied with, though such is not apt to be the case. The disregard which has too frequently been paid to the wishes and intentions of donors, should put man on his guard, in devising property to churches.

THE FIRST AND SECOND CONGREGATIONAL CHURCHES.

In January, 1696, Mr. Nathaniel Clap, of Dorchester, in Massachusetts Bay, a graduate of Howard College, by the advice of the minister of Boston, came to Newport and preached till his death. It was not, however, till the year 1720, that a church was gathered and organized, and Mr. Clap was ordained and installed its pastor. November 20th, the church consisted of the following fourteen male members, viz.: Nathaniel Clap, John Reynolds, Thomas Brown, Culbert Campbell, Ebenezer Davenport, William Sanford, Richard Clark, Job Bisset, Joshua Statson, Kendal Nichols, (he was an influential merchant of Newport, and died Sept. 18, 1767, aged 81 years,) John Mayhem, James Carey, Nathaniel Townsend, and John Labeer.

The church under Mr. Clap's ministry flourished, and additions were gradually made to its numbers for about three years, when the sacrament of the Lord's Supper ceased to be administered by the pastor, and at the same time he refused to administer the ordinance of Baptism to a child of Mr. Kendal Nichols, who with his wife were communicants of the church. He thought his church was not pure, and that its members were "not of sufficiently holy conversation" for the holy ordinance.

In the original correspondence, (still extant,) between Mr. Clap and Mr. and Mrs. Nichols, on the subject of his refusal to baptize the infant of the latter, there is assigned no reason for such refusal, but a distrust on the part of Mr. Clap, of the Christian state of Mr. and Mrs. Nichols.

This course on the part of Mr. Clap gave great offence, and was the commencement of a fire that continued to burn for many years. The church and congregation revered their pastor, and admired him as a truly evangelical apostolical preacher, but were displeased with his rigid course of discipline and church government.

In July 20th, 1724, the church addressed a respectful application to their pastor, soliciting his consent to have recourse to other churches for sacramental privileges, if bodily weakness was the only reason of his denying or withholding them, but without success.

Mr. Clap, in answer to a remonstrance from B. Ellery and S. Vernon, Esq., said:

"I came here by the advice of the Rev. minister of Boston. I have continued here by his advice; I have preached the Gospel here. As for you who are trying to drive me away, I would have you to consider the awful account you will have to give for the damnation of the souls that will be lost for the want of my preaching."

Although Mr. Clap was not inclined to assign a plausible reason, or one that was satisfactory to the church, in the singular course which he took in refusing to baptize the child of Mr. and Mrs. Nichols, and subsequently in suspending the holy ordinance of Communion, yet tradition has informed us, that there was a valid reason in his mind, which led him to pursue such a course. It was owing to a remark made to him soon after his taking possession of the parsonage, which he understood was built *expressly* for him by Mr. Nichols. A female member of his church, who called upon him soon after he was quietly settled in his new home, on learning his gratification of the favor which had been conferred upon him by Mr. Nichols, she very indiscreetly remarked, that as long as he remained the pastor of the church, the house was his. On Mr. Clap's interrogating her where she had derived her information of this fact, she replied that she had it from Mr. Nichols. This, no doubt, led him to suspect that a possibility existed of an attempt to dissolve the connection, which at that period was viewed as solemn and as sacred as the marriage contract. The least allusion to such an event was considered in the light of a gross insult. And it has been also said that on Mr. Nichols calling upon Mr. Clap, he was received with coldness, and that he at once put the question to Mr. Nichols, wishing to know of him whose house this was. On being told it was his, he then requested Mr. Nichols at once to leave it.

This shows that he retained a degree of self-respect, however his conduct may be viewed by the pigmies and dwarfs of the present day. In the view of Mr. Clap, it looked like an invasion of his rights, which if not checked in the bud, might lead to disastrous consequences to the church and to the ministry. This is the most probable reason which can be assigned for his singular conduct.

In the year 1745, Mr. Callender published a discourse occasioned by the death of his friend, the Rev. Mr. Clap, in which he pays a high tribute of affectionate veneration to his memory. Mr. Callender's sermon was founded on Hebrews xiii., 7, 8. The prominent traits in his character are faithfully delineated in the following extracts from this sermon:

"The main stroke in his character, was his eminent sanctity and piety, and an ardent desire to promote the knowledge and practice of true godliness in others. As his understanding was above the common level, so was his learning, though he studiously concealed it. He thought his station required more than common instances of innocency, self-denial, and caution. He abounded in contrivances to do good, by scattering books of piety and virtue, not such as minister questions and strife, but godly edifying, and put himself to a very considerable expense, that he might by this method awaken the careless and secure, comfort the feeble minded, succor the tempted, instruct the ignorant, and quicken, animate, and encourage all. He abounded in acts of charity to the poor and necessitous, to whom he was a kind father and guardian. In fine, he was a public blessing, as an able minister of the New Testament, an example of unspotted piety, and an honor to religion. There are two things in which he excelled in so remarkable a manner, that I must not omit them: his care about the education of children, and his concern for the instruction of servants.

"The conclusion of his life and ministry, was a peaceful and happy death, without those raptures which some boast of, but with perfect resignation to the will of God, and good hope and humble confidence in Christ Jesus, who was the sum of his doctrine, and the end of his conversation."

While he was eminently pious, he was at the same time very eccentric. "The administrator of his estate informed the writer, that he found among the papers and dust of his study, which he never allowed to be swept, several hundred dollars, in many little parcels, wrapped in orange peel or paper, which had probably fallen from his table, without observation or subsequent search; 'and likewise, another sum of considerable amount, on the shelves of his closet, in paper, and orange-peel.

"There was likewise a barrel, almost full of tops, which he had purchased of boys in the street, to show his disapprobation of the vain sport. It was his custom to walk out in a black velvet cap, and in a gown girded about his loins. In one side of it he would carry books, and in the other cakes, and with one or the other of which he would generally succeed in purchasing of boys their tops, and would give them kind advice, so that instead of fleeing from him, they loved to see him approach."—*Reminiscences of Hopkins.*

Their next step, July, 1725, was to propose a colleague, as a means of allaying all uneasiness; this, Mr. Clap declined. The church and congregation were determined, and the services of Mr. Bass were obtained for a short season, and after him, Mr. John Adams; this must have been some time in 1727. Mr. Clap, after a while, utterly refused any association with Mr. Adams, and entirely occupied the pulpit on the Lord's day, not giving opportunity to the other to preach. This exasperated the people to such a degree, that nearly half of both churches and congregations withdrew, and met in a separate place, under Mr. Adams' ministry.

In 1728, an *ex-parte* Council of Churches was convened on the 3rd of April, which, after solemn supplication to God for his gracious presence and direction, came to the following result, unanimously agreed in, upon mature deliberation. The Council then went on to say, "that as Mr. Adams had received a valid call to the colleagueship with Mr. Clap, they affectionately advised Mr. Clap and his friends to consent to Mr. Adams' ordination; and if they would not, they recommended the aggrieved party to use the same house of worship, for the time being, one in the morning and the other in the evening, with their respective pastors." Mr. Clap persisted in having no intercourse with Mr. Adams.

Tradition informs us, that when the Council had assembled at the parsonage, to endeavor to adjust the differences which existed between a portion of the church and Mr. Clap, he came from his study with a plate in his hand, containing as many figs as there were ministers present, and after handing them round, until he came to the last, remarked, " here is a fig for you all;" and immediately retired to his study. This illustrates the moral courage of the ministry at that day.

A new church was organized, and Mr. Adams ordained their pastor, April 11th, 1728. The Lord's Supper was administered on Lord's day, May 11th, 1728. The place of worship where Mr. Clap then preached, was situated in Tanner-street, and its occupancy by Mr. Adams, contrary to his wishes, was so displeasing to him, that he would not consent to preach in it again. A new house was erected, which at present is occupied by the Unitarian Society, under the pastoral care of the Rev. Mr. Brooks. When the house was completed, and they had brought him the key, the first question he asked, was, " Is it paid for ?" On being informed that a small balance remained unsettled, he handed back the key, and not until the debt was cancelled would he consent to occupy the house, which was quickly done. Such was the moral principle of that day.

Mr. Whitfield, in his Journal, in his remarks on Mr. Clap, says, " His countenance was very heavenly, and he prayed most affectionately for a blessing on my coming to Rhode Island. I could not but think I was sitting by one of the patriarchs."

Dean Berkley was intimate with Mr. Clap, and often spoke of his good deeds, and exemplary character. He said, " Before I saw Father Clap, I thought the Bishop of Rome had the most grave aspect of any man I ever saw ; but really, the minister of Newport has the most venerable appearance."

The Rev. Mr. Clap continued his pastoral care over the First Church, until his death, though he abandoned the house, as before remarked, to Mr. Adams and his Church.

1733. This year, the Second Congregational Church built a new meeting-house, in Clarke-street.

The Rev. Mr. Adams was dismissed, February 25th, 1729—1730.

April 21st, 1731, the Rev. James Searing was ordained over the Second Church. He died January 6th, 1755, aged fifty years.

May, 1740, the Rev. Joseph Gardner was ordained co-pastor with Mr. Clap, over the First Church, and was dismissed June 10th, 1743.

June 20th, 1744, Jonathan Helier was ordained co-pastor with Mr. Clap, over the First Church, and died May 27th, 1745. He was a very ingenious and excellent man.

October 30th, 1745, the Rev Nathaniel Clap died, at the advanced age of seventy-eight years. His remains lay in the Arnold burial ground, at the rear of the Unitarian Church.

October 29th, 1746, the Rev. William Vinal was ordained pastor of the First Church, and was dismissed September 21st, 1768.

April 11th, 1755, Rev. Samuel Hopkins was intalled pastor of the First Congregational Church.

October 22d, 1755, Rev. Ezra Stiles was ordained pastor of the Second Congregational Church. It was a most curious coincidence that two such minds should have been settled over Newport churches the same year.

At the settlement of these distinguished divines, Hopkins and Stiles, over the churches in Newport, they were in a flourishing condition, and continued so many years, and many additions were made to them; but, in 1744, the difficulties connected with the relations that existed between Great Britain and her American Colonies, began to give warning of the conflict that ensued. Newport began to decline, commerce forsook her wharfs, many dwellings were emptied of their inhabitants, and the churches were in a great measure forsaken. Dr. Hopkins had removed his family; and, in 1776, he himself left, and returned to reside with his family in Great Barrington, Massachusetts.

On the 23rd of October, 1775, the remnant of the Second Society met, and determined it to be inexpedient to continue public worship during the winter, in consideration of the tumultuous and evacuated state of the town. In the following March, their pastor left Newport, and these churches were destitute of ministers, and their members scattered abroad.

Both the houses of worship, during the war, had been used as barracks for the soldiers. The bell of the First Church was carried to England, and the pulpit, pews, and fixtures, were demolished. The Second Church fared but little better; for, though the pulpit was left standing, the enemy had put up a chimney in the middle of it, and destroyed the pews below, and in the gallery.

In the spring of 1780, Dr. Hopkins returned to his parish, to witness a scene of desolation and misery; some of the members of the church and congregation had died, many had sought other homes, and those that remained, were so impoverished and dispirited, that only a few had the moral courage to think of reviving their church. But they were eventually able to succeed.

It has already been remarked, that the enemy had completely destroyed the interior of the church, and their limited resources prevented their refitting it, only in a plain manner. For years there was no paint on the pews, and the impression was visibly seen in the aisles, where the British soldiers had struck the muzzles of their guns. The people of Taunton very kindly gave them the pulpit, which continued to be graced with Hopkins, and his successors, so long as the place of worship was used by the society.

But although there was no outward adorning, yet an amount of piety existed at that period, which more than supplied its place. The female members of his church were many of them eminently pious. There was Madam Osborne, Susannah Anthony, Hannah Johnson, Mrs. Donely, with many others, "whose praise is in all the churches." The writings of Madam Osborne and Susannah Anthony are to be met with in the Sabbath School libraries of the land. They were the "poor of this world, but rich in faith, and heirs of the kingdom which God hath prepared for them that love him." They were to Doctor Hopkins what Aaron and Hur were to Moses, they stayed up his hands, and encouraged his heart under the conflicts and trials which, as a soldier of the cross, he was called to endure. At that period, there was something witnessed like the primitive times, when love bound the church together as one. The world had not then the complete ascendency in the human heart. There was a renunciation of "the world, the flesh, and the devil," and a childlike spirit seemed to characterize the church.

During the war, Dr. Stiles had accepted the presidency of Yale College, although he was not formally dismissed from the pastoral charge till after the peace; consequently, on their return to Newport, the Second Church found themselves without a pastor, and continued in that state till the 24th of May, 1786, on which day the Rev. William Patton was ordained their minister.

President Stiles was one of the most learned men that our country has ever produced. As a scholar, he was familiar with every department of learning. He had a profound and critical knowledge of the Latin, Greek, French, and Hebrew languages; in the Samaritan, Chaldee, Syriac, and Arabic, he had made considerable progress, and he had bestowed some attention on the Persic and Coptic. He had a passion for history, and an intimate acquaintance with the rabbinical writings, and with those of the fathers of the Christian Church. As a preacher, he was impressive and eloquent; and the excellence of his sermons was enhanced by the energy of his delivery, and by the unction which pervaded them. His catholic spirit embraced men of every nation, sect, and party. In the cause of civil and religious liberty, he was enthusiastic. In his discourse on Christian union, he says: "There ought to be no restrictions on the conscience of an honest and sober believer of revelation."

The following appropriate remarks are from the pen of Chancellor Kent, one of Dr. Stiles' pupils.

"A more constant and devoted friend to the Revolution and independence of his country, never existed. He had anticipated it as early as the year 1760, and his whole soul was enlisted in favor of every measure which led on gradually to the formation and establishment of the American Union. He was distinguished for the dignity of his deportment, the politeness of his address, and the urbanity of his manners." President Stiles was for more than twenty years a resident and distinguished ornament of Rhode Island.

December 20th, 1803, Rev. Samuel Hopkins, D.D., died aged 82 years. In his death, the church sustained a heavy loss.

Though not eloquent, as was Dr. Stiles, yet there was a solemnity in his preaching which carried conviction to the understanding and heart, and shewed the sincerity of his mind, as one in whom you could rely. Decision of character was preëminently conspicuous in his whole character—a trait seldom to be met with at the present day. His theological views were somewhat peculiar, and gave great offence, though his opponents were constrained to admit his honesty.

He was a target at which the arrows of malice were thrown, but he stood, as he remarked, "like a brazen wall, unhurt." Charles Cahoone, who was skeptical in his views, and rather eccentric, was disposed to annoy the Doctor by sending persons to him to buy *brimstone*. Such conduct was highly displeasing to the Doctor, but it never deterred him from preaching what he believed to be the truth. Cahoone was a carver, and a specimen of his work may be seen on the roof of the house of Engine No. VI., at the head of King-street. It represents old Breton, an English rigger, dressed in his petticoat, trowsers, and cocked hat, with the pig-tail tobacco hanging out of his pocket. It is a *fac simile* of the person.

"Dr. Hopkins was a distinguished divine. His mind was discerning, and his application was almost unequaled. He sometimes devoted to his studies eighteen hours in a day. One of his peculiar sentiments, was that the inability of sinners is moral, not natural; but this is only saying that their inability consists in disinclination of heart, or of opposition of will, to what is good. Combining the Calvinistic doctrine that God has foreordained whatsoever comes to pass, with his views of the nature of sin as consisting entirely in the intention or disposition of the mind, he inferred that it was no impeachment upon the character of the most righteous Disposer of all events, to say, not only that He had decreed the existence of sin, but that He exerted His own power to produce it. The design being benevolent, he contended that no more iniquity could be attached to this act, than to the bare permission of sin. This is another of his peculiarities. From his view of the nature of holiness, as consisting in disinterested benevolence, he also inferred that a Christian should be willing to perish forever, to be forever miserable, if it should be necessary for the glory of God and the good of the universe that he should encounter this destruction.

"Instead of the Calvinistic doctrine of the strict imputation of Adam's sin, and of the righteousness of Christ, he chose rather to adopt the language of Scripture in saying, that on account of the first transgression, men were made or constituted sinners, and that men are justified on account of the righteousness of Christ, or through the redemption which there is in him. Another of his peculiarities is, that all sin consists in selfishness."

He was a man of large stature, and well proportioned; dressed in the costume of the age, with a full bottomed wig, he presented an imposing appearance.

Sept. 12, 1804, Rev. Caleb T. Tenney was installed pastor of the First Church, and was dismissed May 29th, 1815.

Aug. 23d, 1815, Rev. Calvin Hitchcock was installed over the First Church, and was dismissed August 23d, 1820.

July 25th, 1821, Rev. Samuel Austin, D. D., was installed pastor of the First Church, and was dismissed in 1826. Dr. Austin, previous to his coming to Newport, had been President of Burlington College, Vermont. He was an able expositor of the Scriptures.

He was succeeded by Rev. William Torrey, January, 1827, who was dismissed in May, 1829, rather unceremoniously.

March 24th, 1830, Rev. William Beecher was ordained pastor of the First Church, and dismissed June 23d, 1833.

April 18th, 1833, Rev. William Patten was dismissed from his pastoral charge over the Second Church, after having ministered to his people for the long period of forty-seven years. If great success did not attend his ministrations, if additions were not as numerous as in some instances, nevertheless he was a pious and devoted servant of Christ, and was strongly endeared to the members of his Church.

Dr. Patten was a fine classical scholar. There was no attempt at display in the pulpit; he delivered the *truth*, and left it with God to apply it to the hearts and consciences of his hearers. The reason assigned for his dismission, was that the Church had been long in a declining state. This was not of sufficient weight to dissolve a connection which had existed for nearly half a century. Dr. Patten had spent the energies of his youth in their service; he had reared up a large family in their midst and all his dearest associations were there. It was painful to his mind to be under the necessity of turning his back on the people of his charge, and to take up his residence in a spot where the changes had been so great in the period of nearly half a century, that he scarcely knew any of the inhabitants.

It would have been far better, had the church and society proposed a colleague, and allowed the venerable servant of God to have lived and died in their midst.

Dr. Patten, though dignified in manners, and commanding the respect of all, was yet very companionable, and at times highly amusing. A Mrs. K., a lady from the South, and connected with some of the first families, became insane, and was placed in the family of Rev. William Patten. She was rather disposed to sneer at his pretensions to the ministerial office, which he pleasantly submitted to. Subsequently, Brown University conferred on him the degree of D. D. Mrs. K. continued her attacks, when the Doctor remarked, "Why, Mrs. K., I am really surprised that a lady of your rank and dignity, will condescend so low as to insult a Doctor of Divinity." She appeared greatly surprised at the announcement. "You a D. D.?" "Yes, madam; do you require my credentials?" "No, sir," she replied; and from that moment, as he informed the author, she was always respectful. The Doctor jocosely remarked that this was all the benefit he derived from the Doctorate.

For many years, the Second Church was destitute of a single male member, and was indebted to the Deacons of the First Church for the duties which pertain to that office, in the celebration of the Lord's Supper. In 1833, a project for uniting these two churches in one began to be talked of, and gradually gained favor, until at length, on the 24th of May, 1833, the work was consummated.

On the 26th of Sept., 1839, the Rev. A. Henry Dumont was installed, by an Ecclesiastical Council, the first pastor of the United Church.

The societies being united in one, deemed it expedient to erect a new house of worship, which was accordingly done. This house was solemnly dedicated to the worship of the Triune God, on the 4th of June, 1834.

The present pastor is the Rev. Thatcher Thayer, who succeeded the Rev. Mr. Dumont, and who is highly esteemed by his people.

The two Congregational Churches, up to the time of the death of Dr. Hopkins, enjoyed the most entire harmony. So pure and deep was the sympathy of the two pastors, that they called each other by the appellations of *father* and *son*. The last time that Dr. Hopkins walked out with Dr. Patten, who at that time was comparatively a young man, and accompanied him home, Dr. Hopkins said, "What need have I any more of a cane, since I have your arm;" and gave his cane or long staff, mounted with ivory, into the hands of Dr. Patten, who used it afterwards, and reckoned it among his choice things. They were like David and Jonathan, "pleasant and lovely in their lives," and in their resting place on earth they are not divided. They repose in front of the Spring-street church.

A strong desire is expressed by the family of the late lamented Dr. Patten, that a monument be erected to his memory, and we trust, for the honor of the town, that no obstacles will be thrown in the way of the accomplishment of the object.

At the same time, the church and society over which Dr. Hopkins presided for so many years, should erect a suitable monument to his memory, or join with the family of Dr. Patten in the praiseworthy undertaking.

The estimation in which Dr. Hopkins' writings were held in Scotland, led the College at Edinburgh to confer on him the degree of D.D. It was a high honor, and showed that they highly appreciated his talents as an able theologian.

Dr. Hopkins' salary, for many years, did not exceed $200 per annum, and the parsonage house, which is still standing. His study would only admit of a table, with just sufficient room to move round it; it was there he wrote his System of Divinity, which cost him ten years' labor, and for the copyright of which he obtained $800.

A wealthy lady of his church, Mrs. Wright, was in the habit of furnishing himself and wife, which then comprised his family, dinner three times a week from her own table; and he and his companion would often take tea out, with some of his parishioners, who were always gratified with the visit of their pastor. Dr. Hopkins often remarked that he would not exchange his situation for an increase of salary, so delighted was he with Newport, and the affectionate church over which he ministered.

But few such self-sacrificing spirits are to be met with in this world. It was *the flock*, and not *the fleece* he was after. He had consecrated himself to the work of the Gospel ministry, and in that service he labored until removed by death. He looked for higher honors than earth could possibly confer, as the reward of his labors and toils in the service of his Lord and Master. A faithful minister will proclaim the truth to both saint and sinner; he will not shun to declare the whole counsel of God. The commission which he professes to have received, binds him to the faithful performance of this duty. His office is not one of earthly appointment, if well understood—though many at this day seem to view it so, by the cautious manner in which they wield the weapons of the Gospel, lest the minds of their hearers should be disturbed. It was not so with Hopkins and his associates; they believed that the investiture was from Jehovah, and that obedience was required of all who bore the vessels of the sanctuary. They put their trust entirely in God, and not in man for a blessing on their labors of love. Such were the divines Clark, Callender, Stiles, Hopkins, Brown, Clap, Thurston, and Patten, who graced the pulpits of that day.

1787.—Last Saturday night arrived here Capt. Benjamin Pearce, in the brig Elizabeth, sixty-three days from Copenhagen, bringing a bell of about 1,100 lbs. weight, for the Second Congregational Church of the City of Newport. "The City of Newport" is cast on the bell. It is now in the belfry of the Union Congregational Church, in Spring-street.

THE FIRST BAPTIST CHURCH IN NEWPORT, AND THE FIRST IN AMERICA.

The First Baptist Church in Providence having arrogated to itself the honor of being the first in the State and in the country, it was taken for granted that their claim was a valid one, and none attempted to deny to them the honor. But recently the subject has undergone a thorough examination, which has resulted in giving an entire new version to the subject. A committee was appointed by the church at Providence, to investigate the matter, of which Rev. T. C. Jameson was Chairman, wherein they report that they "are of the opinion that the Baptist church at Newport was formed certainly before the 1st of May, 1639, and probably on the 7th of March, 1638." Instead of submitting to the report, which, according to parliamentary usages, they should have done, they came out with a review of the doings of their committee, and finding themselves driven to the wall by the weight of evidence furnished of the priority of the First Church in Newport, labored to show that it was not in its commencement Anna-Baptist, but Pædo-Baptist.

May 11th, 1639. The existence of this church was matter of public record in Massachusetts:

"1639. The people of Aquedneck, gathered a church in a very disordered way, for they took some excommunicated persons, and others who were members of the church of Boston, and not dismissed."

"The church of Boston sent three brethren with letters to Mr. Coddington, and the rest of our members at Aquedneck, to understand their judgment in divers points of religion formerly maintained by all, or divers of them, and to require them to give account to the church of their unwarrantable practice, in communicating with excommunicated persons, &c. When they came, they found that those of them who dwelt at Newport, had joined themselves to a church there, newly constituted, and therefore refused to hear them as messengers of our church, or to receive the church's letters. Whereupon, at their return, the elders and most of the church would have them cast out, as refusing to hear the church, but all not being agreed, it was deferred."—*Winthrop's Journal*, *1st month*, (March) 24, 1639–40.

From this extract, it appears that this church, from its organization, rejected infant baptism, the supervision of the civil magistrates, &c., and was in fact a Baptist church. On what other ground can we possibly reconcile the conduct of the church at Newport, in thus refusing to receive the messengers which were sent from Boston? Most certainly, if they had been at this period Pædo-Baptist, they would never have rejected those of the same faith and order, but would have extended the right hand of fellowship to their brethren. It is well-known that infant baptism at that day among Pædo-Baptists, was the *sine qua non*, and all who differed in this grand essential were viewed as heretical and worthy to receive thirty stripes, which were subsequently inflicted on Mr. Holmes and others with great severity.

The charge preferred against this church was "in their communicating with excommunicated persons." Now, it is not probable that the church in Newport would receive into their communion, persons of immoral character, but rather individuals that had thought proper to exercise their own private judgment in matters of conscience. This was a point which gave offence to the churches in Massachusetts, and led them to view the church in Newport, as unworthy of their fellowship, having abandoned a vital principle of Christianity. There is displayed a spirit of dictation by the Congregational churches of Massachusetts towards this church, which preëminently characterizes their history. They came to Newport to *brow-beat* this church, but the church would not recognize them as brethren of the same faith and order with themselves. They were Anna-Baptists as early as this period, for in no other sense can we reconcile their conduct towards the churches of Massachusetts, which is well-known were Pædo-Baptist, and held to the ordinance of infant sprinkling as a matter of infinite importance.

The First Baptist Church in Providence has assumed two points, which she is unable to maintain: First, her existence being prior to that of the church at Newport; secondly, that the church was founded by Roger Williams. Comer, the first, and for the early history of our denomination, the most reliable of writers, ascribes distinctly and repeatedly, this priority to the Newport church. He had formed the design, more than a hundred and twenty years ago, of writing the history of the American Baptists, and in that work which he only lived to commence, but which embraces an account of this church, he says in one place, that it is the first of the Baptist denomination; and closing his history of it, he says: "Thus I have briefly given some account of the settlement and progress of the First Baptist church on Rhode Island, in New-England, and the first in America."

From the way in which he asserts it, the priority of the Newport church must have been a universally conceded fact. He was careful to excess, not to record as certain, that on which any suspicion rested, and yet this father of American Baptist history, whose veracity has never been questioned, states that in age it was prior to any other Baptist church in America. It is true, and I was sorry to see it, some later hand has added in a note: "*Excepting that of Providence.*" Who wrote this, I will not say, but no one should touch Comer's writings, unless he is a more reliable witness than that pains-taking and impartial man.

Besides his general carefulness, he was, when he wrote the above, on the most favorable terms with the Providence church, while a difficulty had occurred between him and the Newport church, which caused him the most painful feelings.

This interpretation of the writings of Comer, in order to give the priority to the church at Providence, is most certainly an unchristian act, and shows to what miserable shifts they were driven to obtain the honor which justly belongs to another. This, however, is not the first attempt to pluck the laurels from the brow of the people of Newport, and which they have too long passively submitted to; but a redeeming spirit is at work, which will be put forth in defence of her just and lawful claims, as the first to rear the Baptist standard in this land, as well as the first to publish to the world the great principle of the rights of conscience.

Rev. Mr. Adlam has shown conclusively that the present First Baptist church of Providence has existed only from 1652, and thus it cannot be the oldest of the Baptists in America. Dr. Hague, late pastor of that church, in his "Historical Discourse," prepared with great care, and received with uncommon satisfaction and respect by his people, does not deny a single statement that Comer, or Callender, or Backus have made, but as far as he refers to this subject harmonizes with them.

The First Baptist church in Providence has been called the "Roger Williams' Church," implying that he was its first patron and founder, and this, until very recently, has been the generally received opinion. Stephen Hopkins, Signer of the Declaration of Independence, grandson of Wickenden, uniformly affirmed that Wickenden was the first elder of the existing church, and asserted this in his "History of Providence," published in 1765. Moses Brown, that venerable Nestor of Providence, as he is called by Knowles, always held that his ancestor Chad Brown, was the first elder of the Providence Baptist church. John

Angel, born in 1691, claimed the same honor for his grandfather, Gregory Dexter, ancestor of Nathaniel G. B. Dexter, Esq., of Pawtucket, R. I.

Callender, in 1738, says: "The most ancient inhabitants now alive, some of them above eighty years old, who personally knew Mr. Williams, and were well acquainted with many of the original settlers, never heard that Mr. Williams formed the Baptist church there, but always understood that Mr. Brown, Mr. Wickenden, or Wigginton, Mr. Dexter, Mr. Olney, Mr. Tillinghast, &c., were the first founders of that church."

"This shows that the general opinion of Roger Williams being the founder and first pastor of that church is a modern theory; the farther you go back, the less generally is it believed, till coming to the most ancient times, to the men who knew Williams, they are such entire strangers to it, that they never heard that he formed the Baptist church there.

"Among the evils that have resulted from the wrong date of the Providence church, has been the prominence given to Roger Williams. It is greatly to be regretted that it has ever entered into the mind of any one to make him, in America, the founder of our denomination. In no sense was he so; well would it be for Baptists, and for Williams himself, could his short and fitful attempt to become a Baptist, be obliterated from the minds of men. A man only *four months* a Baptist, and then renouncing his baptism forever, to be lauded and magnified as the founder of the Baptist denomination in the New World! There is another name long, too long concealed by Williams' being placed before him, who will in after time be regarded with unmingled affection and respect, as the true founder of the Baptist cause in this country.

"That orb of purest lustre will yet shine forth, and Baptists, whether they regard his spotless character, his talents, his learning, the services he rendered, the urbanity and the modesty that distinguished him, will mention John Clarke, as the real founder of our denomination in America. And when Baptist history is better known than it is at present, every one pointing to that venerable church, which on one of earth's loveliest spots he established, will say: "This is the mother of us all!"—*Rev. S. Adlam, on the Origin of the Baptist Churches.*

Having presented the proof of the priority of the First

Baptist Church in Newport, we will proceed to notice the most important events connected with its history

Dr. John Clarke was its first pastor.

The first house erected to the worship of God, was built at Greenend ; they sold the house, and built a new one in 1708, on the lot in Tanner-street, now used as a burial place for the pastors of the church. The ground was the gift of John Clarke.

Mr. Obadiah Holmes was the second pastor of this church, and was called to that office very soon after Mr. Clarke sailed for England. In him the church found a bold and fearless advocate for truth, and a faithful and indefatigable pastor ; which office he continued to discharge, until, in 1682, he was removed from the scene of his sufferings and toils by death, in the seventy-sixth year of his age. He lies buried on the Holmes Farm, in Middletown, now owned by Gideon Peckham, Esq., where a tomb is erected to his memory.

Mr. Holmes was educated at the University of Oxford, in England, and seems to have been well adapted to the times in which he lived,—times which tried men's souls. The name of Holmes has now become extinct on the island, but his descendants, in the male line, are still numerous in New Jersey ; some of his descendants, in the female line, are still living in Newport.

After Mr. Holmes' death, the church seems to have been without a pastor, until about the year 1690, when Mr. Richard Dingley became their pastor. He continued with them only four years, when he left, and went to Charleston, South Carolina. After Mr. Dingley left, the church being few in number, and without any one to administer to them the word of life, they concluded to sit under the ministry of the Rev. Mr. Hiscox, of the Sabbatarian Church.

In 1711, this little band were again permitted to go up to the Zion they loved, and sit under the ministry of the Rev. William Peckham, who was ordained to the pastoral care of the church that same year.

Mr. Peckham continued faithfully to discharge the duties of his office, until the increasing infirmities of age rendered assistance indispensable to his own happiness, and the prosperity of the church.

In May, 1718, it appears from the records of the church,

that a Mr. Daniel White was received to her fellowship, by a letter from a church in England, and was soon after invited by the church to assist Elder Peckham in the discharge of his ministerial services; but he proved a very troublesome man, and created a division in the church.

In 1724, a meeting-house was erected for Mr. White, in which he continued to hold meetings for about four years; when, having but one individual member of his church left, he sold the meeting-house, and left the place.

In 1725, the church invited Mr. John Comer to become the colleague of Mr. Peckham, which invitation he accepted, and entered upon the duties of his office the following spring. Mr. Comer was a man of talents, and eminently successful as a minister of Jesus. Under his ministry, the number of the church was increased. He also commenced the records of the church before alluded to, and to him we are indebted for much of her early history. But the prosperity and happiness of the church, under Mr. Comer's administration, was soon interrupted by a sermon, delivered by him on Lord's day, November 17th, 1728, in which he maintained the doctrine of imposition of hands on baptized believers, as indispensable to church membership, &c. This discourse gave great uneasiness to the church, and finally resulted in his dismission, which occurred on the 8th of January, 1729; they, however, parted with their late pastor in love and peace.

The sixth pastor of this church, was the Rev. John Callender, nephew of the Rev. Elisha Callender, of the old Baptist Church, in Boston. Mr. Callender was a native of Boston, and received his education at Harvard University, in Cambridge. He accepted the invitation of this church to become their pastor on the 4th of July, 1731, and on the 13th day of October following, was set apart to that office, by fasting, and prayer, and the imposition of hands. The churches of Boston and Swanzey, by their ministers and messengers, were invited to participate in the services.

Mr. Callender ministered in this church, during the period of almost seventeen years, and was very evidently attended with the approbation and blessing of God. Like his divine master, Mr. Callender was poor in this world's goods, "but rich in faith, and heir to an inheritance incorruptible, undefiled, and that fadeth not away." His passage through this vale of tears, though not protracted to great length, was one of adversity, sickness, and pain. His departure from the toils and sorrows of earth, to that rest which remaineth for the people of God, was on the 26th of January, 1748, in the forty-second year of his age. Mr. Callender not only lived to secure the reputation of the scholar and gentleman, but what is infinitely more valuable, the reputation of a liberal-minded, pious, and devoted christian.

His Historical Sermon, preached in March, 1738, has immortalized his name. It breathes the same spirit of religious freedom and liberality of sentiment, that distinguished the names of Clarke, Coddington, and their associates.

His remains lie in the burial place in Tanner-street, Newport, beside John Clarke, which render it a consecrated spot.

The following inscription was composed by Dr. Moffat, a celebrated physician of Newport:

"Confident of awakening, here reposeth,

JOHN CALLENDER,

Of very excellent endowments of nature,
And of an accomplished education,
Improved by application, in the wide circle
Of the more polite arts, and useful sciences,
From motives of conscience and grace,
He dedicated himself to the immediate service
Of God,
In which he was distinguished as a shining
And very burning light, by a true and faithful
Ministry of seventeen years, in the First Baptist
Church of Rhode Island; where the purity
And evangelical simplicity of his doctrine, confirmed
And embellished by the virtuous and devout tenor
Of his own life,
Endear'd him to his flock, and justly conciliated
The esteem, love, and reverence of all the
Wise, worthy, and good.
Much humility, benevolence, and charity
Breathed in his conversation, discourses, and
Writings,
Which were all pertinent, reasonable, and useful.
Regretted by all, lamented by his friends, and

Deeply deplored by a Wife, and numerous issue,
He died
In the forty-second year of his age,
January 26th, 1748,
Having struggled through the vale of life
In adversity, much sickness, and pain,
With fortitude, dignity, and elevation of soul,
Worthy the Philosopher, Christian, and Divine."

Mr. Callender was succeeded in the pastoral office by the Rev. Edward Upham, who continued with them for more than twenty years, when, by death, he was removed from his labors, to that rest that remaineth for the people of God.

The eighth pastor of this church, was the Rev. Erasmus Kelley. He accepted the call of the church in 1771, and continued in the faithful discharge of his duty until 1778, when the meeting-house being used as a barrack for the troops of King George, he removed to Warren. But, in a few months, the enemy followed him to that place, and burnt the house in which he resided, and destroyed his valuable furniture.

In 1784, Mr. Kelley returned to Newport, and resumed his pastoral labors among his flock. But they were, however, of short continuance, for, on the 7th of November following, he was removed by death.

The ninth pastor was the Rev. Benjamin Foster, D. D. Mr. Foster commenced his labors with the church on the first sabbath in January, 1785, and, on the 5th of June following, was installed to the pastoral office. He contineud with them for three years, when he received and accepted a call from the First Baptist Church in New-York. Mr. Foster was a man of superior intellect, and of high literary attainments. He was well versed in the Greek, Hebrew, and Chaldean languages.

In 1789, the Rev. Michael Eddy became the pastor of this church, the duties of which office he continued to discharge for almost half a century. He possessed a liberal mind, was a pleasant companion, and in the sick-room, and at the bedside of death, he excelled. Mr. Eddy departed this life on the 3d day of June, 1835, in the seventy-fifth year of his age respected and beloved by his friends, in the church and congregation, and by the inhabitants of Newport. If greatness consists in goodness, then was Elder Eddy worthy of the appellation. During his labors of love in the church, he baptized more than five hundred, many of whom have been removed by death, and some remain unto this day. He was assisted one year, by the Rev. J. M'Kensie, of Newport

The Rev. Arthur A. Ross was installed March 11th, 1835, and remained with them a few years.

The present pastor is the Rev. S. Adlam, who continues to be popular with his people.

THE SECOND BAPTIST CHURCH.

In 1656, twenty-one members of the First Baptist Church in Newport, withdrew themselves, and formed the Second Baptist Church in this town. These brethren objected to the original church, in her use of psalmody, restraints upon the liberty of prophesying, and holding the laying on of hands a matter of indifference, which they regarded as binding on all believers.

The grounds for this schism will be looked upon at this day as too trivial to cause a separation. This very church, now, has an organ, agreeably to the directions of the sweet singer of Israel, "Praise Him upon the organ, and let every thing that hath breath, praise the Lord." It shows the progress which has been made in the science of music, by conforming to the letter and spirit of the Bible. It was viewed by these brethren as sin for any to engage in sacred music but the professed members of the church, and this without the least regard to order. A choir was looked upon as an infringement, and at variance with the teachings of the apostles. The tuning fork, the pitch-pipe, was horrible, and when the big fiddle, as it was then called, was introduced into the sanctuary, it was an innovation, which could not for a moment be tolerated. But, alas! those days of scriptural simplicity have fled, and now the organ is thought to be a necessary appendage, and its absence renders the services far less interesting. It is stated, that when Bishop Berkeley was in this country, he offered an organ to the

Congregational Church, in Berkley, Massachusetts, which they refused to accept. It was then presented to Trinity Church, Newport. How are the times changed! The town of Berkley was named in honor of the prelate.

The first pastor of this Church was the Rev. William Vaughan, who continued with them till his death, in 1677.

The second was the Rev. Thomas Baker, who subsequently settled in North Kingston. He was succeeded by the Rev. John Harden, who died in 1700.

The fourth pastor was the Rev. James Clarke, nephew of Dr. John Clarke. He was assisted in the discharge of his pastoral duties by the Rev. Daniel Whitman, who succeeded him in that office, in 1704.

In 1729, Mr. John Comer became a member of this church, and as Mr. Whitman was now aged and infirm, the church invited Mr. Comer to assist him in the ministry. Mr. Clarke died in 1736, aged eighty-seven years.

After the death of Mr. Clarke, the church invited Mr. Nicholas Eyers to become the colleague of Mr. Whitman, in which he continued until Mr. Whitman's death, in 1750. Mr. Eyers died in 1759.

He was succeeded by the Rev. Gardiner Thurston, who continued to discharge the duties of a minister of Jesus Christ with great faithfulness and success for more than forty years, when increasing infirmities of age pressed heavily upon him, and he applied to his beloved flock to procure an assistant, to relieve him from some part of his arduous labors. Mr. Thurston was not distinguished for superior talents; but he possessed, in a very eminent degree, what is infinitely more valuable—a heart deeply imbued with the spirit of his divine Master, which led him to labor untiringly in his service. Under his ministry, the church was united in love, and many were the trophies of redeeming grace, through his instrumentality. He was assisted for a few months by the Rev. Thomas Dunn; after him, by the Rev. William Peckham, a licentiate and member of the church.

In 1799, the Rev. William Collier, of Boston, was invited to labor as the assistant of Mr. Thurston. But in 1801, the venerable servant of God, knowing that the time of his departure was at hand, earnestly entreated his people to procure a pastor, and release him from the responsibilities of his charge. Accordingly, in May of that year, he was permitted to witness the settlement of the Rev. Joshua Bradley as his successor in the pastoral office. Mr. Thurston died the following year, aged eighty-two. "The memory of the just is blessed."

In October, 1807, the Rev. Mr. Gibson became their pastor; which office he held till March, 1815, when he requested and received a discharge from the pastoral charge of the church. Mr. Gibson was very successful in building up the cause of Christ, and many will have occasion to rejoice forever, who were made recipients of divine grace through his instrumentality.

The Rev. Samuel Widown was his successor, who continued with the church until 1817, when the Rev. Mr. Elton was invited to become its pastor, and was ordained on the 11th of June, of the same year. During the year 1820, more than one hundred were added by baptism. In 1822, Mr. Elton, having received a call from the Baptist Church in Windsor, Vermont, requested a dismission, which was reluctantly granted by his affectionate people.

Mr. Elton was succeeded in the pastoral office by the late lamented Gammell, December 10, 1823. Mr. Gammell's career was short, but brilliant; on the 31st of May, 1827, he suddenly expired, in the full hope of a glorious immortality. Mr. Gammell was no ordinary man; what was wanting in classical education, was more than made up in native talent. That stiffness and formality which is often the result of an imperfect training, was not witnessed in his case. There was an independence of character displayed in his public efforts, which showed that he felt his accountability to his God, and not to man. His death was not only deeply afflicting to his family and the church of God, but lamented by thousands who had with pleasure hung upon his lips, as the ambassador of Heaven, and listened to the impassioned eloquence of his soul.

On the 27th of September following, the Rev. J. O. Choules was inducted into the pastoral office. On the 3d of January, 1833, Mr. Choules tendered his resignation as pastor of the church, which was accepted on the 25th of the same month.

In December, 1833, Rev. John Dowling was called to the pastoral charge, which call he accepted. On the 27th of March following, he was publicly recognized as their pastor. On the

20th of July, 1836, Mr. Dowling tendered his resignation, which was accepted.

The Rev. Timothy G. Freeman was invited to become pastor of this church, on the 15th of January, 1837, which invitation he accepted, and was set apart to that office on the 16th of March following.

There is a ministerial fund of $8,000, left by the late Judge Taber, as also $1,000 for a poor fund, for the benefit of the church.

SOCIETY OF FRIENDS, OR QUAKERS.

The exact time when the Society of Friends or Quakers formed themselves into a body for church government, cannot now be actually stated. When William Leddra and Marmaduke Stephenson came to Newport, in the year 1658 or '59, they found their brethren here; and Daniel Gould, the first minister they have any account of in Newport, went to Boston with them, where the two first named were hanged, and Gould severely whipped at the carriage of a great gun, as appears by his account, written by himself, and published in 1700. The first records of the monthly meeting commenced in the year 1676.

But it is evident that they were formed into a society previous to that time, as John Burnyeat, a minister here from England, speaks in his journal of attending a yearly meeting in Newport, as early as 1671; and George Fox the following year, 1672, which was held at the house of William Coddington. In early times, the society was very large. About one-half the population, in 1700, were of that persuasion, and in that year they built the meeting house in which they now worship.

There have been many ministers, and other conspicuous members of that society, who lived in Newport and its vicinity. The most distinguished ministers who appeared among them, were Daniel Gould, John Hewlett, Ebenezer Slocum, Thomas Cornell, Samuel Freeborn, William Anthony, Gov. John Wanton, Joseph Wanton, Dr. Clarke Rodman, John Casey, Christopher Townsend, Joseph Michel, Isaac Lawton, David Buffum, Jacob Mott, and many others. The Mott family have ever been highly respectable; the property has continued in the family from the early settlement of the Island, and the *sixth* Jacob now occupies the homestead. General Nathaniel Greene's mother was Mary, the daughter of Jacob Mott, of Portsmouth, R. I. Like Mary, the mother of Washington, she gave an impress to his character, which rendered him highly distinguished. He was brought up in the religious principles of the Society of Friends, of which his father was a preacher. He early became fond of a military life, and was most active in forming the military company known as the Kentish Guards. General Greene's abilities soon attracted notice, and he was particularly distinguished by George Washington, who deservedly placed great confidence in his talents and judgment. When the army was formed, he was appointed Major-General. Gen. Greene was born at Potowamet, in the township of Warwick, R. I., on the 22d of May, 1742. The estate is still in possession of his family. He died at Savannah, Geo., aged forty-seven years.

Since the Revolutionary war, the Society has decreased in Newport, and on the Island. There are, however, a respectable number, who meet, both at Newport and at Portsmouth, and hold regular meetings in the middle of the week, on Thursdays and Sundays.

Previous to the war of the Revolution, their meeting house was well filled, above and below; but at that time many of its most wealthy members removed to other places, and never returned—and it is now remarked that there are but few settlements of Friends in the State of New York, or in Vermont, where the seed of Rhode Island is not to be found. And it is now easily shown, that within forty years, more of this Society have removed from the Island, than now dwell upon it.

This Society, at one period of the settlement, say from 1660 to 1760, was very influential in the government of the Colony. A large proportion of its Governors and other officers, were of that denomination. Among whom may be enumerated Wm. Coddington, Nicholas Easton, John Easton, Walter Clarke, and Henry Bull, who died the last of the first settlers; and John Wanton, Gideon Wanton, and Governor Hopkins, were all members of the Society.

SABBATTARIAN, OR SEVENTH DAY BAPTIST CHURCH.

This church was constituted in 1671. Several members of Mr. Clarke's church, entertaining conscientious scruples in regard to keeping the first day of the week as the Christian Sabbath, withdrew from the fellowship of that church, and organized themselves into a church, with Mr. William Hiscox as their leader. He died May 24, 1704, in the 66th year of his age.

The second pastor of this church was Rev. William Gibson, of London. He died March 12th, 1717, aged seventy-nine.

He was succeeded by Rev. Joseph Crandall, who died in 1737.

Their next pastor was Rev. Joseph Maxson, who was ordained as an Evangelist at Newport, Oct. 8th, 1732, and preached alternately at Newport and Westerly, serving the church with great faithfulness until his death, which occurred in September, 1748.

Elder John Maxson was the fifth pastor of this church, from the year 1754 until his death, in March, 1778.

Mr. Ebenezer David, who was converted in Brown University, during his collegiate course of study, became a member of this church, and was ordained May 31, 1775. He accepted a place of chaplain in the army, in which office he died, near Philadelphia, March 19th, 1778.

Mr. William Bliss became their next pastor. He was admitted as a member of the church, June 7th, 1764, and was ordained an evangelist at Hopkinton, Dec. 7th, 1779, and was installed pastor of this church, Dec. 25th, 1780. He continued faithfully to discharge the duties of his office until his death, which occurred May 4th, 1808, aged eighty-one years.

Elder Bliss owned a farm at "Green-End," where he resided. His second wife was the sister of Gov. Ward. The relationship of the people of the Island, either by blood or marriage, is quite remarkable, when the matter is investigated. They seem to be one family. Elder Bliss was a fine sportsman, and the neighborhood where he resided furnished much game at that period. The precision with which he took aim, and his great success, led the British, who were often present to witness his skill, to think they had a formidable enemy to encounter in the

Yankees. His remains lay buried in the family burial ground at Green-End.

On the Bliss farm are excavations, known as the "Bliss Mines." Tradition says "it was the work of money diggers," who believed that treasure was hidden there. Of their success we have no means of knowing. It was a judicious remark of an eminent professor, that "the most gold lay under the ploughshare." Some of late have attempted to invest these subterraneous passages with the marvellous, in order to excite interest in the minds of the credulous and unsuspecting. They suggest that it was the chosen retreat of the noted Kid, where he deposited his plunder, and its proximity to the ocean rendered it a safe and convenient retreat from his enemies. This, however, being of recent origin, should be received with caution, as it carries on its front a strong appearance of fiction.

Since penning the above, we have conversed with Captain Jeremiah Bliss, now in the 82d year of his age, (the son of Elder Bliss.) He remarked: "I have often heard my father say that the excavations were made by his father, in the hope of finding treasure, which he imagined was buried there." If there was no tradition on the subject, its first appearance would lead the mind to the belief that it was the work of nature. But on a more careful examination it will be found to have been the work of art, as the drills in the rock are plainly visible. The passage from the "Mine" to Easton's Pond, was undoubtedly designed for a drain to carry off the water. It is, on the whole, quite a curiosity, and worthy of notice for its antiquity, without making it the abode of smugglers.

The last pastor, Rev. Henry Burdick, was admitted as a member of this body, January 30, 1802, and was ordained to the work of the Gospel ministry, December 10, 1807. He continued to labor with them until his death, which occurred October 22d, 1843. Since that period they have had no regular ministrations.

This church, previous to the Revolutionary war, embraced a number of talented and influential men. The Hon. Samuel Ward, who for several years was Governor of Rhode Island, and a member also of the Continental Congress, belonged to this church. But the war scattered them, and greatly interrupted their prosperity. Since that time this church has never been able to recover her former eminence, and for several years past, having but few if any additions, the church has gradually decreased, so that its present number is but eight, who reside in Newport. Their first house of worship was built at "Greene End," near Newport.

THE MORAVIANS, OR UNITED BRETHREN.

In 1758, the Moravians, or United Brethren, constituted a church in Newport. The origin of this church is as follows:

In 1749, two missionaries, Matthew Reutz, and George Haske, stopped at Newport, on their way to Surinam. While here, they formed an acquaintance with the Rev. Timothy Peckham, a Sabbatarian preacher, who kindly received them at his house, and introduced them to several pious persons, who desired them to preach to them the unsearchable riches of Christ. This request was complied with, and at their departure deep solicitude was expressed by their hearers, that a teacher from among the Brethren might be sent to gather a congregation in Newport. These Brethren no sooner arrived at their place of destination, than they wrote to Bethlehem, Penn., and requested that some of the Brethren at that place, if possible, should make them a visit. Soon after two Brethren from Bethlehem made them a visit, and others from time to time, until the constitution of the church, in 1758.

The first pastor of this church was the Rev. Richard Utley.

The second pastor was the Rev. Thomas Yarrell

The third pastor was Rev. Frederick Smith.

These were pastors of the church from its constitution until the year 1765.

The fourth pastor was the Rev. Lewis Rusmeyer, who held this office from 1766 to 1783.

From 1785 to 1802, the Rev. Frederick Smith held the pastoral office of this church.

The sixth pastor was the Rev. Samuel Towle, from 1803 to 1819. Mr. Towle was a most estimable man; he was universally beloved by the church and the inhabitants of Newport, and it is a matter of regret that he and his family were not continued here. It was ascertained after he had left, that the society in Bethlehem would have afforded her aid in Newport, without his repairing to Bethlehem. The infirmities of age prevented his laboring much in the service of Christ; still his presence was consoling, with those of his amiable wife and two lovely daughters, Mary and Louisa, who have all since passed into the eternal world.

His successor was Rev. George G. Miller, who remained with the church but one year.

In 1821, Rev. John G. Herman became the pastor of the church, the duties of which office he continued to discharge until 1823.

The ninth pastor, Rev. Charles A. Van Vleck, served the church from 1827 to 1834.

The tenth and last pastor was the Rev. Charles F. Seidel, who commenced his pastoral relations in 1837. For many years they have been without a shepherd, and the flock has become greatly reduced. But a few are now to be found in Newport, and they have connected themselves with other religious bodies. The influence of this Christian body had a salutary influence on the hearts of the community; the weapon which they wielded was *love*, and this alone will subdue the evil passions of man's nature, and fit and qualify him for heaven.

THE FOURTH BAPTIST CHURCH.

The Fourth Baptist Church in Newport, was organized June 23, 1783. The original members of the church were nine males, and these were chiefly from the Second Baptist Church in this town, who not feeling satisfied to remain in that church, withdrew and formed another.

They believed that "where the spirit of the Lord is, there is liberty," and hence they thought all Christians were called upon to exhort, and to teach in public. "Also, the liberty and duty to prophesy or exhort, in all or any meetings of the church, was most fully recognized and maintained."

The first ministers of the church were Rev. Caleb Greene and William Moore, who were ordained November 27th, 1796, and were succeeded by John Ormsbee, a member of the Baptist church in North Providence.

Mr. Ormsbee was ordained the 14th of September, 1821, and removed to Wickford in 1822. Between this time and 1826, Elder Greene and Elder James Graham, preached with them a short time, the last being invited to become their pastor, but was under the necessity of returning to Beauford, S. C., in consequence of the decease of the minister of the church in that place. Mr. Graham was a highly acceptable preacher.

The next minister was James A. McKenzie, who was ordained to the pastoral office, August 12th, 1830. Mr. McKenzie was succeeded by the Rev. Samuel Robbins, of Buxton, Me., November, 1835.

This church can now hardly be said to have an existence, no more than the Sabbatarians and the Moravians. It is painful to see churches which have once existed, lose their visibility.

METHODIST SOCIETY.

Previous to the year 1805, Newport was occasionally visited by Methodist clergymen, having oversight of that district of country in which Newport was situated.

In December, 1805, the presiding elder of this district was pleased to send to this place the Rev. R. Hubbard, who commenced his mission in the First Baptist meeting-house, under the pastoral care of the Rev. Michael Eddy. Mr. Hubbard continued here two years, and was succeeded by the Rev. Messrs. Mervin, Webb, Frost, and Lambert, when the latter was succeeded by Mr. Webb, who became a Local Preacher, and remained with the church nine years. He was succeeded by Messrs. Mudge, Norris, Puffer, Tucker, Kent, Lord, Jansen, Ely, and Cady.

There is also a small church, of the Methodist denomination, in Portsmouth, in the north part of the island, which has a convenient house of worship, and is regularly supplied with the ministry of the word of life.

COLORED UNION CHURCH.

In 1824, several individuals of the people of color, among whom was Newport Gardiner, who subsequently died at Liberia, formed themselves into a religious society, under a written constitution, by the name of the "Colored Union Church and Society, in Newport, Rhode Island." There is also among them a society for promoting the education of colored children and youth, called the "School Friend Association," which sustains an instructress the greater part of the year. They own and occupy a very neat and commodious house of worship. Since the purchase of the house in 1835, it has been raised, and a basement story added, which is occupied as a school-room, &c.

The people of color, in Newport, are a well-bred class, such as you seldom meet with elsewhere.

ST. JOSEPH'S CHURCH.

Soon after the extensive works at Fort Adams were commenced, by the United States, in 1825, Newport was occasionally visited by a Roman Catholic Priest, to look after the spiritual interests of that class of our population, belonging to the Catholic Church, many of whom had been induced to take up their residence in Newport, by finding employment at the Fort.

The Rev. Robert D. Woodley, a native of Virginia, was the first Catholic Priest that organized a congregation in Newport, for the accommodation of which, he purchased of E. Trevett, Esq., in 1828, the school-house, in Barney-street, where divine service was maintained for several years.

Mr. Woodley resigned his charge in 1831, and was succeeded by the Rev. John Corry, who officiated in that congregation, until August, 1837.

In the spring of 1833, Mr. Corry opened a subscription, for the erection of a church, which was commenced the latter part of that same year, and completed in 1836. The house is spacious, and well-finished, and occupies a commanding site at the head of Barney-street. The estimated cost of lot, building, &c., was about $4000; all of which was contributed, and paid by the Catholics, at Fort Adams.

On the 24th of August, 1837, the church was dedicated under the title of St. Joseph, by the Right Rev. Bishop Fenwick, of Boston, Massachusetts. On the following day, the Rev. Mr. Corry, under whose superintendence the church had been erected and completed, resigned his charge of the mission, and was succeeded by the Rev. Constantine Lee.

The Rev. Mr. Corry, in a letter to the Rev. A. Ross, speaking of the people of Newport, says: "It is but just for me to add, that I have never seen a town in the United States, among whose inhabitants there is less *intolerance* and religious bigotry. I have for six years been more or less among them, and during that period none have denied me the common civilities of life, because I was a Catholic priest, but always treated me with the greatest respect." And in proof of the practical existence of religious toleration in Newport, he says: "Our church stood for upward of two years with its windows unprotected by blinds, and during that time not one pane of glass was broken."

The high encomium passed on the people of Newport, by the Rev. Mr. Corry, shews the Catholic spirit which exists there, and which is the fruits of the principle of religious toleration established by Clarke and Coddington, which God grant may ever continue to influence the people. The Catholic population of Newport, numbers about five hundred. A very costly edifice of stone is now in the course of completion, which will prove highly ornamental to the town.

SECOND EPISCOPAL PARISH.

Early in 1833, the Second Episcopal parish was formed in this place, by members of Trinity church. After the due organization of the parish, and an application of the Episcopal Missionary Convocation of Rhode Island, the Rev. John West commenced his labors as the minister of the parish. On the 17th of March, 1833, public worship commenced in the State House, from which the congregation soon removed, to the house of the First Congregational Society, at that time unoccupied. A subscription was immediately opened for building a new church, which as soon as $600 was subscribed, was commenced. In June of the following year, the new church was completed and consecrated. The cost of the building, including organ and furniture, together with the lot, was about $17,000. Of this sum about $11,000 was realized from the sale of pews, and the remainder by a noble act of generosity, contributed and paid by individual members of the corporation.

The Parish has now a fund of nearly $5000 in pews, and of the hundred and twelve pews in the church, at least one hundred of them are sold or rented. At the present date, this parish has been but five years in existence, and the contemplation of its history affords many pleasing evidences that the Divine Head of the Church has poured upon it the continual dew of his blessing. Accessions have been constantly made to the church, and on an average, the additions to the communion have been about thirty a year.

The church from its commencement, has enjoyed great domestic tranquillity and peace. No unhappy difference of opinions has arisen among them, resulting in unfriendly dissensions and divisions, or anything found on the pages of her history, to tarnish the glory and beauty of the Zion of God. The congregation is large, and their attendance on the public and social services of the church, worthy of imitation.

This church has engaged in the cause of missions with a liberality and zeal, becoming the dignity of the Christian character, and the magnitude and importance of the great missionary enterprise. Their annual contributions for home missionary purposes in Rhode Island, amount to not less than $150, and for foreign missions and other benevolent purposes, their contributions equal, if not exceed that sum.

The present Rector of the church, is the Rev. Mr. Watson, a man universally respected by his parish, and whose labors have been eminently successful in advancing the interest of the Redeemer's kingdom in the world.

EPISCOPAL CHURCHES IN PORTSMOUTH.

In the year 1834, a missionary was sent by the Rhode Island Convocation, to Portsmouth, R. I. A parish was organized, under the name of St. Paul's Church, and within one year, a respectable house of worship was erected, and with the aid of about $1200 in contributions, from Episcopalians in other places, was entirely paid for. At the same time, a fund was secured in pews for the support of the minister, amounting to more than one thousand dollars. The labors of a zealous, devoted missionary in that place, have been blessed to the gathering of a respectable congregation, and an addition of about forty members to the communion of the church.

The Rhode Island Convocation has contributed towards the support of the minister of the parish, up to the present time, nearly $2,000.

The church of St. Mary's has been subsequently organized in Portsmouth, and a neat and tasteful church of stone erected by the munificence of Miss Sarah Gibbs, the daughter of the late George Gibbs, Esq., an eminent merchant of Newport.

In Middletown, the Third Episcopal Church has been organized, and a neat structure has been erected, called the "Church of the Holy Cross." Rev. Mr. Williams is the present Rector.

THE UNITARIAN CONGREGATIONAL CHURCH.

An Association of gentleman friendly to Unitarian views of doctrine, was formed in this town, October, 1835. Their earliest meetings for Divine service, were held in the State House; in the course of the following month, they purchased of the Fourth Baptist Society in this place, the church in Mill street. This church had originally belonged to the First Congregational Church and Society, over which the celebrated Dr. Hopkins presided for many years as pastor.

A charter was granted to this Association by the General Assembly of the State, at their January session, in 1836, incorporating them as "The Unitarian Congregational Church," in Newport. Soon after this, the society commenced rebuilding and remodelling the old house in Mill-street, worshipping in the mean time at Masonic Lodge, in Church-street. The work was completed in the Spring of 1836, and for elegance, neatness, and taste in its internal arrangements, is perhaps unequalled in Rhode Island, excepting Trinity church. The new house (for only the frame of the old building had been retained, together with the corner-stone, bearing the inscription, "For Christ and Peace,") was dedicated on the 27th of July that same year. The Rev. Charles T. Brooks of Salem, Mass., was called as the first pastor, in Jan., 1837, and ordained June 14th of the same year. The organization of a church was begun in the summer of 1837. The Communion of the Lord's Supper was first administered on Sunday, October 3d, and continues to be administered monthly.

The Rev. Mr. Brooks married a daughter of the late Benj. Hazard, Esq., of Newport, and continues the able and efficient pastor of this church, respected and beloved for his amiable traits of character, which preëminently distinguish him in the varied walks of life.

CHURCHES OF THE CHRISTIAN DENOMINATION.

There are three churches of this denomination on the Island, —two in Middletown, and one in Portsmouth. The first church in Middletown was organized Oct. 14th, 1828. Their first pastor was the Rev. Harvey Sullings, who served the church with acceptance for nearly five years from its constitution.

They own a very neat and commodious house of worship, about three miles from Newport, erected soon after the organization of the Church.

The house of the Second Society stands on the east road, about three miles from Newport.

The church in Portsmouth was constituted Oct. 16th, 1834. Its first pastor was the Rev. Salmon Tobey. His ministry commenced with this people in April, 1834, and continued for two years, during which time six members were added to the church.

His successor in the pastoral office of this church was the Rev. John Taylor. He commenced his labors with them on the 1st of June, 1837. The house in which they worship was erected in 1821, by voluntary subscription, and is called the Union Meeting-House. It is pleasantly located on the east road about six miles from Newport.

FRIENDS' MEETING-HOUSE.

"The first date upon record of a new meeting-house at Portsmouth, is of a monthly meeting being held at our new meeting-house 2d month 28th, 1702."

There was a house built prior to this, "which was sold and afterwards converted into a barn." As the records of the Society were mostly destroyed, the exact date of the first house cannot be ascertained.

The yearly meeting formerly commenced at Portsmouth on Saturday, but the change in the mode of traveling has led to the commencement of the services at Newport, as being more convenient for the Society.

CENTRAL BAPTIST CHURCH, NEWPORT.

In 1847, a portion of the Second Baptist Church seceded, organized a Church, and invited the Rev. Henry Jackson to become their pastor. He accepted the invitation, and is still laboring among them. Their place of worship is in Clarke-street, formerly the Second Congregational house, where the late Rev. William Patten, D. D., labored for nearly half a century.

The spirit which has characterized the various religious bodies on the Island, has been as catholic as could have been expected in the nature of things. It was not to be presumed that where a diversity of sentiment prevailed, there would be necessarily a perfect agreement in all things; but they have rather agreed to differ on non-essentials, regarding practical

Christianity as the sum and substance of evangelical religion. No where does the character of the Saviour appear more lovely and attractive, than when his divine power was exercised to soothe and mitigate the evils of hunger and nakedness, with all the attendant miseries which flesh is heir to. And the gratitude which is evinced by the subjects of His compassion, was in some degree equivalent to the sincerity which prompted these humane and benevolent acts. In truth, there is no blessing like sympathy;

> "It soothes, it hallows, elevates, subdues,
> And bringeth down to earth its native heaven.
> Life hath nought else that may supply its place;
> Void is ambition, cold is vanity,
> And wealth an empty glitter without love."

LIST OF SUBSCRIBERS.

The Hon. John H. Clarke, United States' Senator, Rhode Island
George B. Holmes, Rhode Island
E. Carrington, Rhode Island
Thomas Burgess, Rhode Island
N. B. Crocker, Rhode Island
The Rt. Rev. J. P. K. Henshaw, D.D., Bishop of Rhode Island
J. H. Eames, Rhode Island
Thomas F. Carpenter, Rhode Island
W. S. Greene, Rhode Island
E. Dyer, Jun., Rhode Island
William Grosvenor, Rhode Island
J. Balch, Jr., Rhode Island
W. B. Burdick, Rhode Island
N. Smith, Rhode Island
Allen Brown, Rhode Island
H. N. Slater, Rhode Island
Benoni Harris, Rhode Island
R. Newcomb, Rhode Island
George Z. Earl, Rhode Island
Marshall Woods, Rhode Island
E. P. Mason, Rhode Island
E. B. Burges, Rhode Island
Thomas Sukill, Rhode Island
S. Ang. Arnold, Rhode Island
C. G. Dodge, Rhode Island
B. J. Brown, Rhode Island
R. J. Arnold, Rhode Island
James R. Brown, Rhode Island
Benjamin Cowell, Rhode Island
The Hon. A. C. Greene, United States' Senator, Rhode Island

John H. Ormsbee, Rhode Island
B. D. Weeden, Rhode Island
Resolved Waterman, Rhode Island
Alpheus Burges, Rhode Island
Prince Davis, Rhode Island
Richard Waterman, Rhode Island
Nelson H. Mowry, Rhode Island
H. C. Gardiner, Rhode Island
H. B. Lyman, Rhode Island
H. W. Bradford, Rhode Island
Hartford Tingley, Rhode Island
William S. Patten, Rhode Island
John I. Hall, Rhode Island
George Grinnell, Rhode Island
Albert S. Gallup, Rhode Island
T. D. Round, Rhode Island
Charles Potter, Rhode Island
S. Dorr, Rhode Island
Baker T. Wesson, Rhode Island
J. C. Brown, Rhode Island
S. G. Arnold, Rhode Island
A. D. Smith, Rhode Island
W. C Snow, Rhode Island
James Mulchahey, Rhode Island
John C. Tower, Rhode Island
Samuel Merry, Rhode Island
George Alexander, Rhode Island
Benjamin Allen, Rhode Island
Alexander Eddy, Rhode Island
W. B. Sayles, Rhode Island
Lewis L. Miller, Rhode Island
Hon. N. R. Knight, Rhode Island
J. D. Burgess, Rhode Island
Gideon Palmer, Rhode Island
Hon. Charles Jackson, Rhode Island
Ebenezer Wood, Rhode Island
William H. Bogman, Rhode Island
R. A. Webster, Rhode Island
James T. Hawes, Rhode Island
Honorable A. Simons, Rhode Island

John B. Herreshoff, Rhode Island
Samuel Dexter, Rhode Island
Edward R. Young, Rhode Island
Menzies Sweet, Rhode Island
William Fletcher, Rhode Island
Bailey W. Evans, Rhode Island
Thomas Vernon, Rhode Island
Nathaniel G. B. Dexter, Rhode Island
Henry Marchant, Rhode Island
Honorable Tristam Burges, Rhode Island
H. Foster, Rhode Island
Samuel Marlor, Rhode Island
Hezekiah Allen, Rhode Island
William P. Bullock, Rhode Island
Samuel Osgood, Rhode Island
John B. Ames, Rhode Island
Thomas Greene, Rhode Island
Thomas C. Hartshorn, Rhode Island
A. Caswell, Rhode Island
Elisha Harris, Rhode Island
Earl Carpenter, Rhode Island
William T. Pierce, Rhode Island
C. L. Bowler, Rhode Island
H. Barker, Rhode Island
E. Ham, Rhode Island
Miss Goddard, Rhode Island
W. A. Clarke, Rhode Island
William Gardner, Rhode Island
Benjamin Watson, New-York
Rev. Evan M. Johnson, New-York
Right Rev. Benjamin T. Onderdonk, D.D., New-York
Rev. Samuel Sebury, D.D., New-York
Charles H. Russell, New-York
Rev. S. H. Tyng, D.D., New-York
T. R. Minturn, New-York
R. R. Ward, New-York
J. Ward, New-York
Rev. G. T. Bedell, New-York
Honorable J. Prescott Hall, New-York
C. A. Busteed, New-York

John Bristed, New-York
Rev. William Berrian, D.D., New-York
Rev. William E. Eigenbrodt, New-York
David P. Hall, New-York
Rev. C. S. Henry, New-York
R. B. Minturn, New-York
Rev. Ed. Y. Higbee, D.D., New-York
Right Rev. J. M. Wainwright, D.D., New-York
Commodore M. C. Perry, United States' Navy
August Belmont, New-York
Rev. J. F. Schroeder, D.D., New-York
William D. Mumford, New-York
B. A. Mumford, New-York
Rev. Francis L. Hawks, D.D., New-York
A. Bloomer Hart, New-York
Major-Gen. Winfield Scott, United States' Army, New-York
Rev. W. H. Lewis, D.D., New-York
Rev. B. C. Cutler, D.D., New-York
Rev. Francis Vinton, D.D., New-York
Rev. Benjamin Evans, D.D., New-York
Rev. Lewis P. W. Balch, New-York
Rev. Jesse Pound, New-York
Right Rev. Henry J. Whitehouse, D.D., New-York
M. W. Dwight, New-York
Gold S. Silliman, New York
John S. Stone, New-York
Isaac Pardee, New-York
W. A. Muntravers, New-York
R. S. Howland, New-York
W. Everett, New-York
Cornelius R. Duffie, New-York
Clement C. Moore, New-York
William J. Hoppin, New-York
G. Curtis, New-York
S. Cahoon, Jun., New-York
Thomas D. M'Gee, New-York
Rev. Benjamin I. Haight, D.D., New-York
Samuel Hazard, New-York
Joseph Harrison, New-York
Thomas R. Hazard, Portsmouth, Rhode Island

J. H. Gilliot, New-York
John Caswell, New-York
R. W. Buloid, New-York
R. Buloid, New-York
R. M. Olyphant, New York
S. A. Crapo, New-York
Hamilton Hoppin, New-York
Peleg Hall, New-York
George Collins, New-York
Frederick A. Farley, New-York
Mrs. R. H. Thurston, New-York
Silas Holmes, New-York
George S. Coe, New-York
L. P. Robinson, New-York
James E. Gorton, New-York
William Childs, New-York
James Fellows, New-York
Richard Cornell, New-York
James S. Tilley, New-York
P. M. Abercrombie, New-York
Thomas A. Whitaker, New-York
James Jacobs, New-York
C. A. Talbot, New-York
S. H. Cahoon, New-York
J. Greenwood, New-York
Henry B. Melville, New-York
George O. Tupper, New-York
G. L. Willard, New York
Z. Ingalls, New-York
A. G. Peckham, New-York
Stanton Bebee, New-York
Edward Anthony, New-York
Isaac H. Cady, New-York
A. B. Thomas, New-York
C. B. Le Baron, New-York
John Davol, New-York
J. A. Sprague, New-York
Nehemiah Knight, New-York
Philip Tillinghast, New-York
William Brenton Greene, New-York

Edwin Hoyt, New-York
Elbert J. Anderson, New-York
Mrs. Martha M. Anderson, New-York
L. M. Roffman, New-York
Waldon Pell, New-York
Henry H. Ward, New-York
R. H. M'Curdy, New-York
Isaac Otis, New-York
H. C. De Rham, New-York
Charles Marsh, New-York
C. L. Anthony, New-York
Mrs. Auchmuty, New-York
Robert W. Aborn, New-York
G. M. Gardiner, New-York
James N. Olney, New-York
Charles Congdon, New-York
M. H. Grinnell, New-York
Joseph Bridgham, New-York
John Jay, New-York
George R. Sheldon, New-York
Isaac Arnold, New-York
Thomas T. Sheffield, New-York
D. H. Gould, New-York
John E. Bigley, New-York
W. A. Work, New-York
C. V. Spencer, New-York
T. W. Wilber, New-York
John F. Phillips, New-York
H. T. Wetmore, New-York
N. Geffry, New-York
D. S. Kennedy, New-York
William Ellery Sedgwick, New-York
S. T. Caswell, New-York
C. H. Van Brunt, New-York
John D. M'Kenzie, New-York
Francis B. Cole, New-York
William H. Douglass, New-York
Pierre C. Kane, New-York
Samuel Johnson, New-York
Robert T. Douglas, New-York

E. Douglas, New-York
T. J. Carr, New-York
C. G. Snow, New-York
P. G. Taylor, New-York
Henry Ruggles, New-York
Samuel Ward, New-York
Hon. George Bancroft, New-York
Stephen William Smith, New-York
J. H. Mahony, New-York
A. Gracie King, New-York
Howard C. Cady, New-York
James Edwards Smith, New-York
Edward Dodge, New-York
C. Jenks Smith, New-York
Rev. Thomas H. Skinner, Jun., New-York
W. B. Lawrence, New-York
Rev. G. Spring, D.D., New-York
Rev. Erskine Mason, D.D., New-York
Rev. J. M'Elvoy, D.D., New-York
Rev. W. W. Phillips, D.D., New-York
Rev. W. Patton, D.D., New-York
Rev. Joseph C. Stiles, New-York
B. D. Silliman, New-York
R. W. Dickinson, New-York
A. A. De Motte, New-York
Charles Dickinson, New-York
John B. Ward, New-York
Rev. George Potts, D.D., New-York
Rev. John M. Krebs, New-York
George Dickinson, New-York
Rev. I. S. Spencer, D.D., New-York
Ralph Malbone, New-York
Rev. M. W. Jacobus, D.D., New-York
Rev. Samuel D. Burchard, D.D., New-York
Rev. John Knox, D.D., New-York
William Dumont, New-York
Rev. Samuel H. Cox, D.D., New-York
Rev. John M. Macauley, New-York
Rev. N. J. Marselus, New-York
Rev. James Benjamin Hardinbugh, D.D., New-York

Thomas Adams Emmet, New-York
C. Champlin, New-York
J. J. Lyons, New-York
Samuel R. Johnson, Brooklyn, Long Island
Ezekiel Ostander, New-York
John H. Baker, New-York
P. Balen, New-York
J. Rich, New-York
S. Knowlton, New-York
E. K. AlBurtis, New-York
Horace Southmayd, New-York
Rev. Henry Chase, New-York
Rev. S. H. Cone, D.D., New-York
A. C. Wheat, New-York
Rev. William R. Williams, D.D., New-York
John C. Thatcher, New-York
John H. Ormsbee, Jun., New-York
Samuel P. Robinson, New-York
Samuel J. Jacobs, New-York
James Robinson, New-York
Right Rev. John Hughes, D.D., New-York
William Richmond, New-York
Cyrus H. Fay, New-York
David Buffum, New-York
Rev. Ira R. Steward, New-York
T. B. Stillman, New-York
Benjamin Babcock, New-York
Charles D. Rhody, New-York
Courtlandt Palmer, New-York
Rev. E. H. Chapin, New-York
Rev. M. S. Hutton, D.D., New-York
Rev. J. M. Mathews, D.D., New-York
Robert S. Slocum, New-York
J. Guidicine, New-York
W. Ames, New-York
Rev. N. Baird, D.D., New-York
Theodore Dehore, New-York
John R. Van Nest, Jun., New-York
H. William Channing, New-York
Samuel L. Bush, New-York.

E. Martin, New-York
John Blunt, Brooklyn
J. W. Brinley, New-York
Edward Brinley, United States' Navy
Ezra Jones, New-York
L. W. Gibbs, New-York
Edward Macomber, New-York
W. W. Russel, New-York
W. C. Russel, New-York
Edward J. Manee, New-York
Joseph W. Taggart, New-York
J. H. Weston, New-York
D. Bigler, New-York
Rev. James M. Macdonald, New-York
John C. Guldin, New-York
James Coggeshall, New-York
Isaac T. Hopper, New-York
John H. Bevier, New-York
W. C. Rowers, New-York
Philip S. Crooke, Brooklyn
Blandina Dudley, Albany
Rev. J. H. Hobart, New York
A. Le Barbie, New-York
W. B. Ogden, New-York
B. B. Grinnell, New-York
Robert A. Durfee, New-York
George S. Easton, New-York
P. W. Engs, New-York
Edward Minturn, New-York
Augustus Whiting, New-York
J. Thorndike, New-York
Benjamin B. Hawkins, Rhode Island
E. F. Newton, Rhode Island
Timothy Coggeshall, Rhode Island
J. Thayer, Rhode Island
George Jones, Rhode Island
R. P. Lee, Rhode Island
M. H. Gould, Rhode Island
T. R. Hunter, Rhode Island
Charles Hunter, Rhode Island

Hon. H. Clay, Ashland, Ky.
James Atkinson, Rhode Island
Samuel B. Vernon, Rhode Island
Thomas Brinley, Rhode Island
Alfred Hazard, Rhode Island
R. B. Lawton, Rhode Island
Charles Sarriall, Philadelphia, Pa.
William V. Taylor, Rhode Island
Rev. D. R. Brewer, Rhode Island
Rev. Thomas R. Lambert, United States' Navy
Levi H. Gales, New Orleans
Sarah Bailey, Rhode Island
Joseph I. Bailey, Rhode Island
Henry Bull, Rhode Island
D. C. Millett, Rhode Island
S. Gibbs, Rhode Island
Rev. W. Williams, Rhode Island
N. B. Crocker, Rhode Island
Hon. Byron Diman, Rhode Island
William G. Hammond, Rhode Island
William H. D'Wolf, Rhode Island
E. King, Rhode Island
Mrs. T. H. Sweet, Boston, Ms.
Robert R. Carr, Rhode Island
Mrs. L. M. Breese, Rhode Island
Mrs. George Engs, Rhode Island
John Hopper, Rhode Island
Rev. H. Potter, D.D., Albany, New-York
Samuel Brown, Rhode Island
Jenny Lind, Stockholm
H. Allen Wright, Rhode Island
De Lancey Kane, New-York
Albert Sumner, Rhode Island
Charles Lyman, New-York
T. Tompkins, Rhode Island
William B. Spooner, Rhode Island
Mrs. I. D. M. Perry, Rhode Island
Henry Waterman, Rhode Island
Thomas Brownell, United States' Navy, New York
Alexander Burgess, Rhode Island

W. B. Burdick, Rhode Island
Mrs. James, Rhode Island
Samuel Allen, Rhode Island
James B. Bliss, Rhode Island
D. H. Braman, Rhode Island
Jeremiah C. Bliss, New-York
John O. Patton, New-York
John W. Richmond, New-York
William R. Andrews, New-York
W. R. Danforth, New-York
Hon. Charles T. James, United States' Senator, Rhode Island
J. Bullock, New-York
Washington Hoppin, New-York
Edward Seagrave, New-York
William Wiley, New-York
Edward J. O'Brien, New-York
Bernard O'Reilly, New-York
William C. Chapin, New-York
William Newton, New-York
D. T. Swinburne, New-York
Samuel Adlam, New-York
James Fitton, New-York
William Sanford Rogers, New-York
Major G. W. Patten, United States' Army
Col. Gates, New-York
James Cook Richmond, New-York
Jacob Babbitt, New-York
Honorable John Brown Francis, Rhode Island
Joseph L. Gardner, New-York
Charles Smith, New-York
Robert Rogers, New-York
Charles C. Burdick, New-York
Rev. J. Stokes, New-York
George J. Bailey, New-York
Oliver Potter, New-York
Edward Van Zandt, New-York
Joseph Sherman, New-York
Albert Sherman, New-York
William J. Roberts, New-York
T. W. Sherman, United States' Army

Joseph Joslen, New-York
James Brickhead, New-York
Mrs. Harriet L. Murray, New-York
William Littlefield, New York
A. B. Belknap, New-York
R. L. Maitland, New-York
O. J. Chafee, New-York
J. P. Darg, New-York
A. Robeson, Jun., New-York
R. S. Satterlee, New-York
Alleyne Otis, New-York
Richard Peterson, New-York
Benjamin J. Cahoone, New-York
Marshall C. Slocum, New-York
Andrews Norton, New-York
Robert S. Hone, New-York
J. S. Hone, New-York
Hon. Levi Woodbury, New Hampshire
Samuel Powel, Rhode Island
James Burdick, New-York
James C. Forsyth, New-York
R. R. Hazard, Jun., New-York
Mrs. R. Moss, Philadelphia, Pa.
Joseph L. Moss, Philadelphia, Pa.
Henry Lazarus, Philadelphia, Pa.
David Sears, Jun., New-York
Jacob A. Herritt, New-York
Henry Brewerton, New-York
Rear-Admiral Wormeley
Mrs. Morrish Samuel, New-York
Mrs. Julia Lawrence, New-York
G. H. Calvert, New-York
Hon. Stephen A. Douglas, United States' Senator, Chicago, Ill.
Miss Minis, Savannah, Georgia
Joseph Few, New-York
Isaiah Rogers, New-York
Felix Peckham, New-York
Jos. B. Weaver, New-York
J. G. Weaver, New-York
David G. Cook, New-York

George M. Dexter, New-York
M. A. D'Bruen, New-York
Richard C. Derby, New-York
E. A. Sherman, New-York
A. Ritchie, New-York
T. Riddell, New-York
A. G. Stout, New-York
J. M. Middleton, New-York
J. S. Pringle, New-York
Nathaniel Greene, New-York
Henry A. Middleton, New-York
P. A. Stockton, New-York
R. M. Mason, Rhode Island
Samuel Allen, New-York
Isaac Gourd, New-York
George Tiffany, Baltimore Md.
S. W. Butler, New-York
W. J. Munro, New-York
R. B. Cranston, New-York
E. M. Munro, New-York
S. A. Gardner, New-York
Amelia De Jongh
Damaris C. Chace, New-York
E. G. Wallop, New-York
John Bull, New-York
G. G. King, New-York
A. N. Littlefield, New-York
George W. Taylor, New-York
Joseph Thomas, New-York
Elisha Atkins, New-York
Mrs. Stephen Bowen, New-York
R. M. Staigg, New-York
Thomas Aston Coffin, New-York
Charles Dereny, New-York
Capt. MacKinnon, R.N., Lymington
Arnold Wilbur, New-York
William S. Vose, New-York
Stephen Hammett, New-York
Joshua Appleby Williams, New-York
Edward A. Hassard, New-York

Daniel Boone, New-York
Edwin Wilbur, New-York
John Ross Dix, New-York
W. P. Congdon, New-York
Nathaniel Holt, New-York
Wymbuley Jones, New-York
Mrs. G. Jones, New-York
Charles Russel, New-York
Ruth C. Thurston, New-York
G. W. Sherman, New-York
C. Rhodes, New-York
A. J. Potter, Bath, Me.
William Bailey, New-York
Joseph Case, New-York
Giles Mardenbro' Eaton
Honorable Frank Pierce, President of the United States
Wanton S. Carr, New-York
Oliver Hull, New-York
William Burnet, New-York

John H. Clarke

J. P. K. Henshaw

H. N. Slater

S. Ang Arnold

A. C. Greene

B. D. Weeden

W. R. Knight

Chas Jackson

James T. Harris

A Simons

Henry Marchant

Wm Tam Burges

Elisha Harris

Samuel Seabury

S. H. Tyng

T. Ward

G. T. Bedell

J Prescott Hall

C. A. Busted

Wm Benson

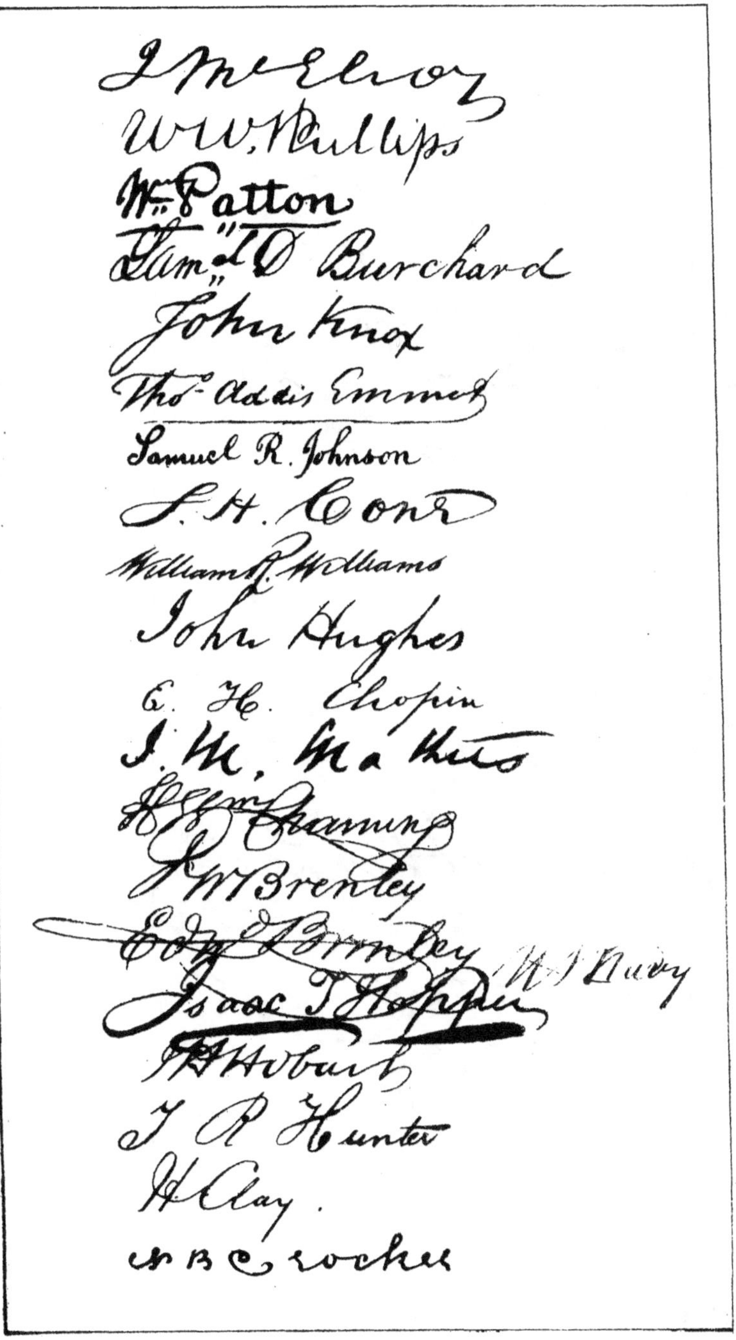

J. McElroy

W. W. Phillips

Wm. Patton

Saml. D. Burchard

John Knox

Thos. Addis Emmet

Samuel R. Johnson

S. H. Cone

William R. Williams

John Hughes

E. H. Chapin

I. M. Mathews

H. E. W. Channing

J. W. Brenley

Edw. J. Brinley

W. T. Dwey

Isaac T. Hopper

J. H. Hobart

J. R. Hunter

H. Clay

N. B. Crocker

Byron Duncan
Wm. H. C. Wroff
Jenny Lind
Chas. T. James
Major G. W. Patten
John Brown France
Levi Woodbury
David Leavitt
S. A. Douglas
R. M. Mason
Amelia De Jongh
Captain MacKennon
Frank Pierce
Ohio Hull
D. C. Mallett
Wm Wiley
Gideon Palmer
W. Everett
Geo. Grinnell
B C Cutler

David L. Hall

C. S. Henry

Jona. M. Wainwright

M. C. Perry

Francis L. Hawks

Winfield Scott,

Benj. Evans

Frances Vinton

Lewis P. W. Balch

Henry J. Whitehouse

R. S. Howland

Thomas D. McGee

R. M. Olyphant

M. H. Grinnell

John Jay

N. Geffroy

George Bancroft

G. Spring

Erskine Mason

Jno. Davol

Whoever the author may be, however, and whatever may be his bodily state, he has clearly no need of a physician to "minister to a mind diseased." In an intellectual sense, the "invalid" lays about him with uncommon vigor, uttering novel opinions with boldness, wit tempered by wisdom, and wisdom sharpened with wit.—*Home Journal.*

He shows a sensibility to the beautiful, and a heart to love what is noble and true. We have followed the wanderings of his mind, often with the deepest attention, always with interest. We have once or twice caught ourselves in supposing that the writer of the "Reveries of a Bachelor" might have had a hand in the authorship.—*Evening Post.*

This work reminds us of the "Reveries of a Bachelor," that much-read and justly commended work of Ike Marvel. The "Musings of an Invalid," like the "Reveries of a Bachelor," show great perception of character, as well as a very happy faculty of conveying his impressions to the reader. No one can read this work without positive benefit, and acquiring more enlarged and truer ideas of the value of life.—*Gazette of the Union.*

A better book than the "Reveries of a Bachelor."—*Day Book.*

Those who have read the "Lorgnette" papers and "Reveries of a Bachelor," by Ike Marvel, with pleasure, can not but enjoy those "Mutterings and Musings," and all who read them, will credit them with great merits.—*New Yorker.*

His pages are not without wisdom. They are crowded with terse and vigorous sentences, and prove a reflecting mind and a philosophic nature.—*Christian Examiner.*

This is one of the most delightful books we have looked into. There is no mistaking the source of these "Musings;" they spring from a kindly heart and an original, refined intellect. To us they seem like the "Reveries" of an old acquaintance (Ike Marvel.)—*Morning Star.*

Rarely have we been treated to so fresh, piquant, and nervous a volume. Every sentence is bold, startling, and replete with vigor, and bears the impress of a keen, sensible, and original mind.—*Long Island Star.*

This book is something altogether unique in the literary world. One moment it reminds us of Charles Lamb, then of some other writer who has charmed us; but in the end we are compelled to fall back upon the conviction, that it is decidedly original. It is full of the deepest and most wholesome thought, while a vein of the richest humor enthralls you. These "Musings" must be the thoughts of a sick chamber—the veritable siftings of no ordinary mind, breaking loose from disease now and then, as a fair struggle is given between the strong mind and a feeble body. The man who wrote this volume must be well worth knowing, if his identity could be once established. To chat with a mind like that, one hour each day, would be a treat indeed. We have quite set our heart on finding out who the author is. This bears evidence of being his first literary effort; may the rest only equal it.—*Peterson's Ladies' National Magazine.*

FANCIES OF A WHIMSICAL MAN.

BY THE AUTHOR OF "MUSINGS OF AN INVALID."

1 vol. 12mo, cloth, - - - - - - - - - - $1 00

OPINIONS OF THE PRESS.

"The Musings of an Invalid," by the same writer, were well received by careful and judicious critics, and are gaining for their unknown author an enviable reputation. The present work will, we predict, secure a still wider popularity, and be more acceptable to that class of readers who appreciate well-drawn and faithful strictures of the fashionable foibles of modern society, written in a forcible, piquant style.—*Merchants' Magazine.*

Our attention has been called to this book, because it has been severely abused in certain quarters, where every thing which is not radical, or which does not savor of infidelity and the "Progress" which is identical with an attempt to destroy all the institutions of civilization and religion, is habitually condemned. We confess that the title did not much prepossess us in favor of the work; but we must also confess that having once opened it, we very soon arrived at the conclusion that it is one of the very best books of the day, and that the author, who is unknown to us, is assuredly a man of no ordinary promise. As a specimen of sarcasm and irony, this little book has rarely been excelled. And the author not only thinks soundly and conservatively upon all subjects, but he writes with a vigor and directness which are exceedingly refreshing in this age of *namby pambyism.*
If there be any fault to find with the author, it is in the severity of his sarcasm and the unsparing manner in which he lashes the follies, and vices, and absurdities of the day. But even this is atoned for in the manly and fearless defense of right and of the old-fashioned principles of religion and equity which pervades this book.—*New York Courier and Enquirer.*

We noticed at some length and with decided favor, the previous work by this author, the "Musings of an Invalid." The invalid has laid aside his chamber *negligeé* and come forth as quite a stout and eupeptic man.
The present work has all the spirit of its predecessor, and a far broader range. It is full of pithy thoughts and sharp sayings. The tone of the book is earnest, and, on the whole, kindly, respectful to all hearty workers, and somewhat savage upon all ambitious theorists.—*Christian Inquirer.*

This new volume is worthy of the reputation acquired by its predecessor, and will considerably increase the public desire to learn the name of the author. He certainly wields his pen with a rare combination of grace and vigor.—*Pittsburg Saturday Visitor.*

We do not know when we have been more entertained than by the reading of this book. It came to us unheralded from an anonymous source. We opened it, intending simply to glance at the contents, and if they were attractive, to lay the volume aside for future examination and notice. We had reckoned without our host. The first few sketches completely enchanted us, and we found ourselves spirited along from page to page, even to the end. The contents embrace short chapters, the subjects of which are generally suggested by the doings of the day in large cities. The thoughts are original, and they are expressed in equally original language. Sarcasm is a prominent feature of the book; sarcasm, too, of the rarest quality. It also abounds in wit and humor of the best quality.—*Church's Bizarre, Phil.*.

The rich field chosen by the author gives full play to his vigorous and original mind, and piquant or nervous style. Those who have read the "Musings," need not be told that he is just the man to glean and bind up an inimitable sheaf of "Whimsical Fancies." Its perusal will take the frown off the face of "dull care," and thereby cheer and lengthen life, besides communicating many wise, striking, and improvable thoughts.—*Binghampton Democrat.*

We are pleased with this book. There is a quaintness about it that is almost unrivalled. The satire is gentlemanly, yet sufficiently pungent; and the oddities are rather more quaint than grotesque. The author has too much feeling to be severe, and too much generosity of soul to misrepresent.—*Hartford Daily Courant.*

This is a very clever book, by an author, whose previous work, mentioned in the title page, has secured for him a favorable reception on this his second appearance. The sketches are lively and spirited, and the reflections have the great recommendation of never being tiresome, as sensible reflections so often are.—*N. Y. Evening Post.*

There is a vein of quiet, keen wit running through this book, that holds the reader as by a charm. The author is certainly a genius of no common order; and though he modestly conceals his name, we can not doubt that he has entered on a career of authorship that will secure to him the highest literary distinction.—*Daily Albany Argus.*

In this volume we see the same adventurous, original, philosophic and amusing genius at work we had occasion to notice some time ago from the same pen, called "The Musings of an Invalid." The articles are interspersed here and there with things *grave* and *facetious*, with a vein of philosophy running through the whole, which always commands readers. This, we believe, is the second work of this original author, but we hope it will not be the last. There is a *vein* of thought where this material comes from that is *worth working.—New York Christian Intelligencer.*

The author is evidently an unpracticed writer, but a man of mature thought, who, as he becomes accustomed to the pen, will attract a constantly increasing attention from the reading public. He is a little too careless in his thrusts at what he deems the follies and vices of the age; and in his zeal for the truth, sometimes strikes right and left with more vigor than discretion; but in spite of his seeming want of orthodoxy, his heart appears right, and is evidently in his work. The earnestness thus acquired, joined with a caustic humor, and an original and striking faculty of illustration, will cause the book to be widely read, even by those who come more or less under the lash of the writer. Notwithstanding that the author, under the guise of an editor, speaks posthumously of himself, we trust that he will not be thus lost to the world, but appear among the armed host this side of the river of death.—*New York Journal of Commerce.*

SALANDER AND THE DRAGON:

A Romance of the Hartz Prison.

BY FREDERICK WILLIAM SHELTON, A.M.,

RECTOR OF ST. JOHN'S CHURCH, HUNTINGDON, LONG ISLAND.

1 vol. 12mo. Illustrated. Full cloth, - - - - -	$1 00
" " " - - - - -	75
1 vol. 18mo, Sunday-school Edition, - - - - -	50

OPINIONS OF THE PRESS.

Since the days of John Bunyan, there has not been given to the Christian world so beautiful an allegory as this. Its design is to exhibit the pernicious effects of slander, and surely no one can contemplate this odious offspring of the depraved heart as it appears in this fanciful sketch, without abhorring and despising the reality. The names of the several characters are significantly chosen, and the grouping is managed with a fine artistic effect. The style comports with that chaste simplicity which should characterize an allegory, in which the veil should not be so elaborately and closely woven as to hide the modest mein of truth beneath.—*The Independent* (*New York*).

A volume, small and quaint, but very clever; and we have read it, every line of it, at a sitting too, and take the pen in hand to suggest to the reader of this that he go and do likewise. Startled he will be at the title, "Salander and the Dragon," but the first page will reveal the story as an allegory, of which the great master of that species of writing need not be ashamed.—*The Presbyterian.*

I regard this volume as one of the most successful attempts at the Bunyan style of allegorical writing I have ever read. A copy came into my hands not long since, and was read with absorbing interest. I then put it into the hands of my oldest child, a girl some ten years of age, and found that it was read by her with equal avidity, and the characters and delineations well understood—a very good test, I judge, of the success of the author in the execution of the work. No one can read "SALANDER" without being struck at the unveiling of the true character and the disastrous consequences of *Slander*. It ought to find a place in every family.—*New York Christian Advocate and Journal.*

A very ingenious use of the allegory, to illustrate the deformity and evil of *Slander* and *Envy*. The excellent lesson is more impressively set forth by this picturesque representation than by any didactic essay, and is much more attractive to the reader. The author evinces great skill in the management of the story, and steady pursuit of a high moral aim.—*New York Evangelist.*

An allegory well worth reading. Its object is to illustrate, in all its deformity, *Slander*—one of the worst and commonest of the social vices. It is written somewhat in the good old Bunyan style—graphic, poetic, convincing. It will put all malicious gossips to their purgations, who can be induced to read it; and if a portion of the funds of the American Tract, Bible, and Missionary Societies were expended in a cheap edition of a million copies of so practical a book as this, the money would be put to good account.—*New York Mirror.*

An allegory, designed to illustrate the danger of uttering or listening to insinuations and scandalous detraction. We are glad to see the hideous deformity of this vice so faithfully exhibited. It requires only to be seen in its true colors, to excite that detestation which will render its exercise disgraceful, and cause it to be avoided.—*New York Journal of Commerce.*

"SALANDER."—Here is an insinuating title for a book!—Salander!—how it runs in the mind, snaky and salamander-like, as though it were related to some ugly monster! And so it is, while it tells "A Story of the Hartz Prison," truthful enough to be recognized by every one—beautiful enough in grace, and flow, and quaintness of narrative, to fascinate the dullest reader, and yet horrible enough in its characters accessory to the plot to make one shudder that so foul a fiend should ever be imprisoned in a human heart. "Salander, a Story of the Hartz Prison," might have been written by that master allegorist, John Bunyan, to his credit; but, for the credit of our time, it is written by Frederick W. Shelton.

It explains fully how Don Officioso imposed, in the name—a forgery—of the Lord Conscienza, upon Goodman, keeper of Hartz Prison, by representing that this Salander—no other than the green monster, *Slander*—was sent by Conscienza (conscience) for incarceration in Hartz (the heart's) Prison; also how Salander vexed Goodman, until his wife Pryint (pry into it) got into the secret, when off she goes to Bad-Neighborhood, and *confidently* tells Mrs. Blab and a host of scandal-mongers that her husband has *brought home a monster!* This is noised speedily about, laying Goodman and his house under suspicion. To get rid of this, he is obliged to let Salander out of prison, and thus be quit of the imputation of fathering him.

Salander goes forth, cultivates the acquaintance of one Duke d'Envy, and a war is declared upon Goodnaim, a person heretofore in the confidence of all who knew him. During the battles between Salander and his host of ragamuffins and Goodnaim—who stoutly defended himself—the Fairweather Guard and Old Friends of the latter forsook him, but Goodnaim triumphed.—*The New Yorker.*

SALANDER AND THE DRAGON.—Be not startled by this head-line. It is only the title of a book, and that an allegory, by the Rev. Mr. Shelton, of Huntingdon, L.I., a clergyman of the Episcopal Church.

Salander is a monster, born of Envy, and his name, without cover, is *Slander.* Hideous and hateful, his own father is not willing to keep him, but commits him to the custody of another called Goodman, the jailor of the Hartz Prison. The struggle of Salander to get out, the food that he is fed on while in this prison of the *Heart*, the command of Lord Conscienza, that he shall be kept confined, and no one shall know of his existence; how the jailor finally tells his wife that he has this monster, and she insists on seeing him, and promises never to mention his existence to any one, and keeps her promise for a whole week or so, and then hints it to Mrs. Snapit, and she to Mrs. Tattleby, and she to Mrs. Blab, and she to Mrs. Watovit, and so on till all the neighbors came to see the monster, and how he was finally let loose;—all this, and more, is painted with exceeding skill. Salander, once at liberty, goes forth to work mischief. He plots the ruin of the castle Gudnaim, and robs Stella, the wife of the baron, of a priceless jewel which she wore, more precious than any gem which ever adorned the casket of an empress; and when she was robbed, she pined away and died, and a pure and beautiful shaft was erected to her memory by her faithful husband, with this inscription—"She healed the hearts of the sorrowful while living, and broke them when she died." And by-and-by the castle is surrounded by a host of enemies, Malice, and Backbite, and others, led on by Salander; and at last the baron is slain, and Gudnaim razed to the ground. The jailor who let Salander out of prison, is arrested by Conscienza, whom he contrived to put to sleep for a while; but at length being roused, the Lord smites the jailor, who confesses his guilt, and tries to make some amends for what he has done. He goes to the ruins of castle Gudnaim, but he can not find Stella's jewel which Salander stole away; nor can he rear again the ruins of the castle; but he asks where are the baron and his beautiful wife? he will humble himself to them; and he is led into the grave-yard, and is told, they are here! Conscienza seizes him, and gives him into the hands of a dark fiend named *Remorse*, who scourges him to the very verge of life, when he is told to go to God for pardon; and by repentance he seeks and finds peace. This is a scant and unfair outline of the allegory, which may be read and re-read with profit.

It is a sermon that ought to be preached everywhere. It has a great truth in it. Who does not know it? Happy is he who has not felt the bitterness of the mischief which this infernal imp is working in the world. And if Mr. Shelton had done nothing else than to write this book, he would have lived to good purpose. We think the story will be read when he ceases to be heard.—*Irenæus.—New York Observer.*

THE LADIES' ILLUSTRATED KEEPSAKE.

With 13 *fine Steel Engravings.*

EDITED BY PROFESSOR ABBOTT.

1 vol. 8vo, cloth, - - - - - - - - -	$2 00
" gilt extra, - - - - - - - -	3 00
" morocco, - - - - - - - -	4 00

VOLUME II.

12 *Engravings.*

1 vol. 8vo, cloth, - - - - - - - - -	$2 00
" gilt extra, - - - - - - - -	3 00
" morocco, - - - - - - - - -	4 00

THE AMERICAN HISTORICAL ANNUAL.

1 vol. 8vo, cloth, gilt extra, - - - - - - - -	$3 00
" morocco, " - - - - - - - -	4 00

REFLECTIONS ON FLOWERS.

BY REV. JAMES HERVEY.

Illustrated with 12 *beautiful Colored Plates.*

1 vol. 18mo, cloth, extra full gilt, - - - -	$1 00

THE SACRED MOUNTAINS

BY REV. J. T. HEADLEY.

1 vol. 12mo.	Illustrated. Full cloth, - - - - -	$1 00
"	" " gilt edges, - - - -	1 50
1 vol. 18mo.	Without the Plates. Sunday-school Edition, - -	50

SACRED SCENES AND CHARACTERS.

BY REV. J. T. HEADLEY

1 vol. 12mo.	Illustrated. Full cloth, - - - - - - -	$1 00
"	" " gilt edges, - - - - -	1 50
1 vol. 18mo.	Without the Plates. Sunday-school Edition, - -	50

OPINIONS OF THE PRESS.

This work may very properly be considered a companion to the "*Sacred Mountains*," by the same author. Its object is to illustrate and "render more life-like" the Sacred Writings. It is not the author's design to supersede the Bible; but his wish is to excite a solicitude to obtain, and to become intimately acquainted and perfectly familiar with its history, doctrines, and laws; to know its truth, to imbibe its spirit, feel its power, and partake of its salvation; in a word, to prize, in some measure, as it deserves, this treasure, which is indeed beyond price. We predict for it a circulation far beyond any of the author's former works.—*The News.*

This work will add greatly to the reputation of the author. In literary merit, it more than equals his "Sacred Mountains." Mr. Headley excels in his glowing style and vivid descriptions. His works are a rich treasury of all the sublimity of thought, moving tenderness of passion, and vigorous strength of expression, which are to be found in all languages by which mortals declare their minds.—*Daily Globe.*

HISTORY OF THE WALDENSES.

BY REV. J. T. HEADLEY.

vol. 12mo.	Illustrated. Full cloth, - - - - - -	$0 75
" 18mo.	Sunday-school Edition, - - - - - -	50

NAPOLEON AND HIS DISTINGUISHED MARSHALS.

BY REV. J. T. HEADLEY.

1 vol. 12mo.	Illustrated. Full cloth, - - - - - -	$1 00

LUTHER AND CROMWELL.

BY REV. J T. HEADLEY.

1 vol. 12mo. Illustrated. Full cloth, - - - - - - **$1 00**

RAMBLES AND SKETCHES.

BY REV. J. T. HEADLEY.

1 vol. 12mo. Illustrated. Full cloth, - - - - - - **$1 00**

OPINIONS OF THE PRESS.

We have not for a long time sat down to a book with more pleasing anticipations, or found those anticipations more fully realized, than in the perusal of the work before us—and we know it will be hailed with gratification by the many admirers of the talented author. His "Napoleon and his Marshals" was, perhaps, as popular, and found at least as many enthusiastic readers as any book that can be mentioned. We think his "Rambles and Sketches" are destined to be as popular at least as any of his previously published works. There is not a dull chapter in the work, filled as it is with "an infinite variety." The author has ample room and verge enough for the employment of his fine talents to great advantage—and most successfully has he accomplished the task. The biographical sketch of the author is interesting and "well considered," and adds much to the value of the book, which is got up in a very neat and attractive style by the publisher.—*Portland Transcript.*

Mr. Headley is one of the most promising writers of this country, and we have here one of his best books—one on which he can safely rest his fame. It possesses the unfatiguing charms of perfect simplicity and truth. There is a graceful frankness pervading the composition, which engages the interest of the reader in the author as well as in the subject. His rambles about Rome, Paris, and London, exhibit a thousand lively traits of an ingenious nature, upon which a man of taste will delight to linger. We predict for this a sale equal to that of any of the author's works.—*New York News.*

BIOGRAPHY OF THE SAVIOUR AND HIS APOSTLES.

With a Portrait of each, Engraved on Steel.

TO WHICH IS ADDED,

AN ESSAY ON THE CHARACTER OF THE APOSTLES.

BY REV. J. T. HEADLEY

1 vol. 18mo. Fifteen Engravings, - - - - - - $1 00
" " gilt edges, extra, - - - 1 50

LETTERS FROM THE BACKWOODS AND THE ADIRONDACK.

BY REV. J. T. HEADLEY.

vol. 12mo. Full cloth, - - - - - - - - $0 50

THE BEAUTIES OF REV. J. T. HEADLEY.

WITH HIS LIFE.

1 vol. 18mo. Illustrated, - - - - - - - - $0 50
" " gilt edges, extra, - - - - - 75

OPINION OF THE PRESS.

The collection is one of which no author need be ashamed. It consists, indeed, of some of Mr. Headley's most brilliant and highly-finished compositions—of those specimens of his abilities by which he may be judged with the greatest safety to his fame as a word-painter and thinker.—*New York Tribune.*

THEOPNEUSTY:

Or, the Plenary Inspiration of the Holy Scriptures.

BY PROFESSOR GAUSSEN, OF GENEVA.

(Translated by Rev. E. N. Kirk).

A NEW AND ENLARGED EDITION.

1 vol. 12mo. 410 pages, - - - - - - - - $1 00

We wish to make a very distinct and earnest recommendation to our clerical friends, to teachers in Sabbath-schools, and others engaged in the work of instruction, of a volume entitled, "Theopneusty, *or the Plenary Inspiration of the Holy Scriptures.*" The work is by Professor Gaussen, of Geneva, Switzerland, and the translation by the Rev. E. N. Kirk. It is published by John S. Taylor, New York. As an attractive, interesting, powerful, and satisfactory argument on the plenary inspiration of the Bible, we regard it as unsurpassed by any work in our knowledge designed for popular reading. It is stripped of dogmatic terminology, and is full of faith, and love, and beauty. Our faith in God and in His Holy Word has been refreshed and strengthened by the perusal of this work.

HEROINES OF SACRED HISTORY

BY MRS. STEELE.

Illustrated with Splendid Engravings.

1 vol. 12mo. New, revised, and enlarged edition, - - - $1 00
" " " " gilt edges, extra, - 1 50

SHANTY, THE BLACKSMITH:

A Tale of Other Times.

BY MRS. SHERWOOD.

1 vol. 18mo. Illustrated, - - - - - - - $0 50

THE HISTORY OF HENRY MILNER.

BY MRS. SHERWOOD.

1 vol. 18mo. Cloth, - - - - - - - - $0 50

LILY OF THE VALLEY.

BY MRS. SHERWOOD.

1 vol. 18mo. Illustrated, - - - - - - - - $0 50

COMMENDATORY NOTICE BY THE REV. WILLIAM PATTON, D.D.

MR. J. S. TAYLOR:

It affords me pleasure to learn that you are about to re-publish the little work called "THE LILY OF THE VALLEY." Since the time it was presented to my daughter, by the Rev. Dr. Matheson, of England, it has been a great favorite in my family. It has been read with intense interest by many who have from time to time obtained the loan of it. Indeed it has but seldom been at home since its first perusal. I doubt not but all who have read it, will be glad of the opportunity of possessing a copy.

The story is not only natural, but instructive, and well calculated to impress upon the mind important moral and religious lessons. Some portions of the narrative are of the most touching and thrilling character. There is a charming simplicity pervading the work. I feel a strong confidence that you will find an ample sale for the book. It will find its w[illegible] into many families, and be found in the libraries of the Sabbath school. WILLIAM PATTON.

OPINIONS OF THE PRESS.

A very interesting little work of 123 pages. It is a simple, though beautiful, narrative of a young female, some portions of which are of the most pathetic and affecting character—particularly designed for the edification and instruction of young females, and a most excellent work to introduce into Sabbath schools. Its tendency is to kindle the flame of piety in the youthful bosom, to instruct the understanding, and to warm and improve the heart. Its intrinsic, though unostentatious, merits, should furnish it with a welcome into every family.—*Ladies' Morning Star.*

This is a neat and very interesting little volume. The narrative throughout will be read with pleasure, and some portions of it with thrilling interest. The story is natural, and told in very neat language, and with admirable simplicity. It is not only calculated to please and interest tne mind of the reader, but also to make moral and religious impressions upon the heart. We are well assured, if its merits were generally known, that it would find its way into many families and Sabbath school libraries, as it is particularly adapted to please and engage the attention of juvenile readers.—*Methodist Protestant, Baltimore.*

This is a re-publication of a small narrative volume published in England. The narrative is written with beautiful simplicity, possesses a touching, interest, and is calculated to leave a salutary impression. It is well fitted for a present by parents or friends to children, and is worthy of a place in Sabbath school libraries.—*Christian Intelligencer.*

THE POOR VICAR.

(*Translated from the German of Zchokke.*)

1 vol. 18mo. Cloth, - - - - - - - - - - $0 31

JOURNAL OF A POOR VICAR.—Such is the title of a little work translated from the German of Zschokke, and published by John S. Taylor, 143 Nassau street. This Journal is said to have been the foundation of Goldsmith's Vicar of Wakefield, and certainly it is worthy of germing that celebrated work. The author of "The Journal of a Poor Vicar," is well known as one of the most affecting of that class of German writers, who know so well how to halo humble life with the iris of tender and holy sentiment, and this little work is, perhaps, his most successful effort. Nothing can be more beautiful, touching, and purifying than the character he has drawn of the Poor Vicar and his two daughters. We defy any one, with a spark of sentiment, to peruse this Journal without shedding tears. It is a wand that exercises the feelings and emotions of the heart, with irresistible potency. We have read nothing—not even the Vicar of Wakefield—to equal it. The translator has happily presented the spirit of the original. The volume is neatly published, and whoever fails to reads it, fails of a great and long to be remembered enjoyment.

THE SHORTER CATECHISM OF THE REV. ASSEMBLY OF DIVINES.

Vith Proofs thereof out of the Scriptures, in Words at length.

Per Hundred, - - - - - - - - - - $3 00

The above Books will be forwarded to order, at the prices mentioned, *free of postage*, to any part of the United States, on the receipt of orders, *with the money*. Address,

JOHN S. TAYLOR, Publisher,

17 ANN STREET, NEW YORK.

N.B. Any valuable Books to be had in New York, furnished by J. S. TAYLOR, at the lowest cash prices.

REPUBLICANISM VS. JESUITISM!

THE MOST IMPORTANT BOOK OF THE AGE.

CARLOTINA AND THE JESUITS,

By EDMUND FARRENC.

In One Vol. 12*mo*., 432 *Pages.*

JUST PUBLISHED BY JOHN S. TAYLOR,

No. 17 Ann Street, New York,

And for Sale by all Booksellers.

"At the present period, there are but two great powers in the world, the one representing the past, with its attendant burden of ignorance, crimes, and miseries, called *Catholicism*, or *Romanism;* the other contending for the present, and foreshadowing the future, known as Republicanism, or Liberty, or Protestantism. All other powers, either civil or religious, are but secondary constellations, moving in various orbits around these two principles, according to the amount of Liberty or Despotism they contain.

"The past Roman Catholicism—concealing her fondling, Despotism, under the cloak of religion:—the present Republicanism—inscribing on its broad flag, Liberty, and the regeneration of mankind."

CONTENTS.

OPINIONS OF THE PRESS.

From the New-York Evangelist.

CARLOTINA AND THE JESUITS.—A powerfully wrought tale, founded upon and weaving into its narrative, the scenes of the revolution in Rome in 1848, under the title of *Carlotina and the Sanfedeste, or a Night with the Jesuits at Rome.* The principal interest centers in the heroine Carlotina; but the other characters are but thin disguises of the prominent actors in that scene.—Using the vices, arts and terrible power of Popery as the material, the fervid imagination of the author has produced a story of exciting and absorbing interest; while the political and religious sentiments it inculcates, are such as Americans cannot help approving. The reader gets, among the deepest impressions of the book, a profound sense of the evils and terrors of Jesuitism, and is carried far towards the adoption of Father Gavazzi's principle, destruction to Popery.

From the Christian Parlor Magazine.

A book in such an attractive form, so true to nature, will be inquired for, purchased and read. The whole tendency is so happy, the moral and religious tone is so unexceptionable, that we earnestly hope it will gain a wider circulation than even Uncle Tom's Cabin, that now goes rapidly even in foreign languages.

Let every one who can obtain this work read it, if for nothing else than to thank God for our security against so dreadful a snare, and the good fortune of living in a land where civil and religious libery are enjoyed unmolested. May the author of this volume be spared to produce another as interesting and as profitable.

From the Tribune.—Detroit.

It portrays, vividly and truthfully, the recent struggles of the Republicans of Rome, against the damning corruption, lust and wickedness of the Jesuitical Priesthood of the Church and Pope of Rome, in its efforts to perpetuate ignorance and despotism. We heartily wish this little book in every family, and especially in the hands of every American citizen, whether Adopted or Native, Catholic or Protestant; for it matters not in what nation or creed an American citizen may have been born and educated, he owes to the American Government the duty to read, examine, and study well the principles upon which that Government is founded and *must be perpetuated*—he owes it to himself to *think for himself*—to scan, compare, and contrast well, *in his own mind*, the teachings of any and every person who would influence him in his actions as an *American Freeman.*

From the Christian Chronicle—Philadelphia.

In this book Catholicism in its true nature, and history as the enemy of civilization and liberty is sketched in glowing and truthful terms by a pen highly skilful and eloquent. The author charges the miseries of the past in Papal countries upon this very apostate religion, and represents every where, and at all times, as in antagonism with republicanism. His strong positions are not overwrought, but fully sustained by the facts in the case. We are truly glad that one so well qualified has entered on this task. The book will do much to open the eyes of the public on the character of Catholicism, and to prepare for its successful resistance as encroachments are continually made.

From the Christian Observer—Philadelphia.

The woof of this interesting story is composed of two great ideas, which claim the attention of theologians, patriots, and statesmen everywhere: 1st. Catholicism in every country where it controls the popular mind, is in open antagonism with the progress of civilization. It is the foster-mother of ignorance, crime, misery, and despotism. 2d. Its direct antagonist power is Republicanism, inscribing on its broad, open flag the liberation of mankind.

From the Trumpet—Boston.

Catholicism is on the increase; it exercises a great influence on the destinies of the world. All the countries of Europe are more or less swayed, or acted upon, by it. Where Catholicism is paramount, civilization is at a low ebb, as in Mexico, South America, Spain. Religious liberty decreases under Catholicism. That species of religion is double-faced; it accommodates itself to despotism or republicanism to gain its ends, while all the time it is striking at the liberties of mankind. To show these expressive facts is the object of the story before us. The Italian peasantry; the Signora a Jesuistic agent of priesthood; the greedy host wavering between money and liberty, but finally yielding to the latter; the unflinching patriotism of Adrian, dying for his fellow-companions in democracy; the precocious genius of the

Italian boy, Jeronimo, whose devotedness to freedom, and repugnance to Catholicism foreshadows in vivid light, the spirit of coming generations; the innocence, love, and recantation of Carlotina, the talent, ambition, and passions of Father Francisco, a priest, whose eminent faculties, forced into a wrong channel by the compressing hand of the Church, were rioting in vices, instead of progressing in virtues;—all these characters, moving in the circle traced round them by the principles they professed, are painted in keeping with the strictest law of the logic of the human mind, and also in accordance with time, locality, and the teachings of history, the records of the Roman Church, and the late events of the Italian Revolution. Let us have a republican literature.—Let us have books which will impress upon the hearts of the people a love of the institutions of our country, especially our Free Schools; and awake them to the dangers with which Catholocism surrounds them.

From the Literary World.

It is just in the vein and temper to pique curiosity, and set in motion all the elements which belong to the two great worlds of Protestant and (Roman) Catholic readers. The plot is sufficiently involved to keep us in a maze, the incidents crowd on with activity and despatch, and altogether the work is done up in a style so vivid and provocative of attention, that all those who make it a pastime or a business to read, will regard "Carlotina" as a windfall of the first quality. There is a certain foreign flavor in the style which, while it is well suited to the subject, arrests attention pretty much as a smack of the brogue or dialect does in living speech.

From the Western Christian Advocate.

The author of the work—Mr. Edmund Farrenc—informs us that he was led to the writing of it by a conviction of the silent, yet greatly-increasing power of Jesuitism throughout the world at the present time. He has furnished the public with a volume of unflagging interest, and none can get up from its perusal without the conviction of the deep, dark, and everlastingly-hypocritical character of these intriguers against human freedom and liberty.

From the Portland Transcript.

Catholicism and Despotism! Protestatism and Liberty! These are the themes of this work. It exposes the workings of the Church of Rome, and especially of the Jesuits. It comprises many facts in regard to the policy of the church, and the condition of the Roman people. As a tale, although the author professes to have drawn his characters from nature, we think they sometimes overstep the limits; the plot is involved, the incidents numerous and exciting, and the whole work is one that will attract much attention. Geo. Lord, Exchange St. has it for sale.

From the Southern Christian Advocate.

It is designed to exhibit Popery in its moral and political enormities, as the enemy of all righteousness, and a veritable child of the devil. The scene is in Pontifical Rome; the time, the revolutionary outbreak of 1848; and the characters, priests and women, republicans and aristocrats, and a general grouping of the corrupt masses that seem to settle down in the ironically called holy city, as the grand reservoir of all the villainous compounds of creation supplied by sewers from the corrupt sources of all civilized and heathen lands. It seems impossible to transcend the limits of truth in depicting the monstrosities of Popery. Improbable as some of the scenes appear, the fathomless abyss of Popish deceivableness of unrighteousness will yet vindicate their correctness, and justify the sad memorials of the man of sin.

From the Christian Mirror—Portland.

This is a book which will be read. The scene of the transactions which it narrates, is Rome and its neighborhood; the *time* that of revolution, which caused the Pope to flee. The Sanfedesti were a secret society of Jesuits, who plotted every conceivable method but honest and upright ones to repress the spirit of liberty and defeat all efforts to secure it. They even planned and attempted to execute a St. Bartholomew tragedy. Carlotina is a lovely girl, whom a female Jesuit was employed to draw from her lover all the plans and secrets of the patriots, even at the cost of her own honor—a sacrifice which, happily, the girl was not required to make; her unsophisticated mind yielded to the arguments of her lover, and she herself became a Protestant. Here are many affecting developments of the iniquitous, oppressive, and wily character and tendency of the papal system of religion—the demoralizing and tragical results, which, in its working, it brings about.

From the Evening Mirror—New York.

CARLOTINA, OR THE SANFEDESTI.

Such is the title of a work written by Edmund Farrenc, a French exile now in this city, and issued from the press of John S. Taylor. It is the most thorough and pungent expose of Jesuits and Jesuitism, as the enemies of human freedom, that has ever attracted our notice. We shall not attempt an analysis of the plot, nor a description of the characters introduced—not wishing to subtract from the interest of those who will get and read the volume—further than to say the scenes are laid in Italy, at the period of the late revolutions, and that the Jesuits, who figure everywhere prominently, are convicted of producing, through their religious, political, and ruffian organizations, the reaction which, beginning with the strangling of the Roman Republic by France, ended in the subversion of every attempt to give the masses sovereignty in Europe.

English and Austrian diplomacy are exhibited as laboring with this Jesuit brood to overthrow liberty and the people. The origin, creed, and character of the Jesuits, sustained by copious extracts from their own records, are traced in all their blood-thirstiness and infamy. The priest-Jesuit and the woman-Jesuit—the latter, Signora Savina, a polished she-devil—are forcibly limned, also the confiding girl-Chorister Carlotina, who, taught to reverence the church above her conscience, is beset by the priest to worm from her lover, a republican soldier at Rome, the secrets of the republicans, even at the sacrifice of her virtue, is splendidly drawn.

Ciceroacchia, (Brunetti,) the great friend of the republicans; the noble boy Geronimo, who counter-plots against the she-Jesuit Savina, and the soldier lover of Carlotina, are rare pictures, and said to be taken—as we may believe—with the general incidents of the book, from life and fact. The volume abounds with descriptive beauties, and is vigorously written throughout. It shows that liberty has no enemy so dangerous as the Jesuits of the Roman Catholic Church. The volume appears at a time best calculated for it to strike an effective blow at the subtle enemy of our institutions, at work everywhere around and among us. It harmonizes with the eloquent writings of Gavazzi. That it will be widely sought and read, we believe, for it is as candid and manful, as it is earnest and pungent.

From the Daily Times—Cincinnati.

This work is one of the best that has issued from the press of the United States. It is well remarked, that Catholicism and Republicanism are now the two great antagonistic powers of the earth. All other powers, either civil or religious, are but secondary, moving as satelites around these two great centres. Catholicism, representing the past, with its ignorance, crimes and miseries; Republicanism, contending for the present, and foreshadowing the future, and having inscribed on its banner, Liberty, Equality, and Fraternity. This work is deeply interesting, and is truthful in its delineations of character, scenes and events. Read it, and learn to discover the secret schemes and open assaults of the agents of Despotism.

From the National Democrat—New York

If bold writing, vigorous descriptions, an exciting plot, and vividly drawn characters will command attention, it will do it. The book has many fascinations of plot and description. The sketches of character persuade us that the writer is an acute observer, a genial thinker, and a man of much humor as well as sentiment. The characters are drawn with a masterly hand, and the dialogue in general is managed with good effect and dramatic power.

From the Puritan and Recorder—Boston.

This work regards Catholicism and Republicanism as the two great powers now existing in the world; and of course it connects the freedom and happiness of the world with the downfall of the one, and the triumph of the other. The characters are for the most part admirably sustained; and the lessons inculcated are so palpable, that no one can mistake them. It is a work of no inconsiderable talent, and cannot fail to make itself felt in the most important controversy of the age.

From the New York Star.

This work is written to illustrate the powerful antagonism of Catholicism to Republicanism, is well written, and in the delineation of character, nature has been scrupulously portrayed. Each character is complete in itself, and are coincident with the history of the Roman Church, and the late events of the Italian revolution. The book should be in every library, illustrating as it does the struggle now waging between the two great ruling powers of the earth—religious despotism and liberty.

From the Atlas—New York.

The scenes so vividly portrayed in this book were enacted in Rome during the late short and sanguinary struggle for liberty and republicanism in that "Eternal City." In our opinion it gives a very accurate idea of the state of society, and the condition of both the common people and the priesthood in that part of the world. The author takes the ground that the Catholic religion is the natural enemy of liberty and the destroyer of republicanism, and of course his book is written in that spirit. It is a very interesting work.

From the Daily Advertiser—Brooklyn.

This book is evidently intended as the embodiment of great principles, and is one of those very few works where some fiction is well used to portray important truths. The author very well says in his introduction, that at the present period there are really but two powers in the world, the one is Popery and despotism, representing the past, with its attendant burden of ignorance, crimes, and miseries; the other is Protestantism and liberty, civil and sacred, contending for the present, and foreshadowing the future. Those powers he considers as two grand centres, around which all other powers revolve, according to the amount of liberty or despotism which they contain. These remarks, which, for substance, are those of the author, give us a "bird's eye view" of the book. The scene is laid in Rome in the year 1849, during the struggle for liberty which then took place, and which describe, in a most graphic manner, the unholy manœuvering of the Jesuits, male and female, to accomplish their wicked schemes. Many of the incidents are truly startling, all are interesting, and on the whole, it is one of those books which the man who takes it up will be unwilling to lay down until he has finished it.

From Parker's Journal—New York.

This is a noble work, and one well calculated to arouse the attention of the community to that great struggle which is being rapidly brought to a crisis—the struggle, namely, between the Protestant tendencies of liberty, and the tyrannical "stay-where-we-areativeness" of the Roman Catholic Church. The abstract theories of freedom, and the real effects of Jesuit influence are set forth in glowing colors. The plot is ably constructed, and the interest sustained to the conclusion. We wish for Mr. Farrenc the success he merits—more his ambition does not covet. *Carlotina* is a book which every one should read, and which it is the duty of every friend of freedom to promote and circulate.

From the Highland Eagle.

The attractive syle in which this book is written, its plot, progress and consummation, the characters, language, and matter of fact disposition of the colloquial arguments which compose the material part of its history, and the variety of valuable facts that relate to the Roman Catholic religion, which are not to be found in ordinary history, renders this work a fit candidate for public favor. No one can read it without a shudder and a pious indignation at the villainous power of priestcraft as exercised in down-trodden and crushed Italy. With a two-edged sword the author lays open the putrescent mass of corruption, and the reader can behold the skull and bones, the tortures of the inquisition, the soulless, defiling criminality that lurks under the cowl and surplice.

From the News—Norfolk, Va.

The scene of this tale, as its title implies, is laid in Rome in the year 1847, and is designed to illustrate the feelings and principles which prompted the Republican movement throughout Italy at that time. The author says that the characters are portrayed from nature. Whether this be the fact or not, they are drawn with vigor and spirit, and no one can in honesty, whatever he may think of the fidelity of the pictures presented in this work, deny its ability and interest.

www.ingramcontent.com/pod-product-compliance
Lightning Source LLC
LaVergne TN
LVHW011157110826
845150LV00006B/1241